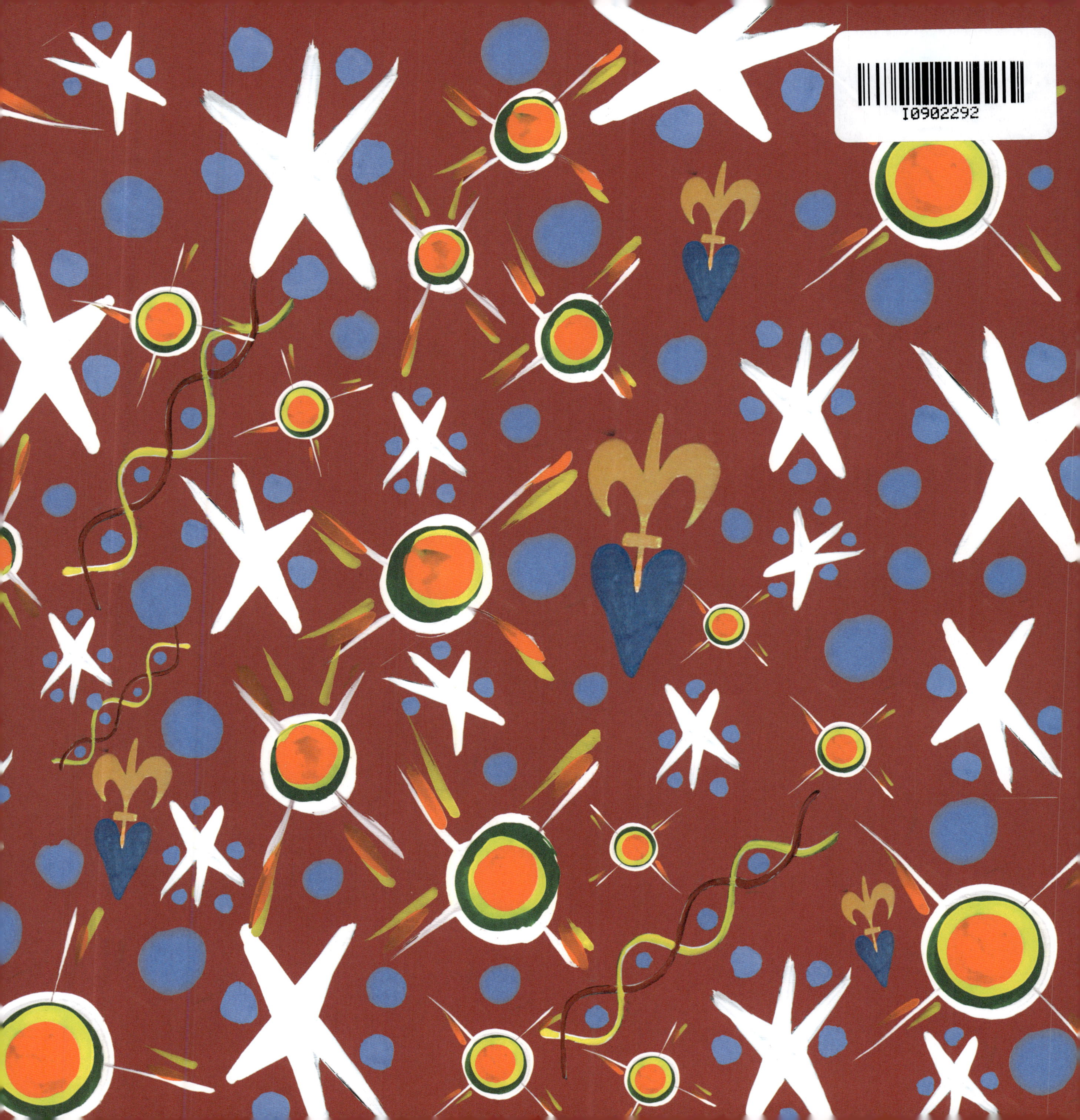

SIMON OF NEW ORLEANS

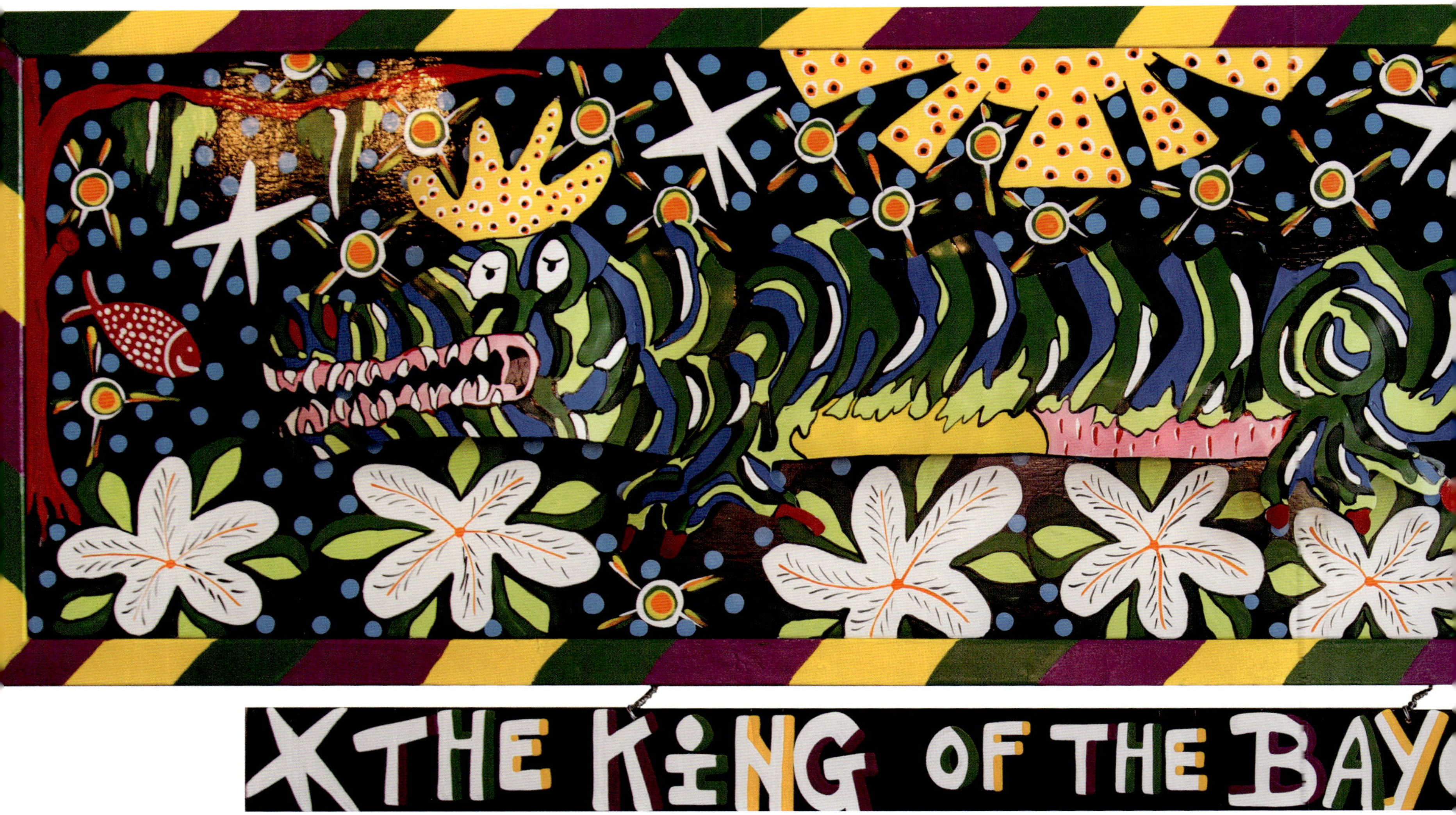
THE KING OF THE BAY

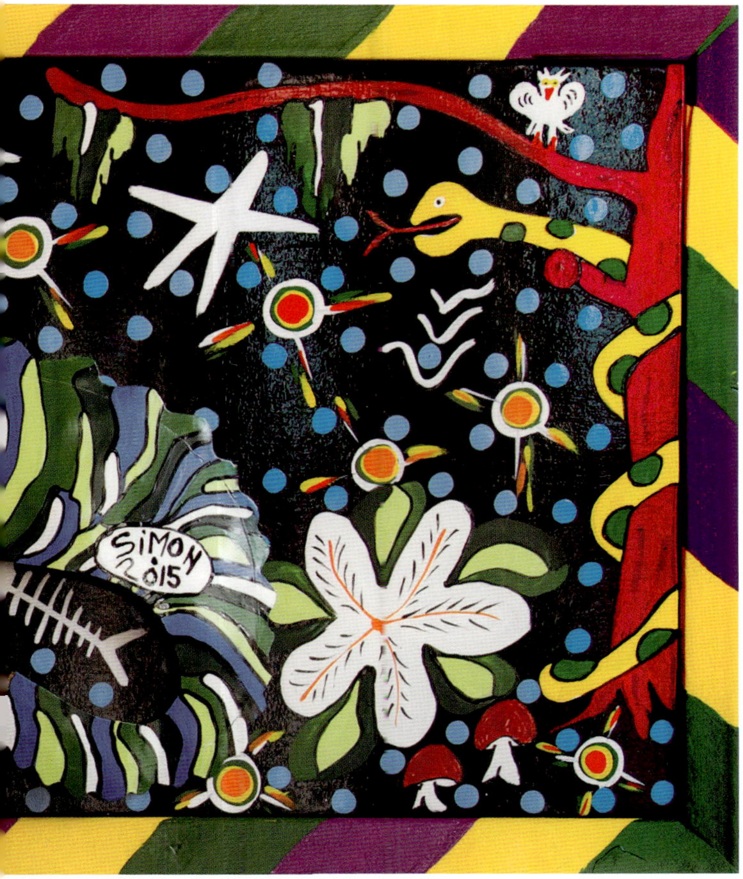

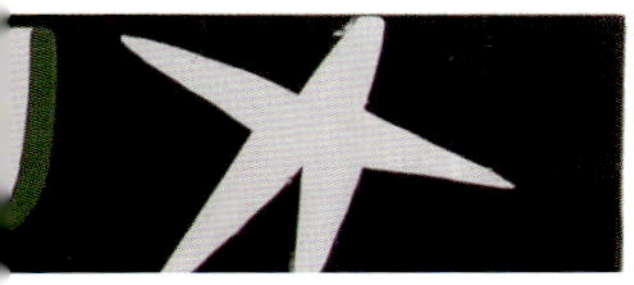

SIMON OF NEW ORLEANS

by

Yvonne Spear Perret

Photography by Paul Perret

RIVER ROAD PRESS

NEW ORLEANS 2016

ISBN: 978-1-941879-07-8

For more information on other River Road Press titles, please visit www.riverroadpress.com.

Printed in Malaysia

RIVER
ROAD
PRESS

Published by River Road Press
PO Box 125
Metairie, LA 70001

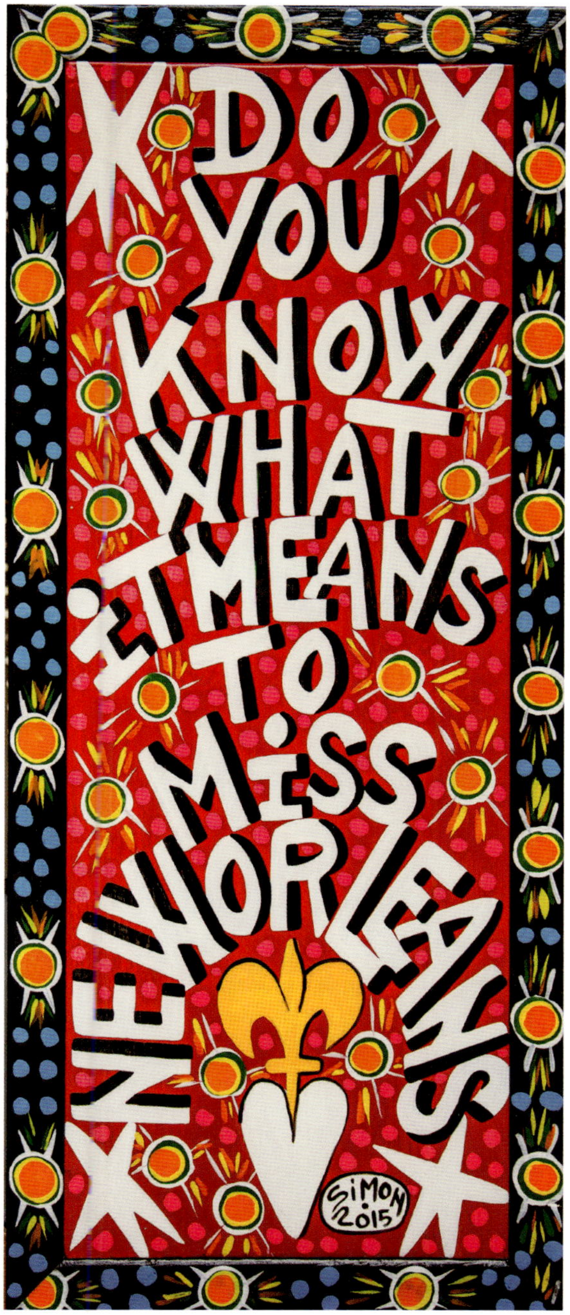

This book is dedicated to Paul Perret—my husband, my friend, and the artist in my life.

I also gratefully acknowledge the support and contributions of Paul III, Cindy, Scott, Simon, and the art-loving community of New Orleans.

—Yvonne Spear Perret

In memory of Shanette Edler, the longtime proprietor—and the heart and soul—of Liuzza's Restaurant. Shanette was a beloved New Orleans icon, a good friend, and a self-made woman who won countless hearts with her giving nature and enduring sense of humor.

—Simon

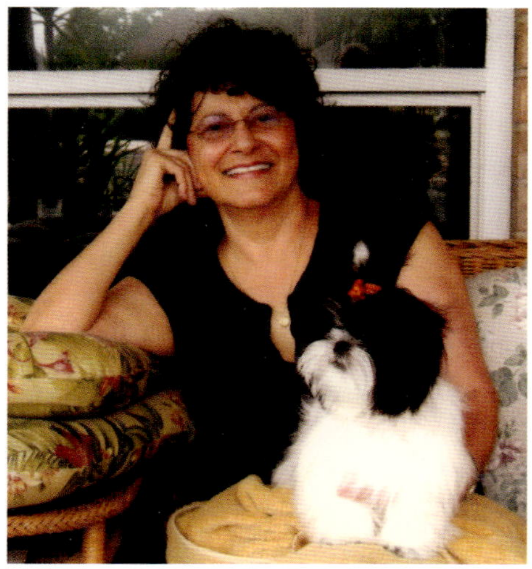

Shanette Bordelon Edler
(1951-2011)

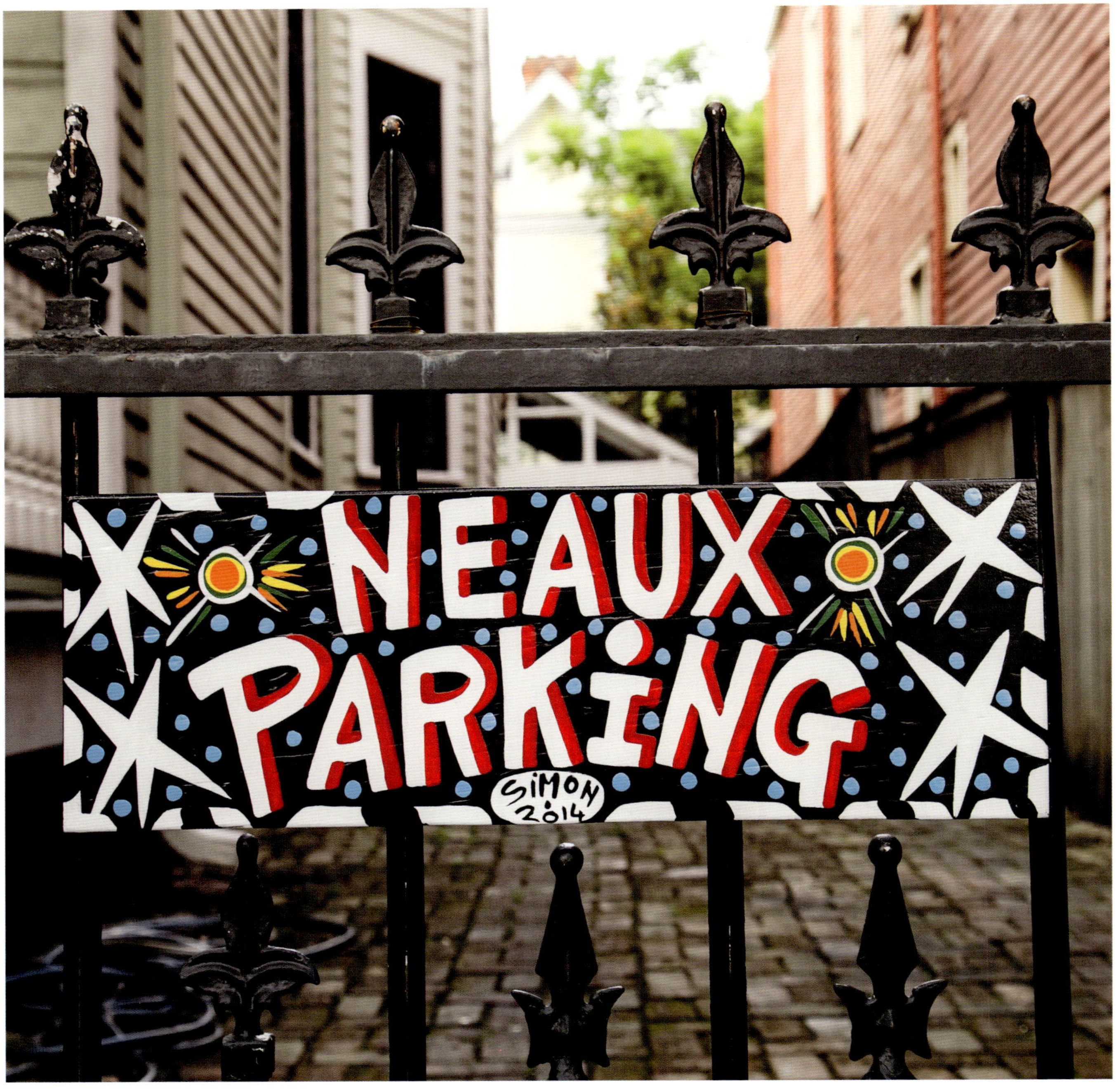
NEAUX
PARKING
SIMON
2014

CONTENTS

FOREWORD

I met Simon for the first time in September 2014, a few days after my arrival in Louisiana. I held a reception at my residence on Prytania Street to introduce myself and meet friends and partners of France. I was greeting the guests when a man of great height, with a long beard, and wearing a bandana on his head gently, modestly, generously handed me a beautiful piece of art painted on wood. Colorful and warm, like his painting, he wished me "welcome" to Louisiana, saying simply, "Here, Mr. Consul General. I did that. It's a painting." I knew then that I was lucky to already own one of his works. I had just met Simon of New Orleans!

Since then, I have gotten to know Simon and his wife, Maria. We are neighbors, and we see each other often. On the weekends, my family often passes by his studio and Maria's antiques shop on Jackson Avenue. We run into each other at festivals and at schools, where he never fails to lend a hand, just as he does for the Consulate General, the Alliance Française, the French-American Chamber of Commerce, and numerous charitable organizations. Simon is a philanthropist, a humanist. It is always a joy to speak and laugh with this French and Louisiana artist, who literally incarnates the spirit and culture of New Orleans. We already own a half-dozen of his works at home. In short, we have been conquered! It is clearly impossible to possess only one work by Simon. Once you've had the good idea to acquire one, it is rare to wait very long before returning to his studio. To see a work by Simon is all it takes to remind you of a smile and faith in your fellow man. Simon's art will warm your home like a cozy fire on a winter night. Put simply, Simon's art makes people happy.

Simon rethinks and redesigns the scenery of the Crescent City. His works are everywhere: in stores, in restaurants, in cafés, at the airport when you arrive. He keeps on painting. He never stops.

How to describe Simon's art? Caribbean colors, with touches of African, French, Spanish, Creole, Voodoo! Funny, spiritual messages painted on wood, proverbs, advice in French and English, all with newspaper articles pasted on the back. Works from him illustrate great celebrations that make up the rhythm of life in the Crescent City: Mardi Gras, Halloween, Easter, Christmas, Jazz Fest, French Quarter Fest, not to mention marriages, births, and all sorts of personal festivities. Simon, like any New Orleanian, never misses an opportunity to enjoy and celebrate life. Simon creates paintings, but also illuminates furniture, restaurants, television studios, and even a (fake) guillotine for Bastille Day.

Legendary characters, the fleurs de lis or the magnolia, stars—all, in Simon's hands, become a permanent invitation to joy, to welcome, tolerance: "Be nice or leave." For Simon, the acts of giving, of sharing, and of compassion for others are the most important human values.

Simon is his art. Simon collided with New Orleans, a city he cherishes and that cherishes him in return, and which he ultimately embodies. He is not a theorist and doesn't bore you with vague concepts. However, it's a fact: here, everyone loves Simon. With his work, he re-embellishes the already sumptuous landscape of a legendary city. Simon is the blending of a man, a city, and its history. It's the story of a man in symbiosis with his cultural environment.

I am proud to know Simon and to pay tribute to him with these few words. I sincerely thank Scott Campbell and River Road Press, Yvonne Spear Perret, and Paul Perret for having respectively published, written, and photographed this beautiful book, a very good antidote against the poison of pessimism and introversion.

Happy reading to everyone and see you soon in the legendary outdoor studio, at the corner of Magazine Street and Jackson Avenue, amid paintings, Zulu lances, and totem poles. Go and greet our friend Simon of New Orleans!

GRÉGOR TRUMEL
Consul General of France in New Orleans
New Orleans, Louisiana
April 2016

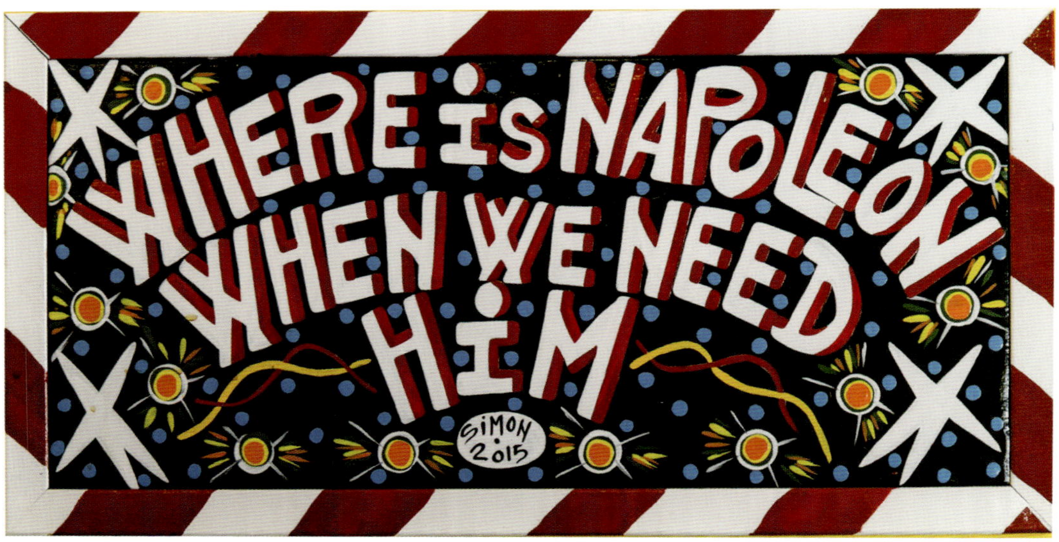

PRÉFACE

La première fois que j'ai rencontré Simon, c'était en septembre 2014, quelques jours après mon arrivée en Louisiane. Je donnais une réception pour me présenter et rencontrer les amis et partenaires de la France, à ma résidence, rue Prytania. Je saluais les invités, quand un homme de grande taille, barbu, portant un bandana sur la tête, me donna gentiment, modestement, généreusement, un beau tableau peint sur du bois, très coloré, si chaleureux, me souhaitant la « Bienvenue ». Il ajouta simplement: «tenez Monsieur le Consul, c'est moi qui fais ça, c'est un tableau». On me dit alors que j'avais de la chance d'être déjà en possession d'une de ses œuvres. Je venais de faire la connaissance de Simon de New Orleans!

Depuis, j'ai appris à connaître Simon et son épouse Maria. Nous sommes voisins, et nous nous voyons souvent. Nous passons à son atelier et au magasin d'antiquités de Maria, rue Jackson, en famille, le week-end, nous nous croisons dans les festivals, dans les écoles qu'il ne manque jamais d'aider, tout comme il aide le Consulat Général, l'Alliance française, la Chambre de Commerce Franco-Américaine et de nombreuses associations caritatives. Simon est un philanthrope, un humaniste. C'est toujours une joie de parler et de rire avec cet artiste français et louisianais, qui incarne littéralement l'esprit et la culture de La Nouvelle-Orléans. Nous avons déjà une demi-douzaine de ses œuvres chez nous. En un mot comme en cent, nous sommes conquis! Il est de toute évidence impossible de posséder seulement une œuvre de Simon. Une fois qu'on a eu la bonne idée d'en acquérir une, il est rare d'attendre longtemps avant de retourner à son atelier. Regarder une œuvre de Simon suffit bien souvent à retrouver le sourire et foi en son prochain. L'art de Simon réchauffe l'intérieur de votre maison mieux qu'un feu de cheminée un soir d'hiver. Il rend heureux, tout simplement.

Simon repense et redessine les décors de la Ville-Croissant. Ces œuvres sont présentes partout, dans les magasins, les restaurants, les cafés, à l'aéroport, quand vous arrivez. Il peint sans cesse, il n'arrête jamais.

Comment décrire l'art de Simon ? Des couleurs caraïbes, des touches africaines, françaises, espagnoles, créoles, vaudous! Des messages drôles, spirituels, peints sur du bois, des articles de journaux collés sur l'envers. Des œuvres qu'on lui achète pour illustrer les grandes fêtes qui rythment la vie dans la *Ville-Croissant* : Mardi Gras, Halloween, Pâques, Noël, Jazz Fest, French Quarter Fest, sans parler des mariages, naissances, et toutes célébrations. Simon en bon Néo-Orléanais ne manque jamais une occasion de se réjouir et de fêter la vie. Simon peint des tableaux, mais aussi des meubles, des restaurants, des studios de télévision et même une (fausse) guillotine pour Bastille Day!

Des personnages légendaires, des fleurs de lys ou de magnolia, des étoiles—deviennent entre les mains de Simon une invitation permanente à la joie, à l'accueil, à la tolérance. «*Be nice or leave*»: pour Simon, le don, l'amour du prochain et le partage sont les valeurs suprêmes.

Simon est son art. Il a rencontré La Nouvelle-Orléans, une ville qu'il chérit et qui le chérit entre tous, et qu'il finit par incarner. Il n'est pas un théoricien et ne vous ennuie pas avec des concepts fumeux. Et pourtant, c'est une évidence : ici, tout le monde aime Simon. Il embellit encore, avec son œuvre, le décor déjà somptueux d'une ville de légende. Simon c'est une rencontre entre un homme, une ville et son histoire. C'est l'histoire d'un homme en symbiose avec son environnement culturel.

Je suis fier de connaître Simon et de lui rendre hommage par ces quelques mots. Je remercie sincèrement Scott Campbell et les éditions *River Road Press*, Yvonne Spear Perret et Paul Perret pour avoir respectivement publié, écrit et illustré ce beau livre, très bon antidote contre le poison du pessimisme et du repli sur soi.

Bonne lecture à tous, et à bientôt, dans le légendaire atelier en plein air, à l'angle de Magazine Street et Jackson Avenue, au milieu des tableaux, des lances Zulus et des totems. Allons saluer notre ami Simon de New Orleans!

GRÉGOR TRUMEL
Consul Général de France à La Nouvelle-Orléans
La Nouvelle-Orléans, Louisiane
avril 2016

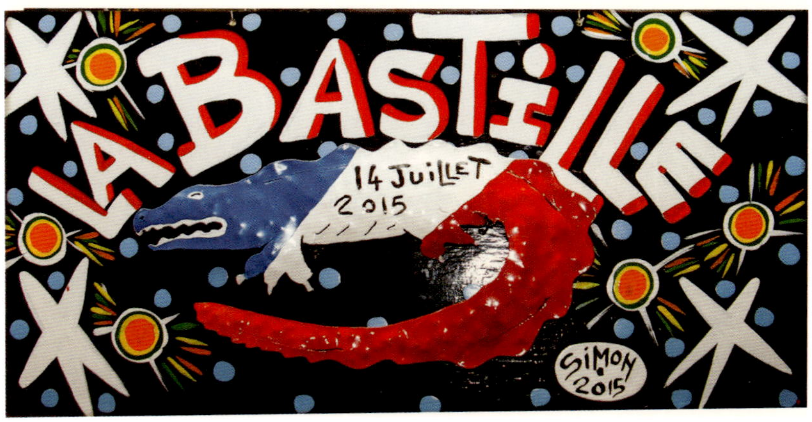

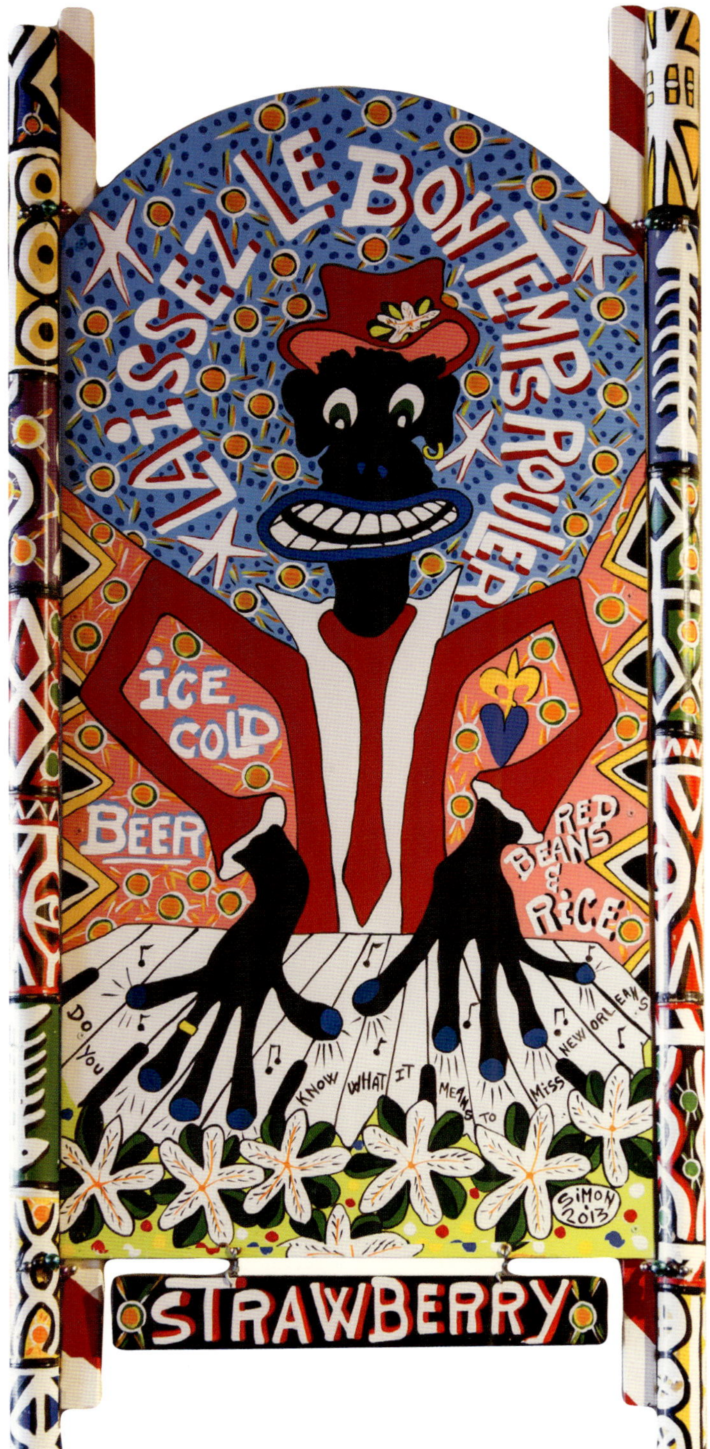
LAISSEZ LE BON TEMPS ROULER
ICE COLD
BEER
RED BEANS & RICE
DO YOU KNOW WHAT IT MEANS TO MISS NEW ORLEANS
SIMON 2013
STRAWBERRY

DÉJÀ VU ART

The prevalence of his signs and artwork throughout the greater New Orleans area ranks second only to that of the ubiquitous symbol of the city's revival, the fleur de lis. Simon (pronounced sih-MOH) Hardeveld is a native Frenchman who has adopted the Crescent City as his own, so much so that he has chosen as his moniker "Simon of New Orleans."

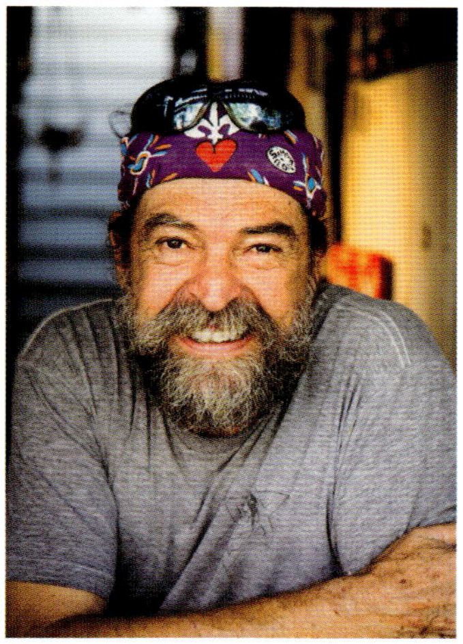

Simon of New Orleans.

His art embellishes the city—from huge billboards decorated with his work to small signboards in neighborhood businesses to French Quarter Festival posters; from the walls of dozens of New Orleans restaurants to the newsroom set of a local television station to the entrance of a hospital's surgery center. Even the artist jests about the pervasiveness of his art. "I like to call it 'Déjà Vu' art," he explains, "because when you see it, you know you've seen it before."

His style is indeed immediately recognizable in its unpretentiousness, intensity, and brightness. It is reminiscent of folk art in its

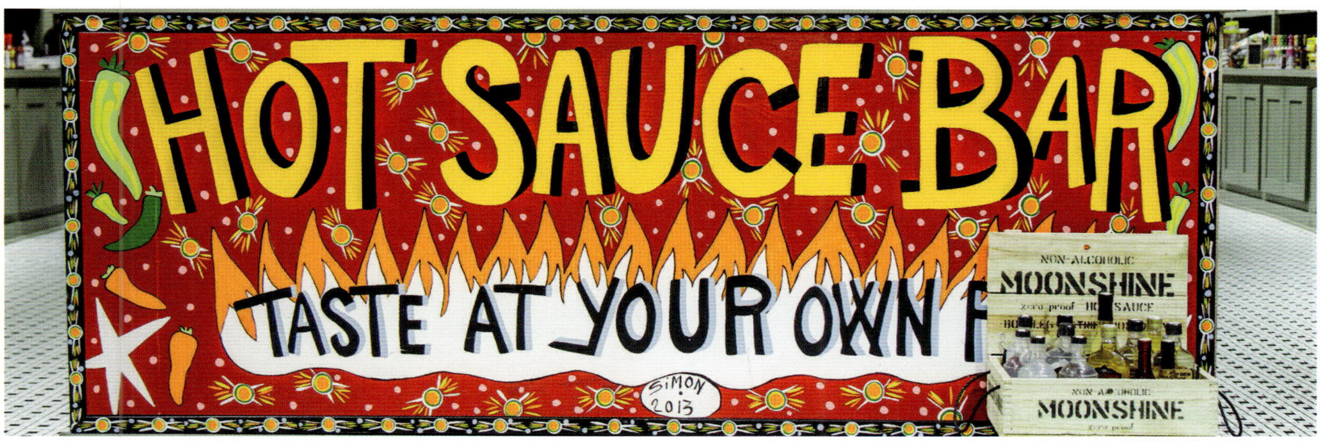

Many businesses feature Simon's custom, hand-painted signs.

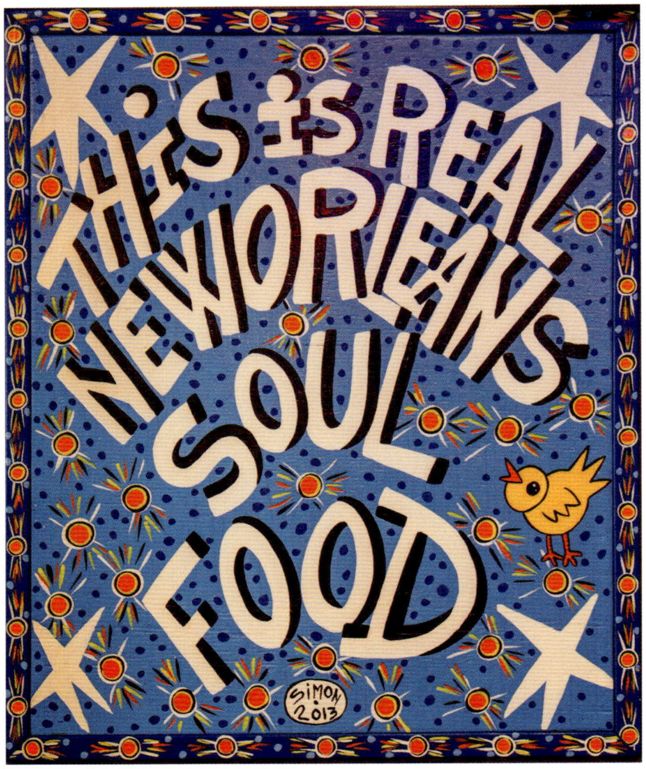

Simon's signs are found in many of the area's restaurants.

elemental design, yet liberally stylized, usually with his three most-recognized symbols: an asymmetric, vaguely personified star; a concentric double-dot or triple-dot, which represents energy; and a squiggle, which he has termed a "chromosome." The colors he chooses are vivid and dynamic, lending a compelling energy to the works. The result is a balance of clarity, innocence, and brashness.

And his work is always New Orleans-centric in subject and feel. "I paint New Orleans," says the artist. "I paint it out of love for the city." His is a deep, abiding love that he is quick to acknowledge. "New Orleans is my inspiration," he says with a thick French accent. "I did not paint before I came here, but since I came here, I cannot stop."

Formerly a chef and restaurateur in his native France, Simon fell in love with New Orleans on his first

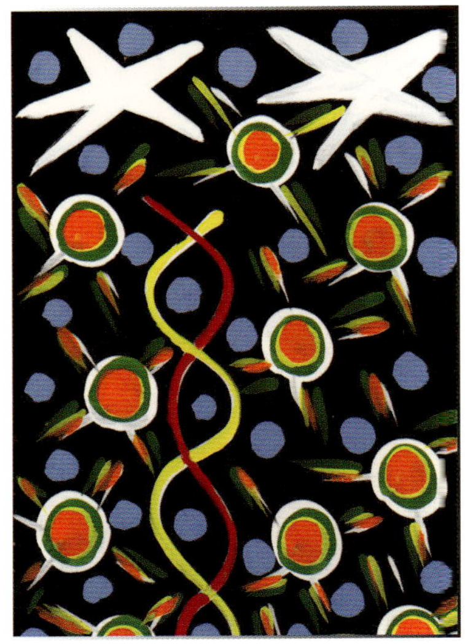

The star, "energy," and "chromosome" elements appear on most Simon creations.

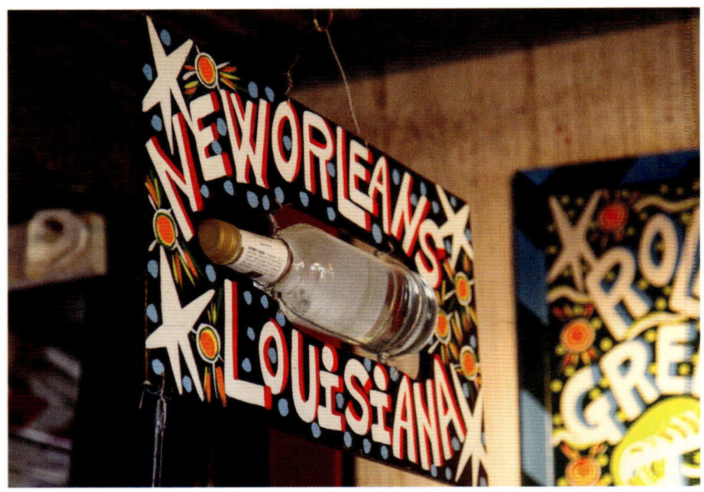

Though popular in other countries, Simon's work remains New Orleans centered.

visit to the Crescent City in the mid-1990s. The attachment has only deepened over the years. He revels in the extensive and enduring arts culture; the spirited, festival atmosphere; and the city's historic ties to France. But what he appreciates most are the people of the city. "Yes, the people first!" he emphasizes with an animated gesture, his right hand signaling the "number one." He loves the populace that has embraced him and his work. "Sometimes I feel like the city's *grand-père*, their French grandfather," he says proudly.

Despite Simon's close connections to the city, the reach of his devotees extends far beyond the New Orleans area. His work can be found in Napa Valley wineries, casinos in Las Vegas, and in private collections on both coasts. His works and fame have also spread internationally as tourists and collectors visit his studio, select a little piece of Simon's New Orleans, and bring it home with them.

Collector Susan Nolan, who has known Simon since 1996, moved to North Carolina after Hurricane Katrina. She took her undamaged Simon pieces with her and has continued collecting. She now owns more than fifty pieces, including artworks, totems, and signs, all of which are prominently displayed in her North Carolina home. By giving pieces as gifts, she has started others off as Simon collectors, beginning with her own family members. The first item on her daughter's Christmas list was one of Simon's signs. Santa came through for her. Her children have travelled the world and lived in Japan and various countries in Europe. They take their Simon pieces with them, and their new friends begin to request his work. "So now Japan has Simon. Europe has Simon. And who knows where else?" says Nolan.

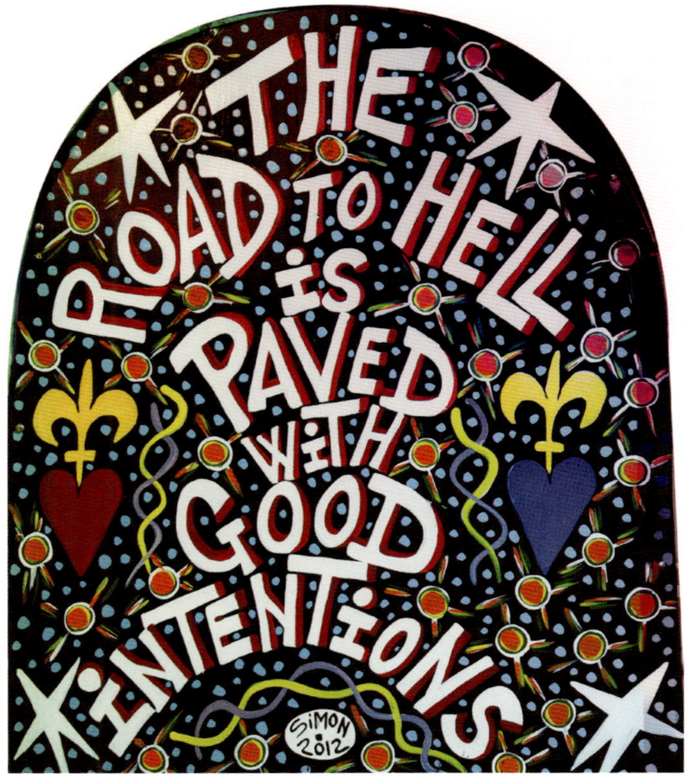

Well-known sayings are given the Simon treatment.

On a recent visit to Portland, Oregon, the Nolans arrived for dinner at an upscale restaurant and Susan spied two of Simon's signs adorning the restaurant walls. One, she recalls, was the iconic "Be Nice or Leave." As

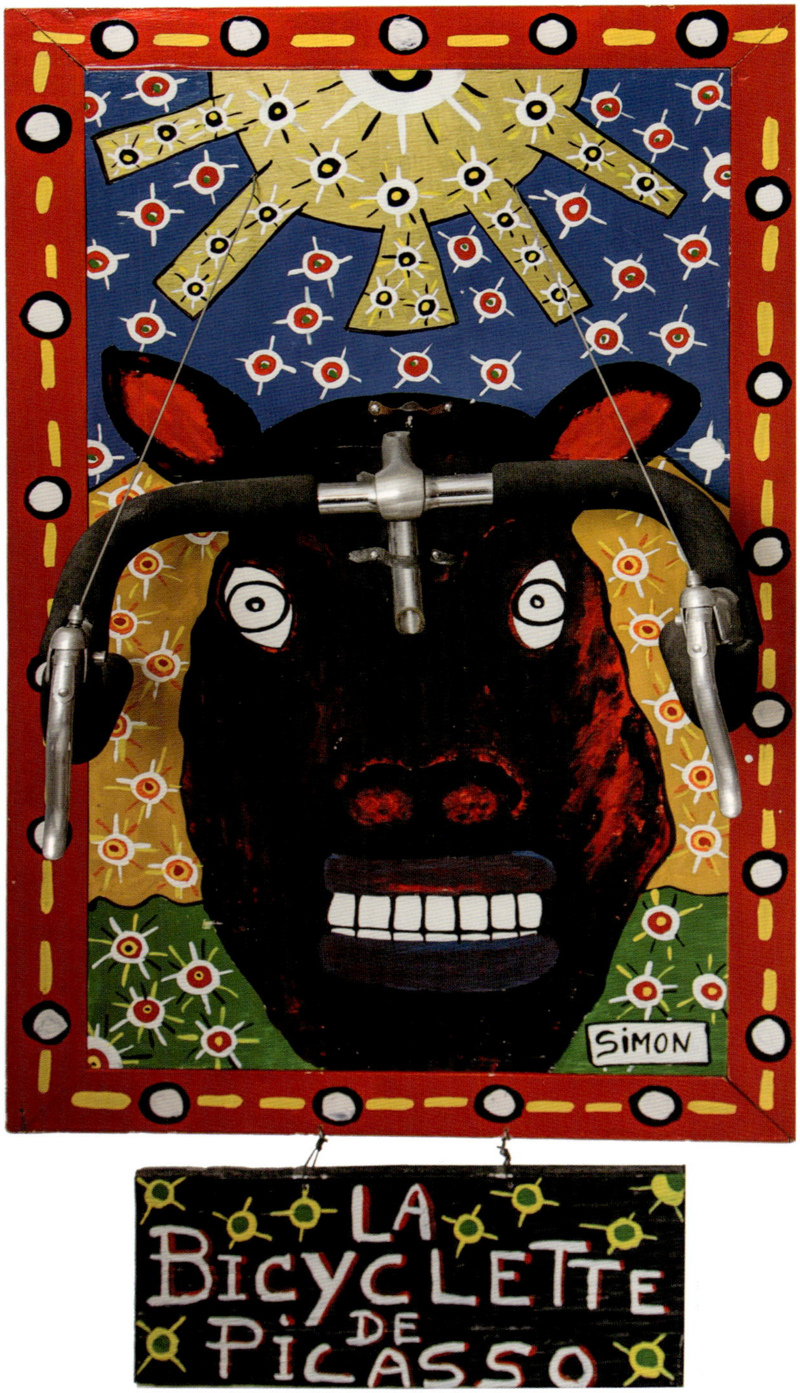

La Bicyclette de Picasso *features the head of an angry bull, complete with bicycle handlebars as the bull's horns. The gear grips on the handles are intact, and the attached cables are threaded through to the back of the painting. It is a functioning mechanism; when the grips are squeezed and released, the entire painting lifts up and down, like a bull rearing its head when readying for a charge. (Fleishmann collection, 1997)*

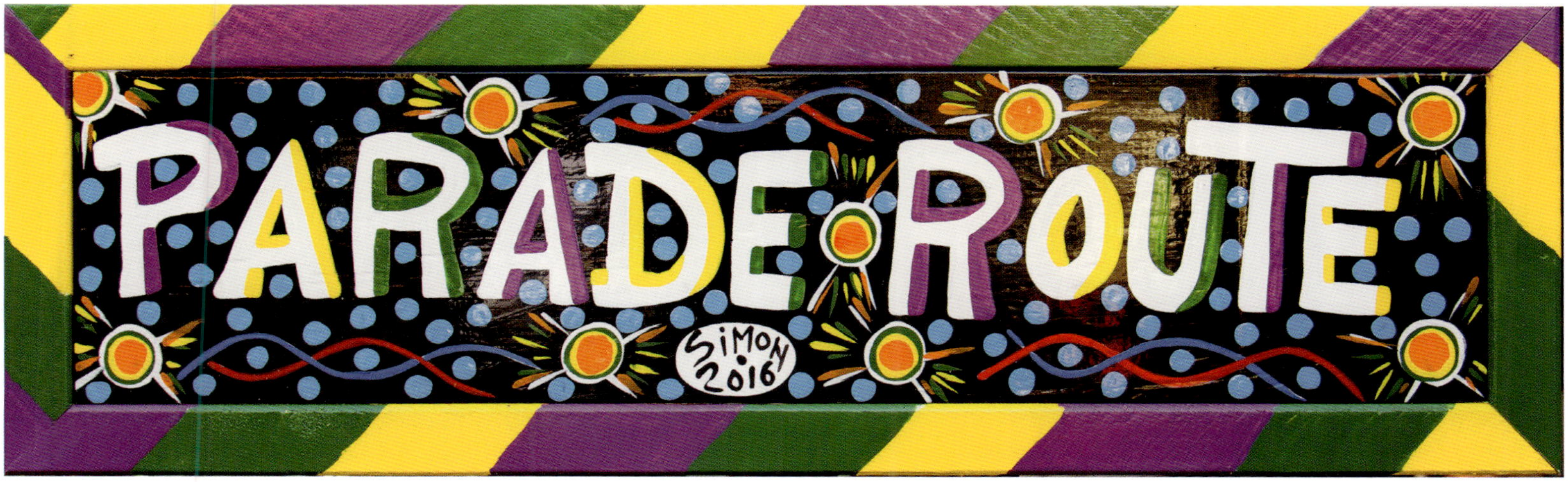

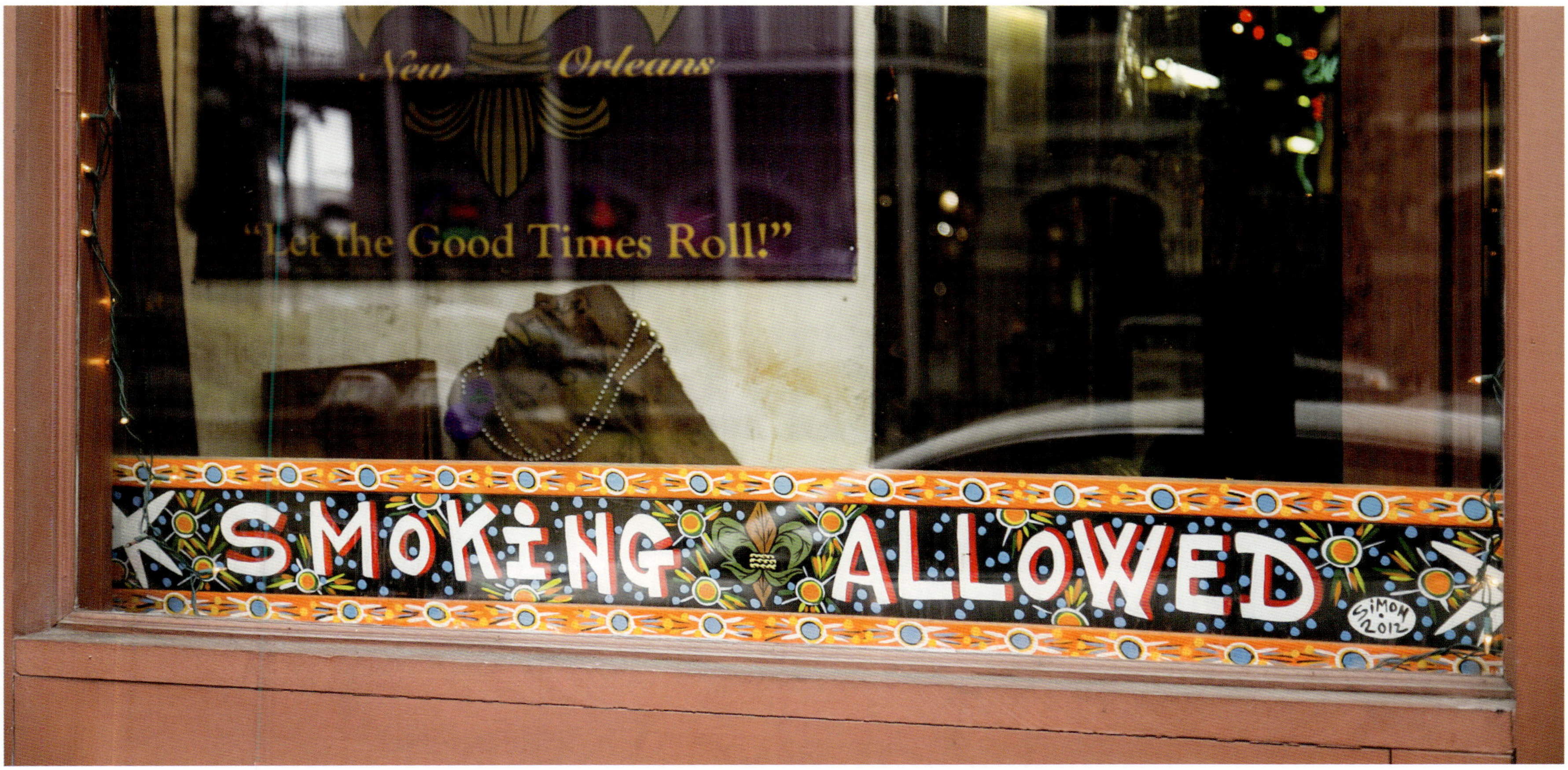

The front window of the Happy Hookah, New Orleans French Quarter.

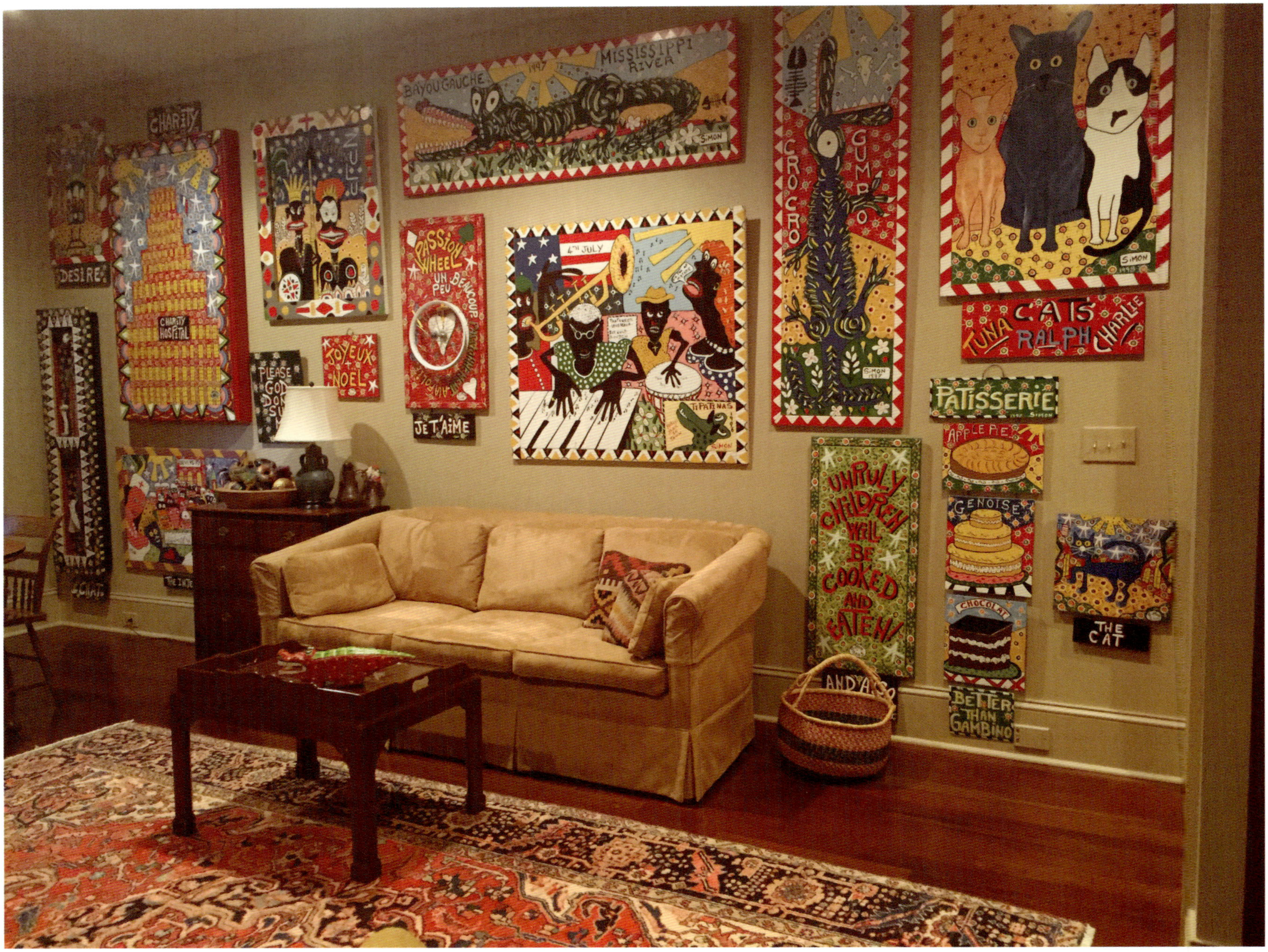

The wall of Tom and Susan Nolan's den in their North Carolina home is covered with Simon's works. (Courtesy Tom and Susan Nolan)

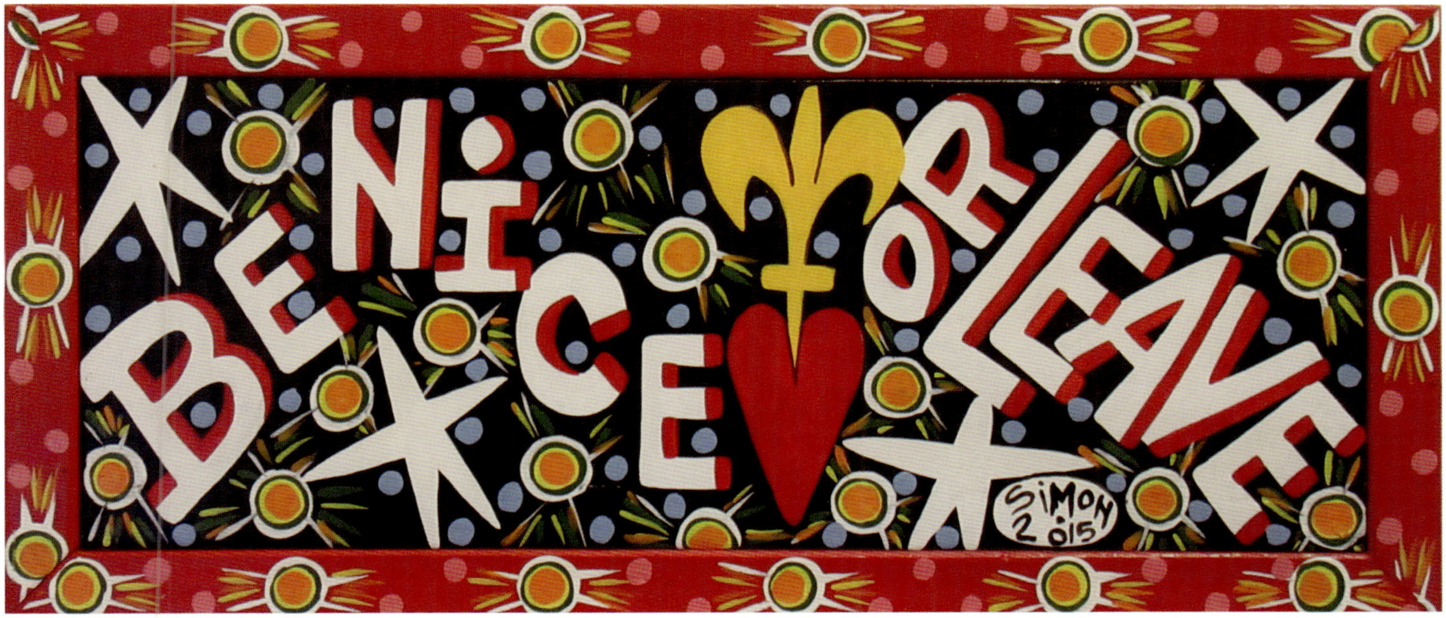

One of Simon's most requested sayings.

she pointed out the signs to her husband, she laughed and remarked, "Look at that! Simon pops up everywhere!"

Yet, despite the worldwide reach of his work, Simon remains a quintessentially New Orleans artist. The city is still his inspiration and his adopted home. "Everything I love is here," he explains. "So, everything I paint is a sign of that love. Painting New Orleans is my passion."

The fact that his passion has had such widespread appeal for other people still astonishes him. "I turn a corner and see one of my signs, and I am so surprised to see it," he says. "How strange—and wonderful—that what I love to do most turns out to be something that so many other people love! I don't go out to them. They just come. How amazing!"

Asked if he ever thought he'd be so well-known and recognized on the streets of the city, Simon scrunches up his face and shakes his head. "Aw, no, no, no," he answers. He then adds, "But it is nice, yes?"

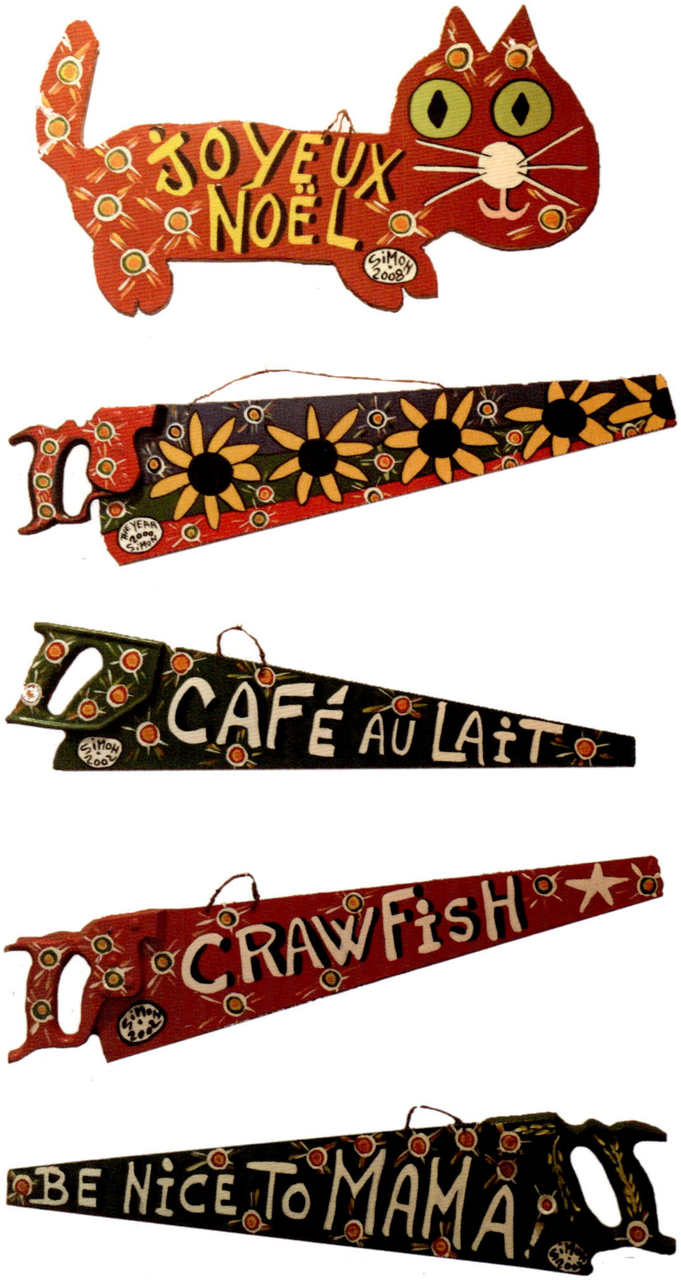

(Courtesy Tom and Susan Nolan)

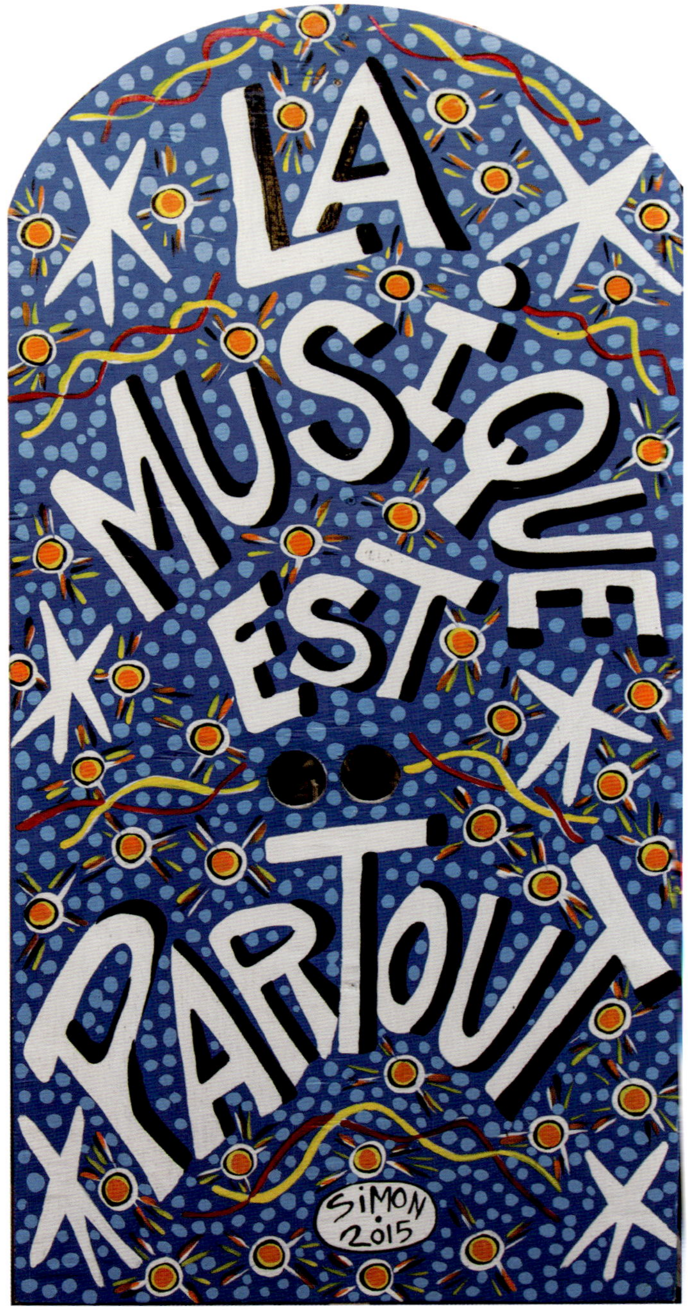

"The Music Is Everywhere."

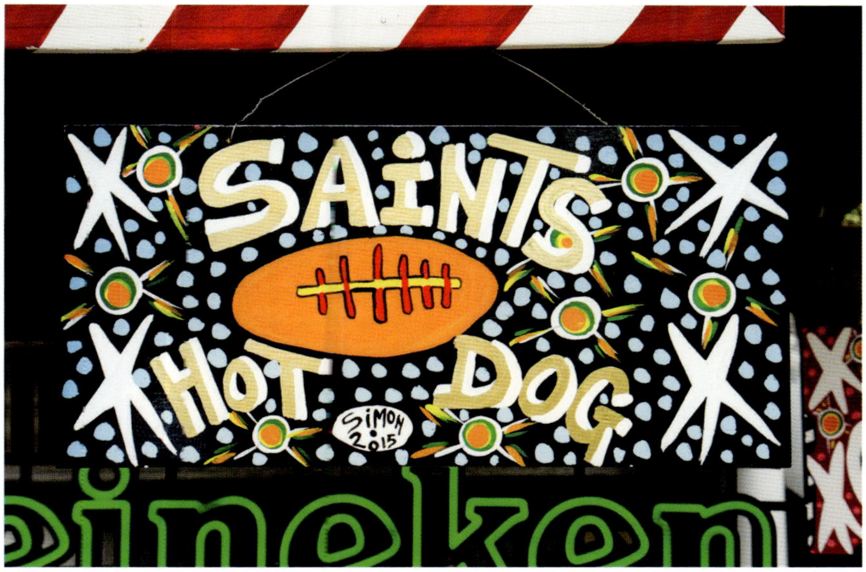
SAINTS
HOT DOG
SIMON 2015

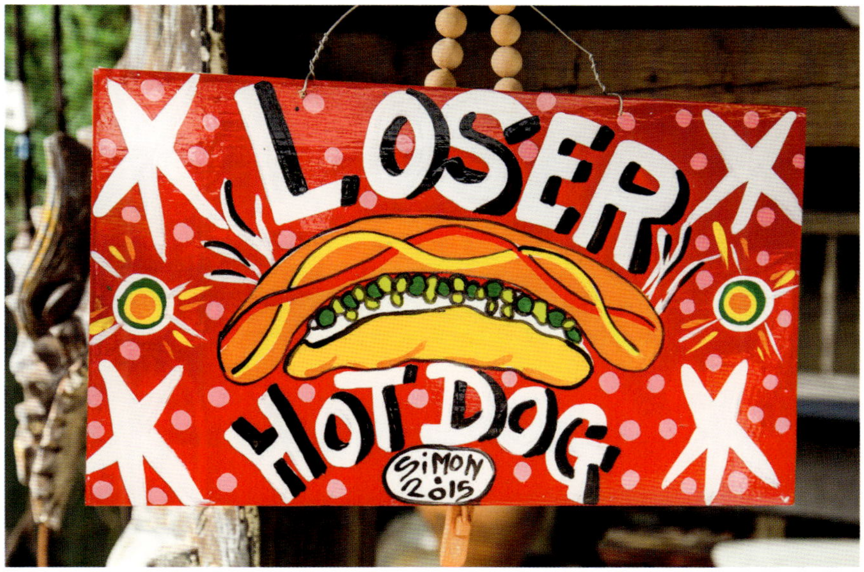
LOSER
HOT DOG
SIMON 2015

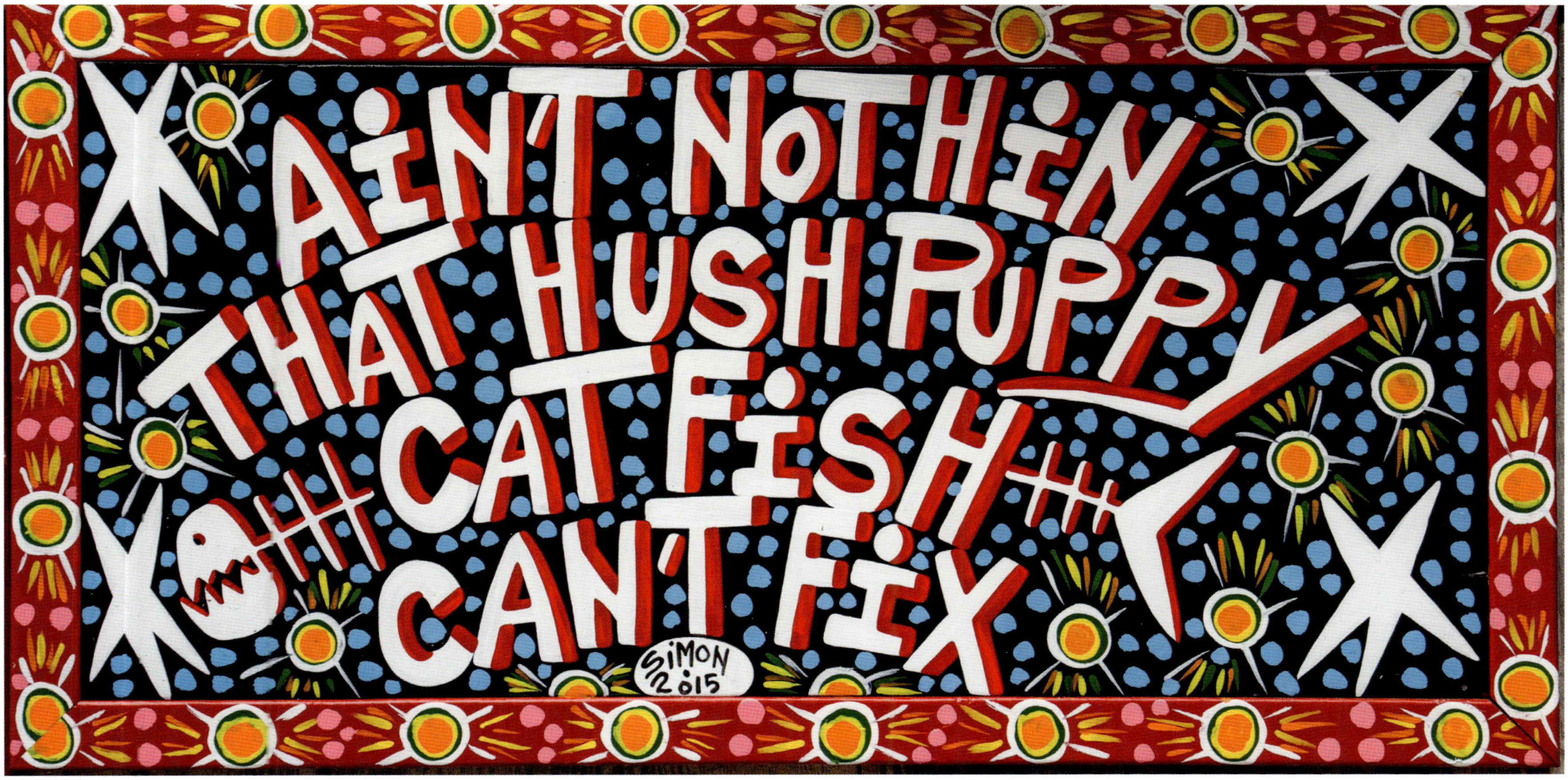
AIN'T NOTHIN
THAT HUSH PUPPY
CAT FISH
CAN'T FIX
SIMON 2015

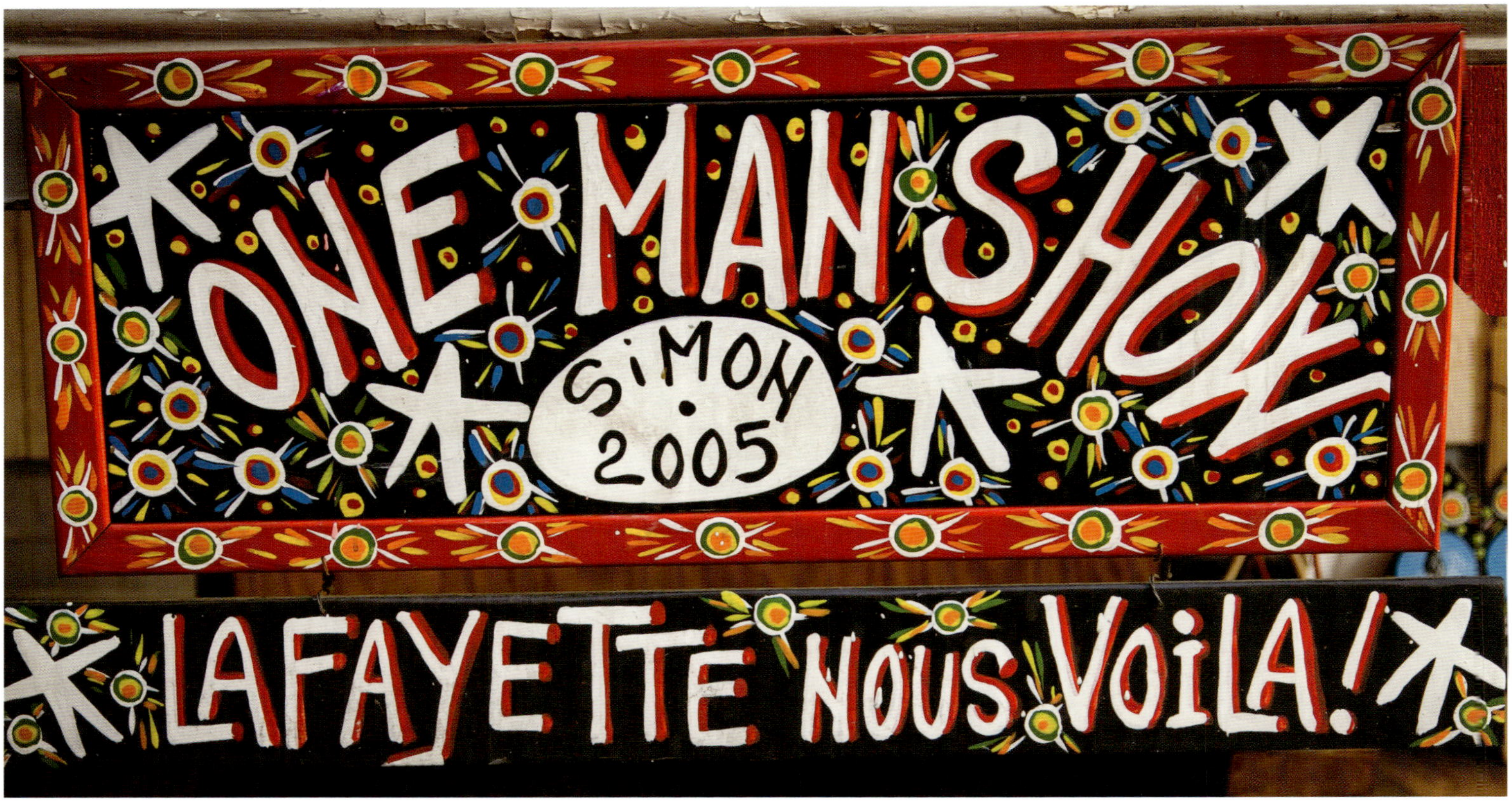
ONE MAN SHOW
SiMON
2005
LAFAYETTE NOUS VOiLA!

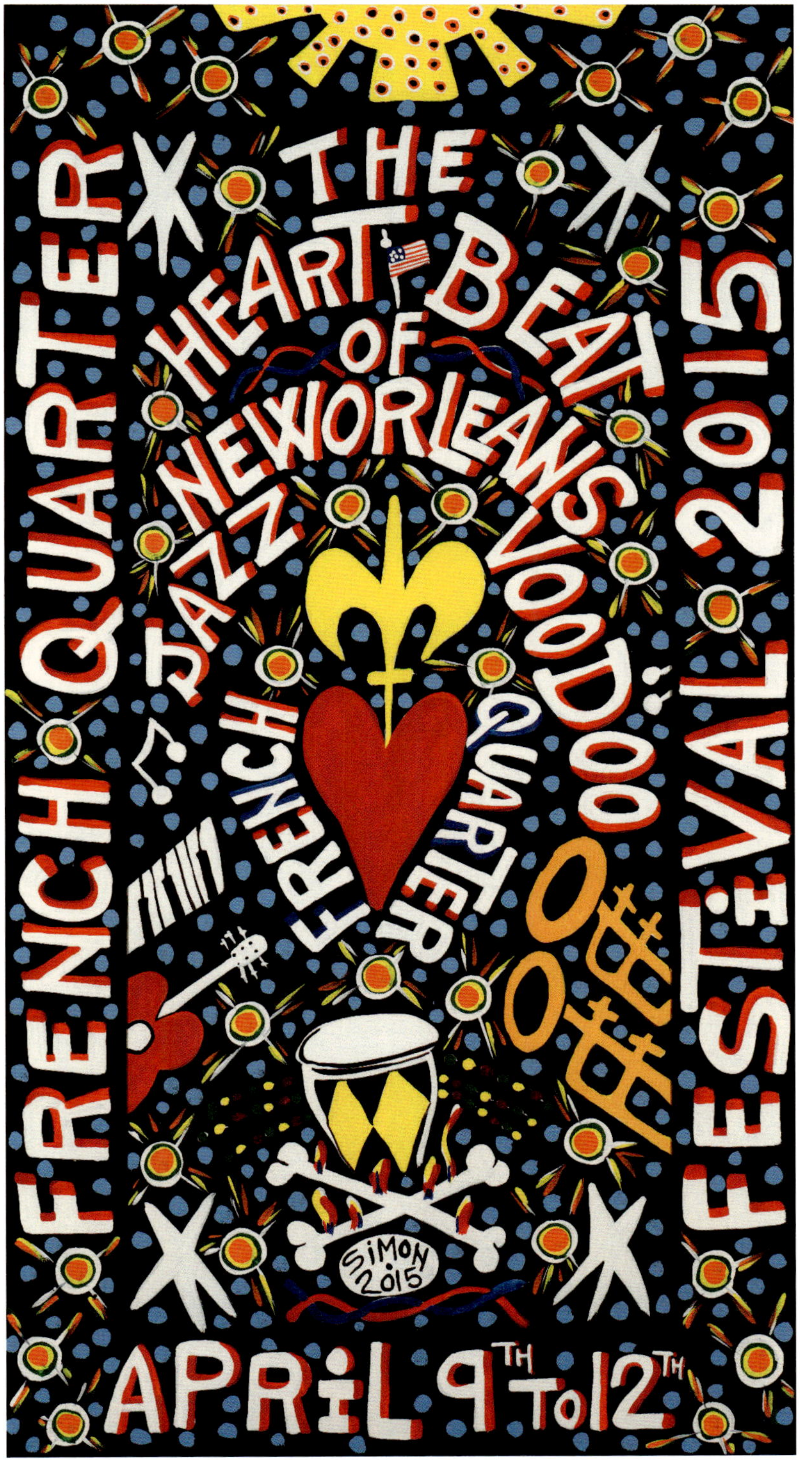

The official poster of the 2015 French Quarter Festival. (Courtesy French Quarter Festivals, Inc.)

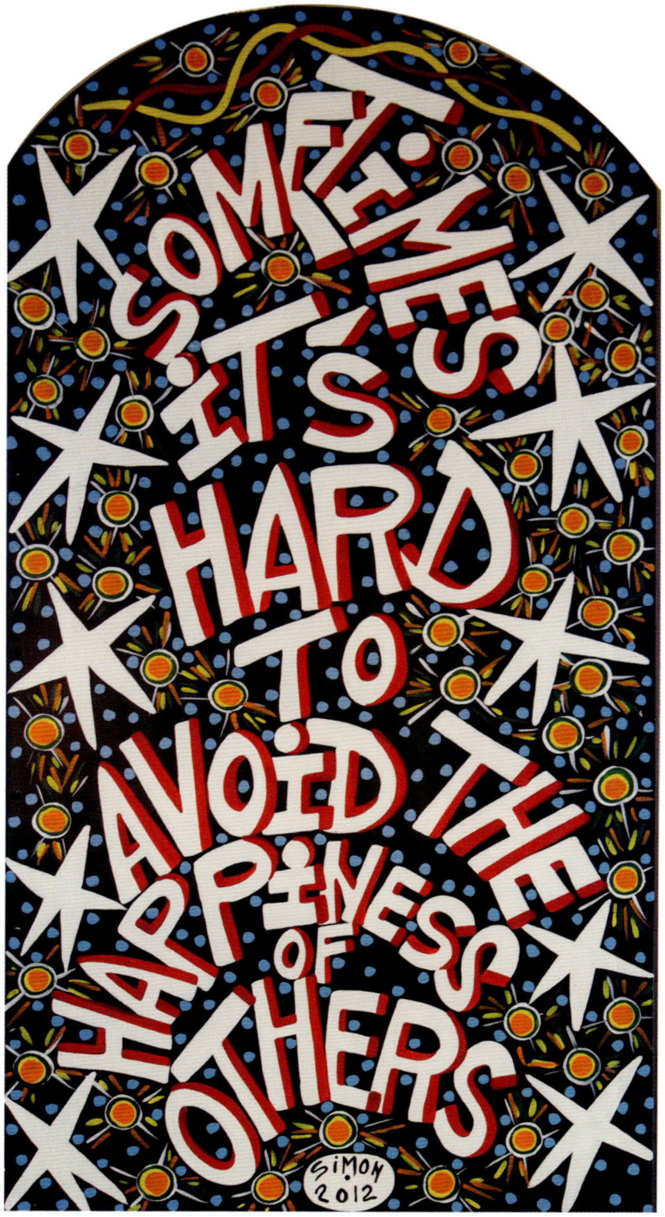

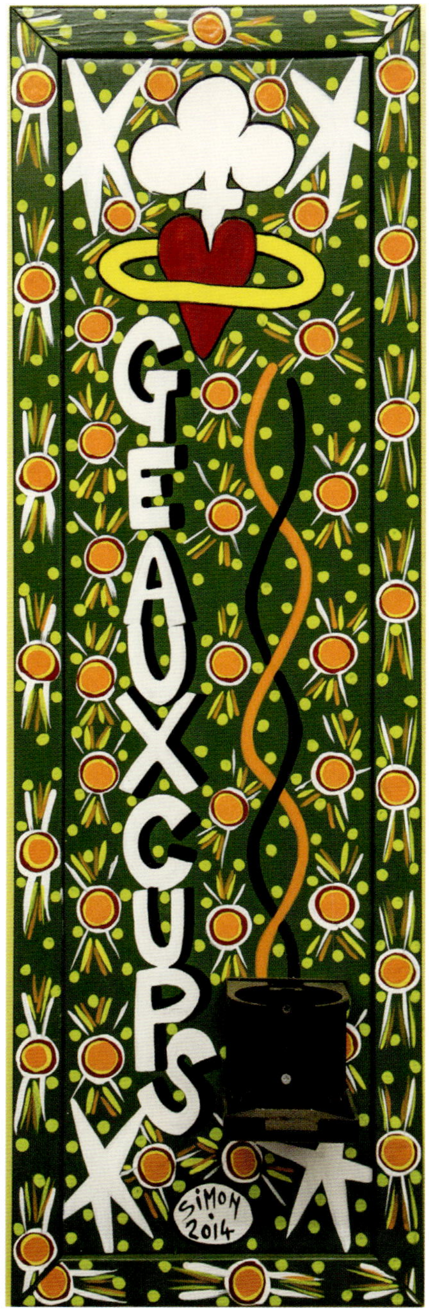

One of Simon's most functional pieces, this go-cup dispenser is found near the doors of many bars in the city.

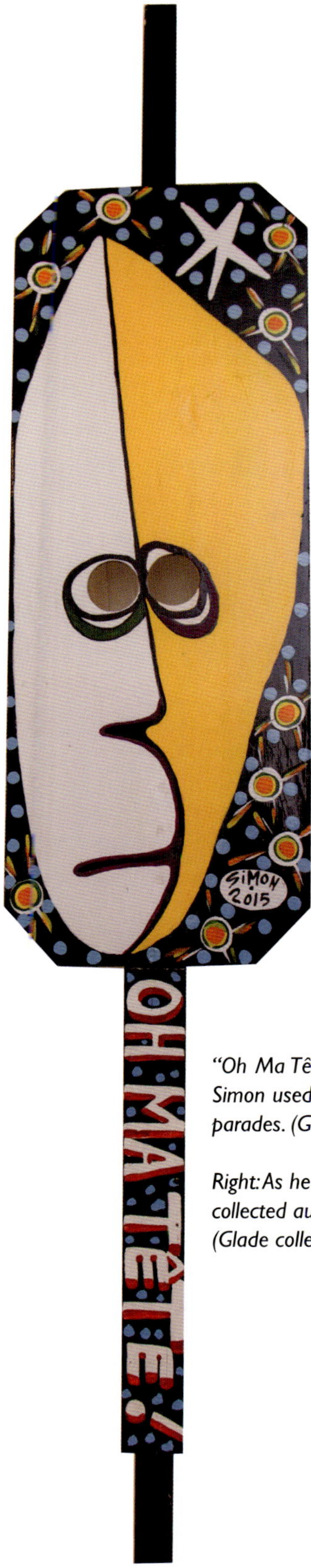

"Oh Ma Tête!" (Oh my head!) proclaims the face board Simon used as his costume during the 2015 Mardi Gras parades. (Glade collection, 2015)

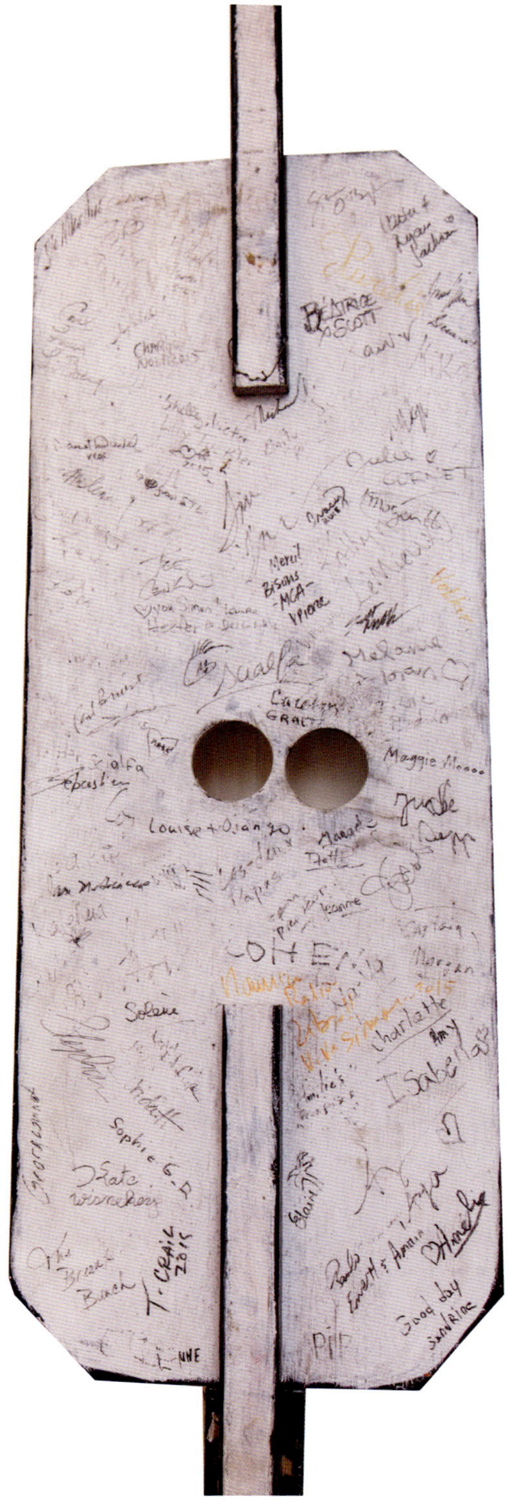

Right: As he walked along the parade route, Simon collected autographs on the back of the board. (Glade collection, 2015)

THE ARTIST

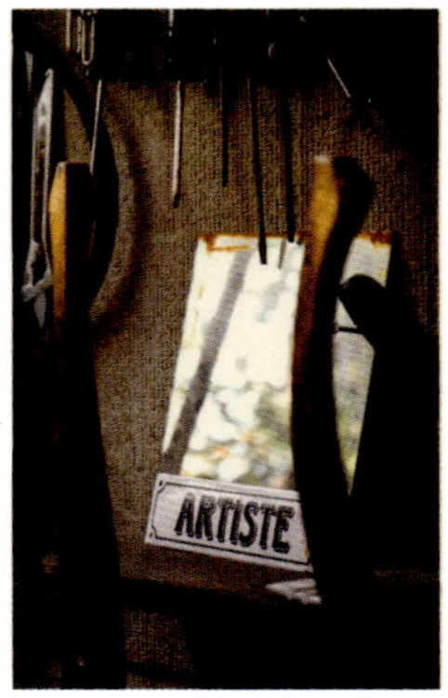

Artists are often stereotypically described as temperamental, brooding, and bohemian. With his decidedly unconventional look, Simon has the bohemian part down pat. Caught up (but never totally confined) in a ponytail at the back of his neck is a mane of long gray hair. An ever-present bandana tied around his forehead helps tame the locks. Peering out from below the bandana are spirited brown eyes. A full beard completes the avant-garde look. His go-to wardrobe consists of sandals, t-shirts, and shorts. Most of his clothing is well-worn, holey in places, and appropriately paint splattered.

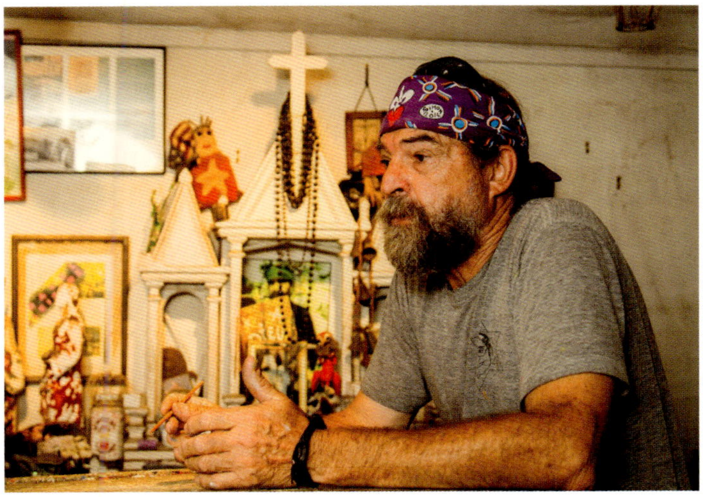

Simon in the office of his Jackson Avenue studio.

As for "temperamental" and "brooding," this artist is neither. On the contrary, he has an unshakeable sense of humor and a wry wit. "I laugh alone," he commented when asked for an insight into his own personality. "I laugh out loud when the mood or situation strikes me as funny, even if there is no one else around." His buoyant character is played out in the upbeat feel of his artwork and the clever sayings on his signs.

"The guy is always smiling," says Katell Oijubin, former owner of a popular Uptown bakery that displayed an entire wall of Simon's signs. "He's just a good soul: kind and gentle and downright nice."

"And ever the optimist," adds Dale Fleishmann, a collector since 1996. "He is one of the happiest people I know, and he likes to spread it around as much as possible."

Indeed, Simon eagerly shares his rose-colored glasses with anyone who could use the

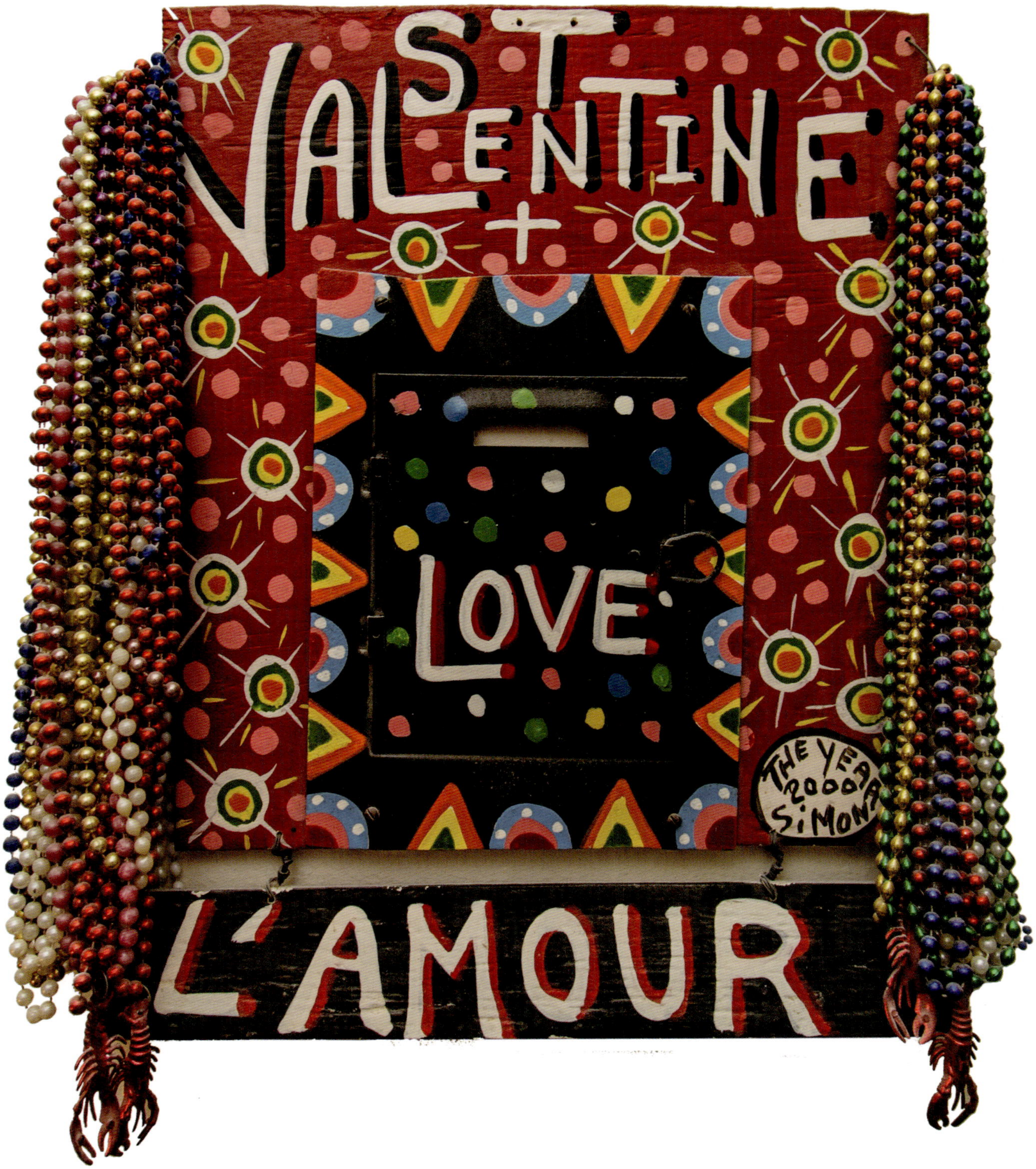
ST VALENTINE
+
LOVE
L'AMOUR
THE YEAR 2000 SIMON

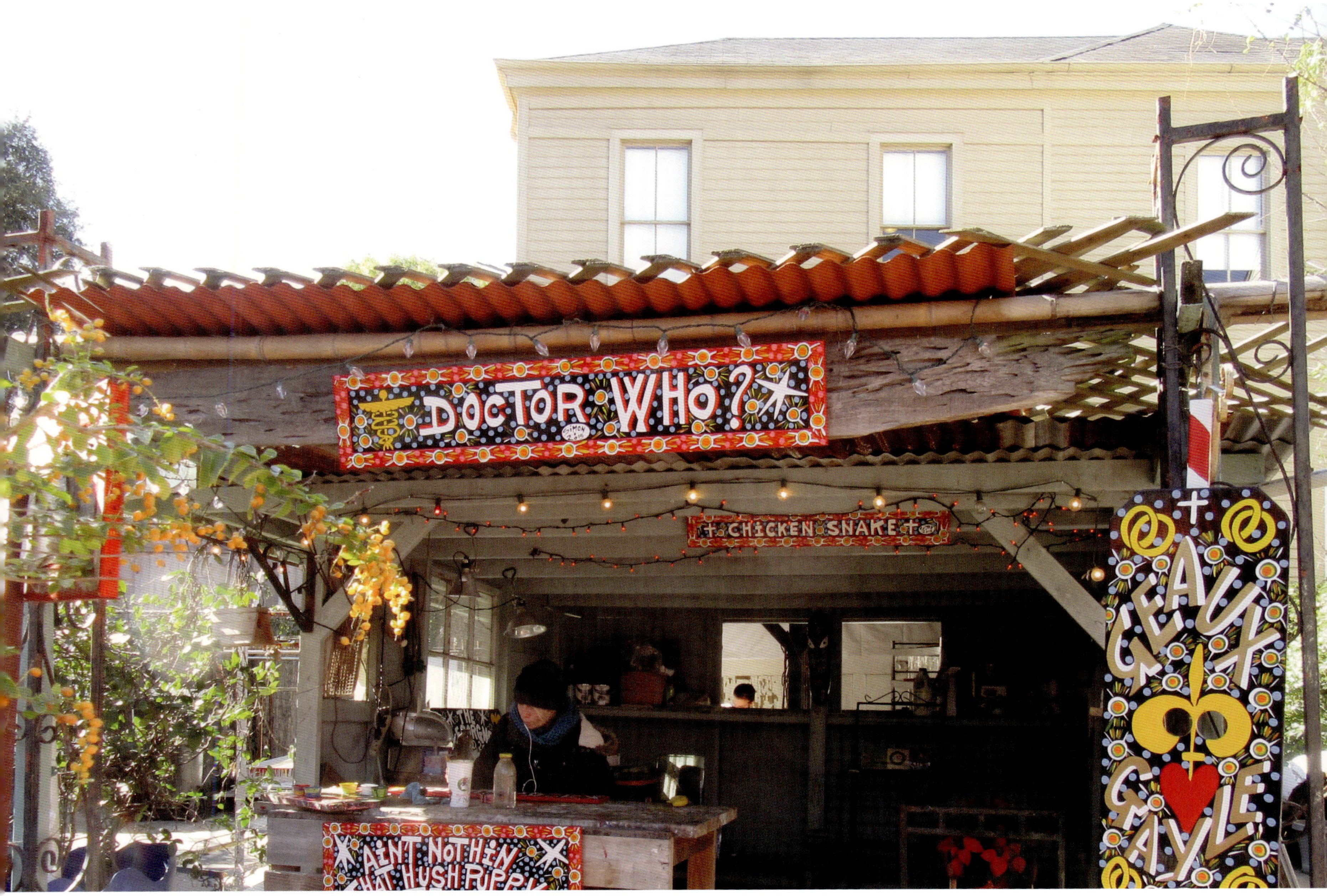

Works-in-progress at one of the open-air sheds at the artist's studio.

encouragement. Skip Murray, owner of Dis & Dem eatery and co-founder of the Dat Dog hot dog restaurants, recalls the uncertainty and doubt that nagged him as he prepared to open his first restaurant on Freret Street. "Would cuisine-savvy New Orleanians embrace a restaurant that built its menu around hot dogs—elaborate though they may be?" he wondered. Murray says that Simon was among his earliest supporters. He recalls Simon's ever-upbeat mantra, "It's gonna be great; it's gonna be great." And sure enough, it was. Not long after opening, Dat Dog had already outgrown its original location and moved to a much larger facility across the street, at 5030 Freret Street. Three additional Dat Dogs have opened in other locations. Having contributed additional works to the décor of the new restaurants, Simon attended each of the grand openings.

Words like "zany" also get thrown around when people search for the right adjectives to describe him. "'Zany' is the perfect word for Simon," says collector Charlie Camm. "'Zany' but also 'uniquely creative,'" he adds.

Murray sums it up: "He's a real New Orleans character with a capital 'C.'"

To borrow a phrase from his own native language: Simon embodies *joie de vivre*. And he revels in the *joie* that is New Orleans.

He is a self-described Mardi Gras junkie, admitting that after catching a couple of back-to-back parades along the St. Charles Avenue route, he has on occasion rushed out

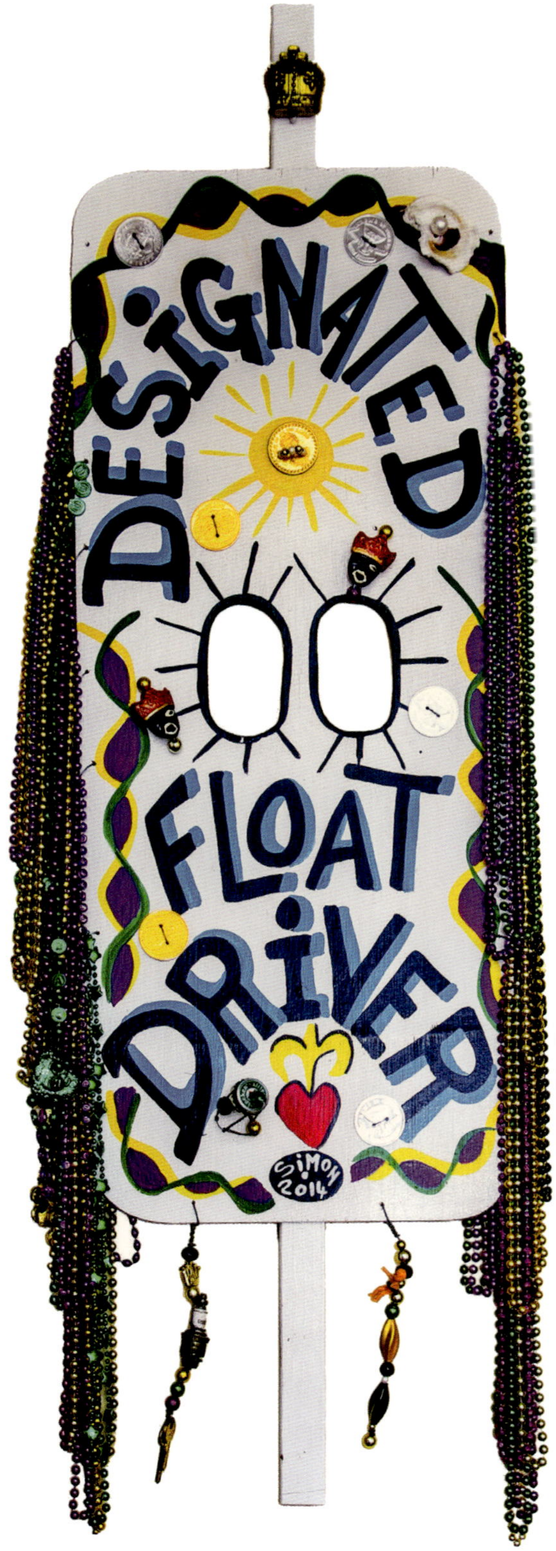

Right and opposite page: These brightly colored hand-held signs function as Mardi Gras costumes.

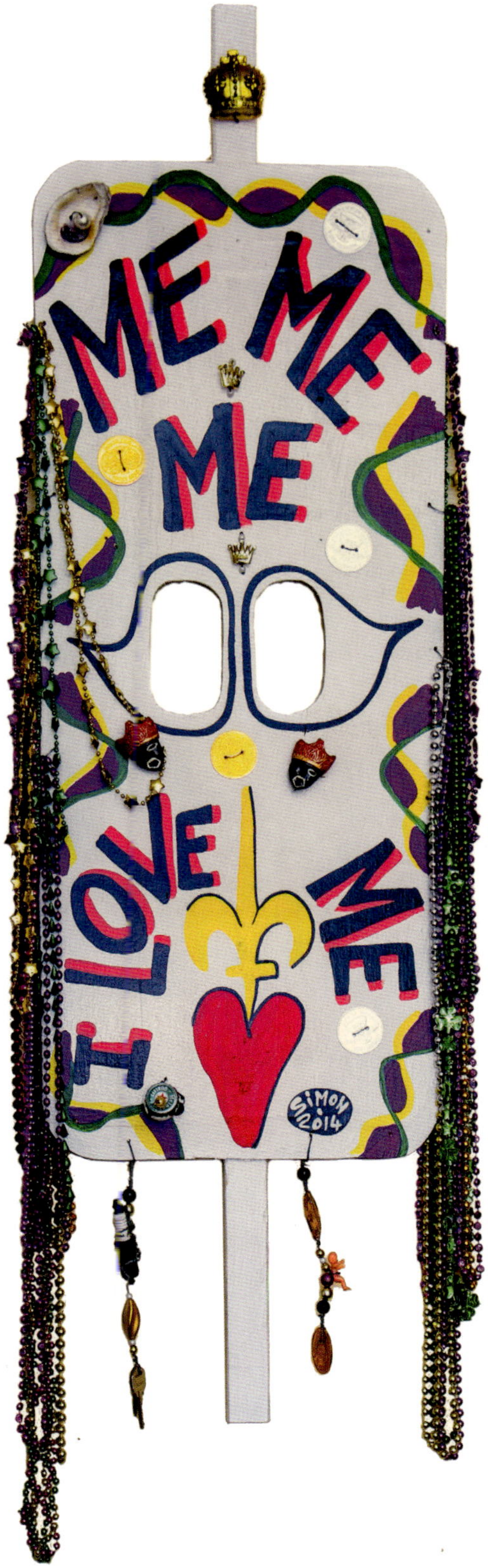

to Metairie to catch more. He has fashioned numerous Mardi Gras get-ups for people to use as costumes. Many of the creations are embellished sign boards with a handle attached at the bottom and two large holes for the eyes so the carrier can hold the board in front of his face and upper body as he walks along the route or stands in place begging for beads.

The St. Patrick's Day parade is another Simon favorite. He has been known to carry (or at times, wear) his artwork along the parade route, then fall in behind the last group of marchers, and eventually finagle his way into the middle of the parade. Along the route he is asked to pose for countless pictures by parade-goers eager to get a selfie with the artist, and he is happy to oblige.

Although Simon left France more than thirty years ago, he still retains a thick, lilting French accent. At best, a conversant with no French-language background can expect to understand most, but certainly not all, of what he says. While he patiently repeats for those who need it, occasionally he is unable to resist the temptation to exploit the pronounced accent for his own purposes.

Dr. Leonard Glade, another longtime collector, tells of the time Simon called the doctor's home and left him a voicemail message. Glade listened to the voicemail over and over again, but he was unable to get past Simon's heavy accent to figure out the message. After replaying it several times, Glade finally realized

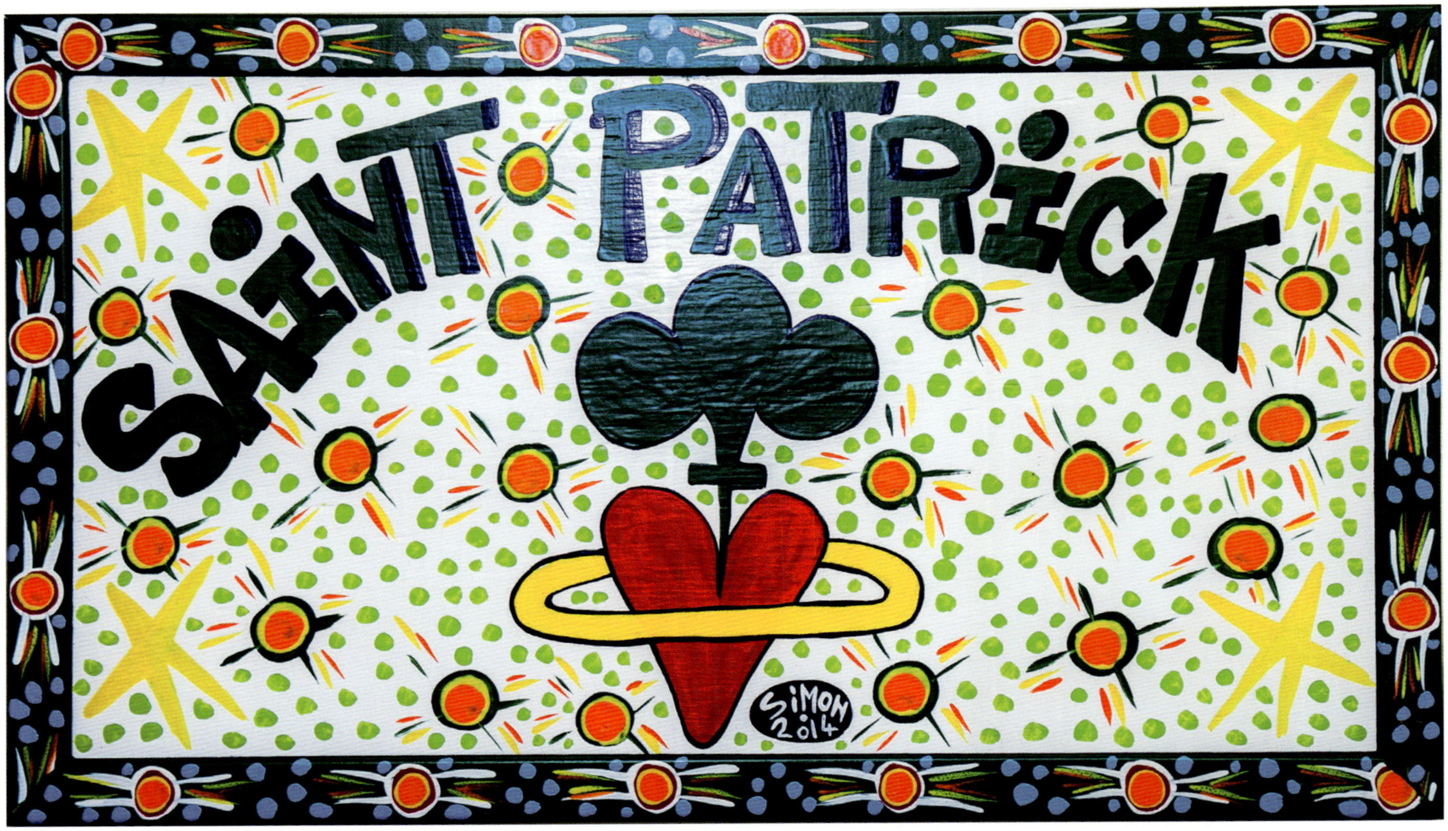

St. Patrick's Day celebrations are a Simon favorite. (Collection of Joey K's, 2014)

that it was not French-accented English words that were perplexing him. It was that the words themselves were French. Simon had left the entire message in his native language. The doctor does not speak French at all, a fact of which Simon was aware. When the doctor called Simon and asked about the message, Simon said that he knew the confusion would prompt the doctor to call him—and sooner rather than later—which is what the artist had wanted from the beginning.

Simon has also been known to exploit the language barrier as an escape tactic if he finds himself involved in a conversation he wants to avoid. Without missing a beat—and often in mid-sentence—he will revert to French, prompting those to whom he is speaking to think they are just unable to understand the point he is trying to make and give up.

With his bewildering accent, his animated hand gestures, and his unorthodox look, Simon not only fits the description of a "character,"

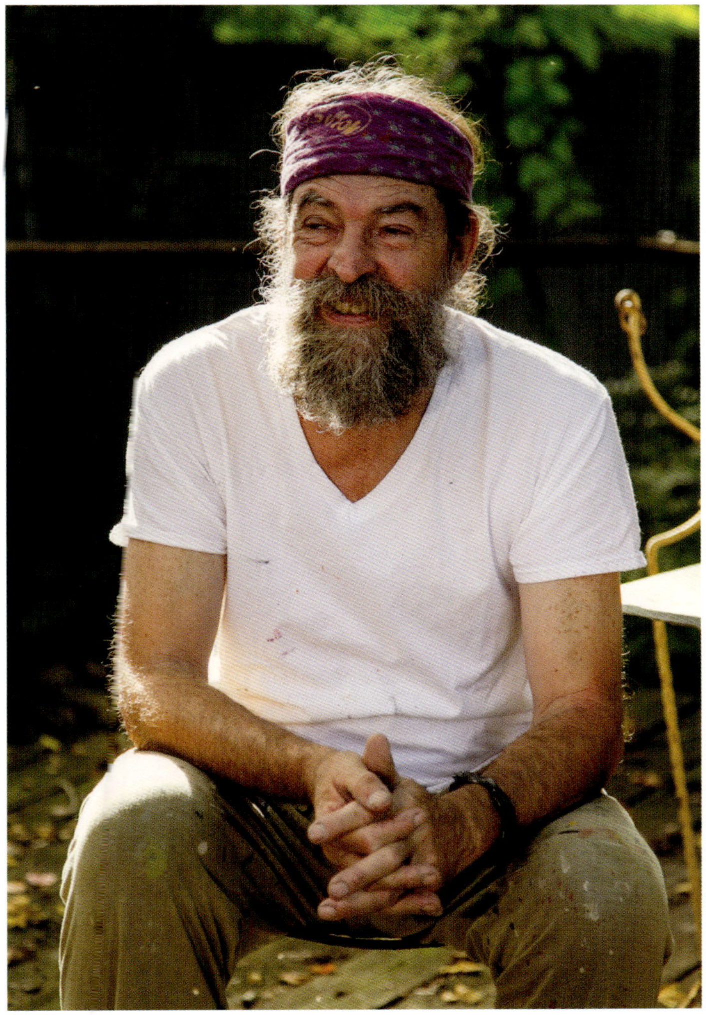

Simon in the backyard of his Broadmoor home.

he acts the part, too.

"I exaggerate," he readily admits. Then holding up his hand as if to swear an oath, he clarifies, "I exaggerate, but I never lie."

Dis & Dem owner Skip Murray provides a perfect example: "Simon was taking a while to finish one of the paintings I had ordered, and I nudged him about it."

"I will have it for you by Wednesday," promised Simon. When Wednesday came and went with no painting, Murray contacted Simon, reminding him about the Wednesday deadline.

"Ah, yes. I said I would have it for you by Wednesday," said Simon. Then he added, "But I didn't say *which* Wednesday."

Glade provides another example. "Simon likes to tell people that I saved his life," says the doctor. "But that's a bit of an exaggeration. I found out that Simon hadn't been in for a check-up in many years, and I finally convinced him to come in. We found and fixed a minor condition that, if left untreated, could eventually have been life-threatening. So to say that I saved his life is an overstatement, but it sounds quite dramatic and makes a good story for him to tell in his inimitable style."

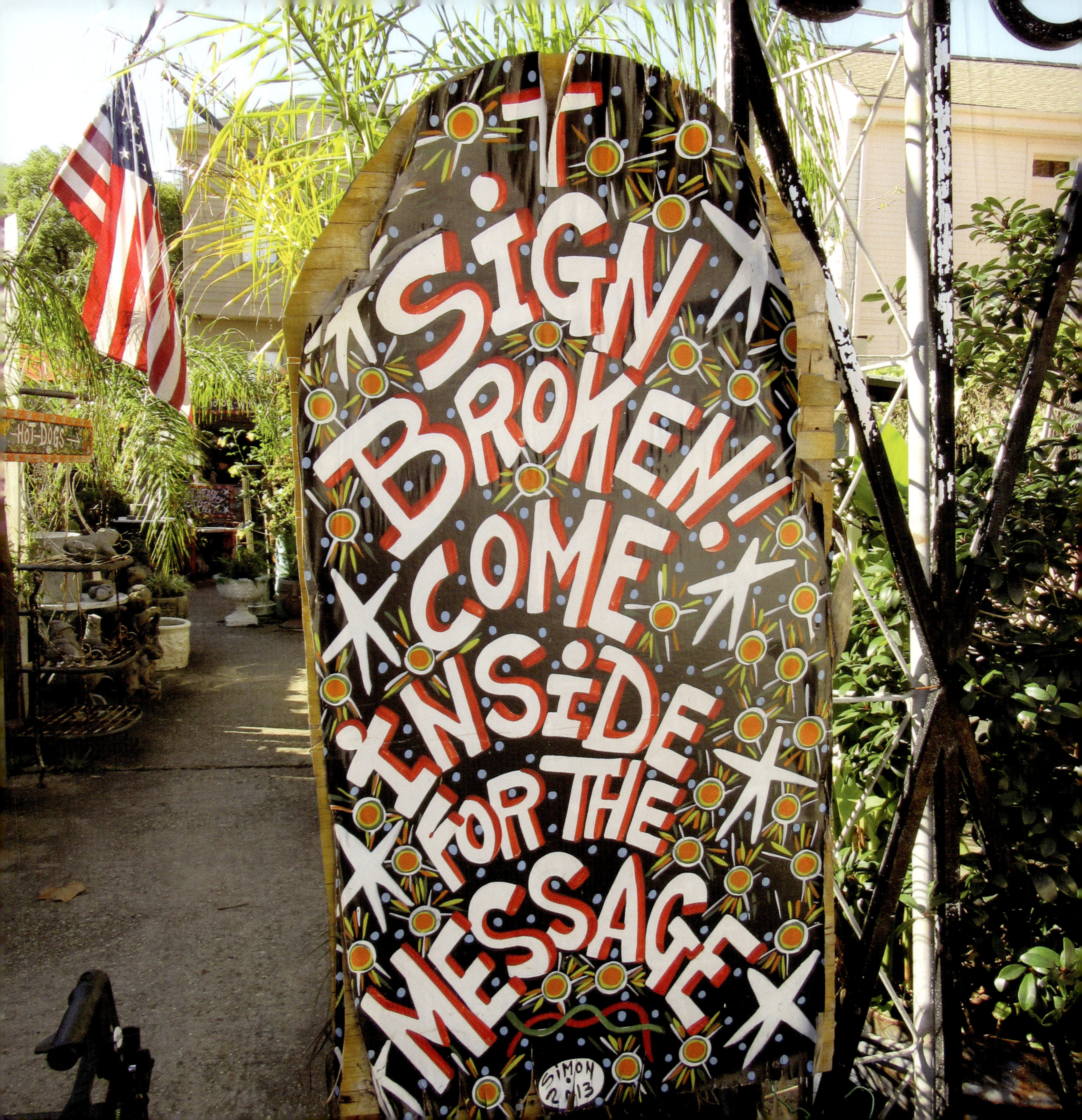
SIGN
BROKEN!
COME
INSIDE
FOR THE
MESSAGE
SIMON
2013
HOT-DOGS

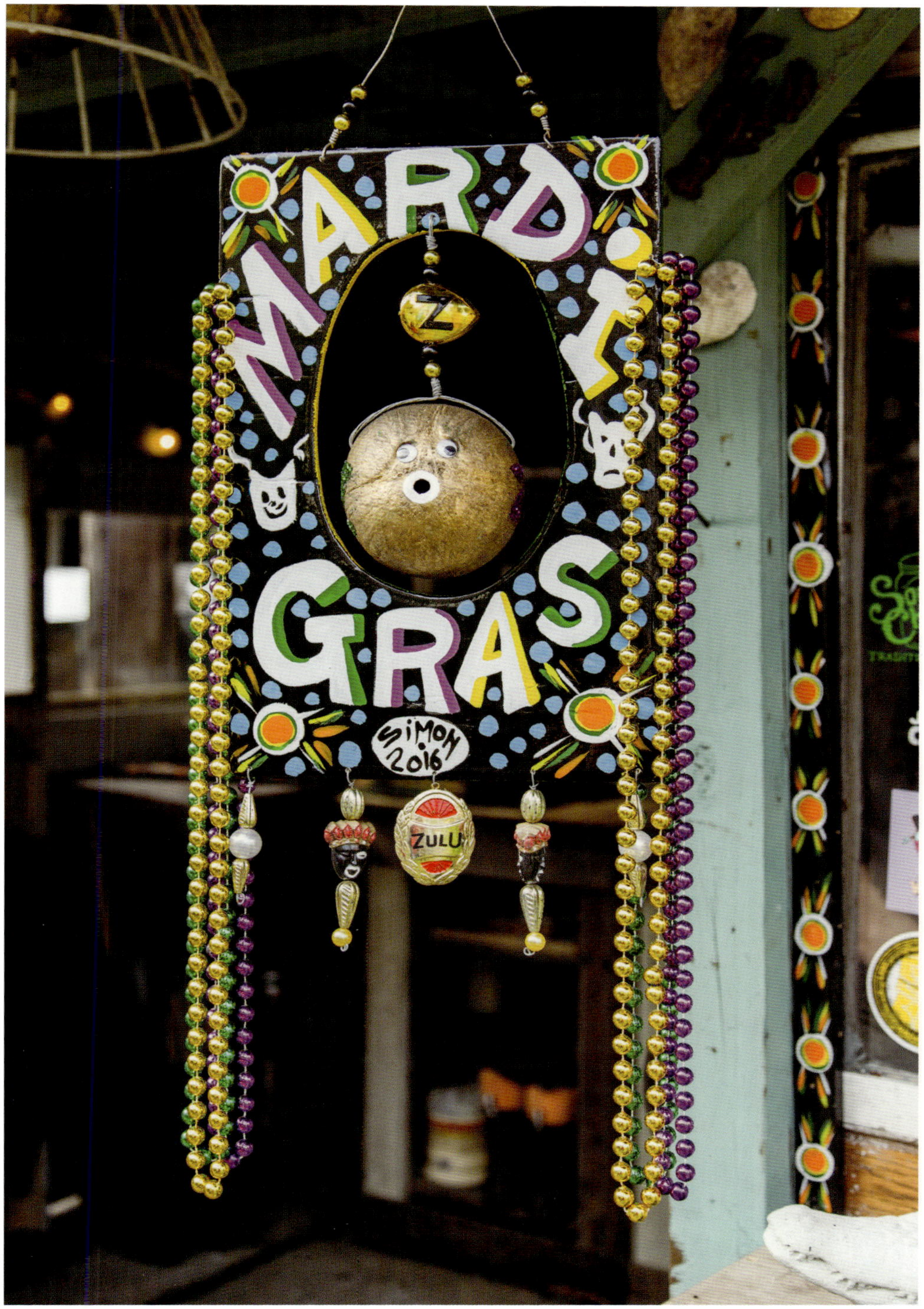

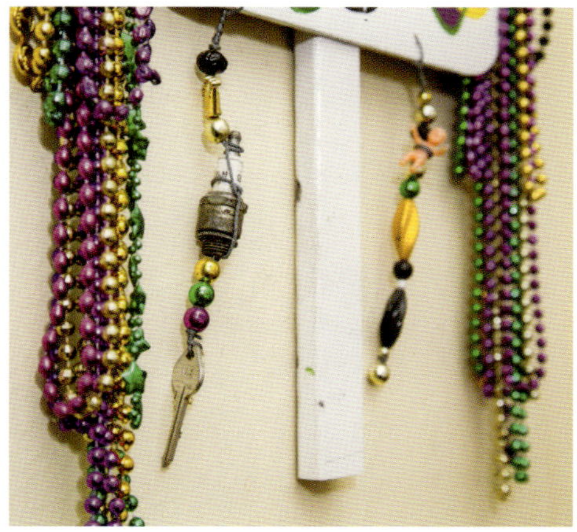

Above: Many of Simon's pieces feature "gris-gris," found objects that embellish the larger piece of art.

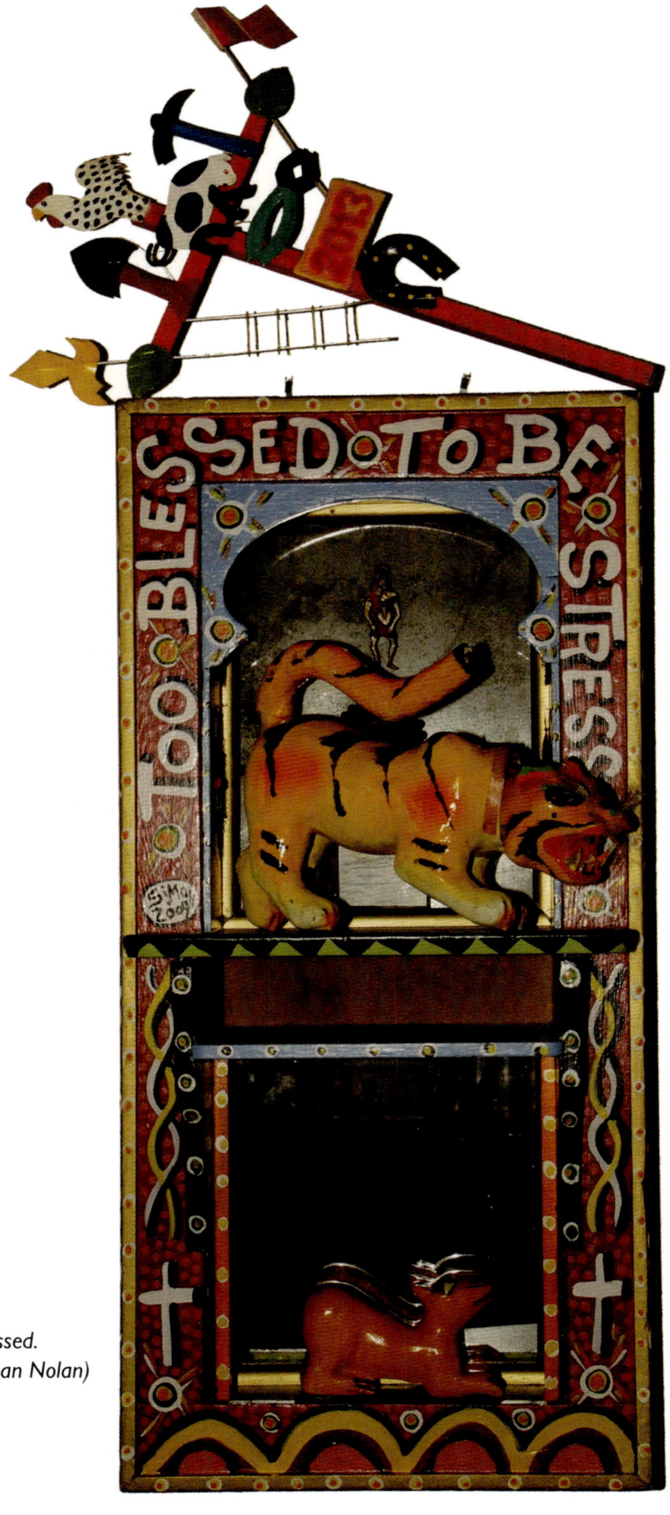

Too Blessed to Be Stressed.
(Courtesy Tom and Susan Nolan)

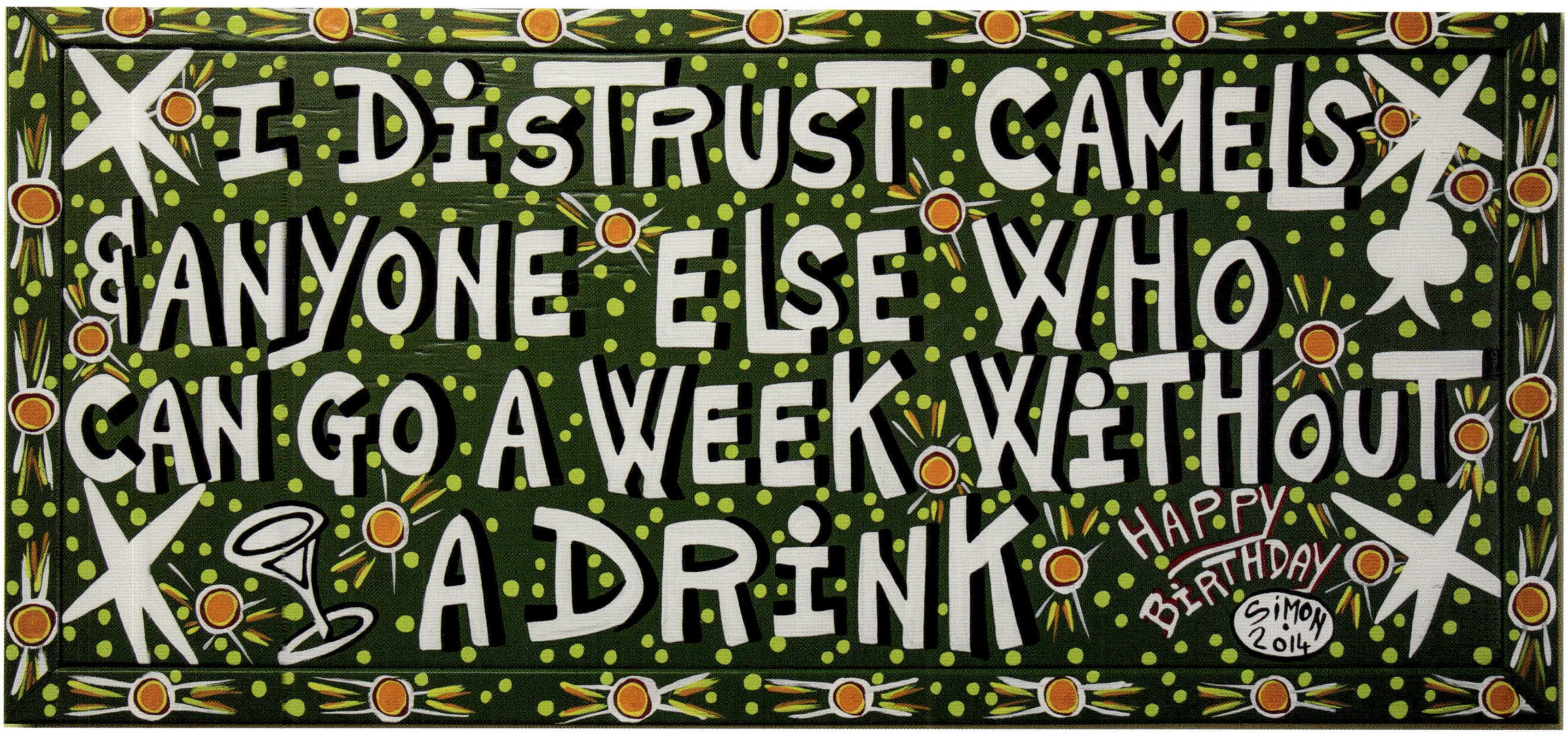
I DISTRUST CAMELS
& ANYONE ELSE WHO
CAN GO A WEEK WITHOUT
A DRINK
HAPPY BIRTHDAY
SIMON
2014

THE ARTIST AND THE NEWS

Simon's rise in popularity has been documented in widespread coverage by the media. An article in *Travel and Leisure* (August 2010) states, "Simon Hardeveld's work draws you in like the biggest, brightest lollipop in the candy store." National publications like the *New York Times*, *USA Today*, and *Lonely Planet* guidebook have featured his work. Regional exposure includes multiple articles in the *New Orleans Times-Picayune*, *Gambit*, the *New Orleans Advocate*, *Cue Magazine*, *Our Louisiana*, the *Uptown Messenger*, *Point of Vue*, and *Time Out New Orleans*.

But Simon's grandest media presence is broadcast live every weeknight on local ABC affiliate WGNO-TV, home of the Simon-crafted newsroom set of *News with a Twist*.

"The news set is living, breathing, dynamic Simon art," explains John Cruse, vice president and general manager of the station. "It is perhaps his greatest artistic achievement," says Cruse, adding that the pairing of the innovative news show and the off-beat artist has been a "perfect marriage." The news show focuses on lighter, local news stories interspersed with unscripted commentary by the show's co-hosts.

Cruse explains that when the idea was first hatched for a new concept newscast, pilots for the show were shot around a bar Cruse had built in his garage. Executives at ABC and Tribune Broadcasting in Chicago, the station's parent company, liked the bar idea. They wanted the set to be recognizable as a New

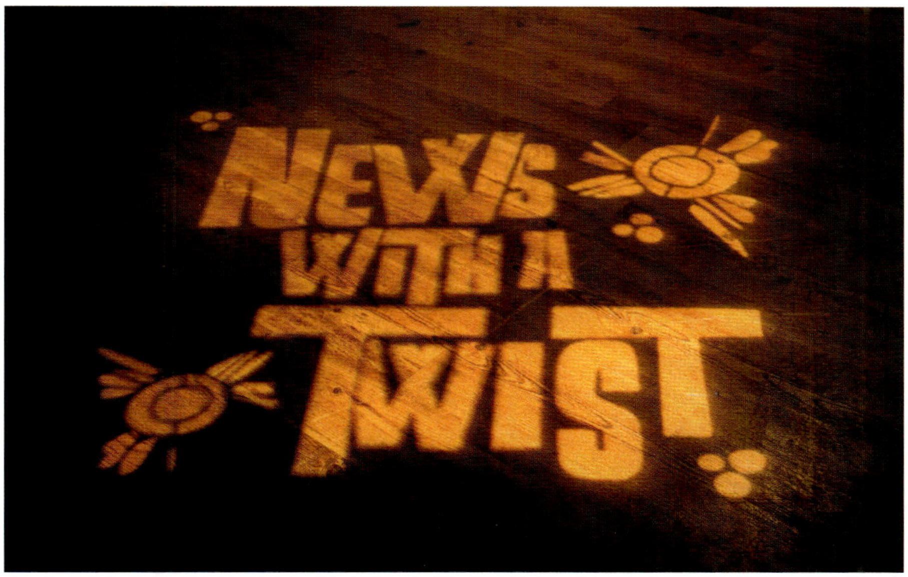

Simon's distinctive lettering is projected onto the floor of the News with a Twist *set.*

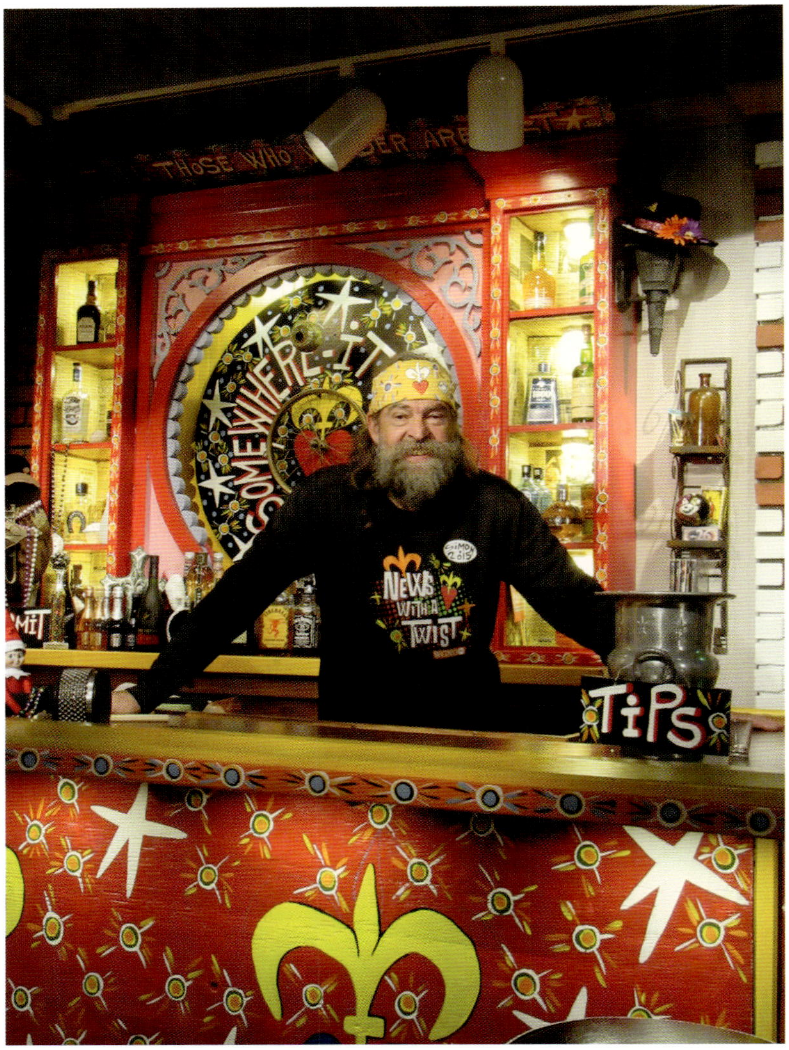

Above: The artist stands at the "bar" of the news set he designed and created.

Right: Perched in a niche of the news set is a guitar emblazoned with the station's call letters.

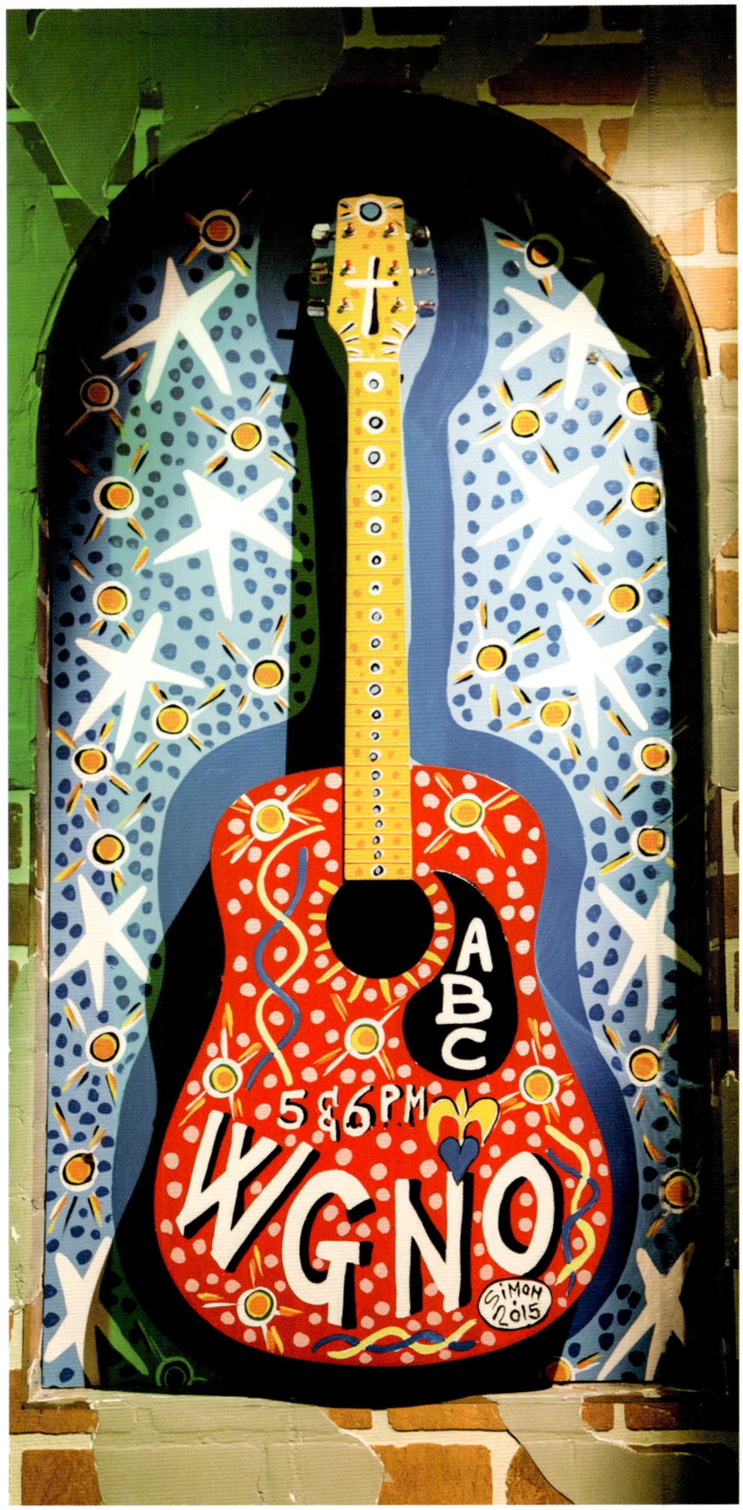

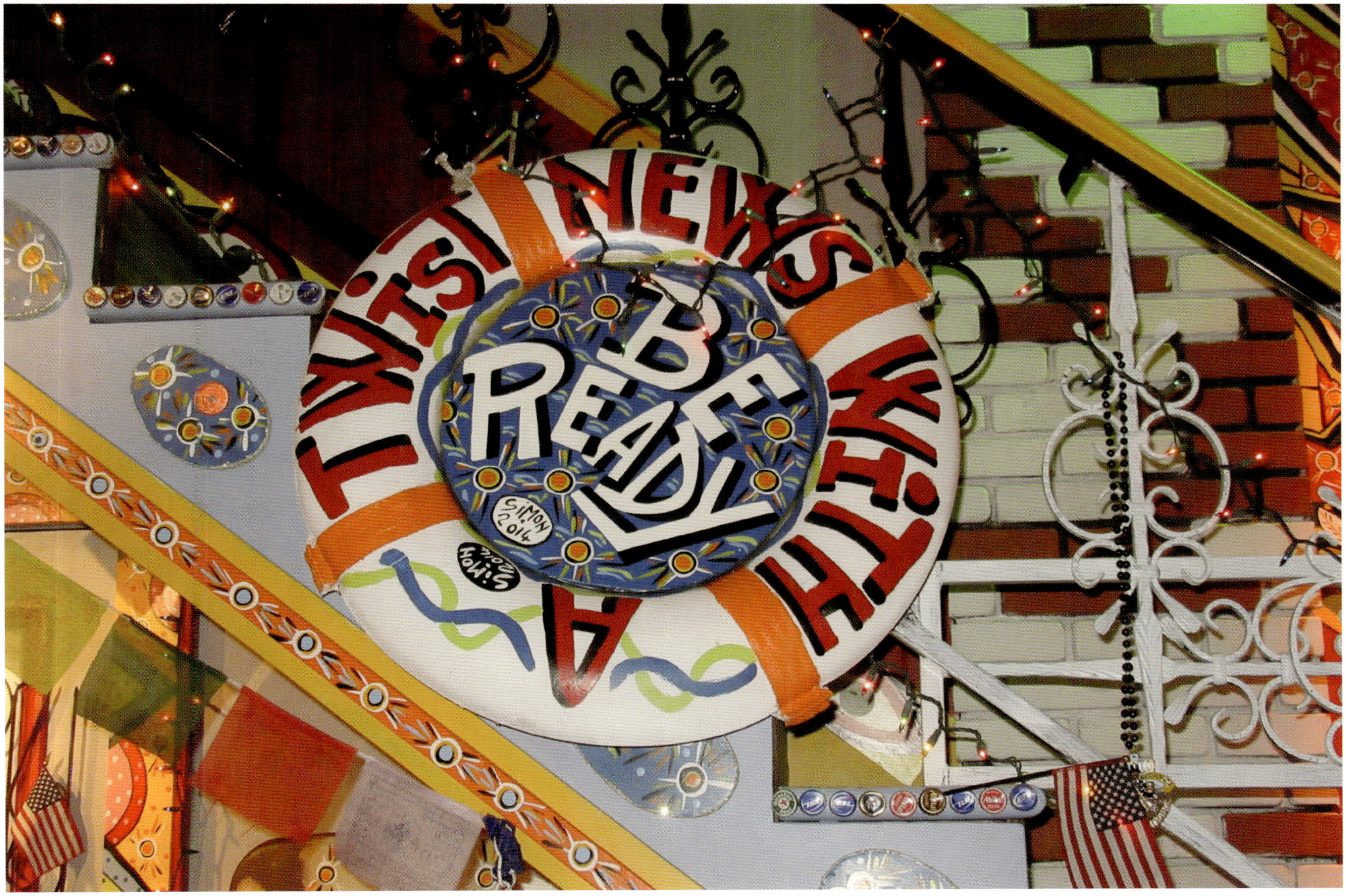

A decorated life preserver tells viewers to "Be Ready."

Orleans bar with a modern-day look. So a news set fashioned after Cruse's bar was built at the station's studio facilities located at The Galleria in Metairie. Upon completion of the construction phase, WGNO executives lined up a local artist to give the set a creative New Orleans touch, but the artist dropped out of the project. So they went looking for another.

At the time, Cruse owned a few of Simon's pieces, and station personnel were familiar with the artist's work from displays at local restaurants. They contacted Simon, and in the fall of 2010 the artist met with Jeff Funk, creative services director for WGNO, who showed him around the newly built, bar-themed set and explained that the management was looking for an artist to "funk it up." Cruse says that Simon understood exactly what they were looking for from the very beginning. (On the other hand, because of Simon's heavy accent, some station personnel confided that they understood little from the artist.) WGNO staff told Simon that everything on the set was open to his design transformation, except

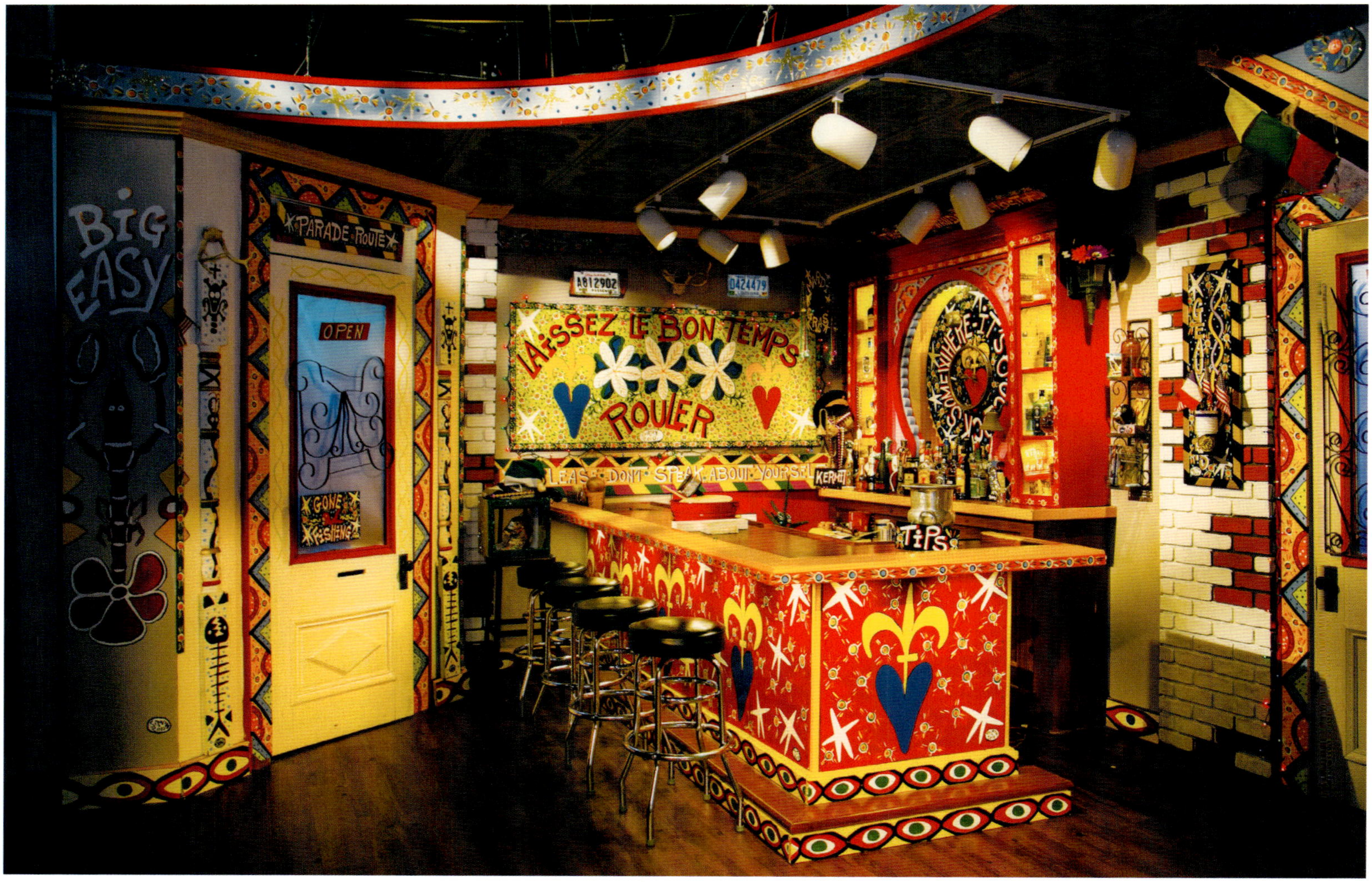

The ABC-TV affiliate's set was designed and created by Simon.

for the copper-colored pressed-tin ceiling. Simon gave them a quote on the spot, and they waited to receive sketches of his ideas for the set.

Simon showed up at the station soon after—not with sketches, but with paints, an assistant, and a six-pack of Heineken—and began to paint. One of the first things he did was to paint the pressed-tin ceiling gray. By the time it was discovered, it was too late. So station personnel decided to just "hang on for the ride" and let the artist create. The result was the popular *News with a Twist* set.

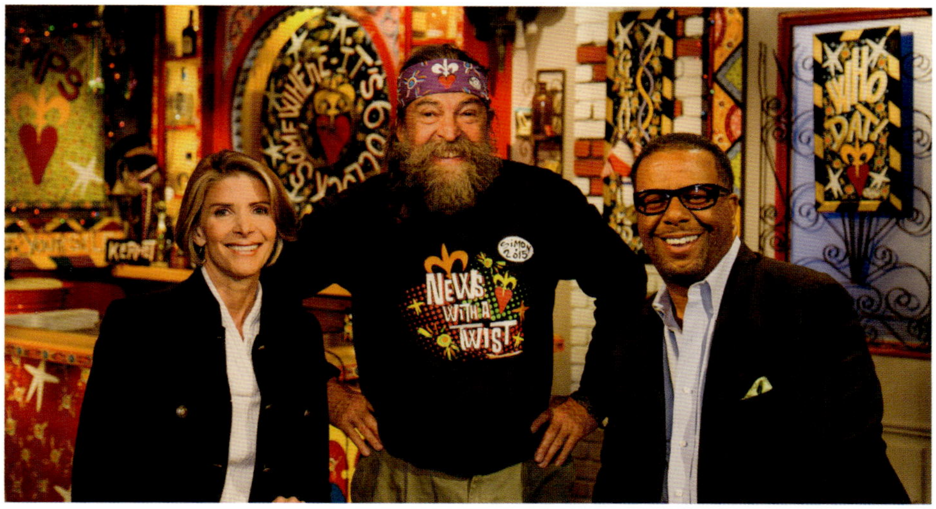

Co-hosts Susan Roesgen and LeBron Joseph pose with Simon.

The first show aired in January 2011, and its unusual set has been a hit with viewers from the beginning. "It has a real New Orleans feel to it," says Cruse. "There's no mistaking it."

Corporate executives in Chicago agree. "They have told us, 'You have no idea what you have here.'" Cruse explains that it is common for viewers to comment on the news content of a show, but only very rarely do they talk about—or even notice—a newscast's set. "But for this one, they do," he says. "The *News with a Twist* set is unique and recognizable. Somehow Simon has captured the essence of the city and decorated the set with it.

"The bands that perform during the shows also love it, especially the stage area," Cruse says. "There's nothing like it on any other news show in the area." Although the stage itself is small, the music reaches viewers across south Louisiana and Mississippi, prompting Jeff Kent, promotions producer for the station, to proclaim it the "smallest stage with the largest audience."

The newscast's longtime co-anchors LeBron Joseph and Susan Roesgen are also fans of the studio's decor. Joseph (known as LBJ) says, "Simon's unique use of bold color, humor, and the repurposing of items has helped to create an identity for our show unlike any other in the market. In fact, I can't imagine the *Twist* set in any other configuration that would better reflect what we are.

"What's interesting is that when we have visitors to the station they absolutely love what it looks like," Joseph continues, "and everyone breaks out the phones to take a

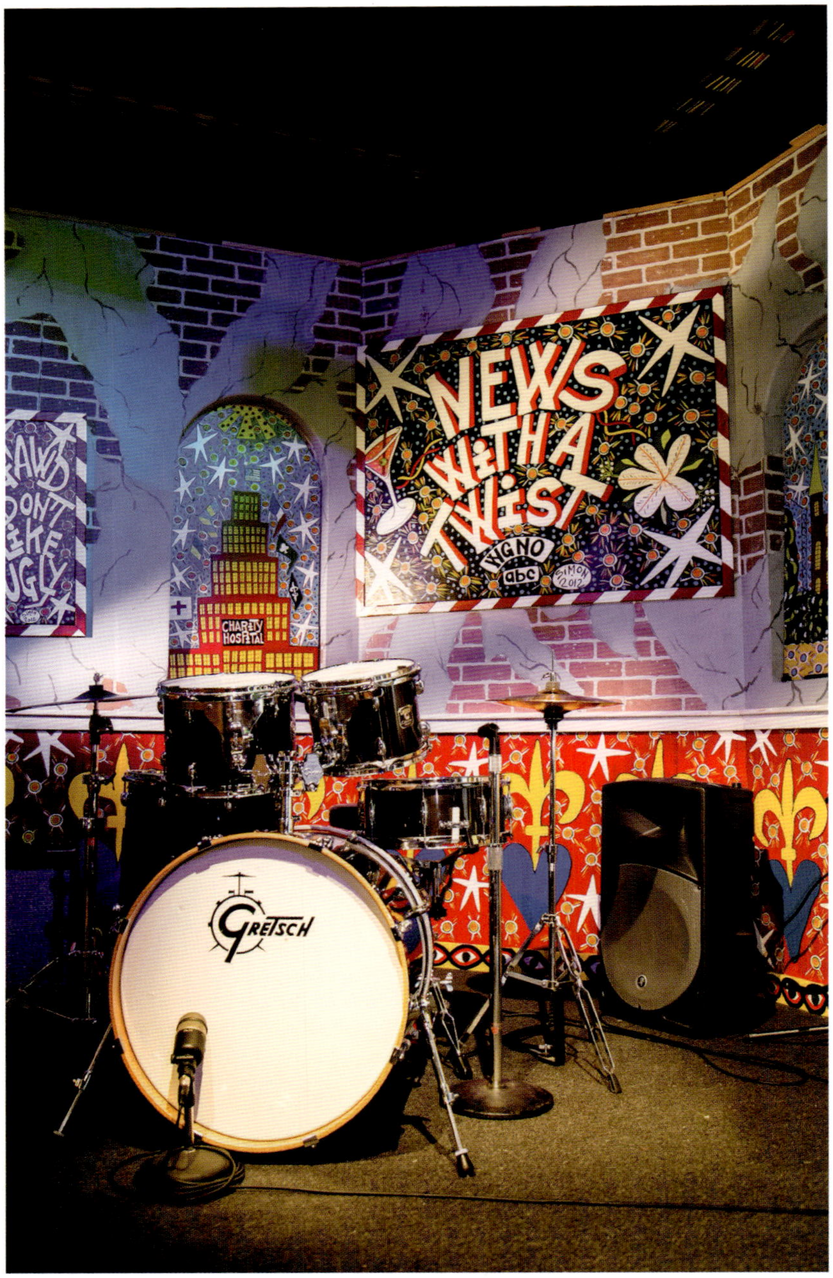

The stage on the news set is popular with local musicians.

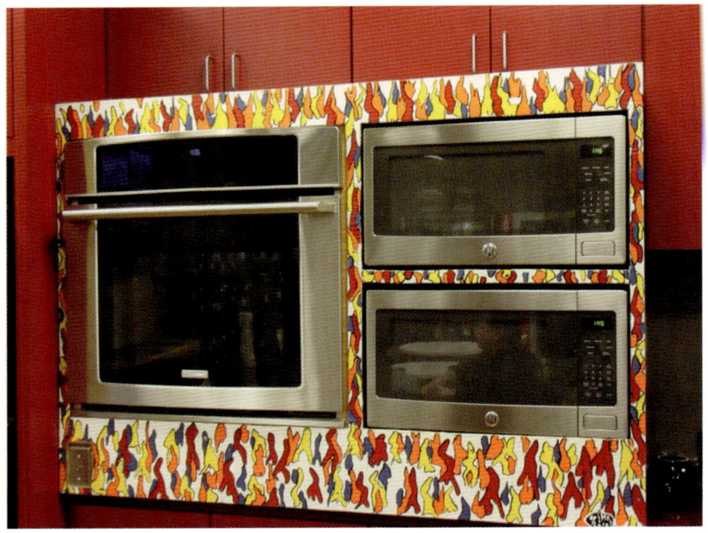

The Simon-decorated kitchen area is used for filming cooking segments on WGNO's news shows.

selfie or picture of the set. That is the reaction from locals and visiting celebrities as well.

"Finally, we always take time to explain that the set has developed and grown over the years, and every brush stroke was painted by Simon. There is no template or wallpaper; the entire set lives. That Simon continues to stop by and bring seasonal pieces is also a big plus, and we're ever excited," Joseph concludes.

Co-host Susan Roesgen adds her comments on Simon's art in general: "Charming, clever, and whimsical—Simon's work is all that and much more. Look closer, and you'll see an attention to detail that rivals Seurat's. No open space is left unadorned. Every canvas becomes a kaleidoscope of patterns and color."

Then, reflecting on the artist himself, she

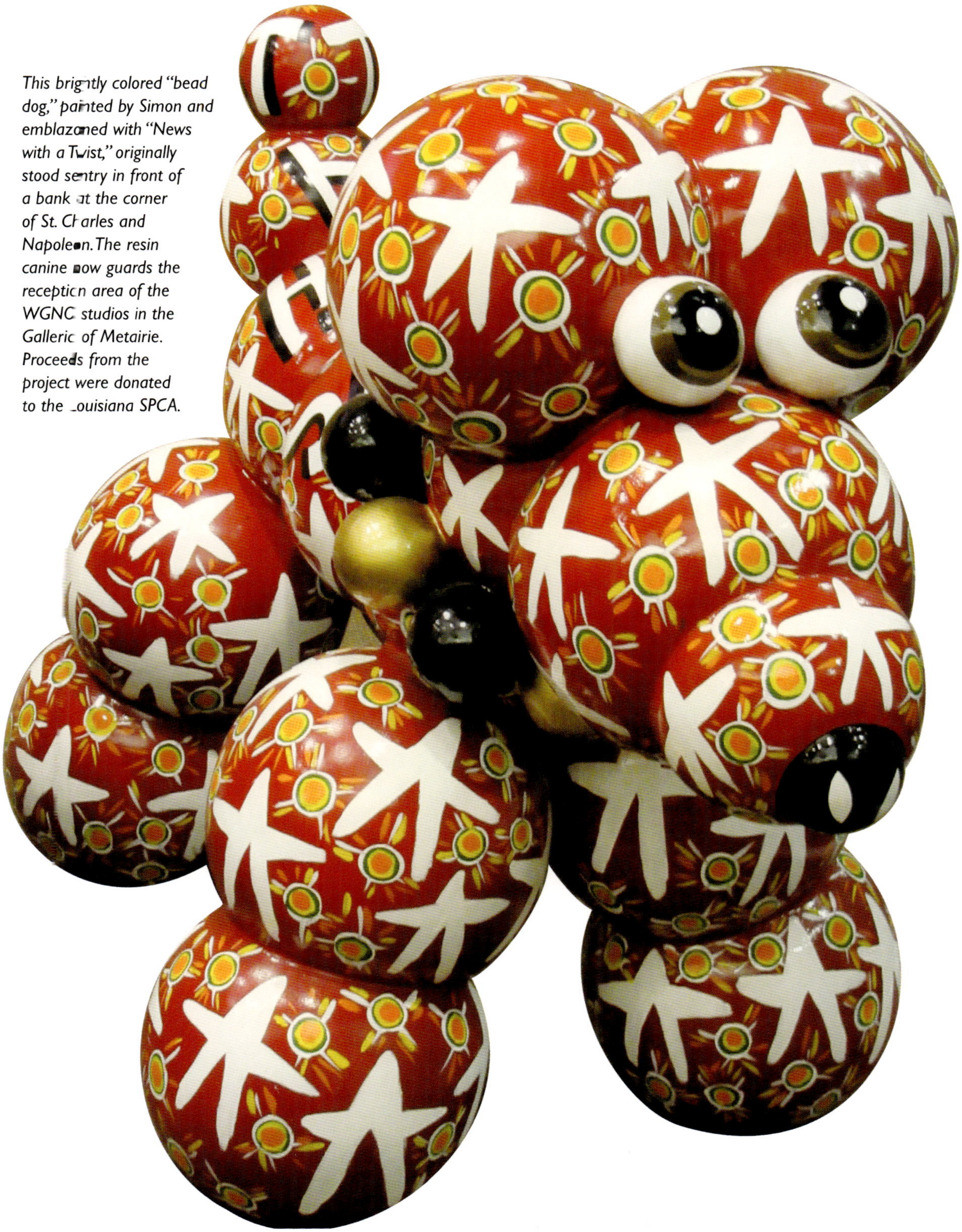

This brightly colored "bead dog," painted by Simon and emblazoned with "News with a Twist," originally stood sentry in front of a bank at the corner of St. Charles and Napoleon. The resin canine now guards the reception area of the WGNO studios in the Galleria of Metairie. Proceeds from the project were donated to the Louisiana SPCA.

adds, "Simon, like his art, is a gentle and cheerful presence with a deep soul."

"He is just a good person," agrees Cruse. "Honest and trusting. And unlike so many other artists, he doesn't hide away. He is sociable and has a great personal touch that resonates with so many people."

The WGNO billboards with Simon's signature style dot the metro area and have been quite effective in bringing fans to both the news show and to Simon's art.

With the fifth anniversary of *News with a Twist* in January of 2016, the station ran a weeklong anniversary celebration of the show, during which Simon and his work were prominently featured.

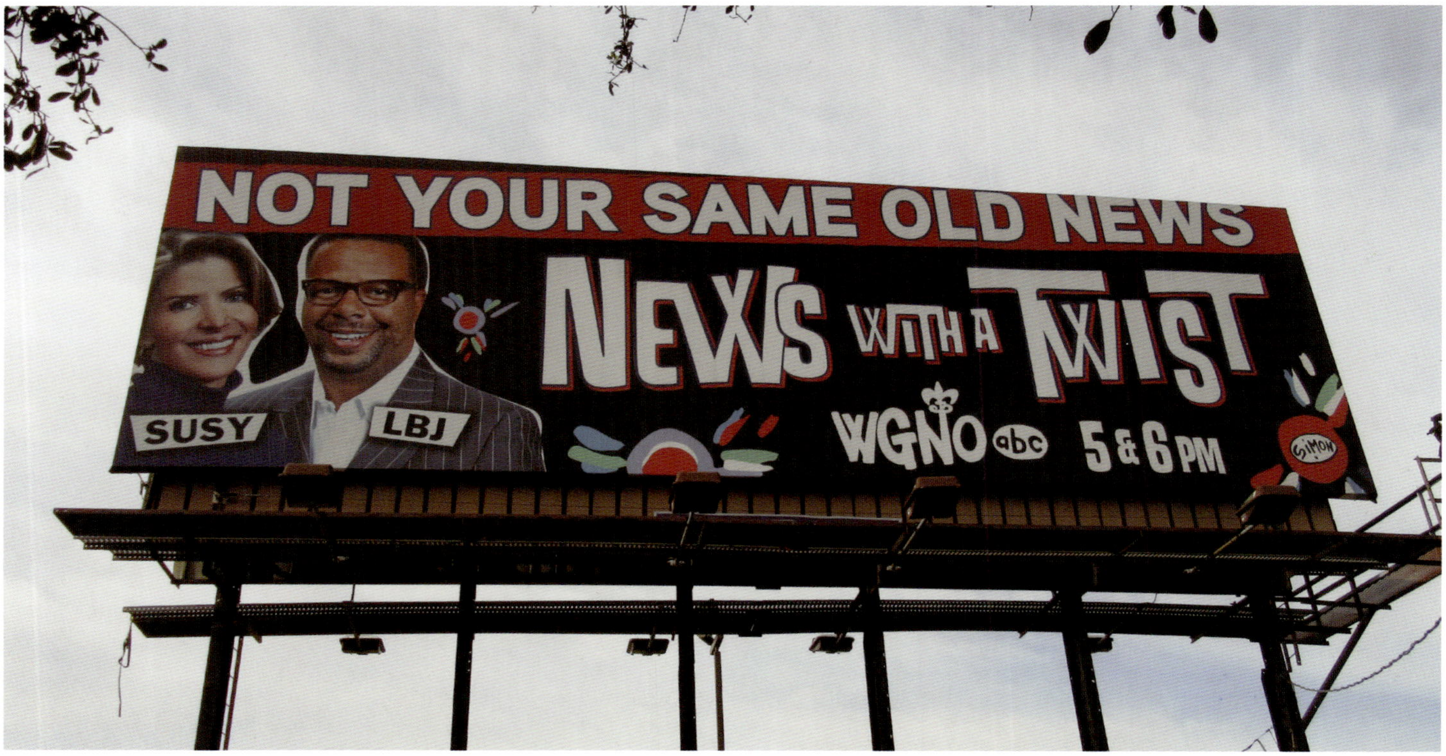

WGNO billboards feature Simon's art. (Photo by author)

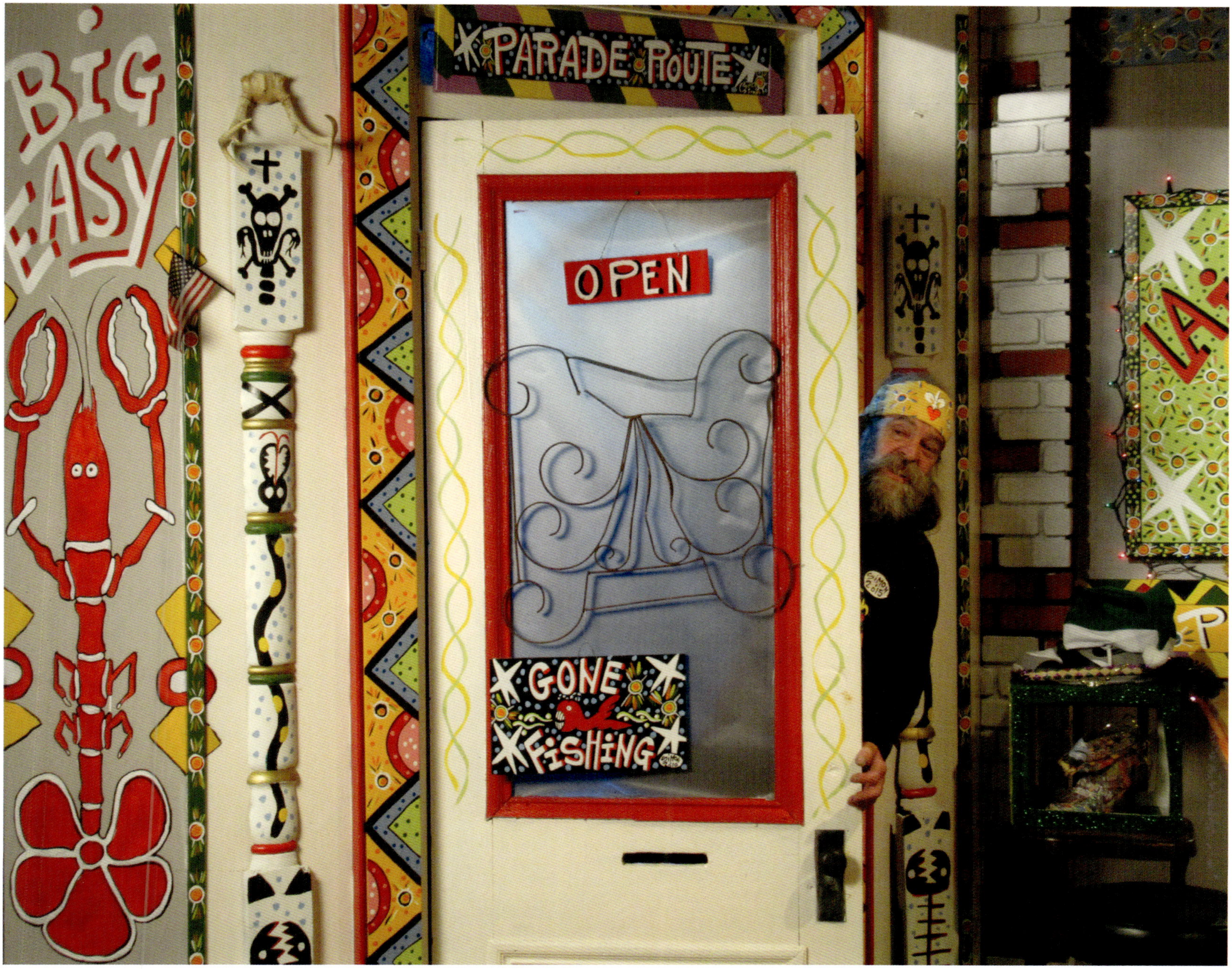

Simon poses behind the door he created for the set.

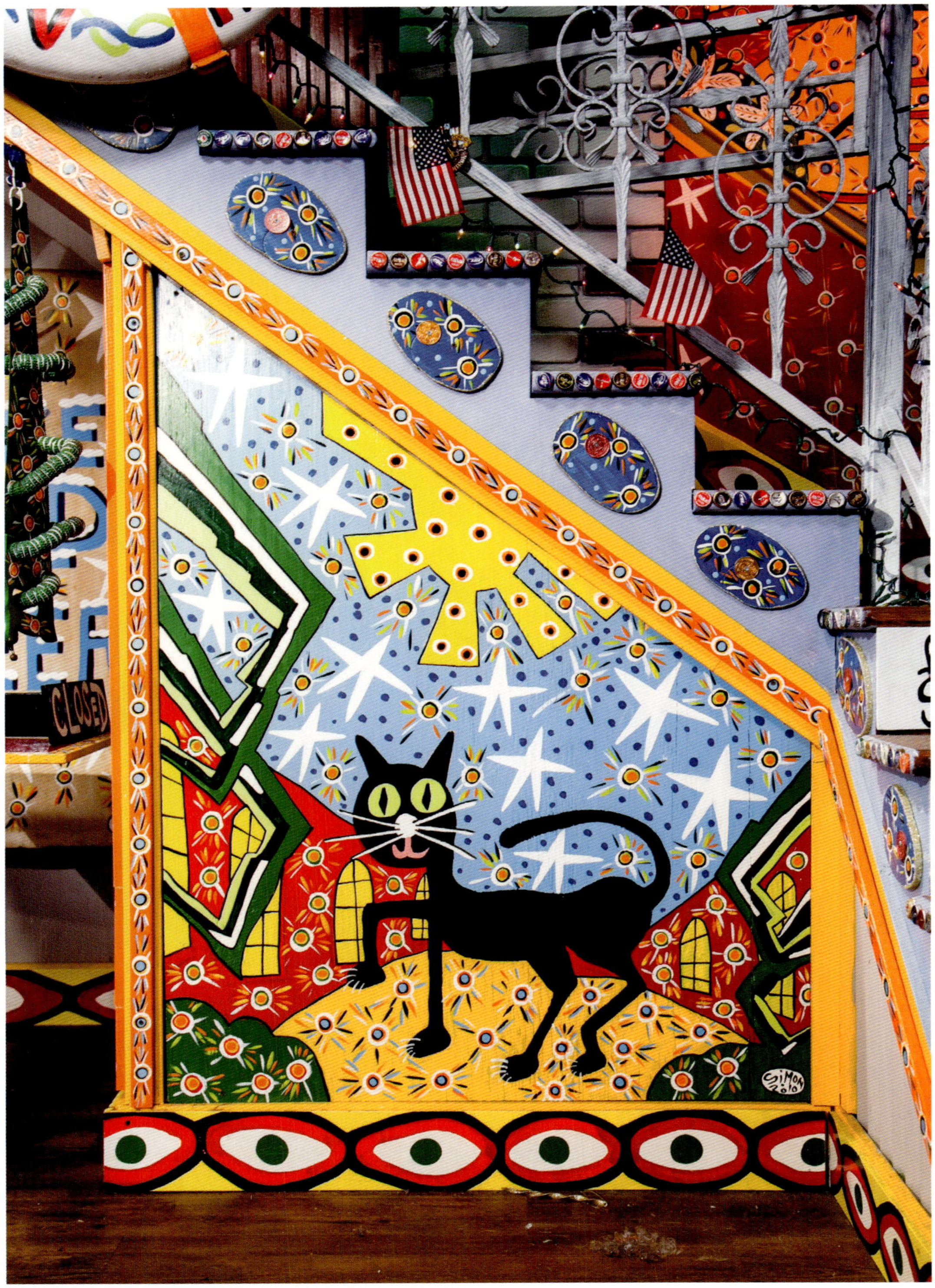

A black cat brings luck to the stage of WGNO's News with a Twist *set.*

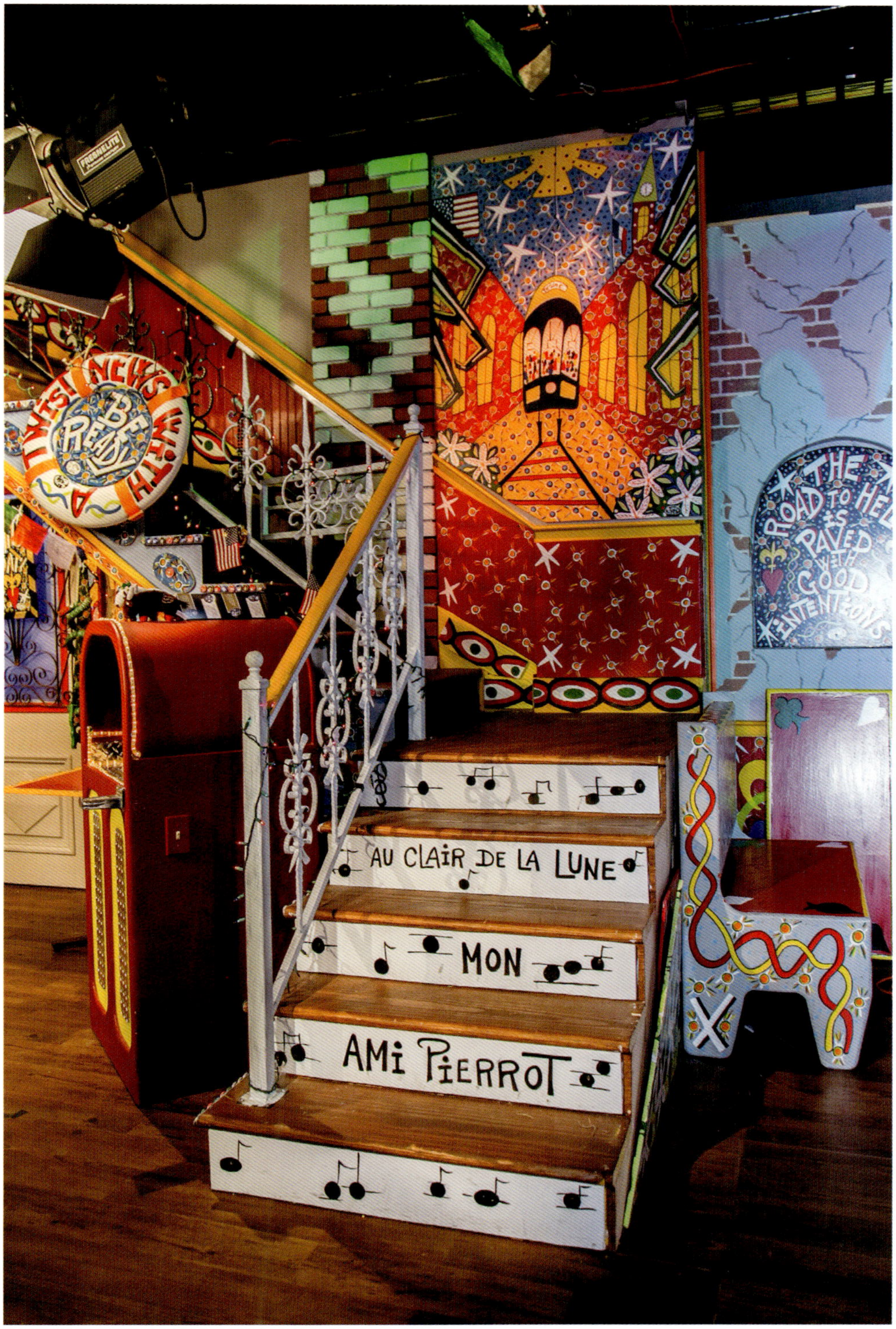

Next to the music stage on the WGNO News with a Twist *set, a streetcar named "Desire" cruises through Uptown with palm fronds lining the route. A clock tower in the background displays 6:00, one of the start times for* News with a Twist. *The risers on the stairs display the first two lines of the French folk song "Au Clair de la Lune" ("By the Light of the Moon").*

THE ARTIST AND THE COMMUNITY

Since first moving to the city in the mid-1990s, Simon has forged many ties to the New Orleans community, especially the local French community.

"Simon is part of the tradition of French heritage that thrives in New Orleans and throughout Louisiana," says Grégor Trumel, Consul général de France à La Nouvelle-Orléans. "He is our own local ambassador of French culture."

"And personally I love his art," adds Trumel, pointing to the Simon artwork that is displayed in the consul general's residence. "My wife feels the same way. And why not? You can't help but feel happy when you see his work." The *Bienvenue* ("Welcome") piece was Simon's gift to the consul general and his family upon their arrival in the city and is prominently displayed in the living room of the consul's residence. It is only one of many Simon works in the two-story house on Prytania Street. The artist occasionally stops by and drops off an additional piece, like a seasonally themed sign.

The French consulate in New Orleans has a long history. Established in 1803—before Louisiana even became a state—it pre-dates the French embassy in Washington, D.C. Simon's affiliation with the consulate in New Orleans also goes way back. Béatrice

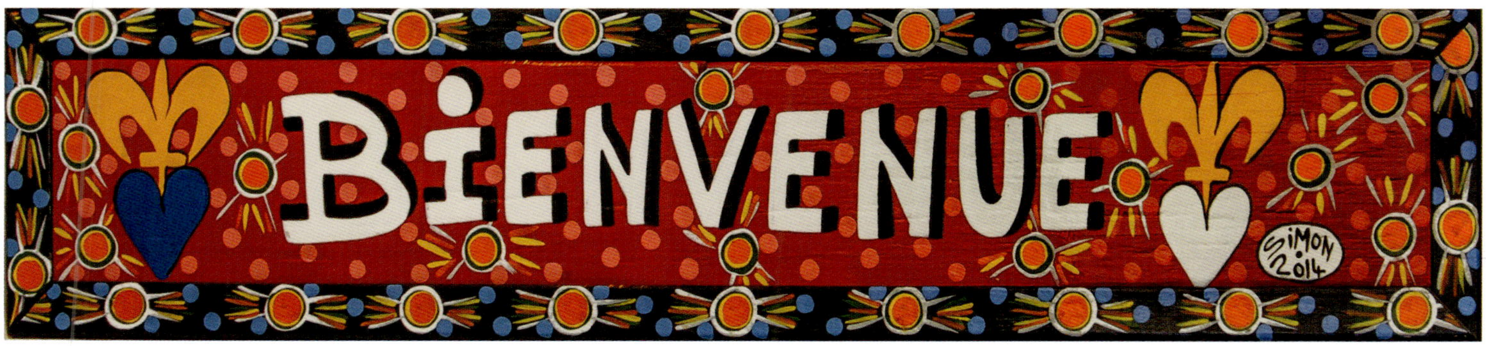

Simon presented this sign to the consul general upon his arrival in New Orleans. (Photo by author)

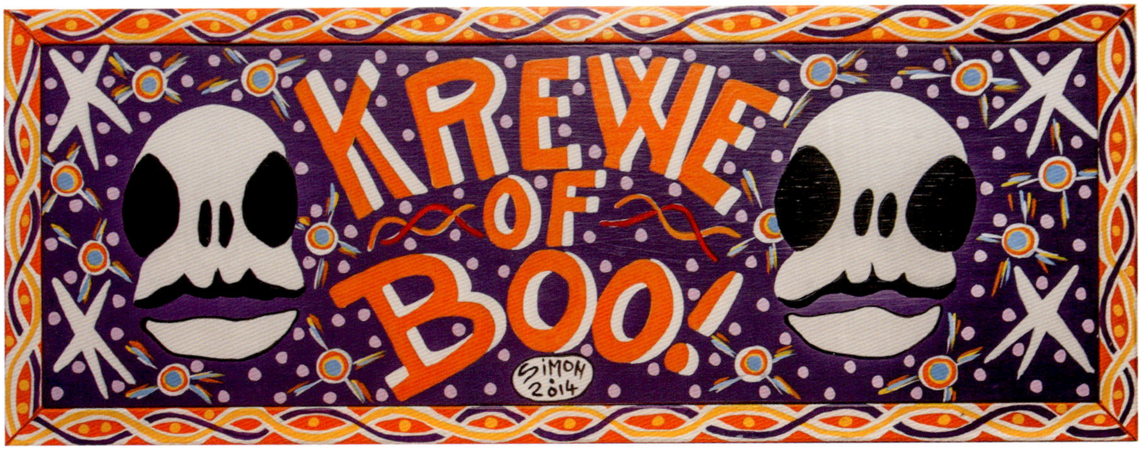

The Halloween sign Simon brought to the consul general's family is displayed in the residence's living room. (Photo by author)

Germaine, cultural attaché at the consulate, recalls one particularly memorable occasion when Simon helped welcome a previous consul general. Simon arrived at the reception carrying a painting with a flamboyant handlebar moustache extending far to the sides of the piece, in an obvious caricature of the consul general, who himself sported a long handlebar moustache. It caused quite a ruckus at the reception. Though the consul general himself was not particularly amused, the other guests enjoyed it immensely, and the tale has become part of consulate lore.

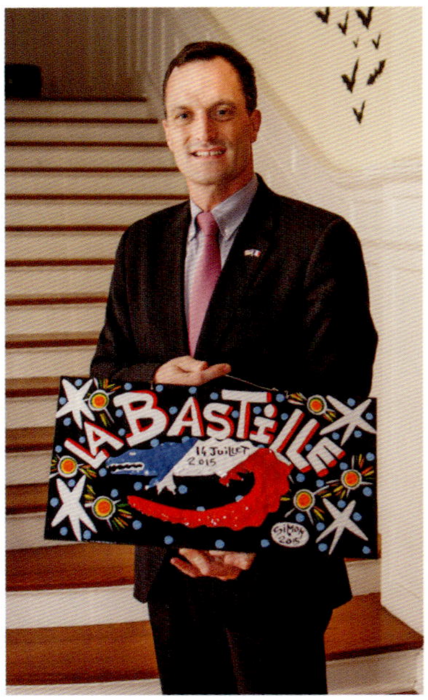

Consul General Grégor Trumel shows off one of the works Simon presented to his family. (Photo by author)

Germaine met Simon more than twenty years ago when he was working at Bush Antiques on Magazine Street. "He is a valuable liaison for the French community in New Orleans," she says, adding that he is proud of his French heritage and is always ready to help when asked to contribute time or talent to local programs that the consulate sponsors. He also has a special fondness for the city's French schools. Simon designed a school logo for Lycée Français de la Nouvelle-Orléans (the French School of New Orleans). The design is used on items that the school sells for fundraising activities. He has hosted art seminars at his

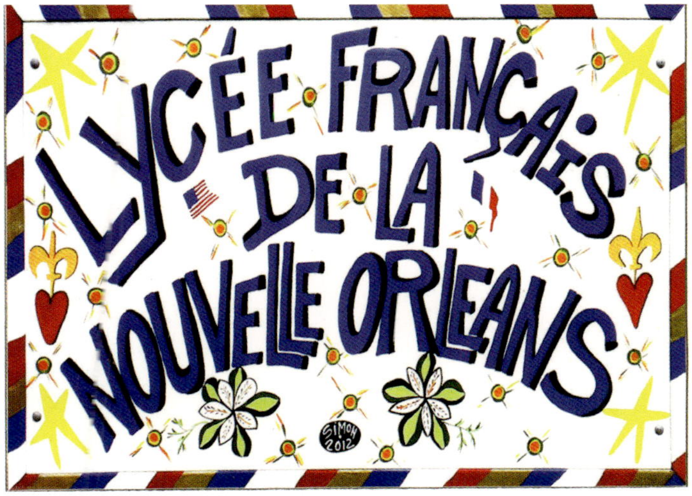

Simon designed a Lycée Français logo, which is displayed at the school's entrance

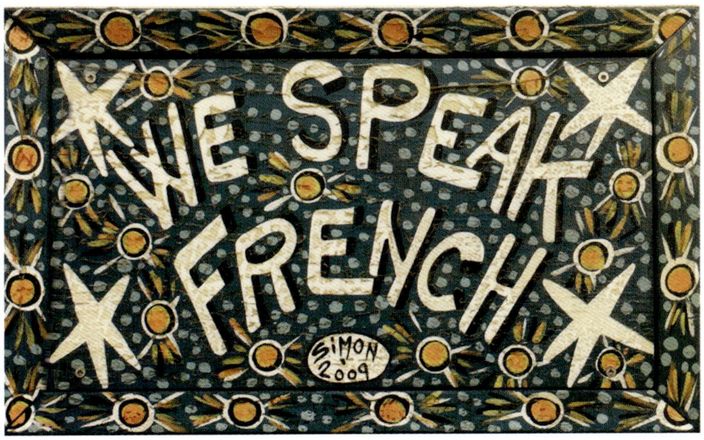

Right: This trio of "Store Open" signs is a small sampling of the hundreds of other such signs by Simon in businesses across the metro area.

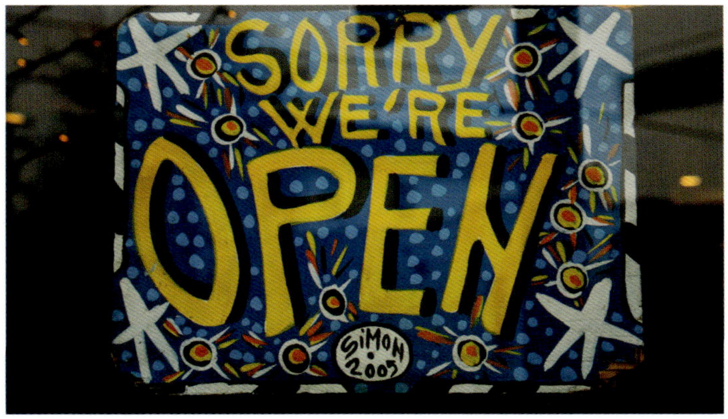

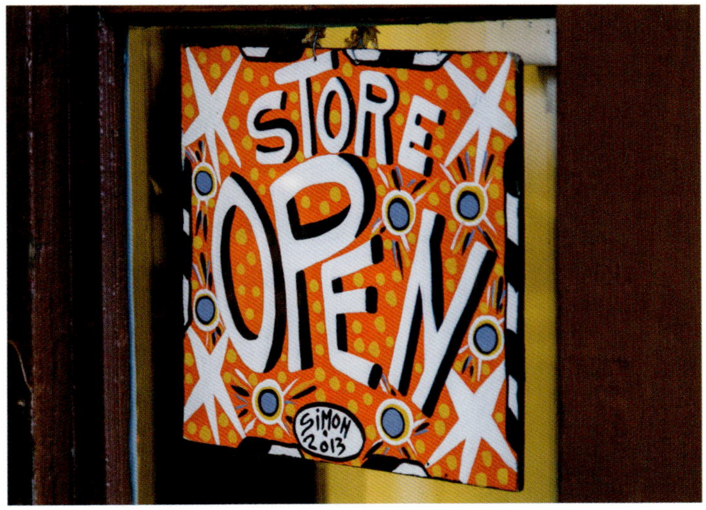

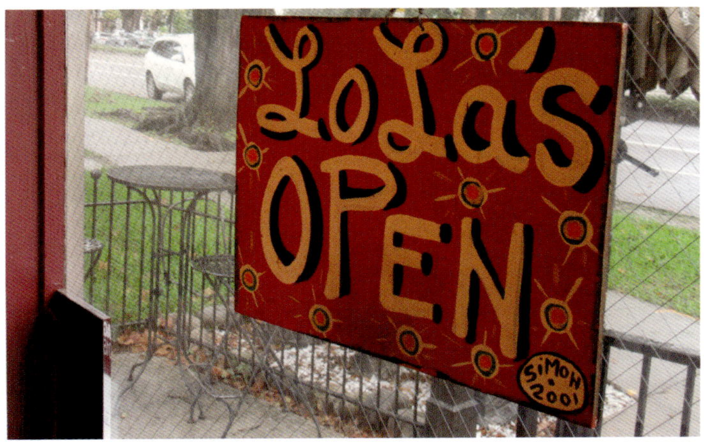

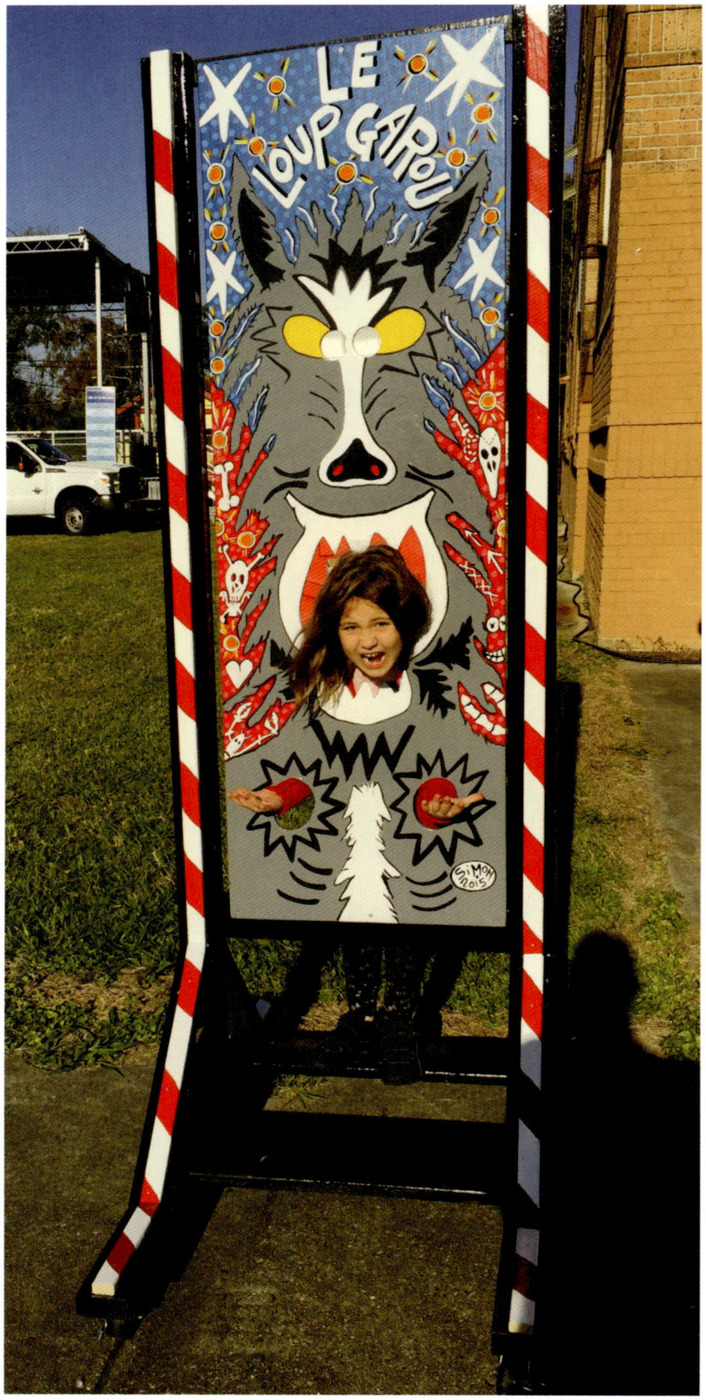

studio for the students, teaching them the basics of his designs and encouraging them to follow their own inspirations. Together they created a large mural, which was auctioned off to benefit the school. He does similar work for other French schools, including Ecole Bilingue de la Nouvelle-Orléans.

"Simon is generous," says Germaine. "He is more interested in sharing than in selling. And he is a great connection for us and the community because he is such a nice person and his works are so well known. Who does not know Simon? Who does not know his work?" she asks rhetorically. "Sometimes it seems that every business in the city has at least one of his 'Open/Closed' signs, if not more pieces."

She is a fan of his work herself and has his paintings in her home. She says that Simon keeps up with both local and world events and finds a way to capture them in his art in a way that makes people smile.

Simon also uses his humor in favor of some of the city's more iconic and best known attractions. As an enthusiastic fan of the city's festivals, Simon remains actively involved in creating artwork especially for these events. He has been an official French Quarter Festival poster artist for the last few years, and his

Kindergartener Tallulah Campbell poses in the clutches of the Loup Garou, Lycée Francais' school mascot. The larger-than-life photo board was donated to the school by Simon. (Photo by S. Campbell)

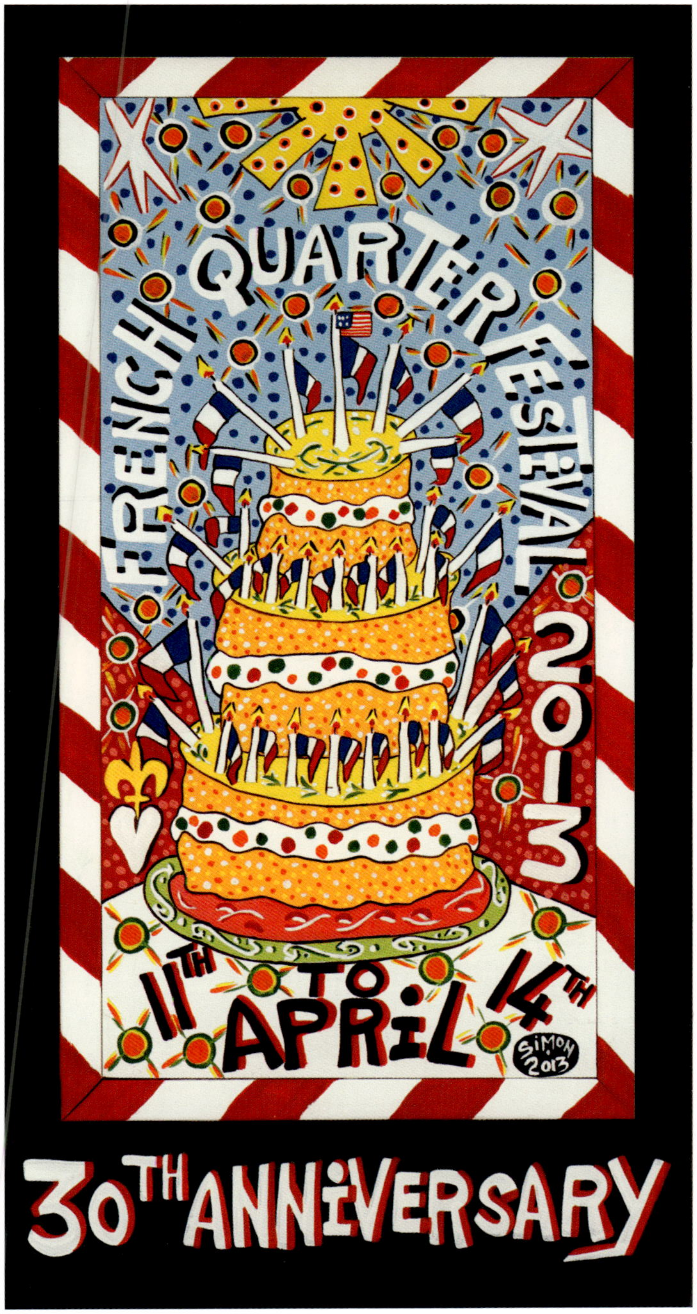

posters have consistently sold out. The sales help fund the festival, making it possible to keep it open to the public and admission free.

His association with the French Quarter Festival began in 2013 when festival director Marci Schramm approached Simon and asked if he would consider designing and painting a special poster to commemorate the festival's thirtieth anniversary. "He said he would be thrilled to do it," remembers Schramm. "We brainstormed a concept, and he made it clear from the beginning that he was doing this as a friend and supporter of the festival, and that he would not charge us for the painting." He is actively involved in helping with publicity for the festival, and each year he donates the original poster art for the organization to use at its auction.

"In addition, at our thirtieth anniversary press conference he announced that he would paint a new piece every year, 'forever,' to support the French Quarter Festival," says Schramm. "So each year now, fans look forward to seeing him in his festival artist booth in the middle of Jackson Square, where he personalizes and autographs the posters, sells original works, and charms everyone he meets."

In 2015, the festival staff made an additional

Simon designed the 2013 French Quarter Festival poster in honor of the fete's thirtieth anniversary and donated it to the organization. (Courtesy French Quarter Festivals, Inc.)

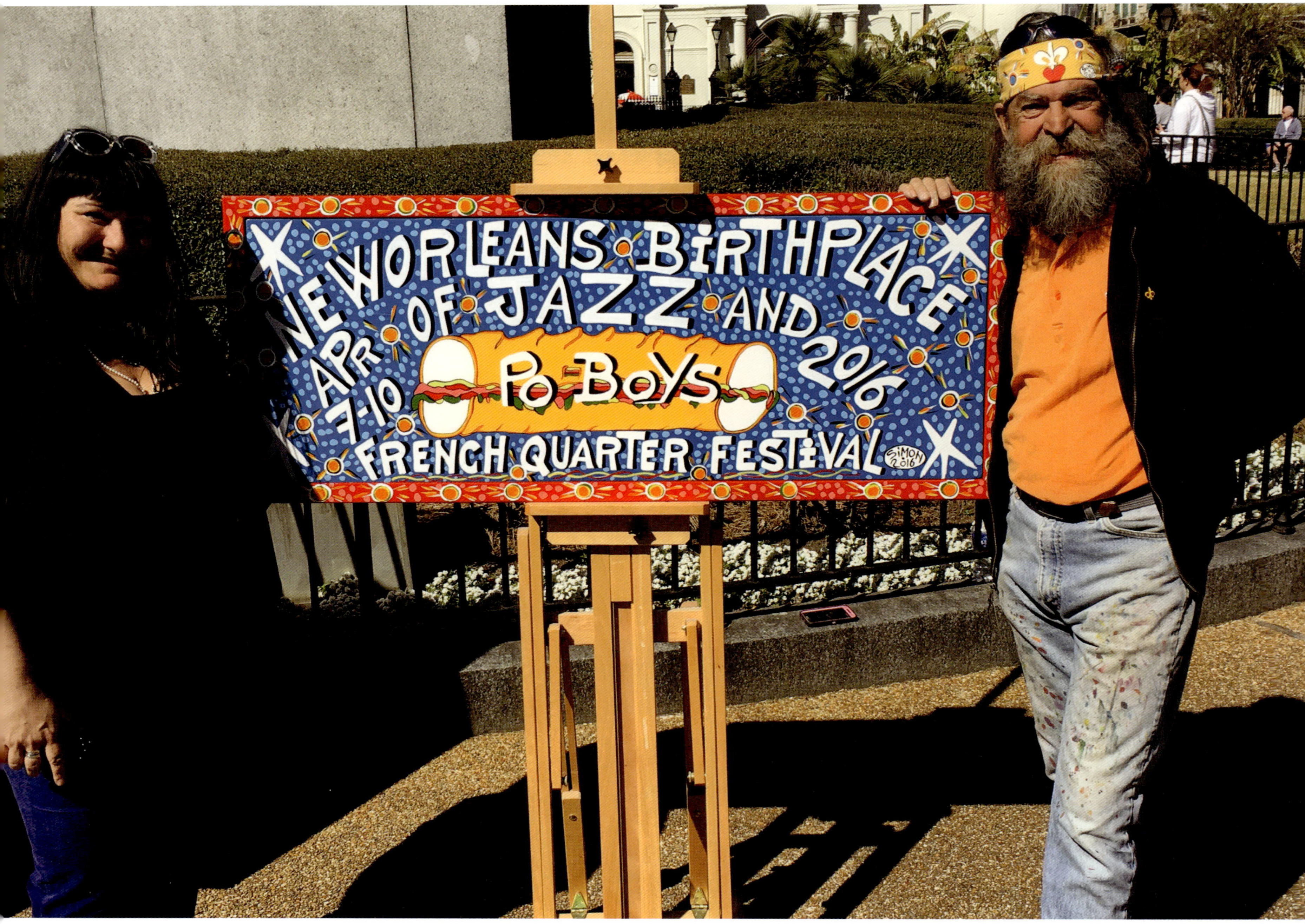

Simon and French Quarter Festival Director Marci Schramm unveil the 2016 festival poster in Jackson Square.

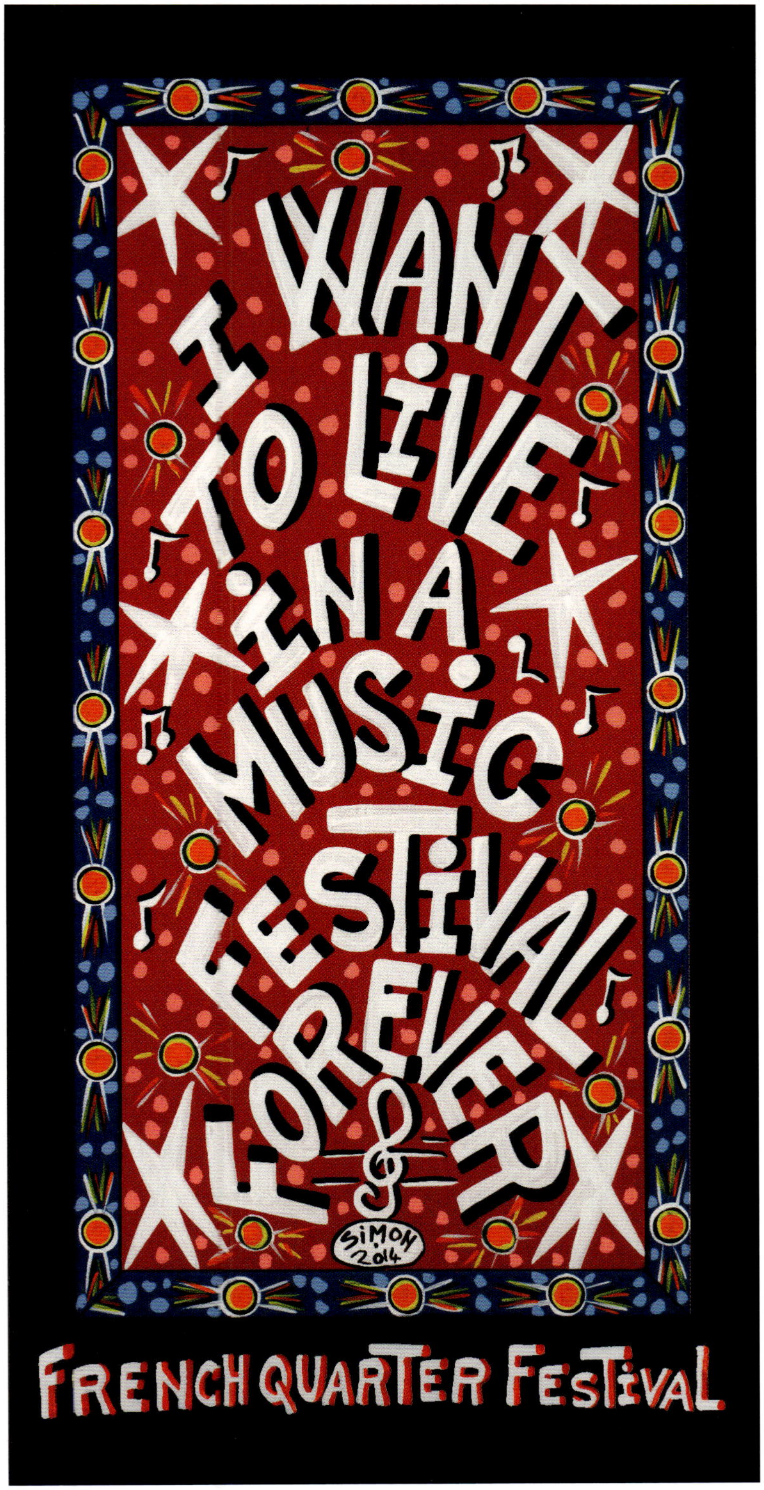

The 2014 French Quarter Festival poster features one of Simon's favorite sayings. (Courtesy French Quarter Festivals, Inc.)

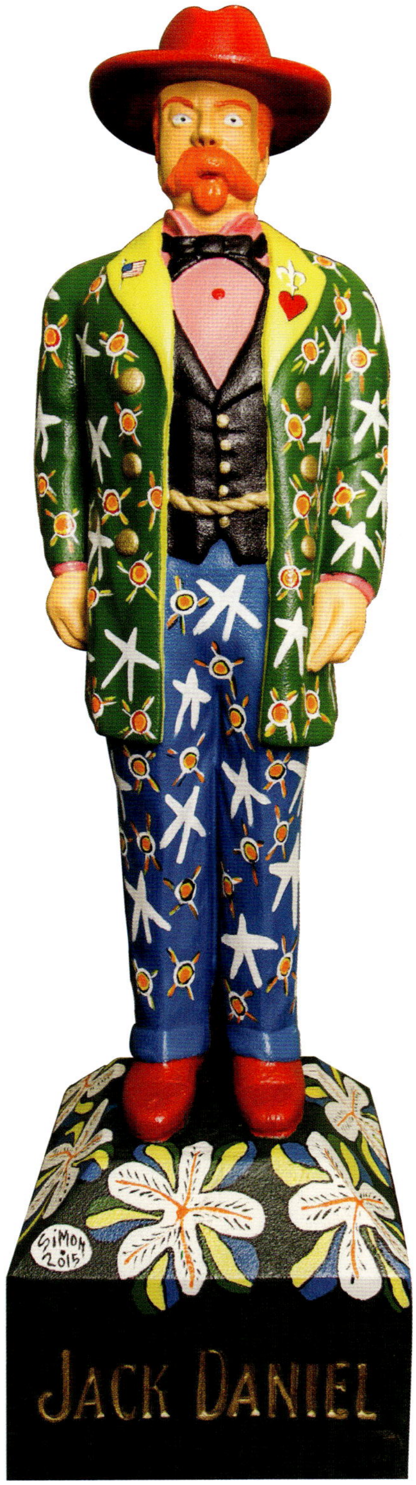

The artist was asked to paint this seven-foot-tall statue of the Jack Daniel's founder for the 2015 French Quarter Festival. Jack Daniel's was a sponsor for the festival.

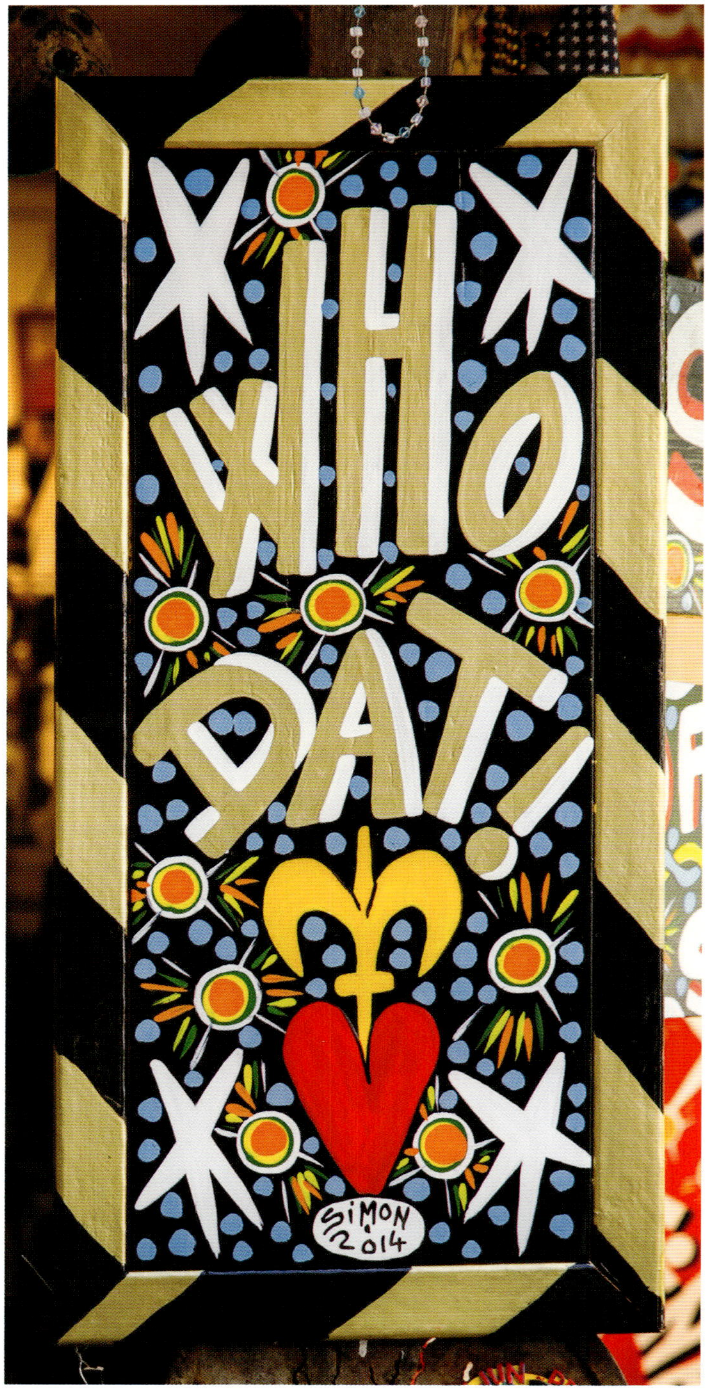

request. Besides asking him to create the poster, they also asked him to paint a seven-foot-tall statue of Jack Daniel to promote their new sponsor. Simon didn't hesitate. "Yes," he said. "Bring me a bottle of Jack Daniel's and the statue, and we'll have some fun." And they did.

"He's an original," says Schramm, "a real character, and he has a heart of gold. Now that I have gotten to know him and his wife, Maria, I am a huge fan and consider them friends. They are just the kind of people who truly embody the spirit of New Orleans."

And like any good New Orleanian, Simon is a full-fledged Saints football fan—through good games and bad. At a recent Monday morning quarterbacking session, he animatedly bemoaned the woes of the team's field-goal kicker, long since released from the team. "All the kickers on the other teams, they kick the ball like this," he says, demonstrating a kick with a smooth follow-through. "Voila! Field goal!" he declares, raising both hands. "Not our guy," he laments. "No, no. He kick like this," says Simon, demonstrating a kick with a wobbly follow-through. "No field goal. No points," he says, shaking his head in exasperation.

Like any good New Orleanian, Simon is a full-fledged Saints football fan. Many of his creations feature the team's colors of black and gold.

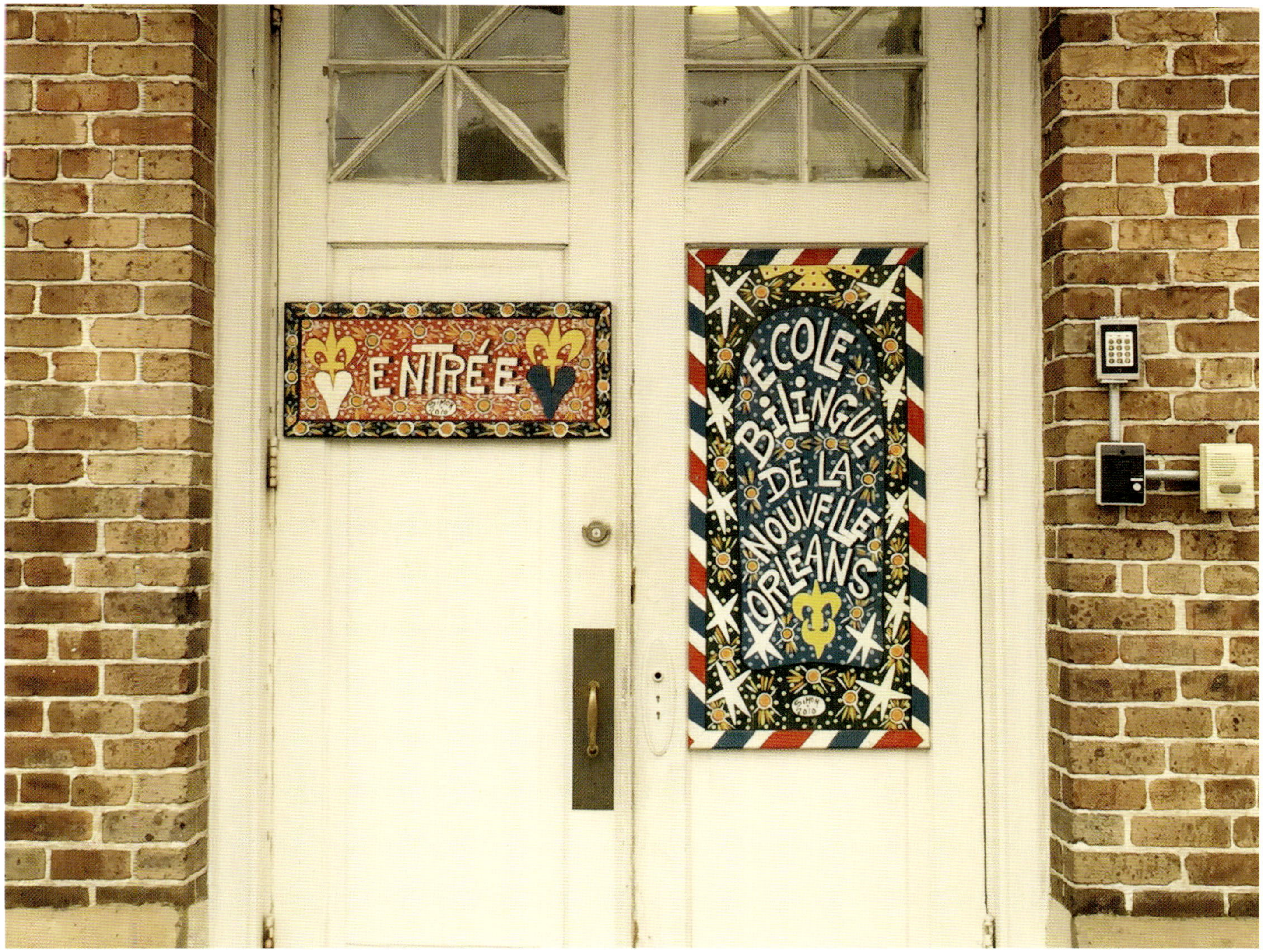

These signs designate the entrance to Ecole Bilingue de la Nouvelle-Orléans.

PAINTING NEW ORLEANS

Though most widely known for his signs, Simon's artistic media run a wide gamut, from small, embellished found objects to huge architectural pieces. Yet despite the disparate types of works, there are common themes that run throughout. In addition to the obviously central theme of New Orleans and its traditions, recurring topics include the Cajun and Creole cultures, the Louisiana-French connection, religious influences on the city, parodies of current events, and the works of master artists of long ago. There are also numerous uniquely themed pieces, obviously inspired by some singular insight. But overarching all is the one thread that ties the entire body of work together—the element of humor. Some pieces are gently irreverent; some are bitingly sarcastic; some are cleverly witty; but all are humorous.

The element of humor emerged from the very beginning in the full-sized folk-art paintings that were among Simon's first types of works, and thus are now some of the most collectible. From the beginning, he often used his art to lampoon current events. A found object painted to look like a missile is affixed to a wooden board and titled "For Saddam." A bawdy Mardi Gras signboard

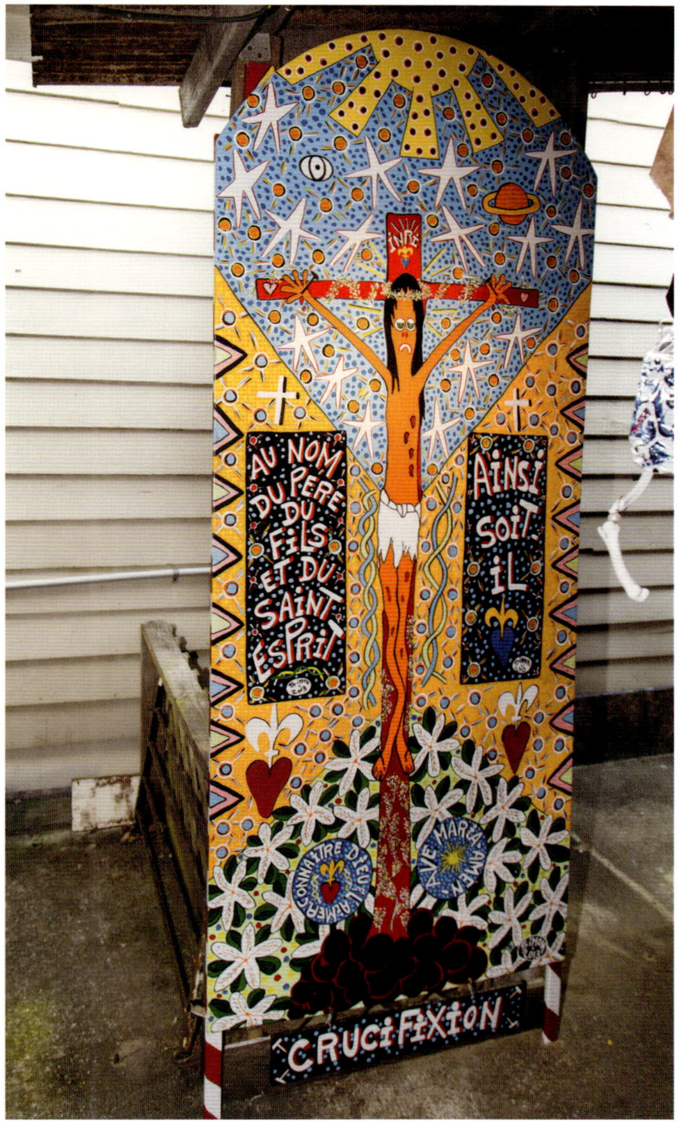

Religion is a common theme in Simon's body of work.

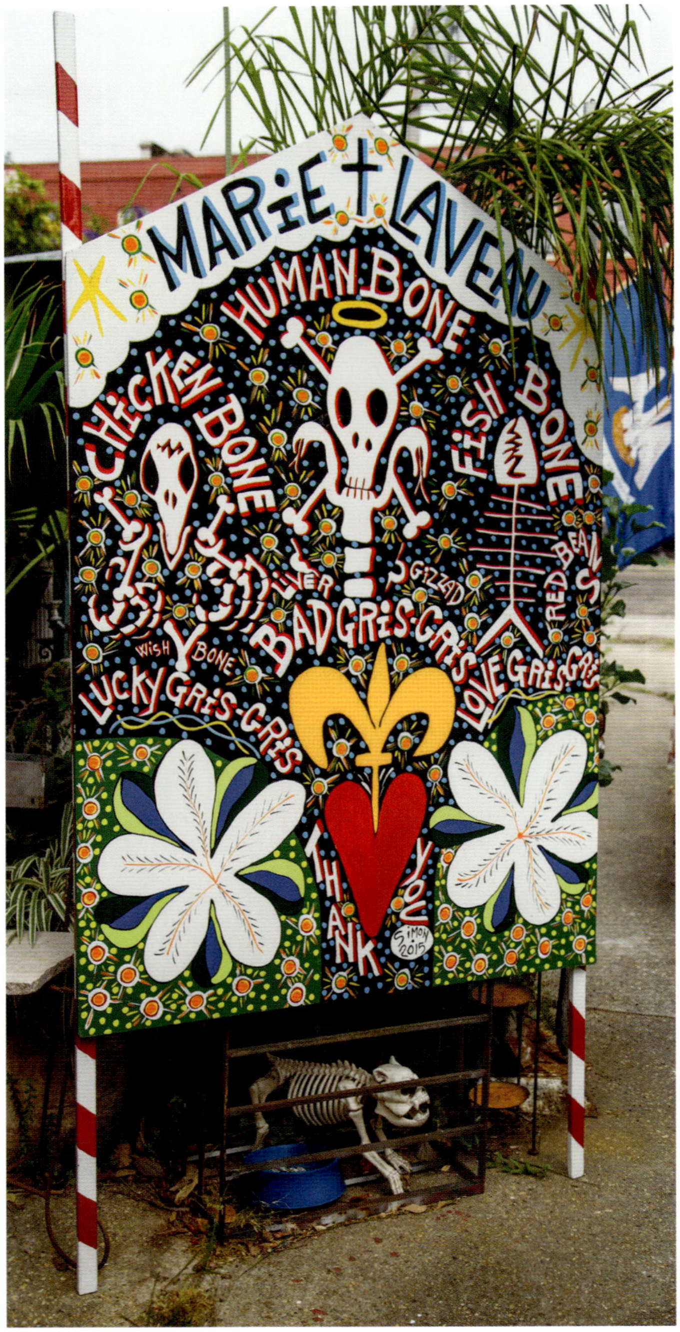

Voodoo-themed pieces are popular with customers.

satirizes the Bill Clinton/Monica Lewinsky affair.

Whatever the format, Simon incorporates humor. Free-standing art pieces have been created from items like full-size front doors, coconuts, liquor bottles, candles, bird cages, saws, and window frames.

Some of the most playful pieces are the objects d'art which he creates from found objects and the large wood-board paintings that incorporate them. Keys, spark plugs, king cake babies, Mardi Gras beads, and oyster shells are among the types of embellishments used to accent his larger works. Simon calls these small objects "gris-gris," and he boasts that they are not bought but are truly "found" objects. Though he finds many of them himself, just as many are brought to him by fans who say, "I found this on the sidewalk and I knew you would like it." He stores most of the objects in a cabinet he himself found discarded on the sidewalk. It resembles an altarpiece or church front but has drawers and nooks where he stores the overflowing collection.

But nowhere is the humor more in-your-face evident than in his most recognizable medium: his signs. Fashioned in oil-based enamel paints applied to gessoed wood or pressed tin, Simon's signs are the most popular and most familiar of his works.

Given any occasion, any sentiment, any sage advice, there's a sign for that. And, of course, each is delivered via a hefty dose of wit or sarcasm. There are signs that

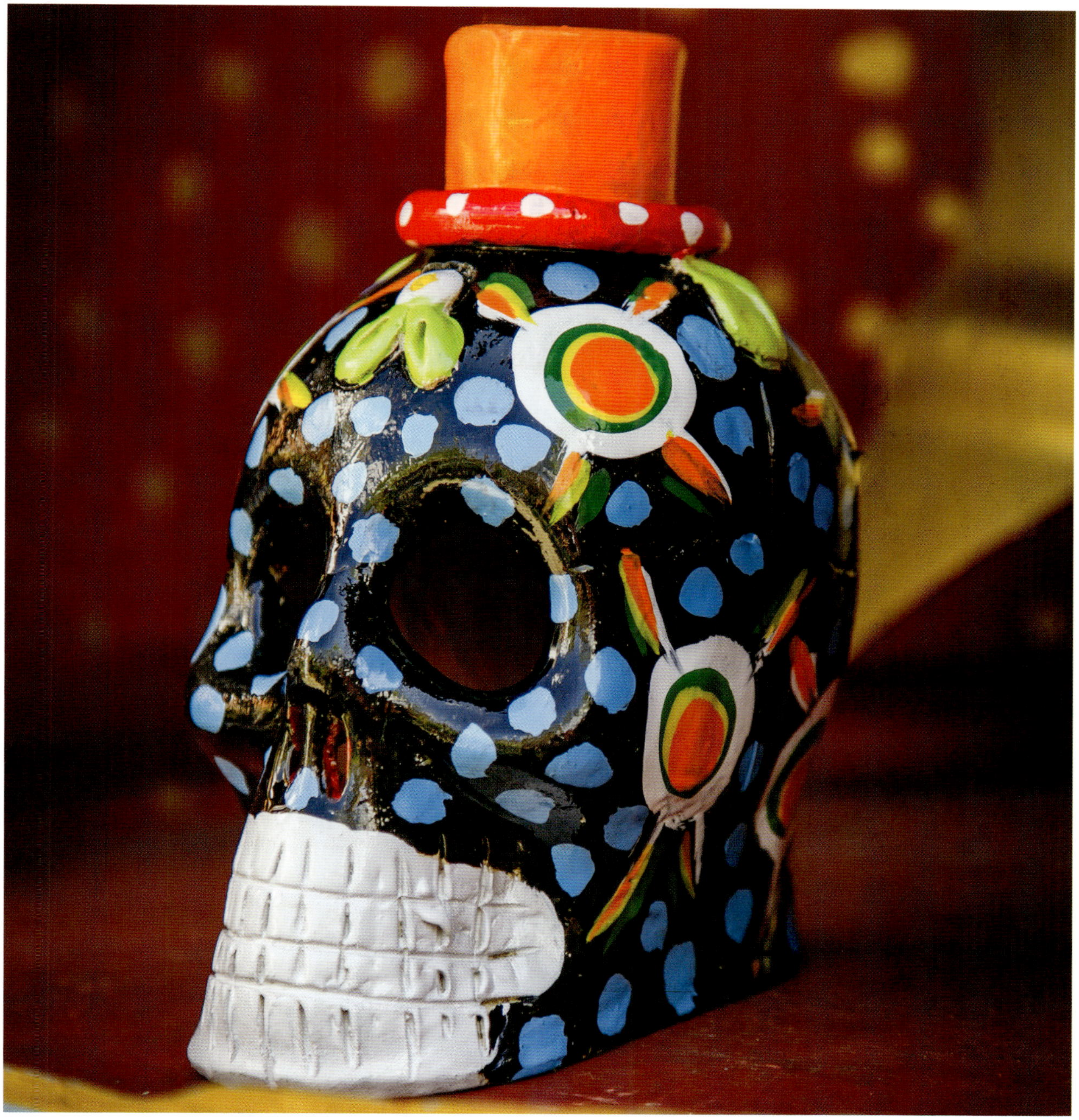

A whimsical nod to the "Day of the Dead."

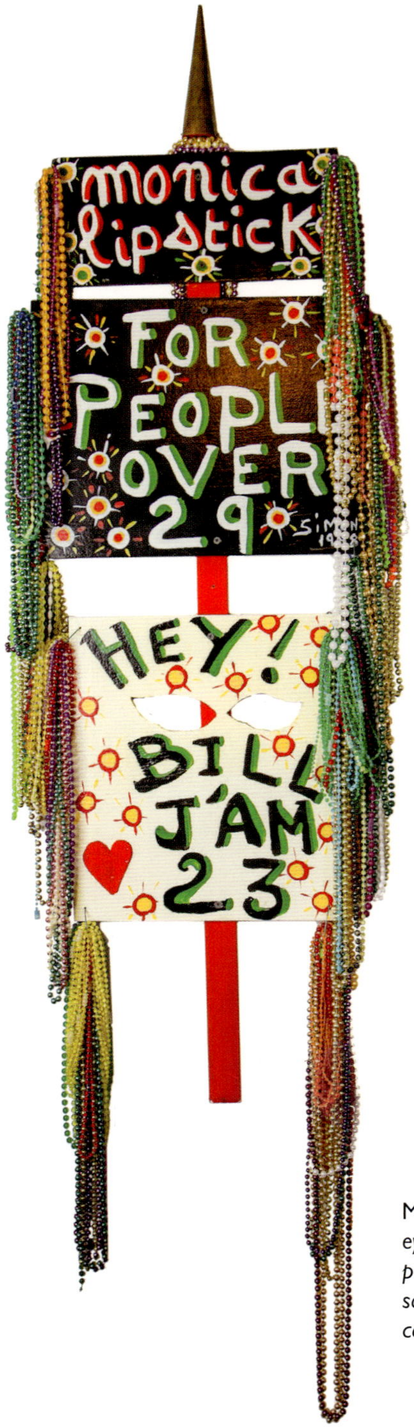

insult: "How can we miss you if you never leave?"; signs that inform: "What's Said on the Porch, Stays on the Porch"; signs that warn: "No advice needed. No suggestions wanted. Got it under control"; and signs that offer succinct tidbits of wisdom: "Nobody Beautiful Ever Hurries." The spiritual gets a hearty nod, encompassing just about every denomination: "Shalom, y'all," "Thank you, Jesus," and "VooDoo, Good Gris Gris."

Signs that remain consistently popular and top the most-requested list include "Laissez Les Bon Temps Rouler," "Red Beans and Rice," and "Do You Know What It Means to Miss New Orleans?" Also popular is "Be Nice or Leave"—a pointed directive displayed on the walls, transoms, and front doors of literally hundreds of New Orleans homes and businesses. Its popularity spiked after the levee failures of Katrina, when residents were too busy putting their lives back together to put up with any additional negative vibes.

Signs pop up in unexpected places. "Too Blessed to Be Stressed" proclaims a Simon-crafted sign at Ochsner Baptist Medical Center. "Every Day Is One-Day Surgery" announces the sign in Touro Ambulatory Surgery Center.

Although Simon is identified with many of the witty sayings proclaimed on his signs, he doesn't claim credit for originating any of them. Many were already in vogue or

Monica Lipstick, *one of Simon's politically satirical pieces, is a Mardi Gras costume body panel complete with eye openings. An obvious parody on the Monica Lewinsky debacle of the mid-1990s, the* Monica Lipstick *piece proclaims that it is "For People Over 29." Surrounding the eyeholes to be held at face level is the message, "Hey! Bill, J'am 23" (Hey! Bill, I am 23). The board also sports a painted heart and Mardi Gras beads cascading down both sides to resemble long tresses of hair. (Fleishmann collection, 1996)*

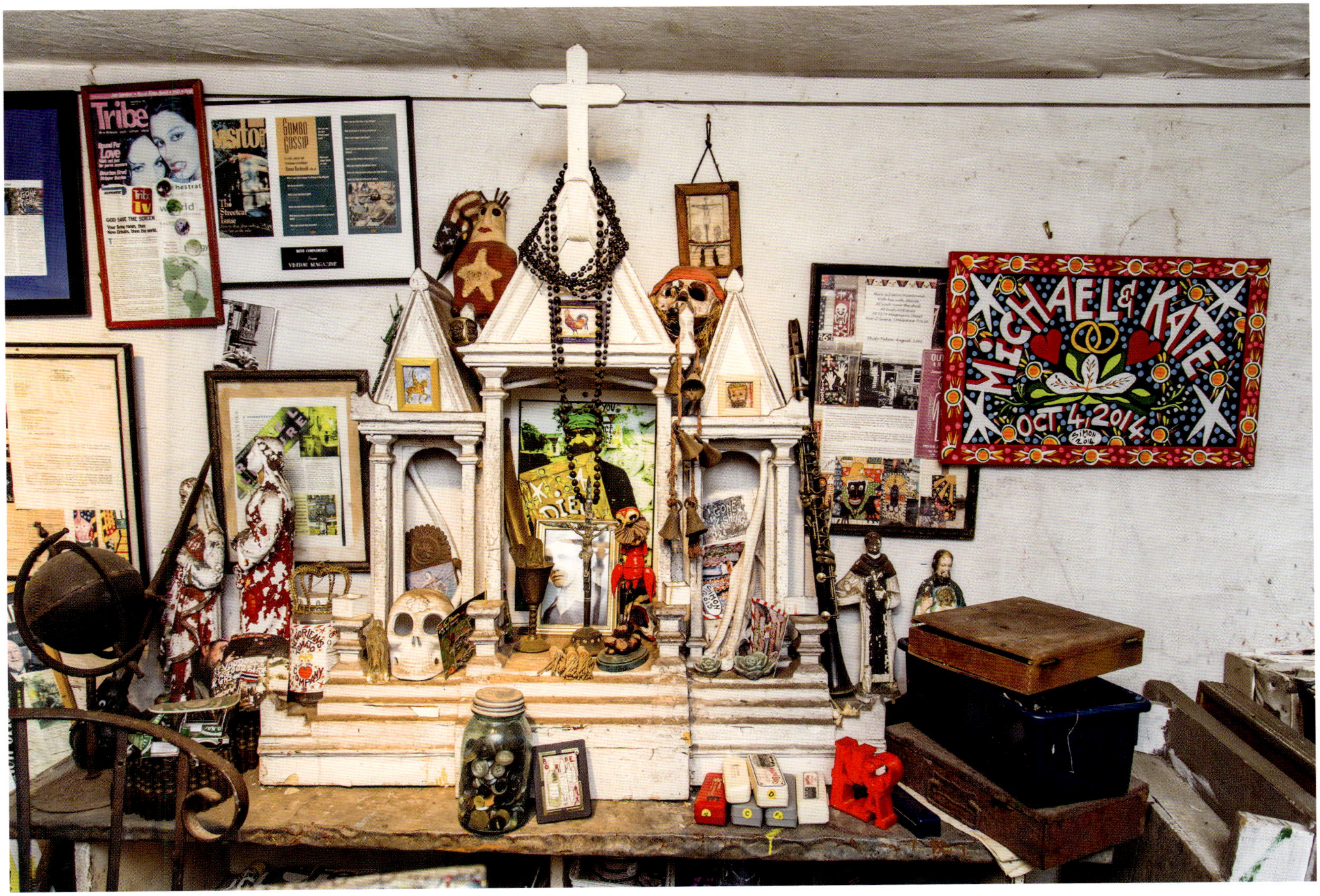

Simon's cabinet for storing found objects is a found object itself.

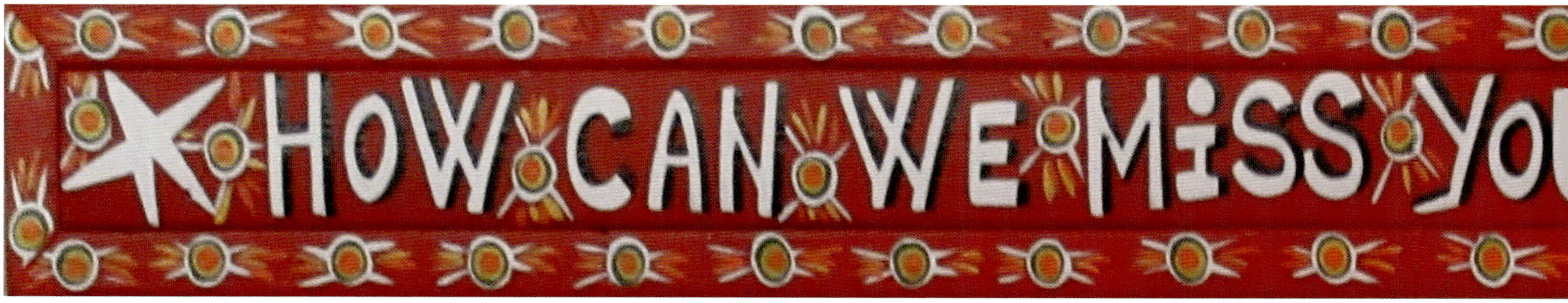

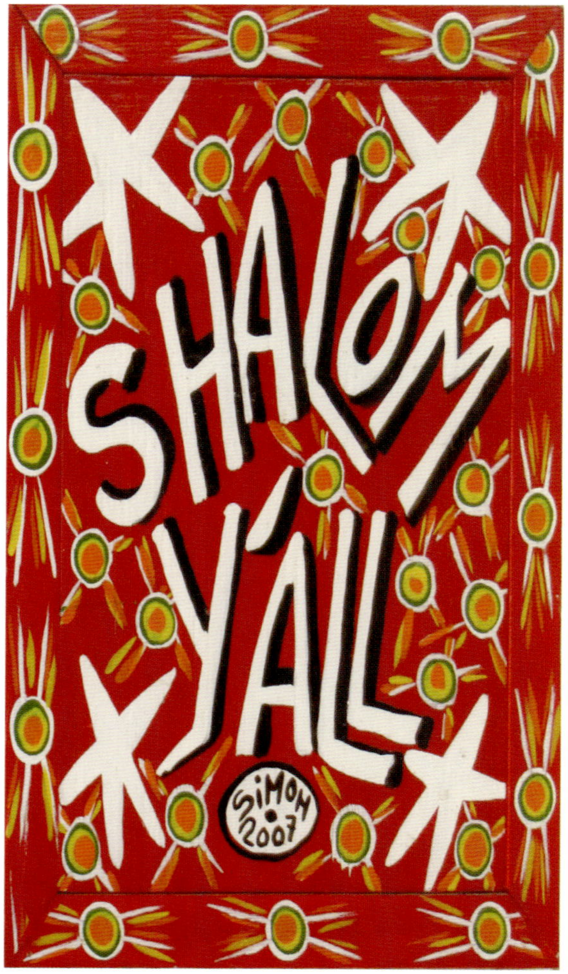

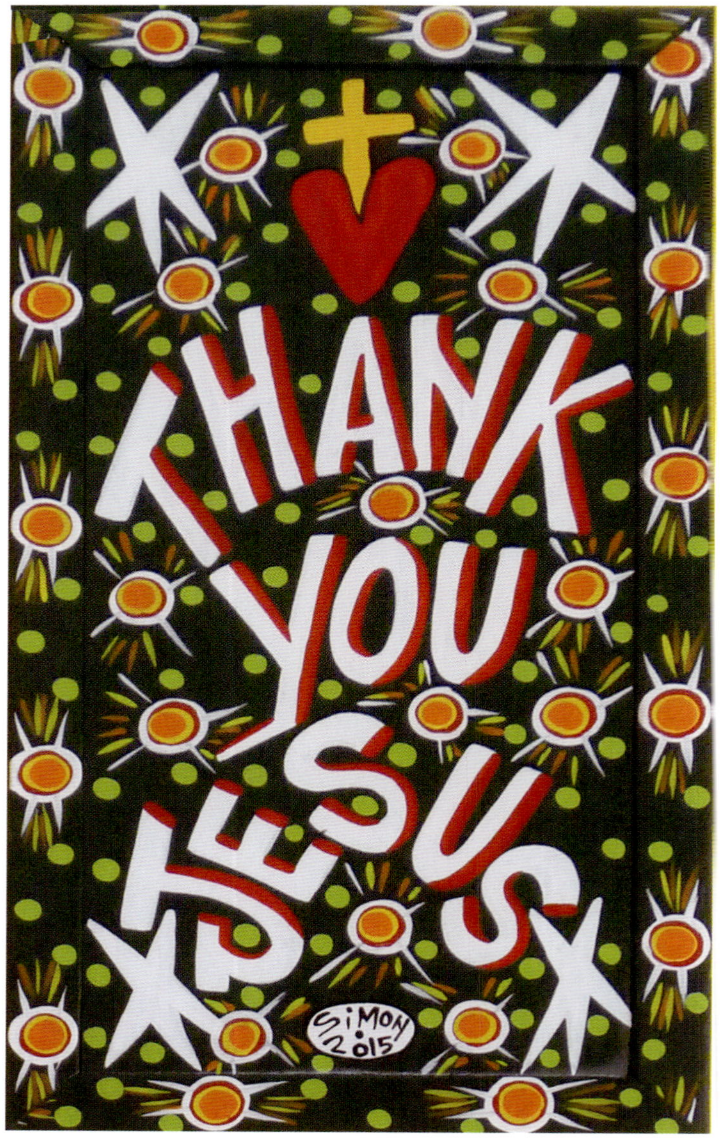

Top: Sarcasm is a popular theme.

Above and right: The spiritual gets a hearty nod.

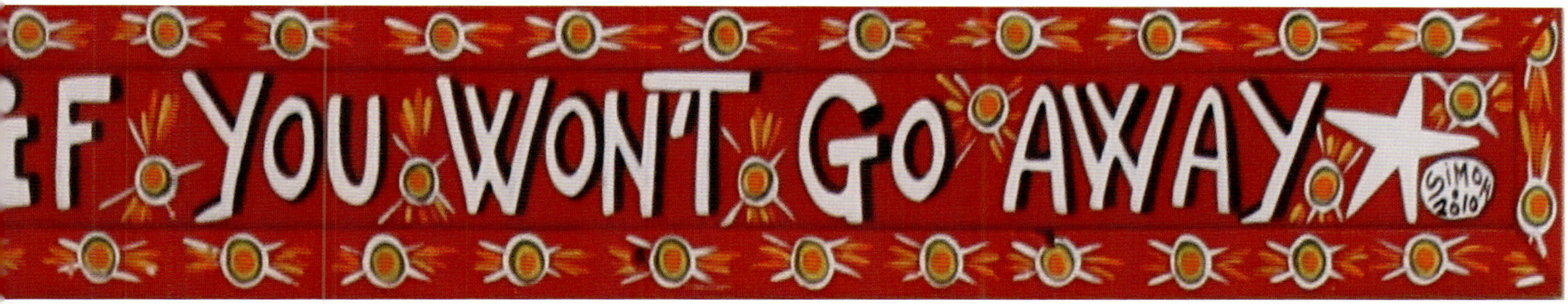

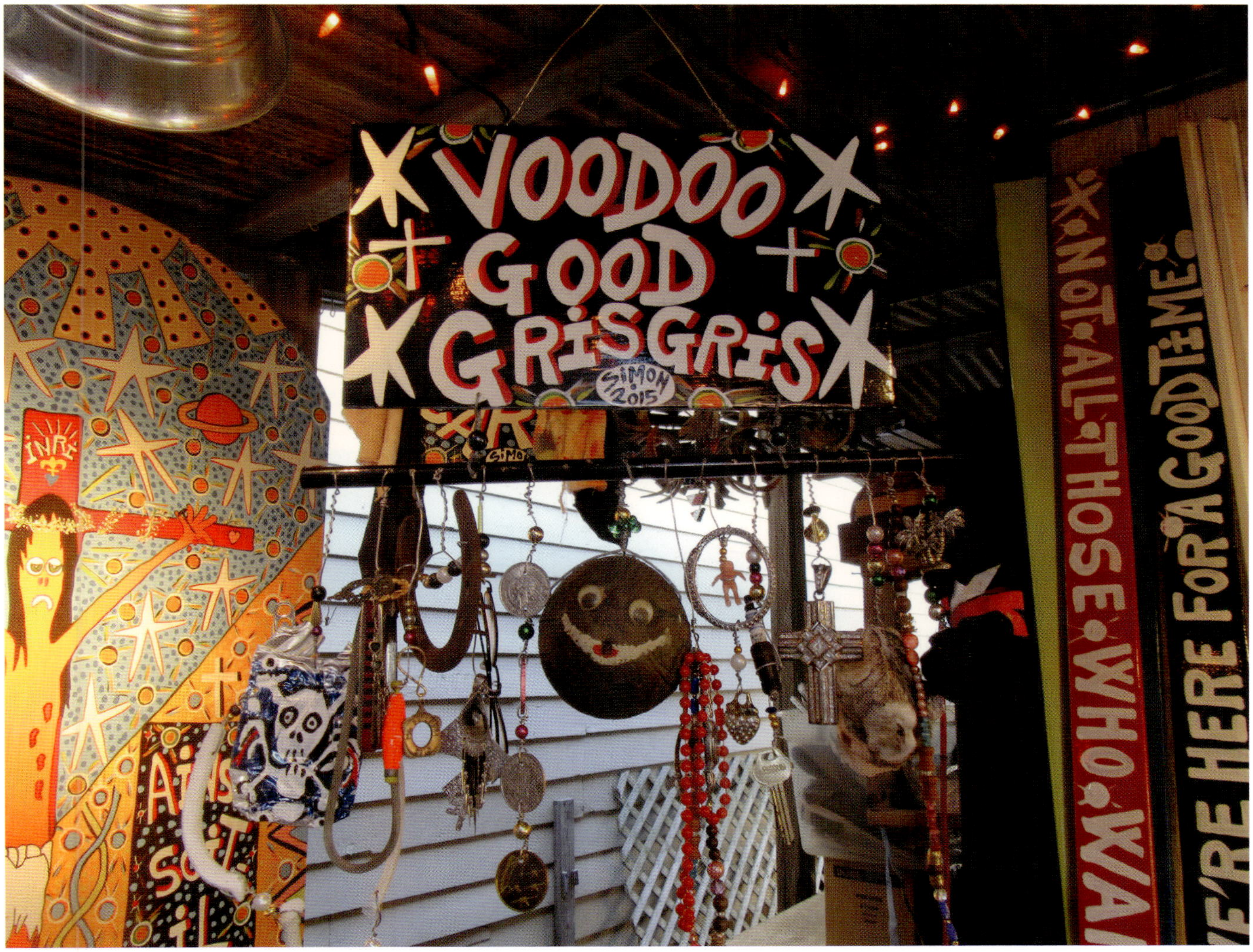

Simon often references voodoo in his works. Among the items chosen for Voodoo, Good Gris Gris *are a pirate-themed beer can, a harmonica, a horseshoe, eyeglasses, beads, doubloons, a king cake baby, a bejeweled cross, and oyster shells.*

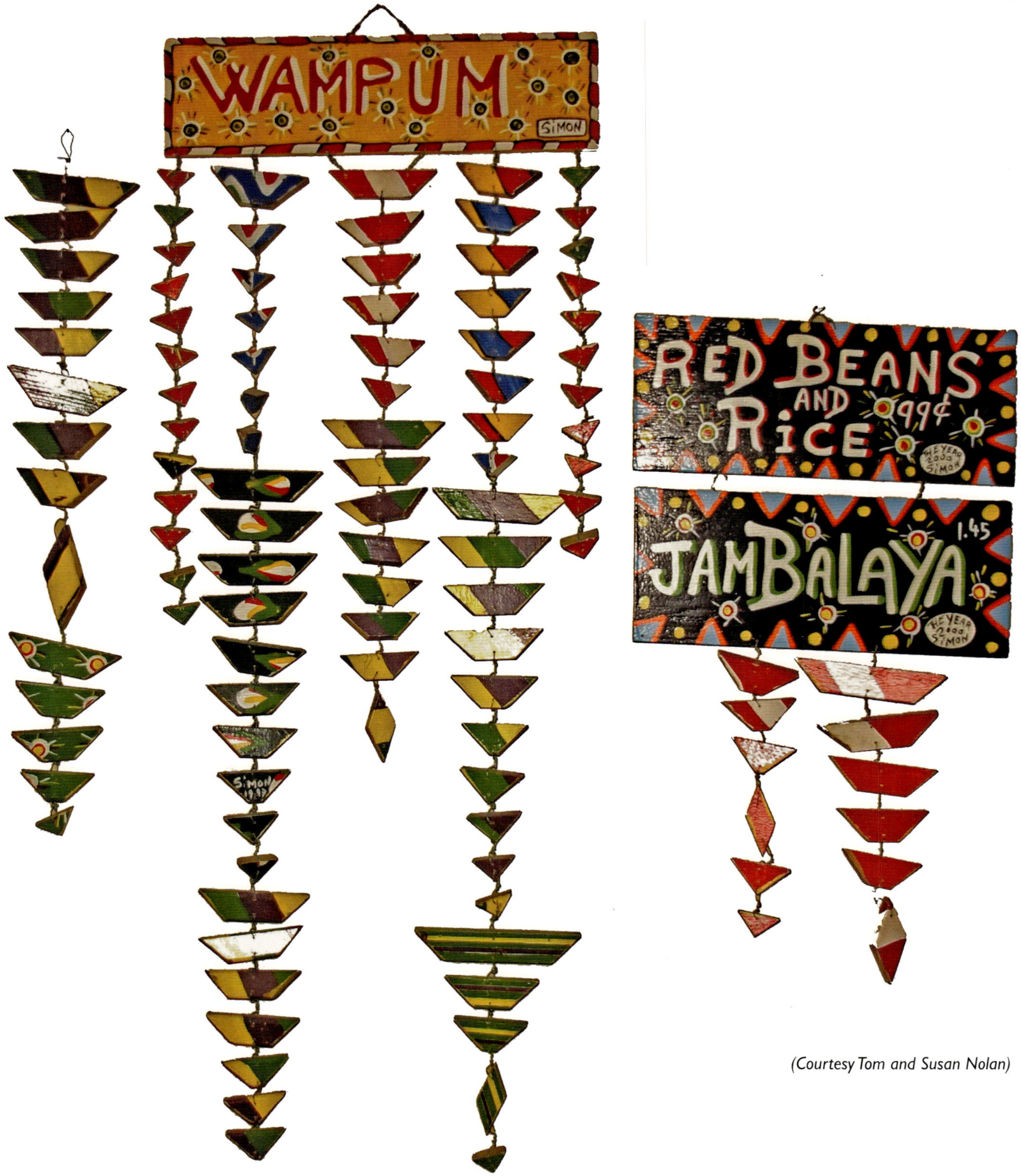

(Courtesy Tom and Susan Nolan)

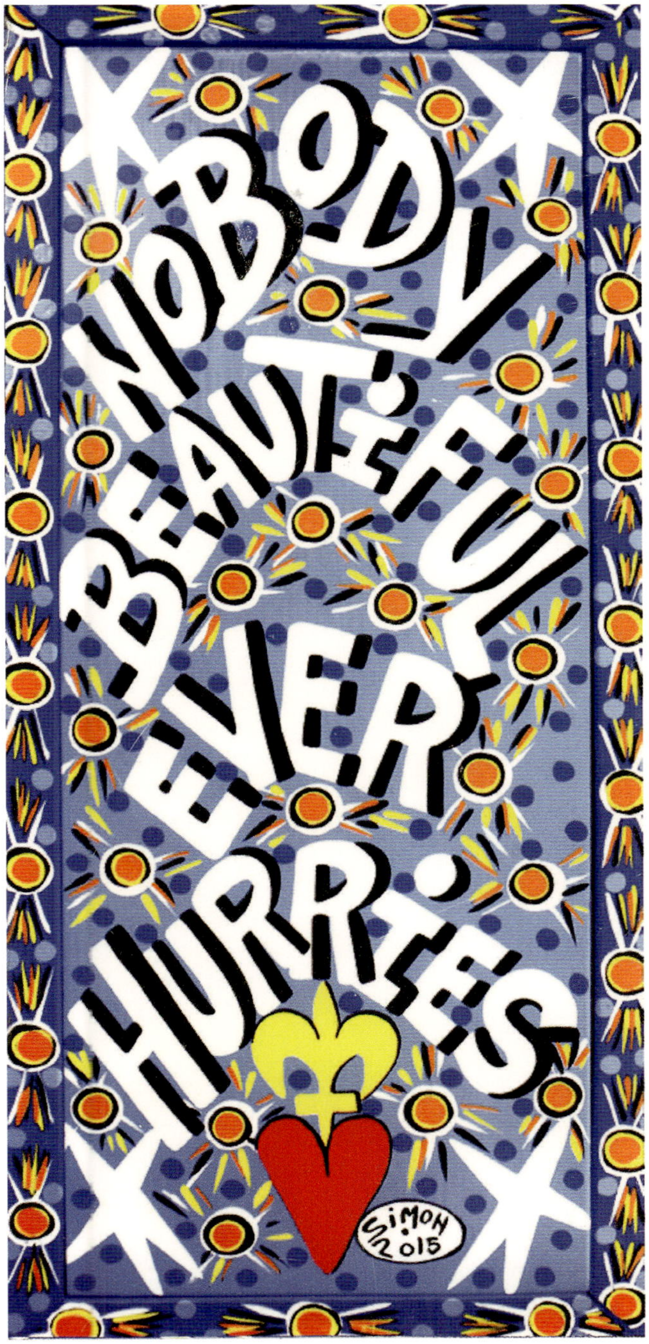
NOBODY
BEAUTIFUL
EVER
HURRIES
SIMON
2015

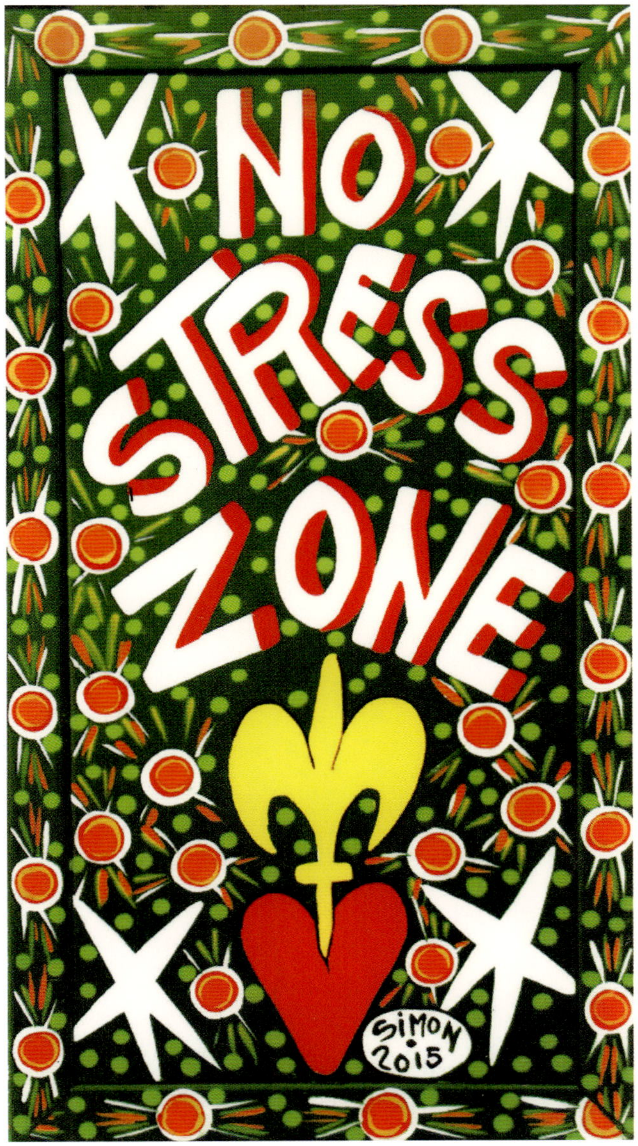
NO
STRESS
ZONE
SIMON
2015

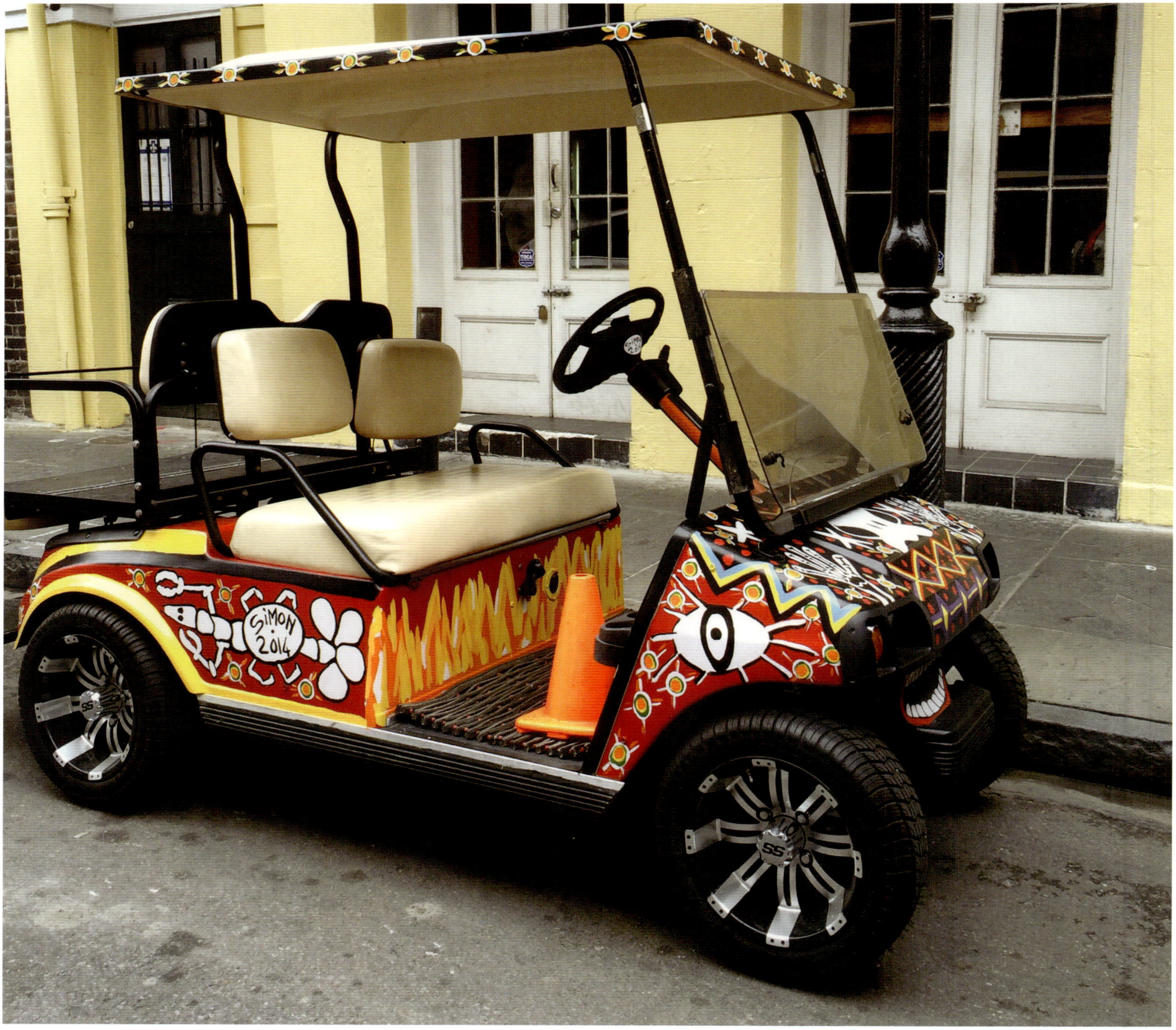

Another unusual "canvas," this golf cart was painted as a fundraiser for a local non-profit.

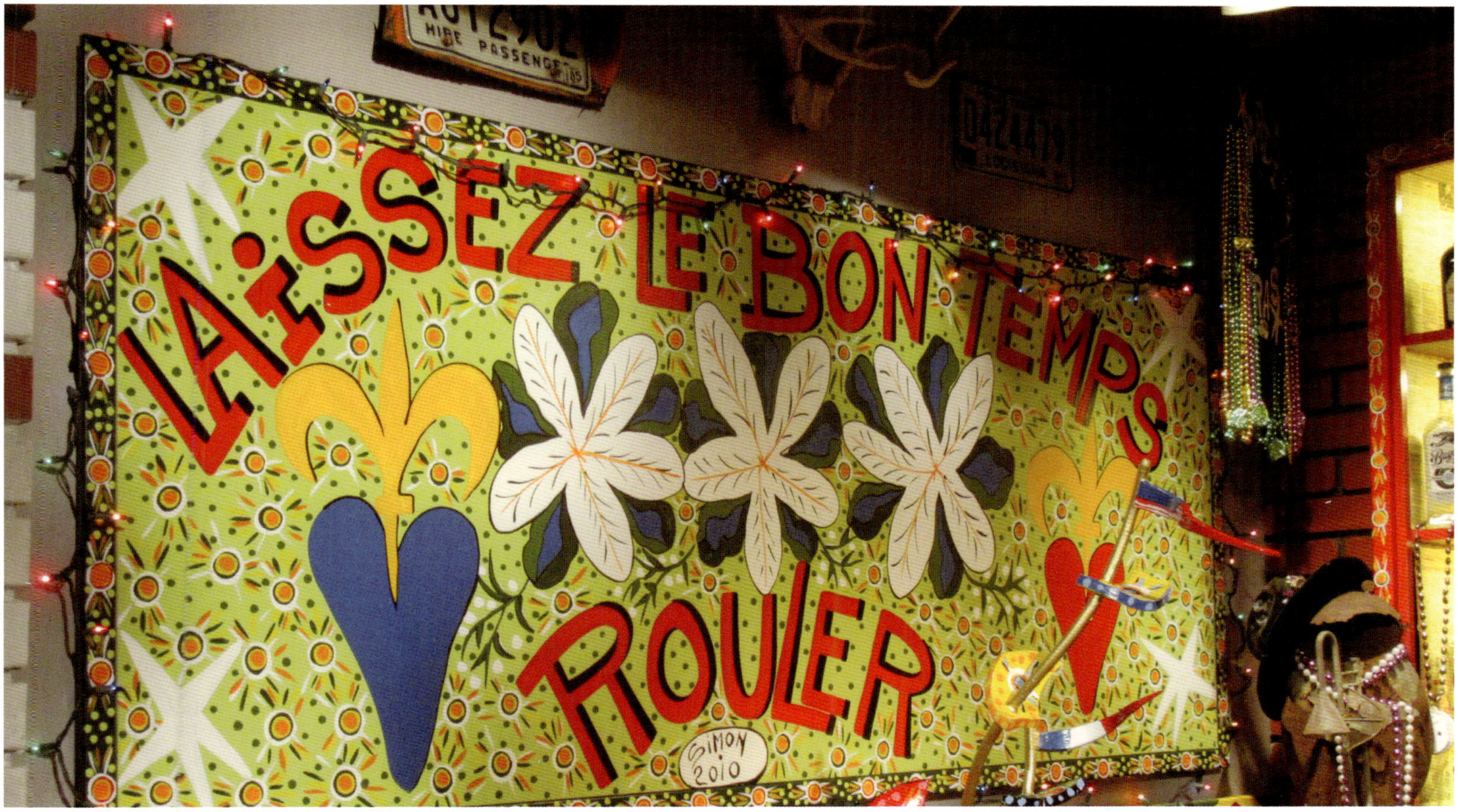

A large version of one of Simon's most popular signs decorates the set of WGNO-TV's News with a Twist.

suggested by customers. He does accept credit, however, for making them so widely known.

A growing percentage of his works are pieces that have been commissioned by collectors to commemorate life events like weddings, birthdays, baptisms, "sweet sixteen" celebrations, and graduations. As a result, there is an increasingly longer wait time for these personalized, custom-made signs—a year or more. But for thousands of people, it is worth the wait to have an event memorialized in a piece by Simon.

Some people find a way to get commissions done a little faster. A local dentist had ordered a commission from Simon years ago, but it was long overdue. The dentist found that a patient who had come to his office knew Simon. He told the patient that if he could get Simon to complete the painting,

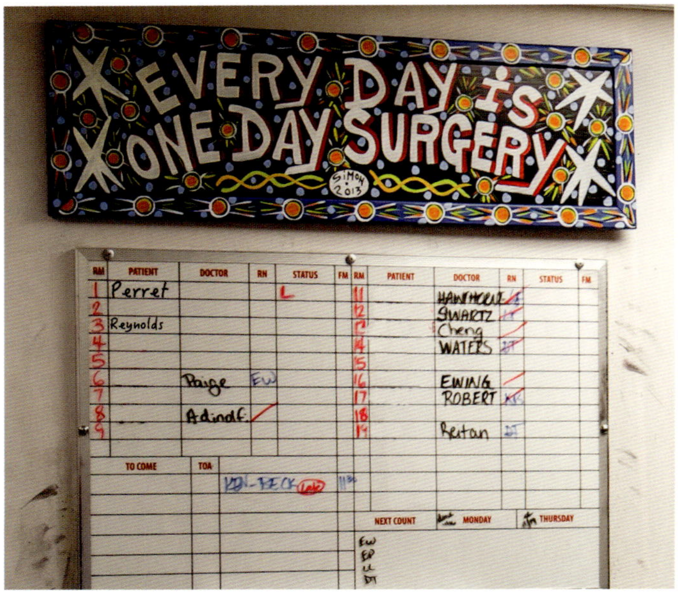

This sign greets visitors to Touro Ambulatory Surgery Center.

he wouldn't charge him for the dental work. The incentive worked. The dentist received his art, and the patient received his dental work gratis.

Some of the events Simon memorializes are rather unusual. On more than one occasion he has been asked to commemorate a divorce. In another, he had painted a piece to commemorate the engagement of a pair of soon-to-be newlyweds. The sign included painted images of the bride, the groom, and their dog. Months later, the woman told Simon the engagement was over and confided to him that it had ended abruptly and bitterly. He requested that she return the sign, and she complied. Simon proceeded to make a few "adjustments," like covering the former fiancé's name and image with a fresh coat of paint. However, he kept the cute rendering of her dog, apparently a more faithful companion than the ex-fiancé.

Over the years, Simon's work has continued to evolve. Some of his more recent works have included "totems," sculptures made from full-sized oil drums which are stacked two or three high and welded together. Windows, circles, and arches are then cut out of the metal barrels. Imposing in size, the totems are painted with the same bright colors he uses on his other works. The resulting art can be anything from a fanciful representation of the St. Louis Cathedral to a utilitarian piece capable of storage to a whimsical snowman totally out of his comfort zone in the New Orleans heat.

Oddly enough, it was a fortuitous theft in the middle of the night that led to Simon's inspiration to begin designing and creating totems. One evening years ago, Simon had placed trash in an old fifty-gallon oil drum and hauled it to the curb to be emptied as usual by trash collectors the next day. But sometime in the early-morning hours after the trash had been emptied, someone made off with the can. A search of the neighborhood eventually turned up the purloined barrel, and Simon hauled it back home. But he was left with the inspired realization that if oil drums were desirable enough to steal, then surely—after creative embellishment by the artist—they would be desirable enough to sell. And they were.

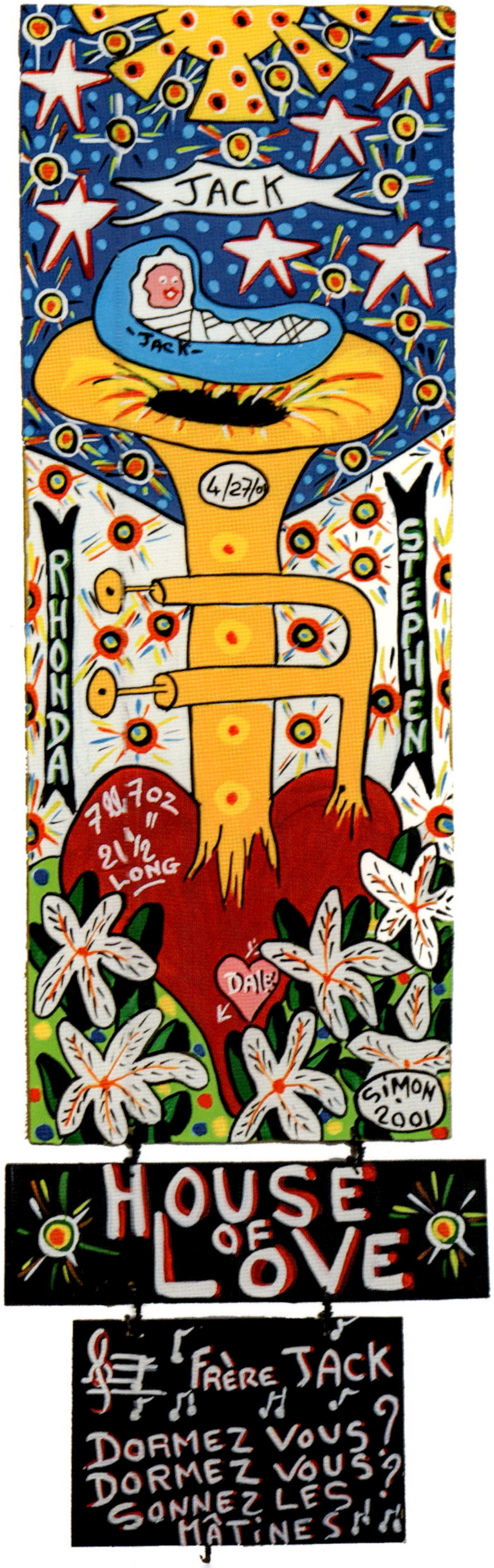

Not all collectors have enough room to display these large totems, so the artist has also created some mini-totems using recycled balustrades from demolished houses and painted them to look like small totems.

Simon was directed from totems to clocks when collector Susan Nolan attempted to make a grandfather clock from a kit. "It turned out downright ugly," she readily admits. "I tried to hide it in out-of-the-way places in my house." Finally, she sent it to Simon with an assortment of bottle caps she had collected and told him, "Do whatever you want." She loves how it turned out. "He did a fabulous job of transforming that ugly clock into a work of art." The clock now stands in their front room.

One of Simon's permanent pieces is a large collection of pillar candles that are half-melted and appear to be one large conglomeration of wicks and wax drippings. Simon explains that he and his wife used the candles after Hurricane Katrina when they had no electricity. Now they light the candle collection only for happy occasions, like birthdays, anniversaries, and artistic achievements. "It was a reminder to us of a very sad time, but we have turned it into a celebration of happy times. But we save it only for really special occasions." A sign over the candles says, "God is free. Candles expensive."

Few artists can match the sheer variety found in Simon's body of work. His painted banners announcing upcoming festivals frequently span the entire width of Magazine

House of Love *was painted to commemorate the birth of the collector's grandchild. Baby Jack seems to be entering the world through a trumpet, which is rooted in a large heart. Included are the parents' names and the grandmother's name along with the baby's birth weight and length. The title of the French song "Frére Jacques" has been changed to "Frére Jack," followed by some of the song's lyrics. (Fleishmann collection, 1996)*

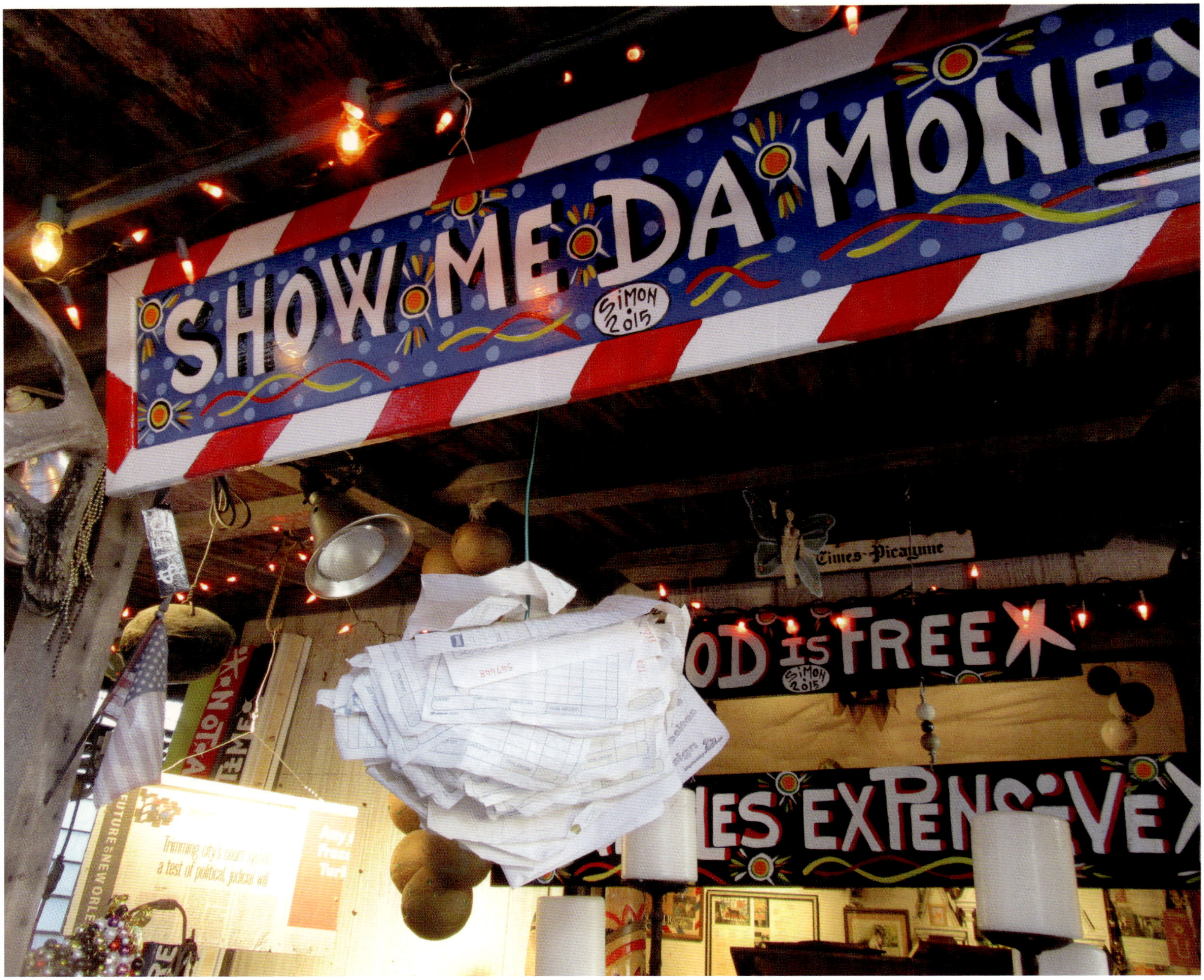

The spindle holds an ever-increasing collection of orders for Simon's commissions.

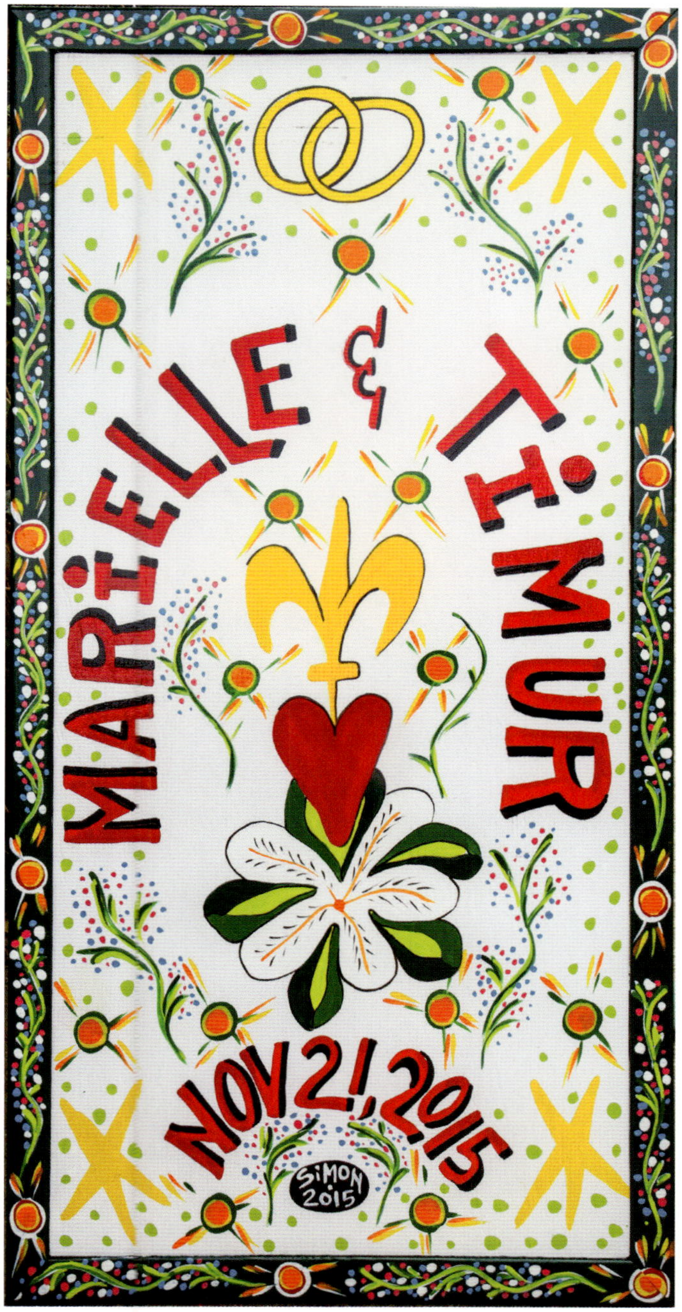

Weddings are a popular subject for commission requests.

Street, high above the busy traffic passing below. He managed to turn a nondescript golf cart into a work of art to be used at a local charity's fundraising event. The International School of Louisiana displayed and then auctioned off a freezer door emblazoned with "Ice Cold Beer." Four-foot-long mini-pirogues, decorated in a seafood motif, are destined to hold mounds of crawfish and shrimp still steaming from the boiling pot. His illustrations brighten the pages of a cookbook titled *Fun, Funky & Fabulous* by Jyl Benson.

Asked to design the 2015 "geaux-cups" for the perennially popular strawberry lemonade drinks at the New Orleans Jazz & Heritage Festival, Simon commented, "After twenty years of painting in New Orleans, for me this cup is like an Oscar award!" He spent time at the Fest autographing the cups for fans, and the cups sold beyond the expectations of the festival officials.

A delightful, curbside mini-lending library on Magazine Street offers neighbors a selection of good reads. The city-designed street sign at Laurel and Webster Streets in Uptown New Orleans just wasn't jazzy enough, so a Simon-designed version adds a little character to the corner.

Simon likes to say that he "paints New Orleans." With his art so bountiful and wide-spread across the city, it seems at times that he has literally done just that.

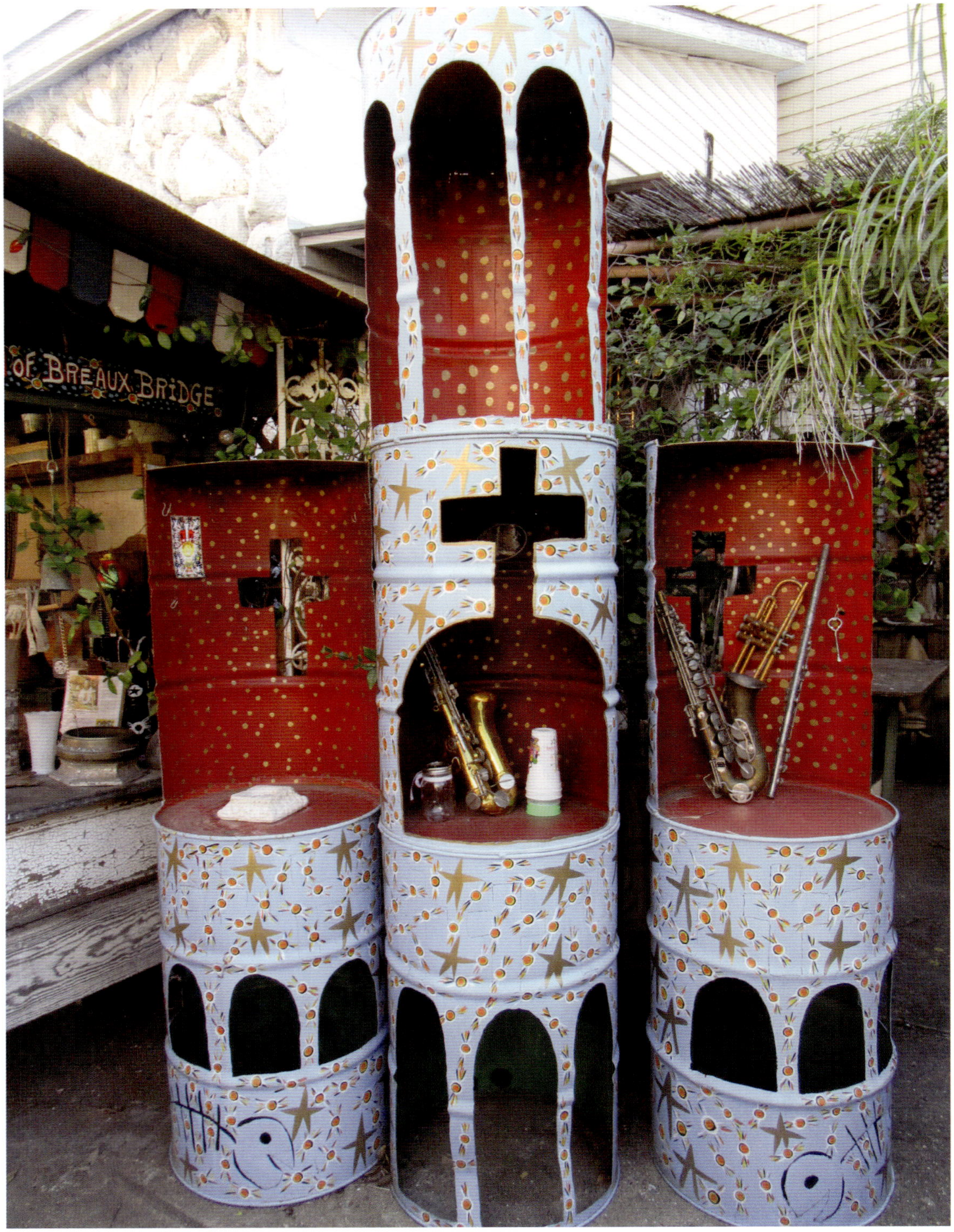

A triple-columned representation of St. Louis Cathedral.

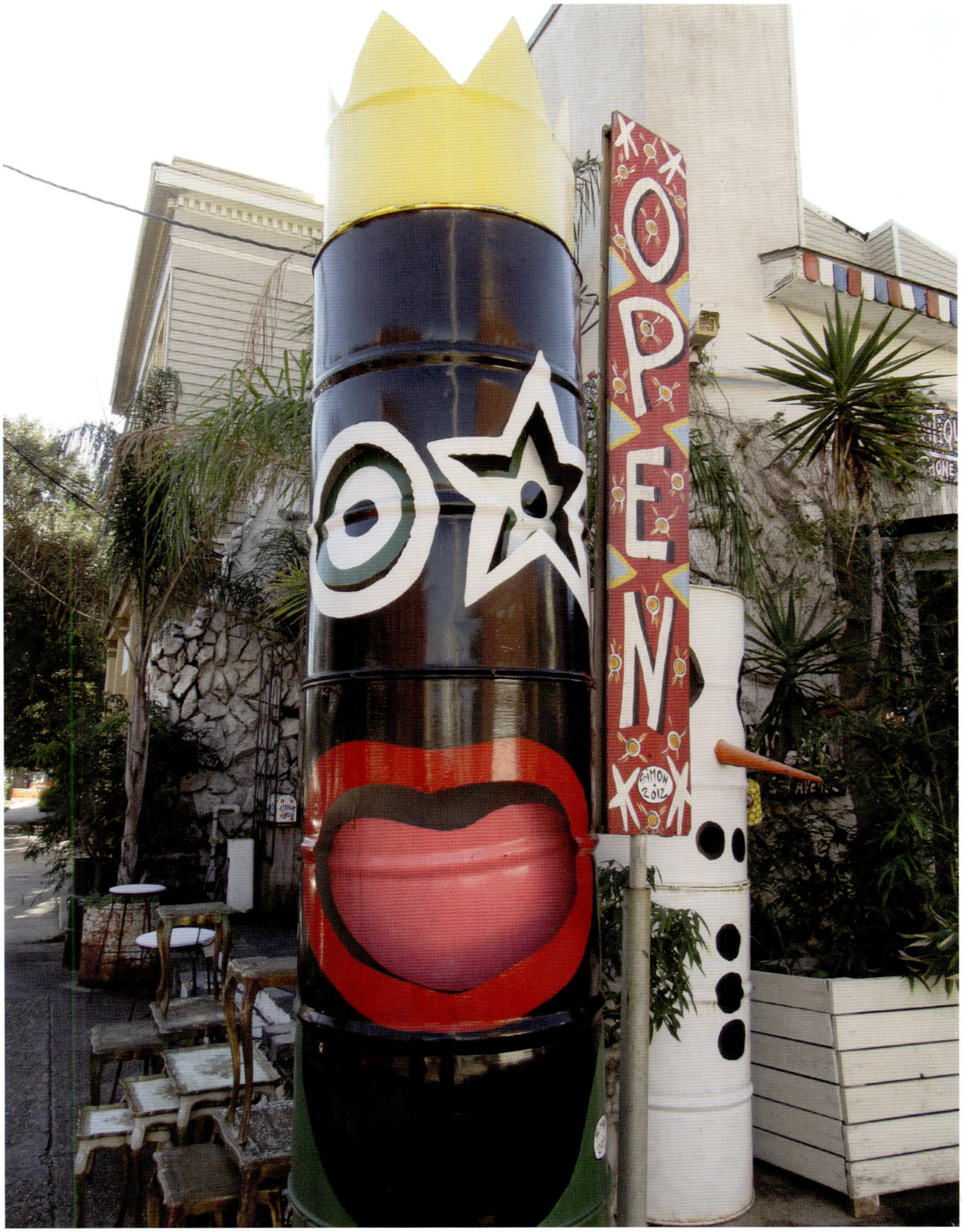

A "Zulu" totem.

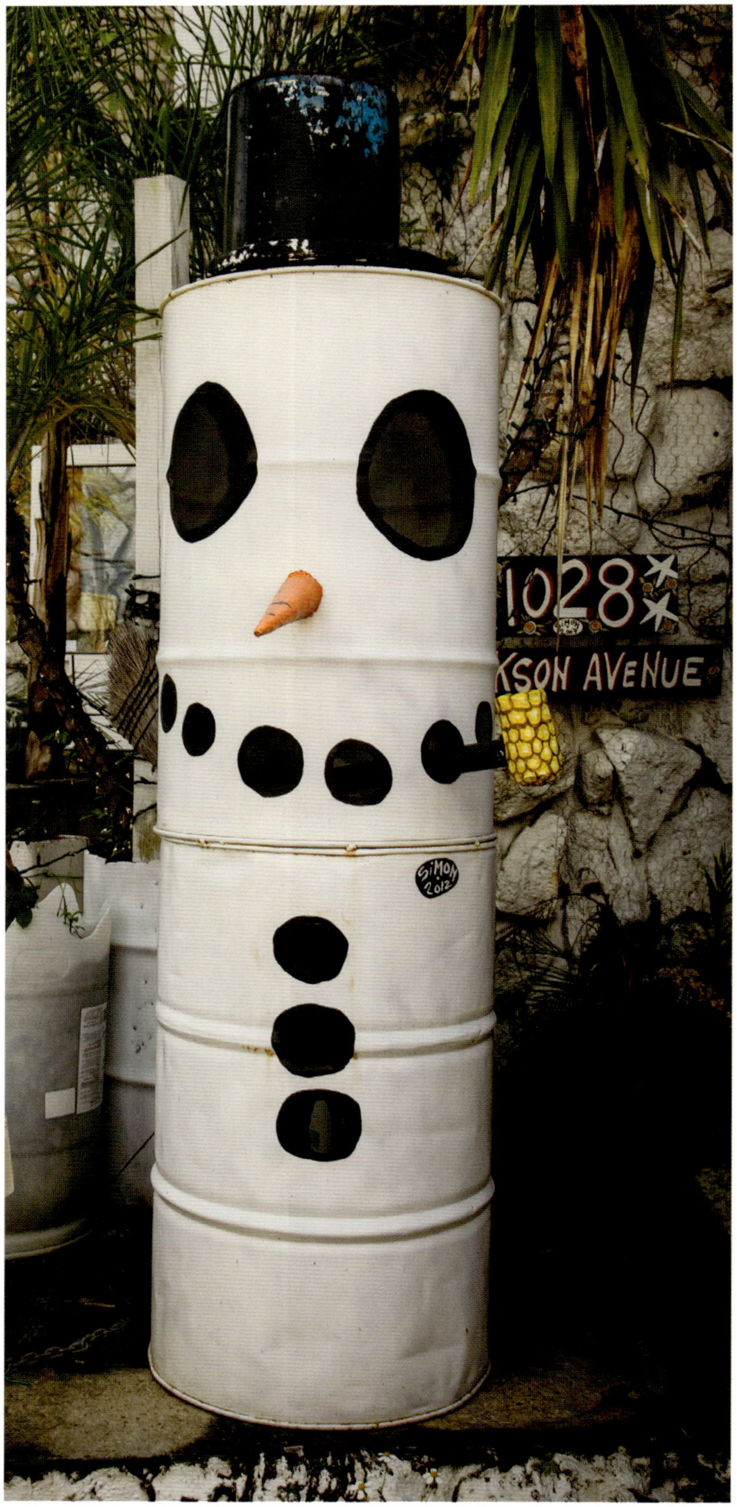

A snowman totem tolerates the New Orleans heat.

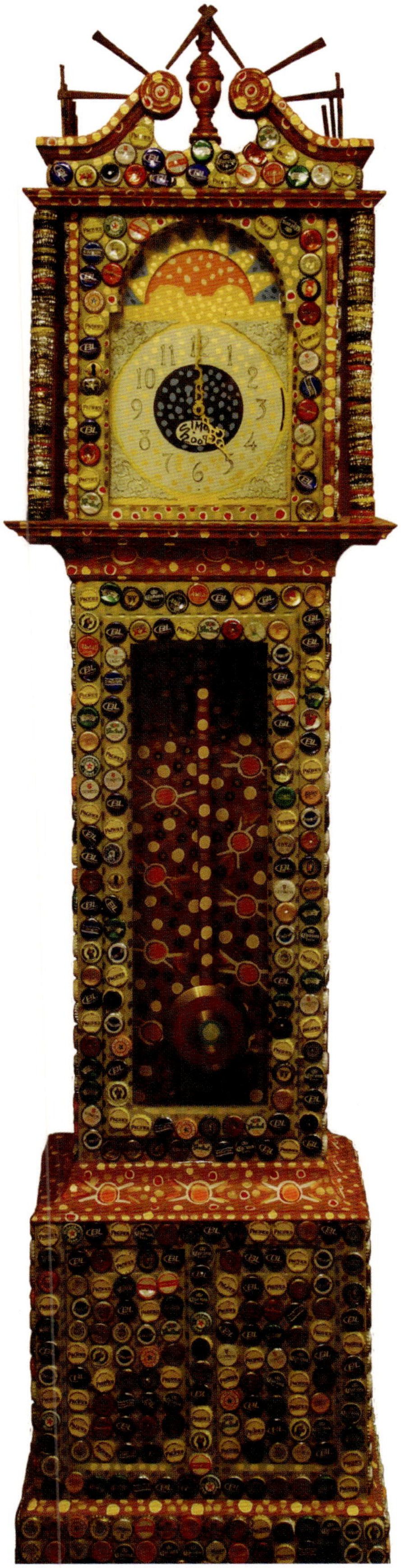

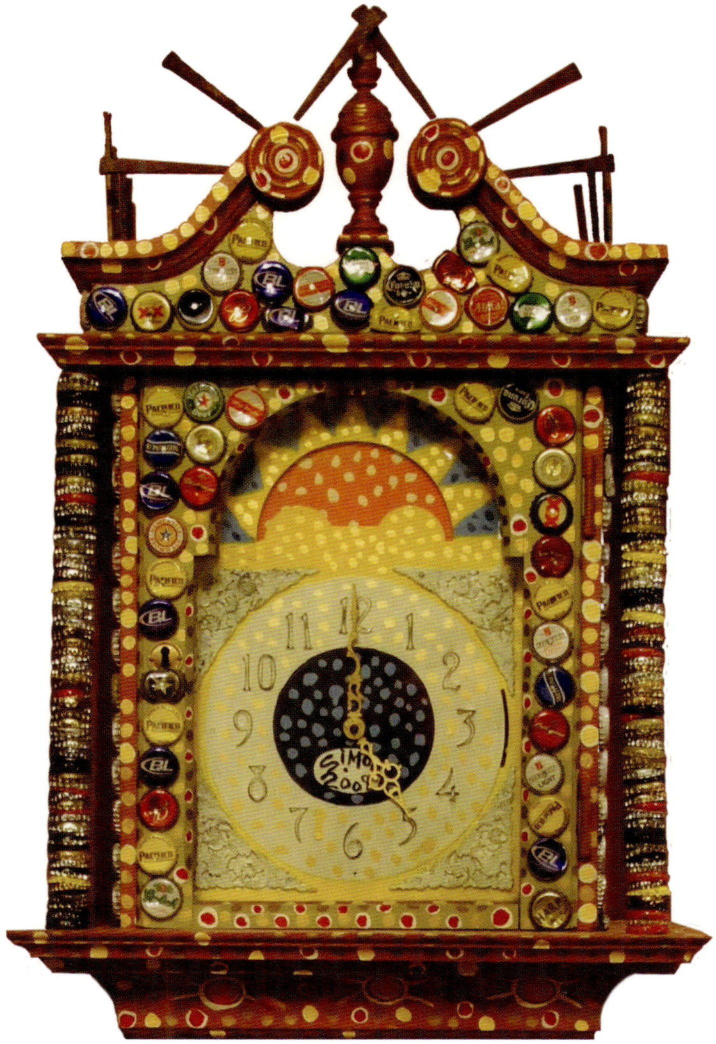

Left: A collector asked Simon to rescue an "ugly" grandfather clock made from a kit. It is now a "work of art," says the collector. (Courtesy Tom and Susan Nolan)

Above: A close-up of the clock face.

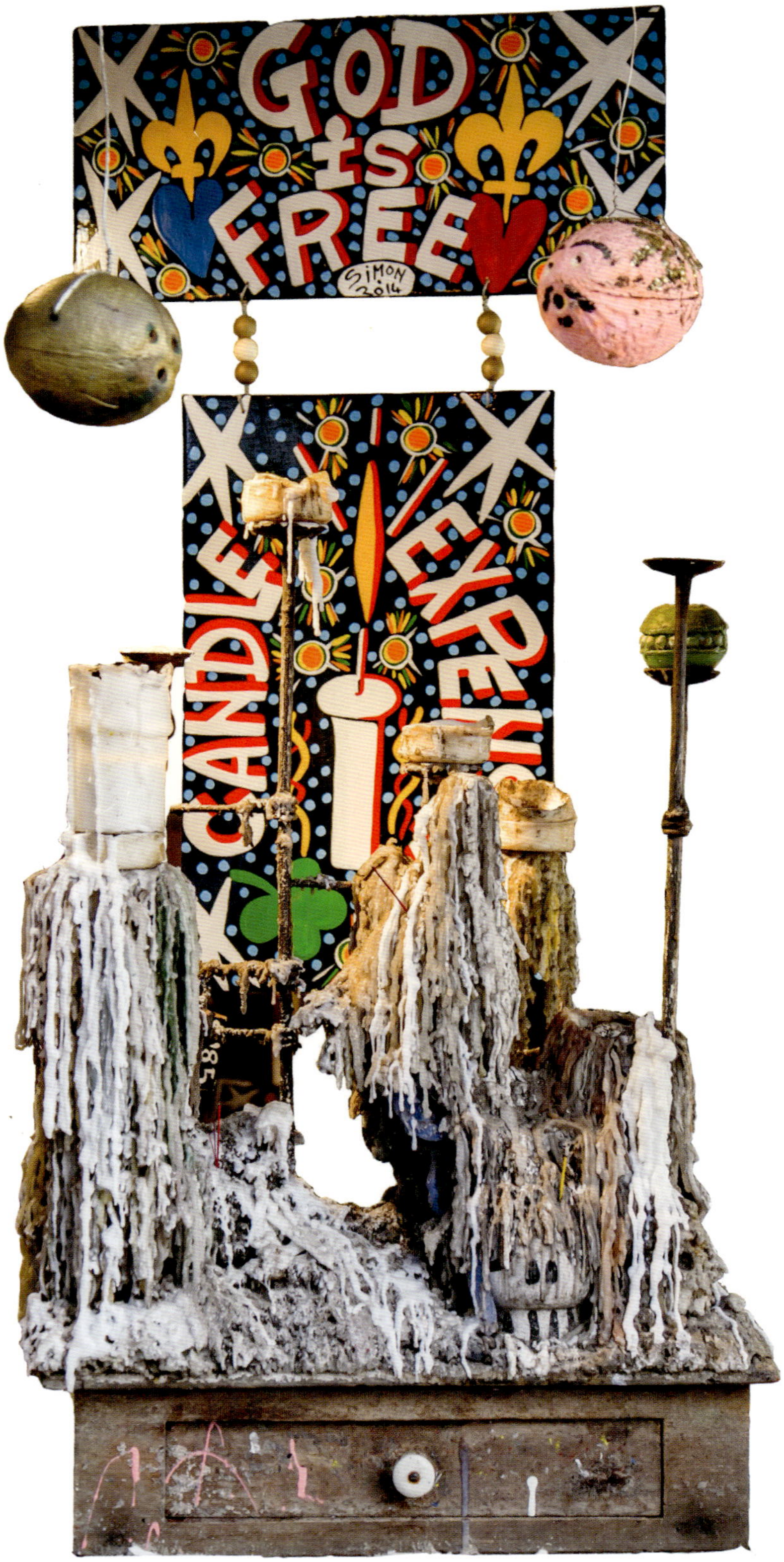

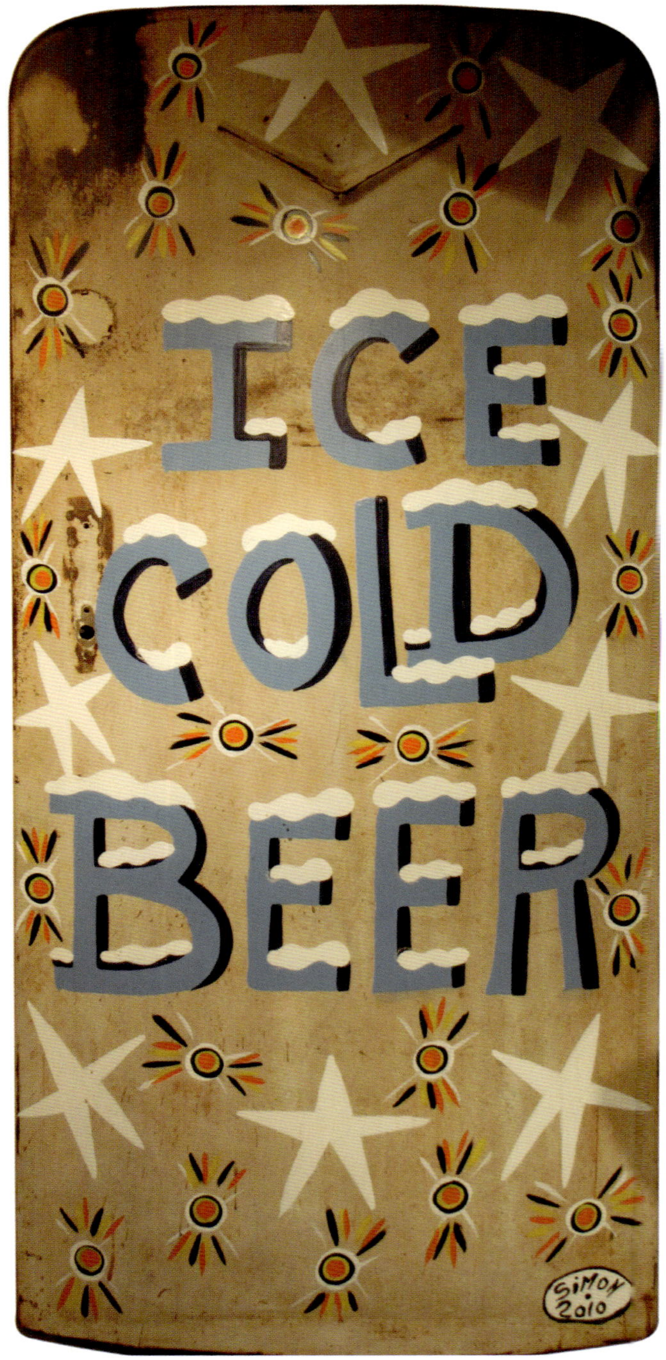

Above: Discarded objects, like this freezer door, are transformed from trash to treasure.

Left: This candle collection, once a Katrina reminder, is now a place to celebrate happy moments. "God Is Free. Candles Expensive."

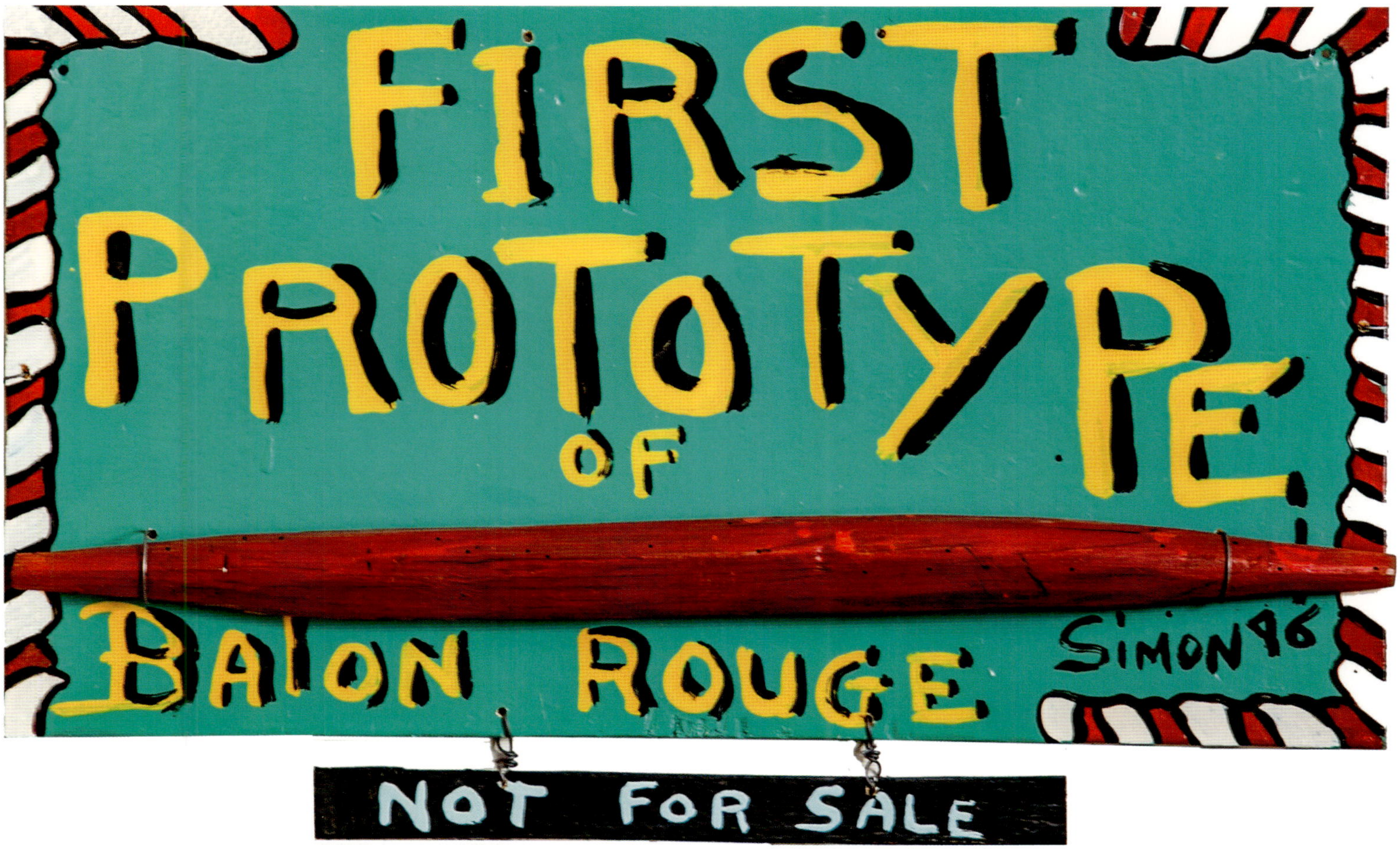

One of Simon's earliest pieces is this humorous take on the origin of the name of the state's capital, Baton Rouge.

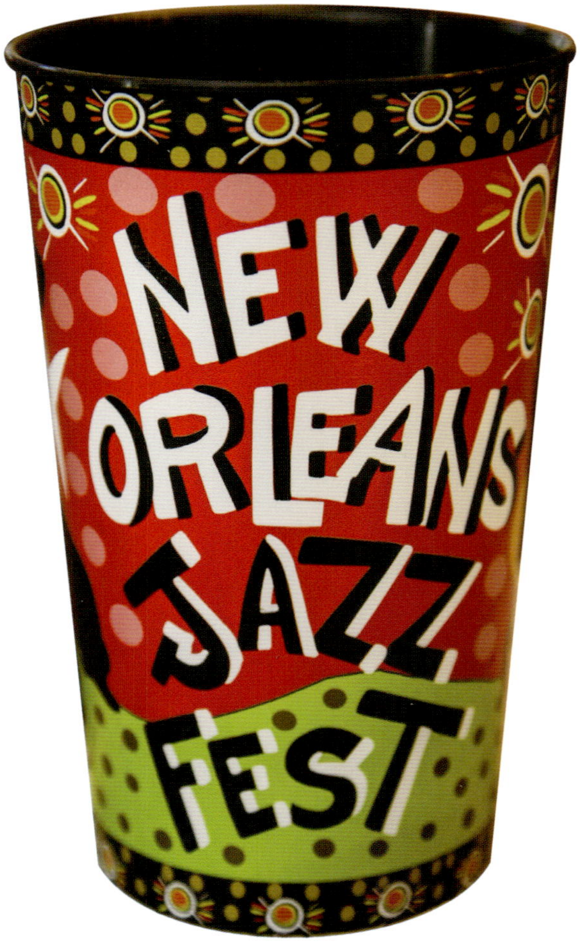

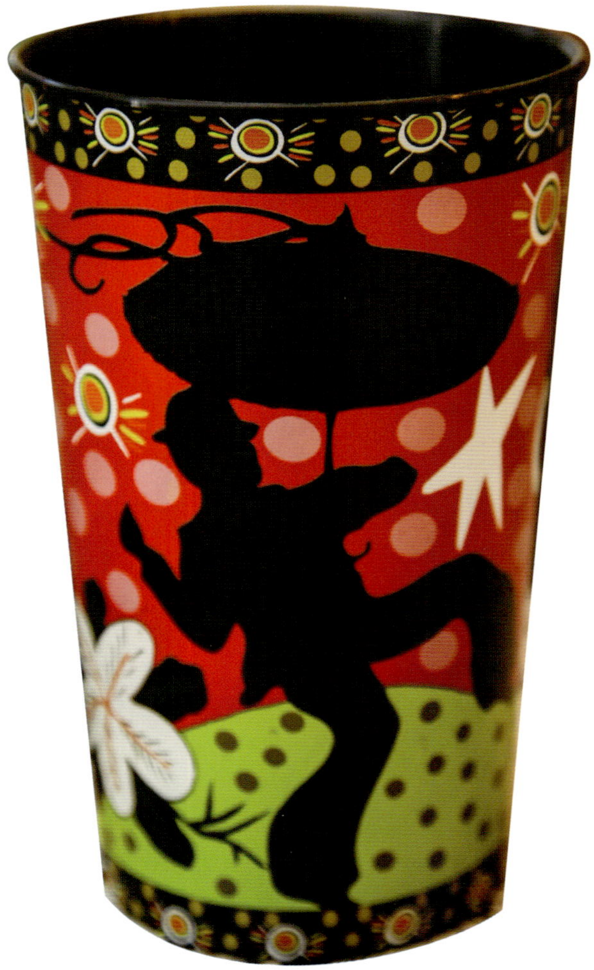

Above: Simon was commissioned by the New Orleans Jazz & Heritage Festival to design "geaux-cups" for the fest's popular strawberry lemonade drink.

Right: The back of the Jazz Fest geaux-cup.

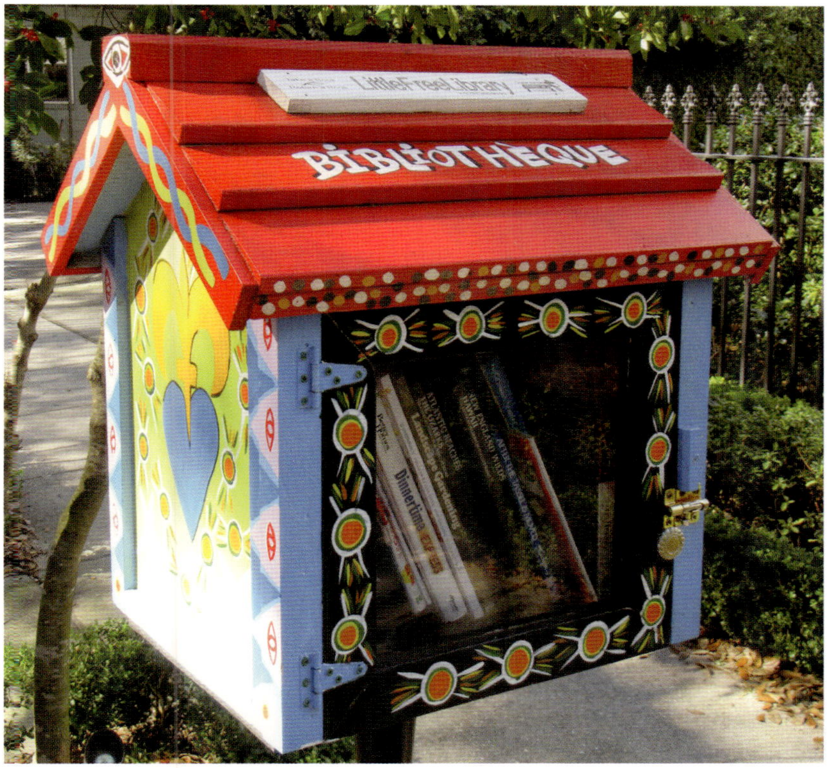

Above: A brightly painted curbside lending library on Magazine Street tempts passersby.

Right: The back side of the Magazine Street lending library. (Photos by S. Campbell).

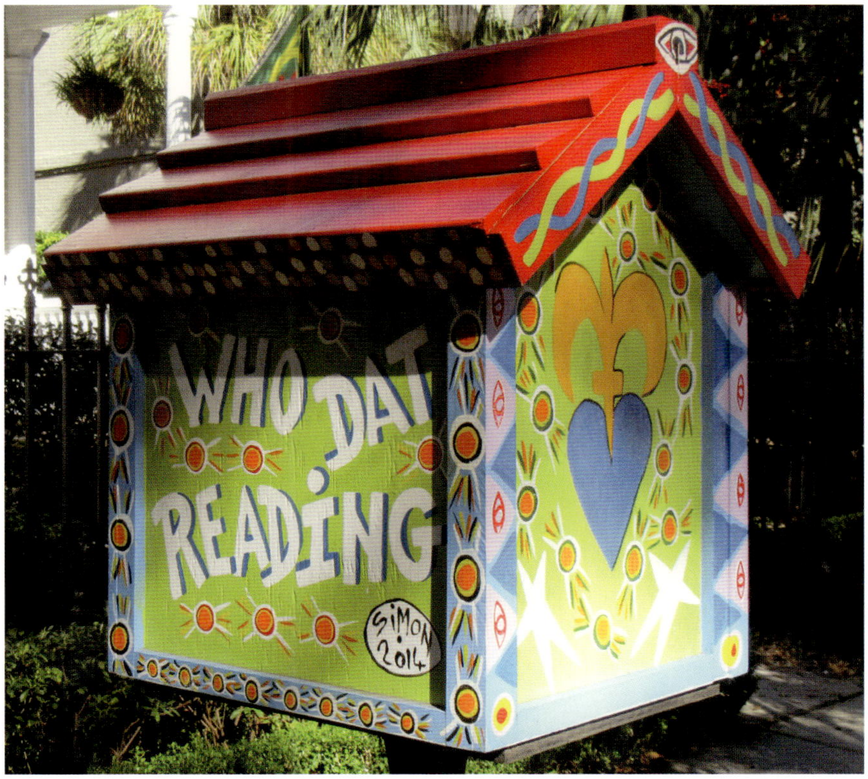

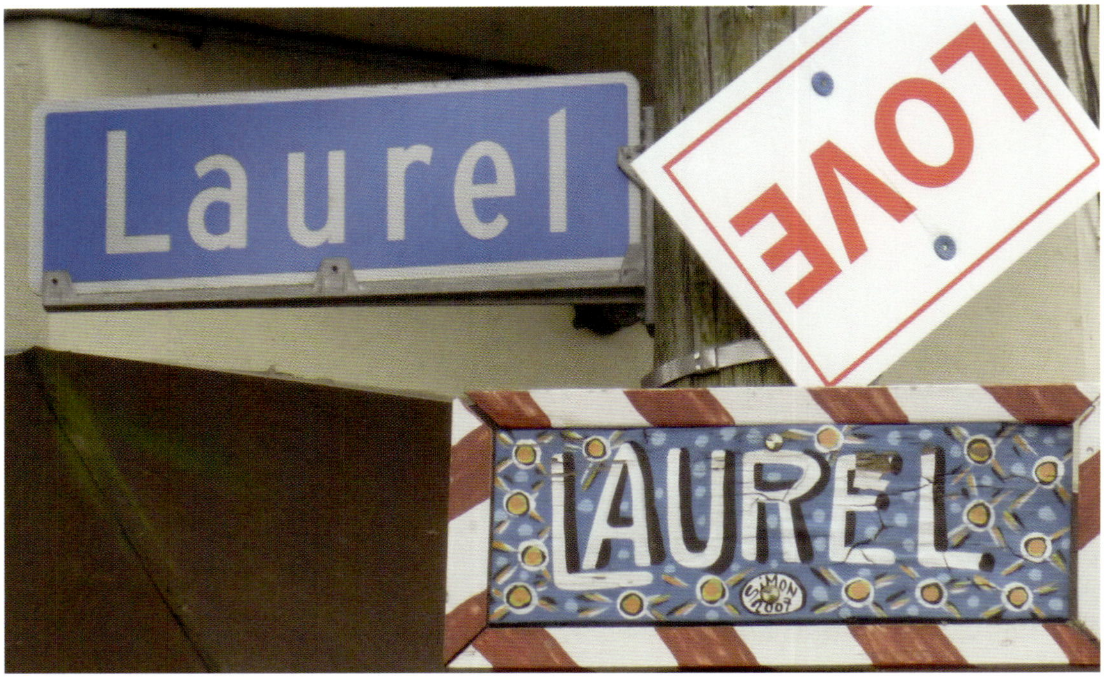

Simon was asked by area residents to "jazz up" their street sign. (Photo by author)

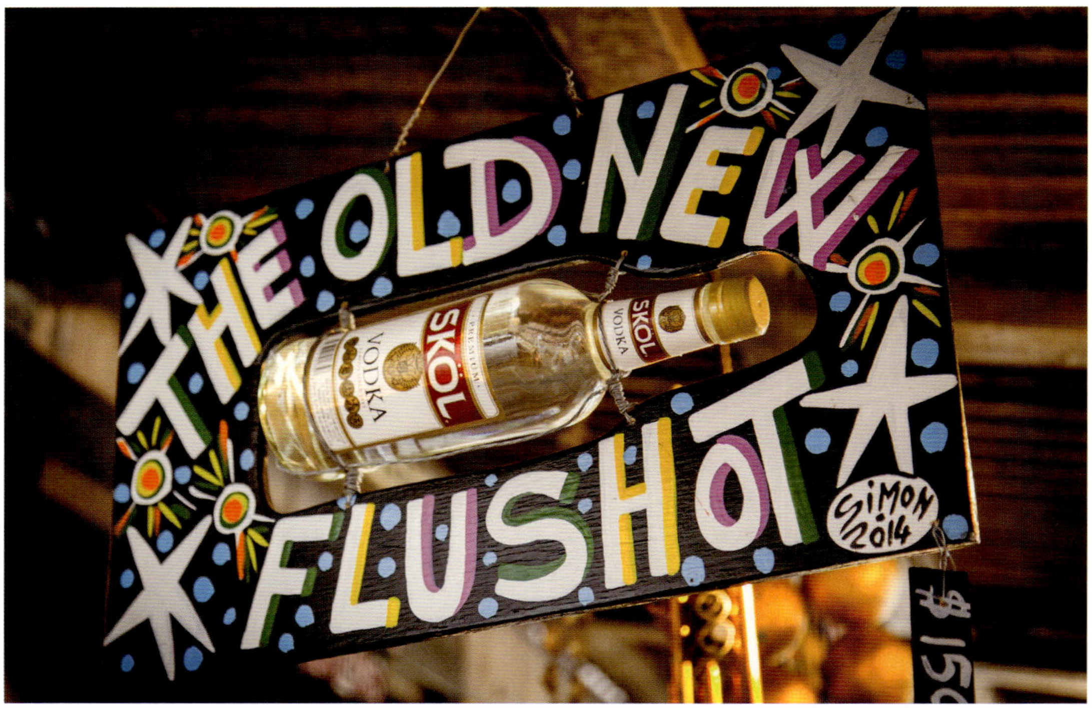

The Old New Flu Shot. The element of humor pervades Simon's work.

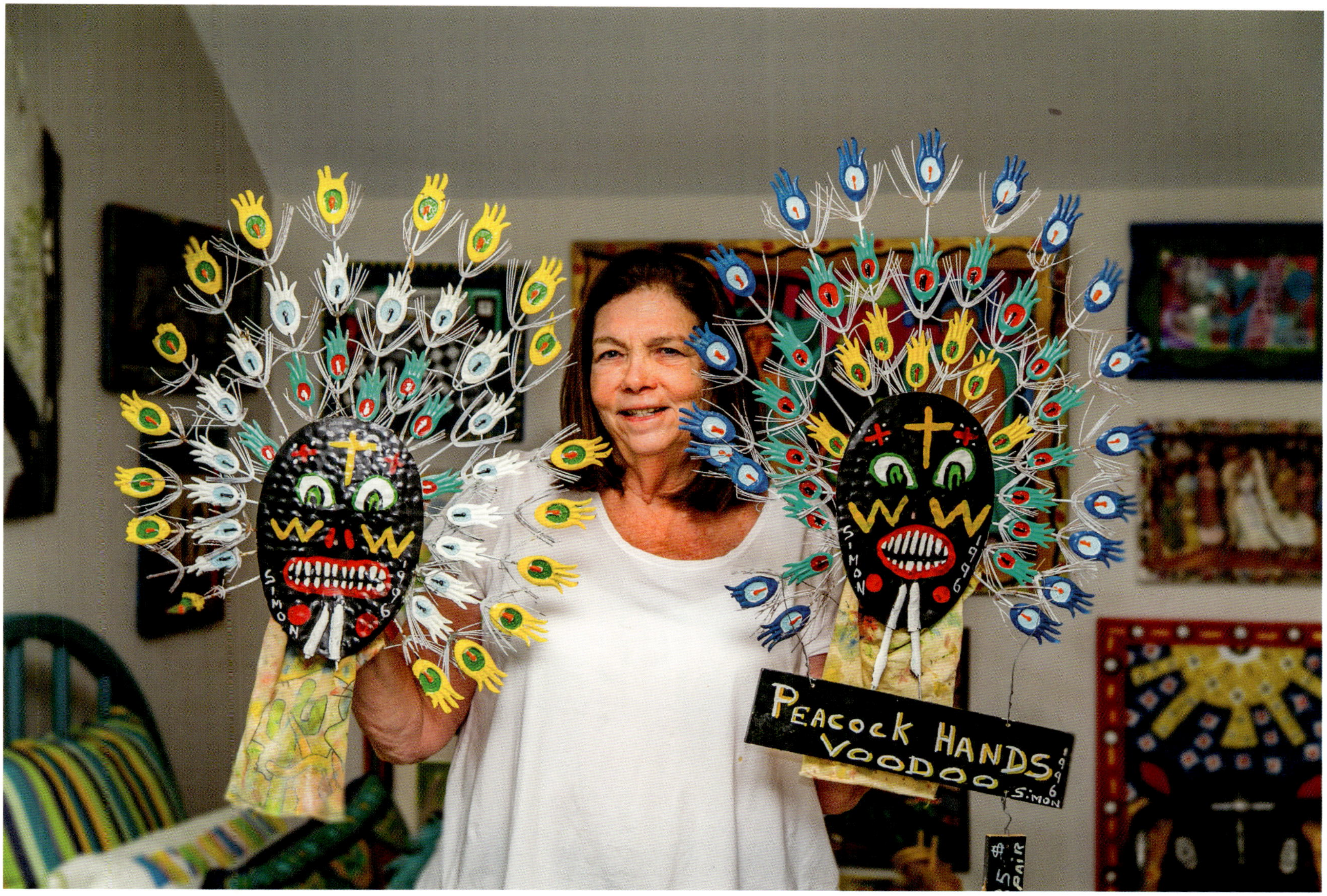

Collector Dale Fleishmann models the peacock "hands" Simon crafted as part of a Mardi Gras costume. The hands are formed from hundreds of wire pieces cut to specific lengths and welded in place to represent the fanlike shape of peacock tails. The "hands" were then painted to resemble peacock plumes. Fleishmann reports that the hands were a hit as a costume, but they made bead-catching a little complicated. (Fleishmann collection, 1996)

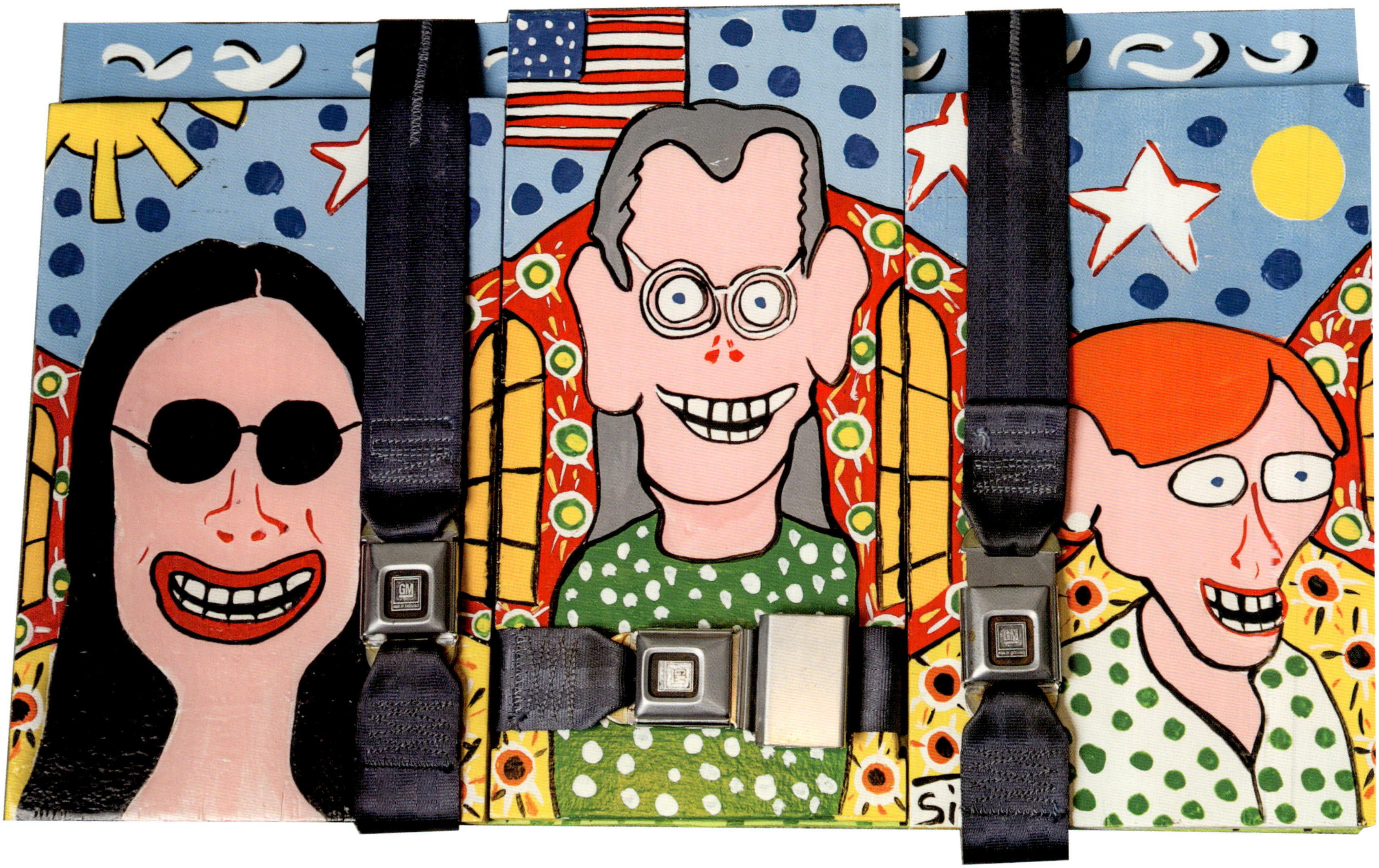

Above and opposite: At first glance The Train Ride *seems like a single piece of art depicting three faces. But the piece has three hinged wooden flaps held secure by functioning seat belts and buckles taken from an old car. When the buckles and belts are released, two of the flaps open outward, one to the left and the other to the right. The third hinged flap opens upward. The open flaps reveal a second painting.*

The double work tells the tongue-in-cheek story of a train ride taken by the collector. The story goes that Dale Fleishmann had boarded a train with two of her friends and after taking her seat, she had searched and searched for her seatbelt Laughing, her friends informed her that trains don't have seatbelts. She was stunned. Already nervous about traveling by train, she tried to back out of the trip but was shamed into it by her friends, who promised her that they would arrive at their destination safely (and they did). However, she has since taken a good deal of ribbing about the seatbelt search. When Simon found out about it, he crafted the piece to commemorate the incident and to continue teasing Fleishmann. (Fleishmann collection, 1998)

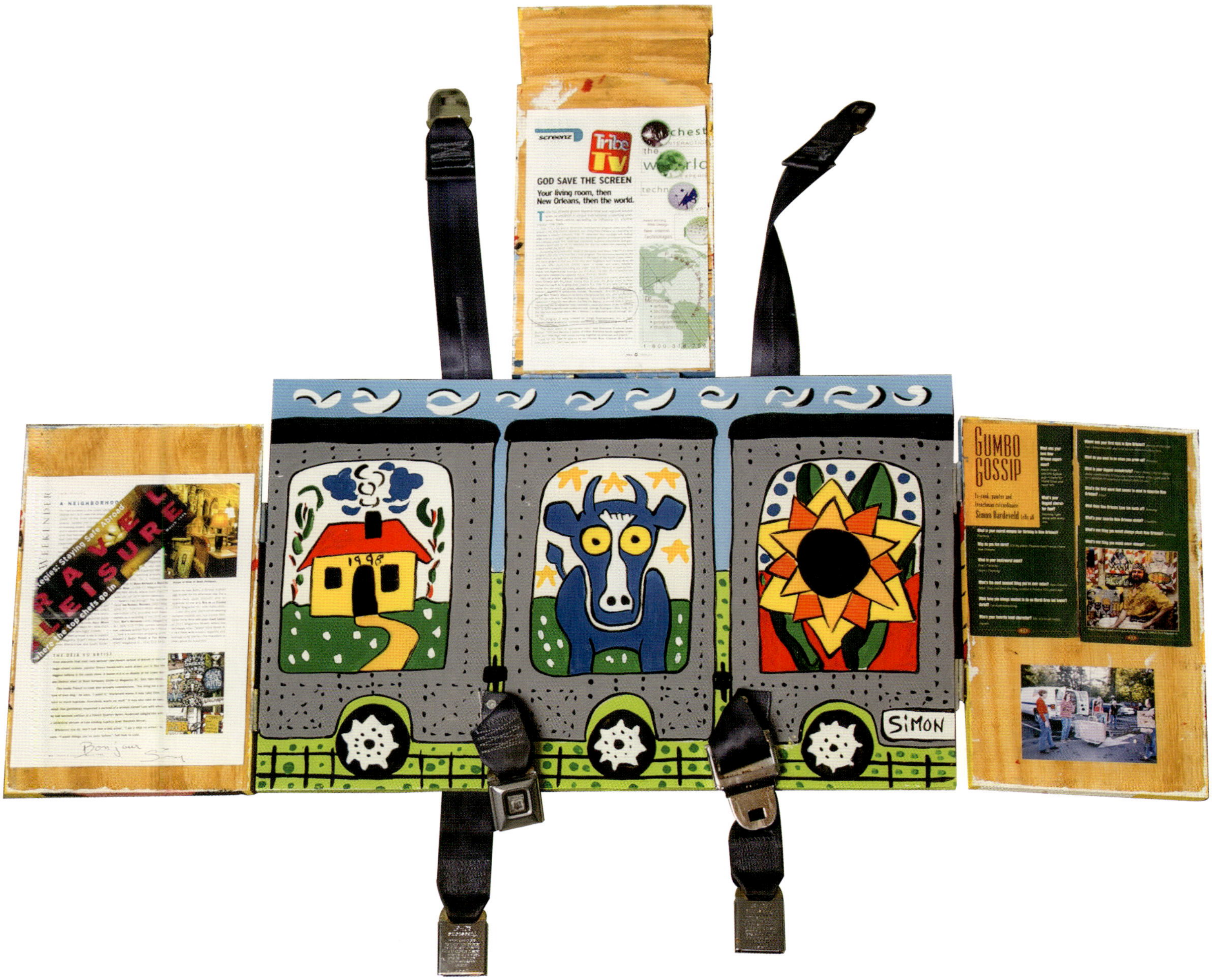
screenz
Tribe TV
GOD SAVE THE SCREEN
Your living room, then New Orleans, then the world.
GUMBO GOSSIP
1998
SiMON

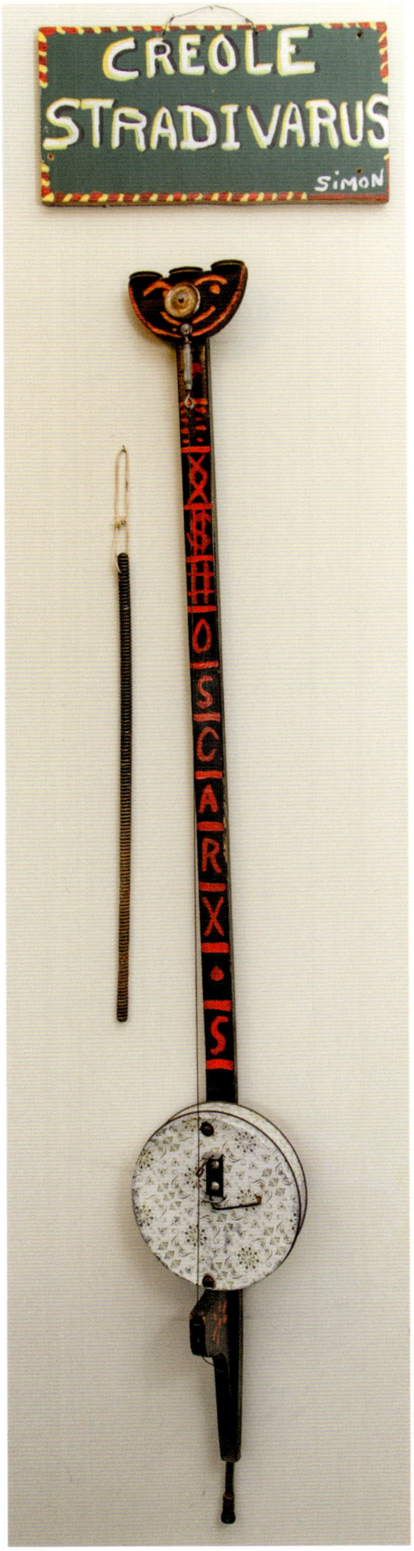

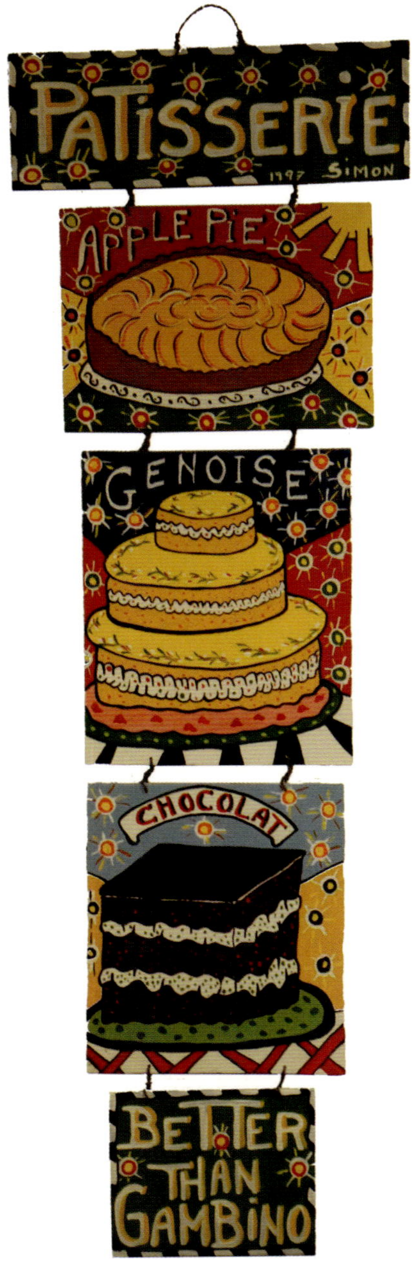

Above: Patisserie *tempts with apple pie, genoise, and chocolat—all apparently "Better Than Gambino." (Courtesy Tom and Susan Nolan, Nolan collection, 1997)*

Left: Creole Stradivarus *[sic] is an oversized Cajun fiddle and bow. The pieces are fashioned mostly of wood, but the head (or drum) of the fiddle is made from a cookie tin. The "bow" is a threaded metal rod. Inscribed along the neck of the instrument is the word "Oscar." Simon explains that when he gets an honor or completes a piece that he is happy with, he feels like he has won an Academy Award. It is a large piece measuring over five feet high. (Fleishmann collection, 1996)*

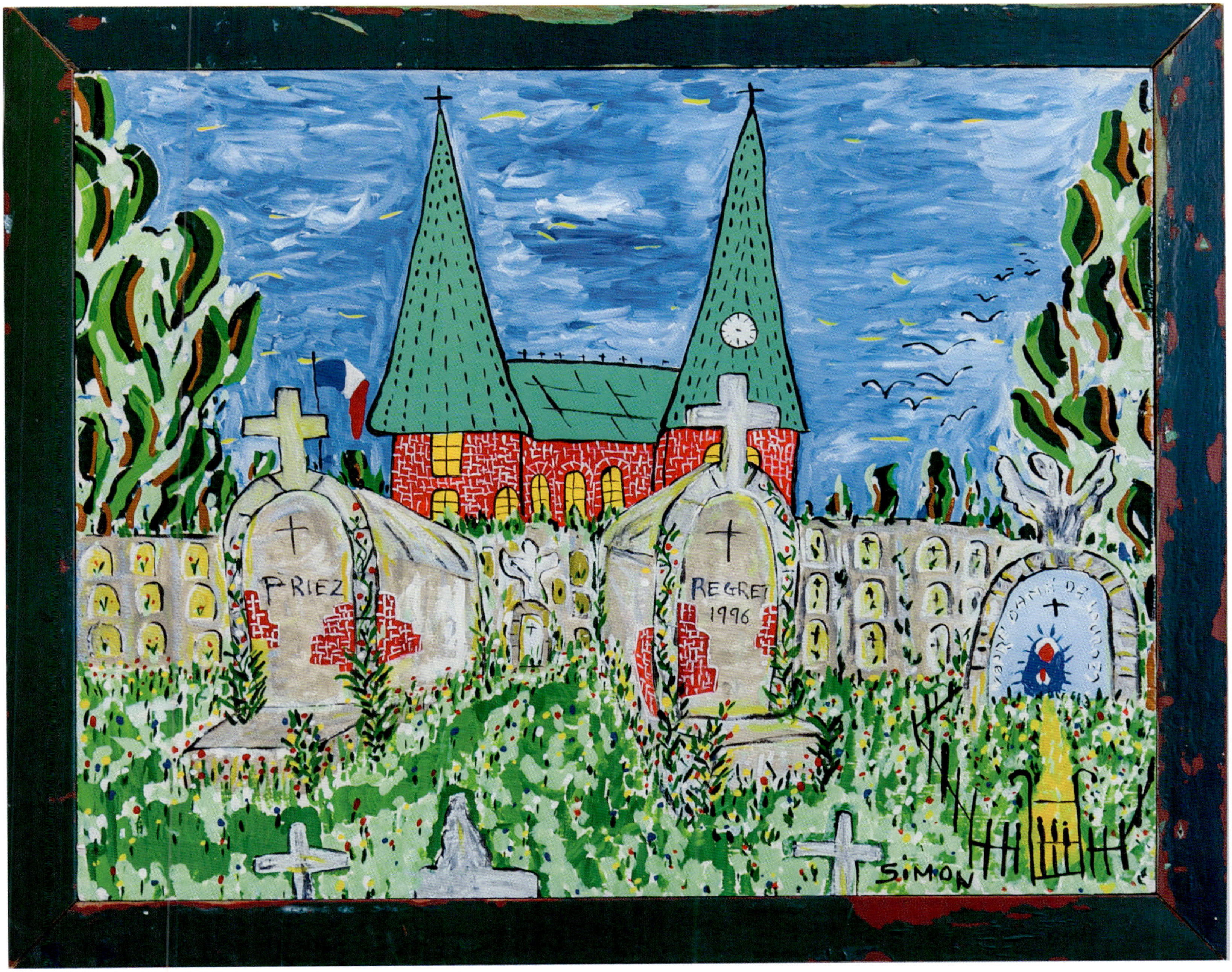

Dominating the foreground of the painting of a small country church is the parish graveyard, typical of many New Orleans-area cemeteries with above-ground tombs and wall "oven" vaults. Prominently featured are two tombs, each of which is inscribed with an admonition for the living. One advises the observer to "priez" (pray); the other to "regret" (repent or regret). To the right is a shrine to Notre Dame de Lourdes (Our Lady of Lourdes). Simon points out that he studied the look of New Orleans cemeteries before painting the piece. "I try to make it right," he says. (Fleishmann collection, 1996)

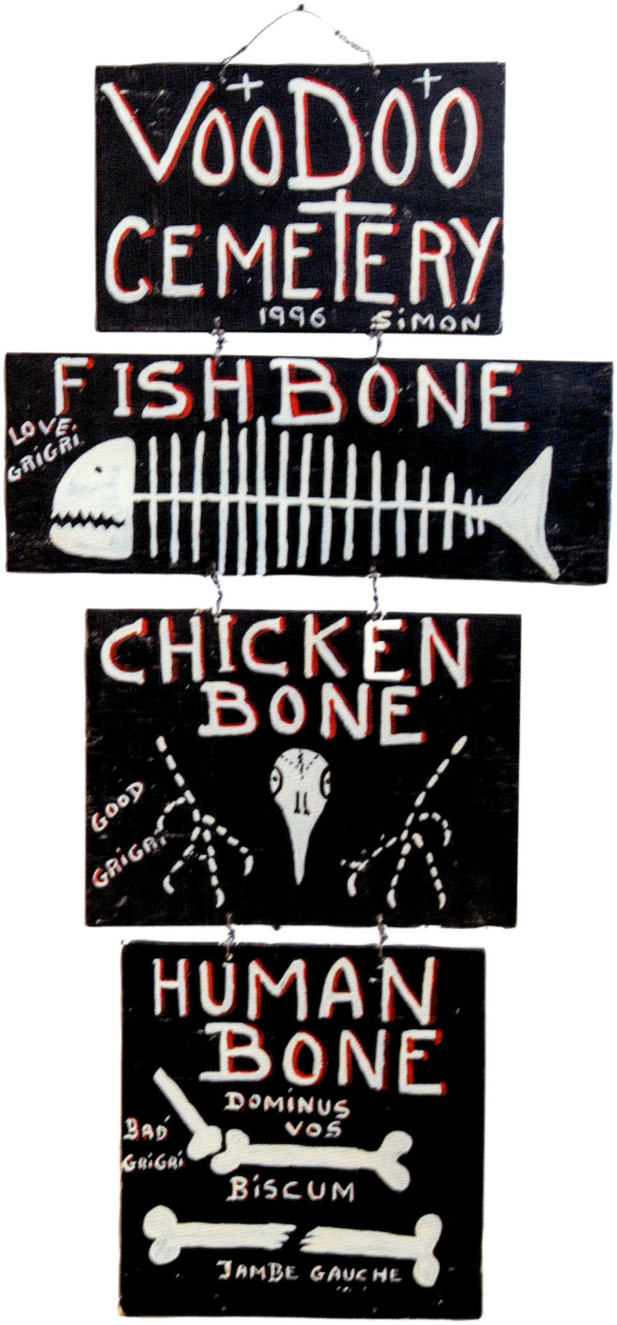

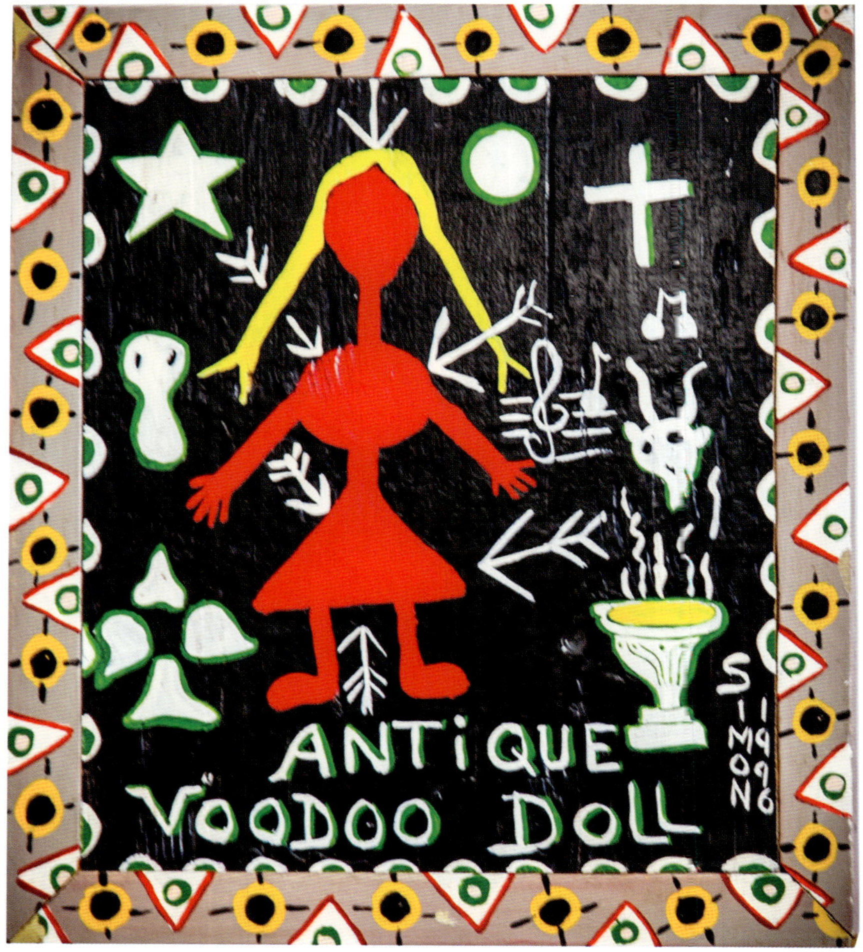

Above: Antique Voodoo Doll *features the silhouette of a doll with arrows that indicate possible insertion points for the pins. Also included in the painting are all the necessary ingredients for a good voodoo: bones, a boiling cauldron, an animal skull, music, a cross, and a star. (Fleishmann collection, 1996)*

Left: Another cemetery-themed piece entitled Voodoo Cemetery lists three types of GriGri: Love GriGri, Good GriGri, and Bad GriGri. Beneath a drawing of a leg bone is the label "Jambe Gauche" (left leg). Also included is the phrase "Dominus vos biscum," a slight derivation on a phrase from the Catholic mass "Dominus vobiscum," meaning "The Lord be with you." Whether intentional or not, in its present spelling, the phrase painted on the art piece translates to "Lord, you laugh," which seems perfectly appropriate for a Simon painting. (Fleishmann collection, 1996)

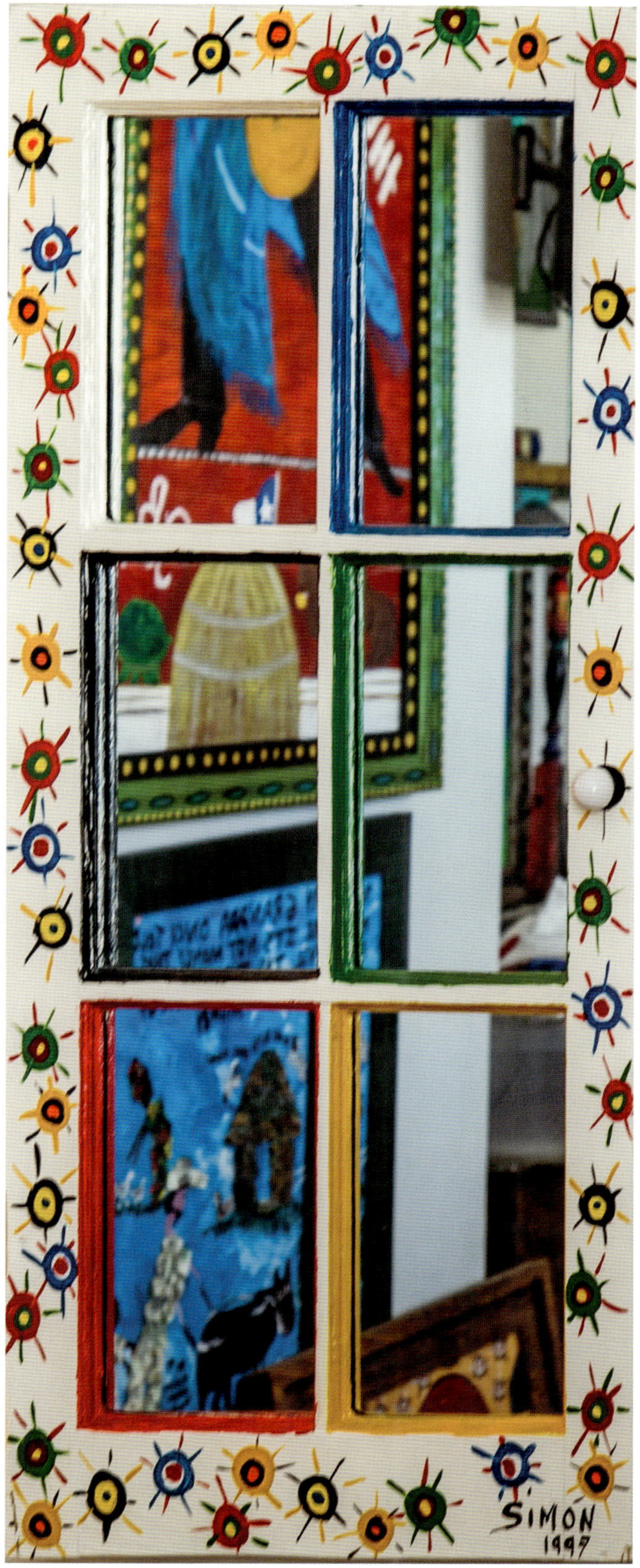

The Mirror *is fashioned from an old cabinet door that originally held six glass panes. The clear panes have been replaced with mirrors, and each section of mullions has been painted a different color. The outside of the frame is adorned with Simon's signature symbols. The white, ball-shaped pull from the original door is still attached. (Fleishmann collection, 1996)*

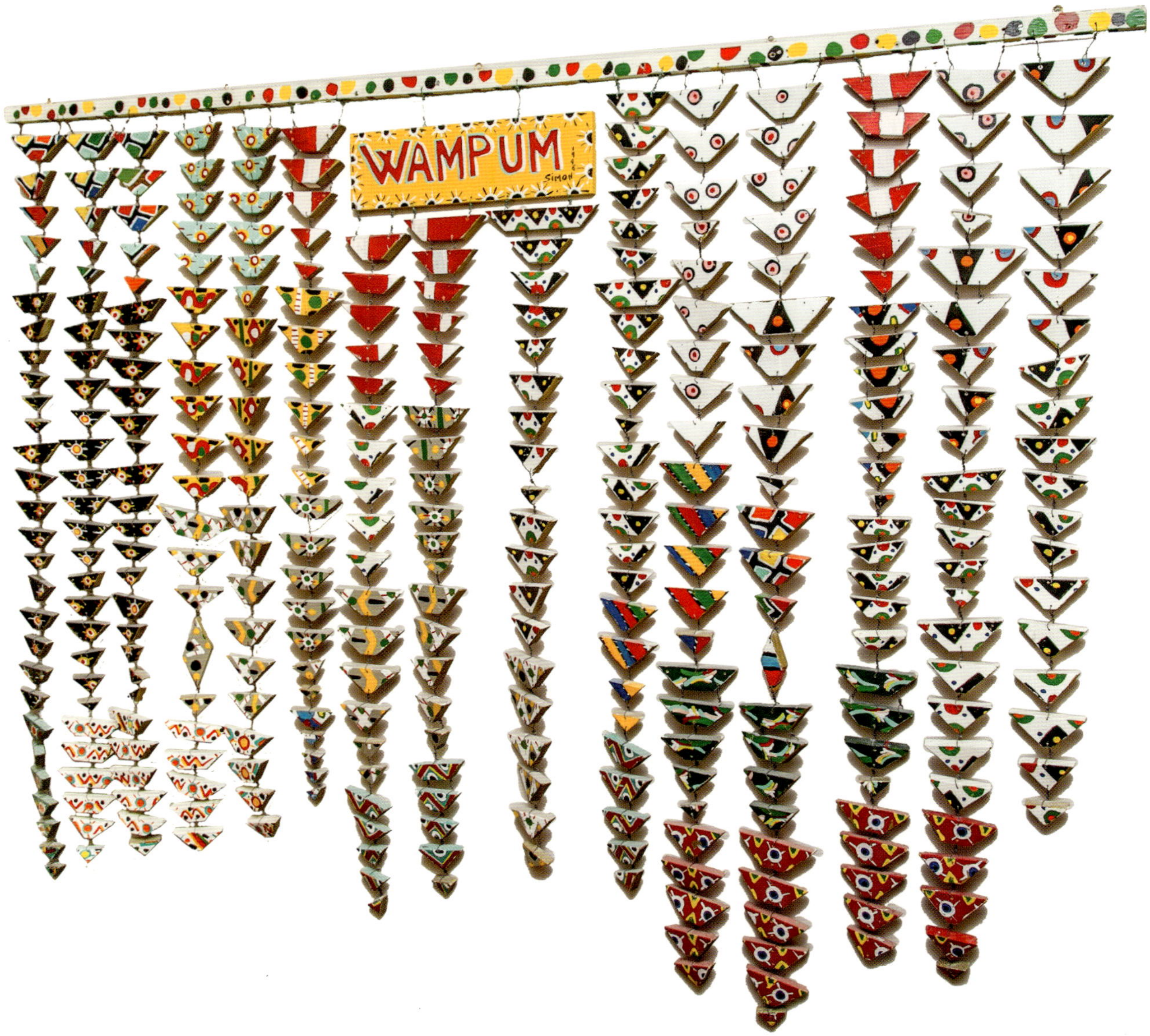

The impressive and imposing wall hanging Wampum *is fashioned from more than three hundred individual polygonal pieces strung together with wire. When constructing the wooden frames for his artwork, Simon noticed that there were always triangular- or trapezoidal-shaped pieces left over from mitering the corners. He began to collect them and supplemented them with additional pieces to create the wall hanging. The term "wampum" refers to the Native American practice of stringing together shells or other valued objects, which were then used as a type of currency, as adornment, or as ceremonial items. (Fleishmann collection, 1996)*

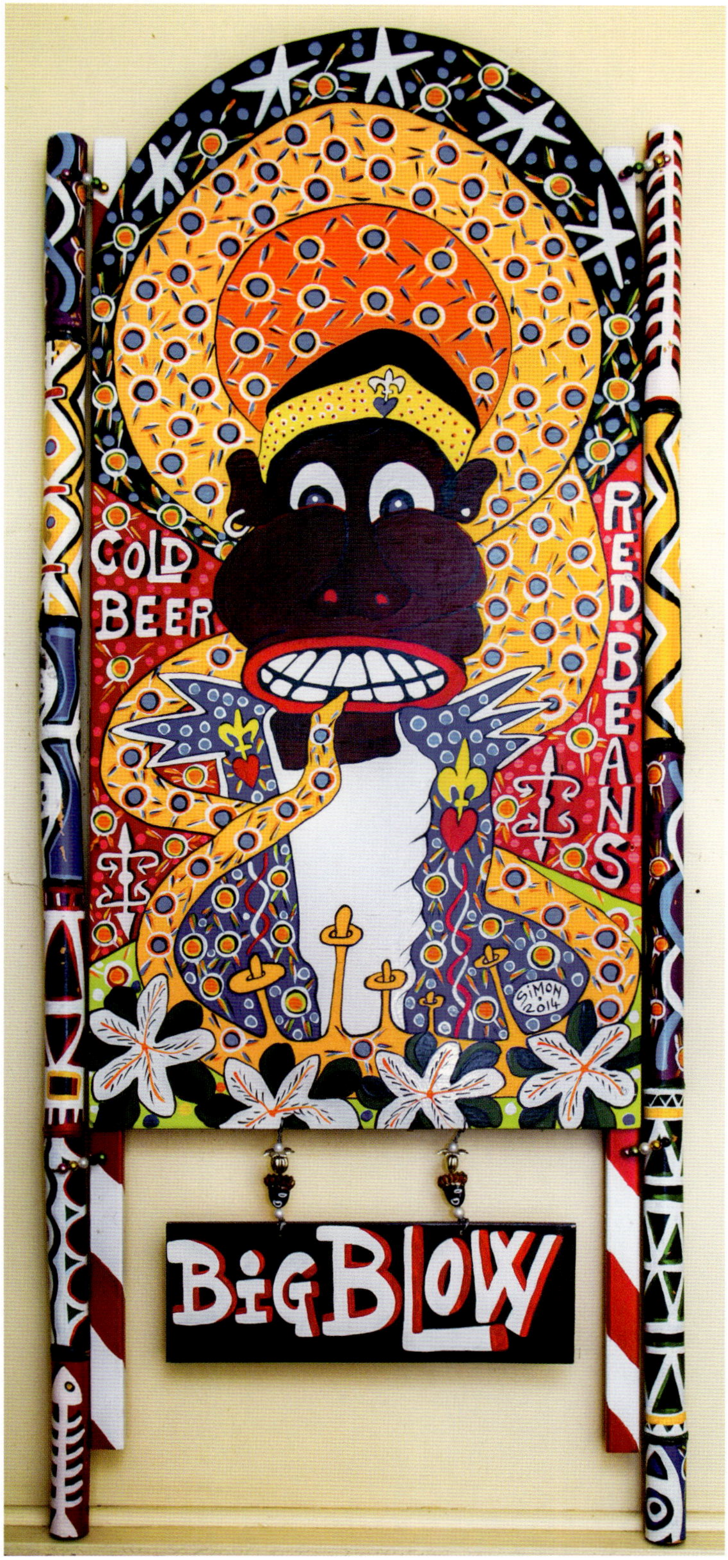

Big Blow depicts a tuba player and his instrument, which is curled snakelike around his torso. The bell of the tuba forms a halo around the player's head. "Cold beer" and "red beans" are inscribed on either side of the player. The piece is approximately four feet tall and is mounted (with Mardi Gras beads, no less) to two round, brightly colored broomstick-like poles. The title of the work is suspended from the bottom of the main piece with Zulu beads and medallions and is centered between the side poles. (Joey K's Restaurant, 2014)

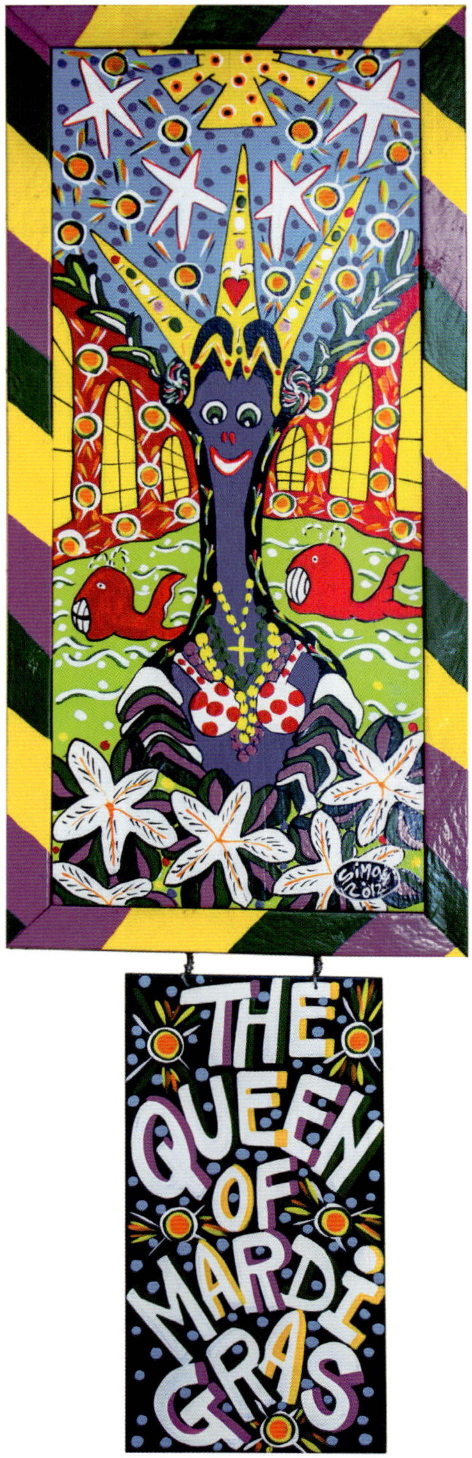

Blue women (instead of Blue Dogs) are a frequent subject for Simon's paintings. The Queen of Mardi Gras *presents a blue queen sporting a polka-dot bikini top, Mardi Gras beads, and a tall three-pronged crown. She appears to be riding down a street, as she is framed by the windows of buildings in the background, but the only occupants on the street are two spouting whales. (Joey K's Restaurant, 2012)*

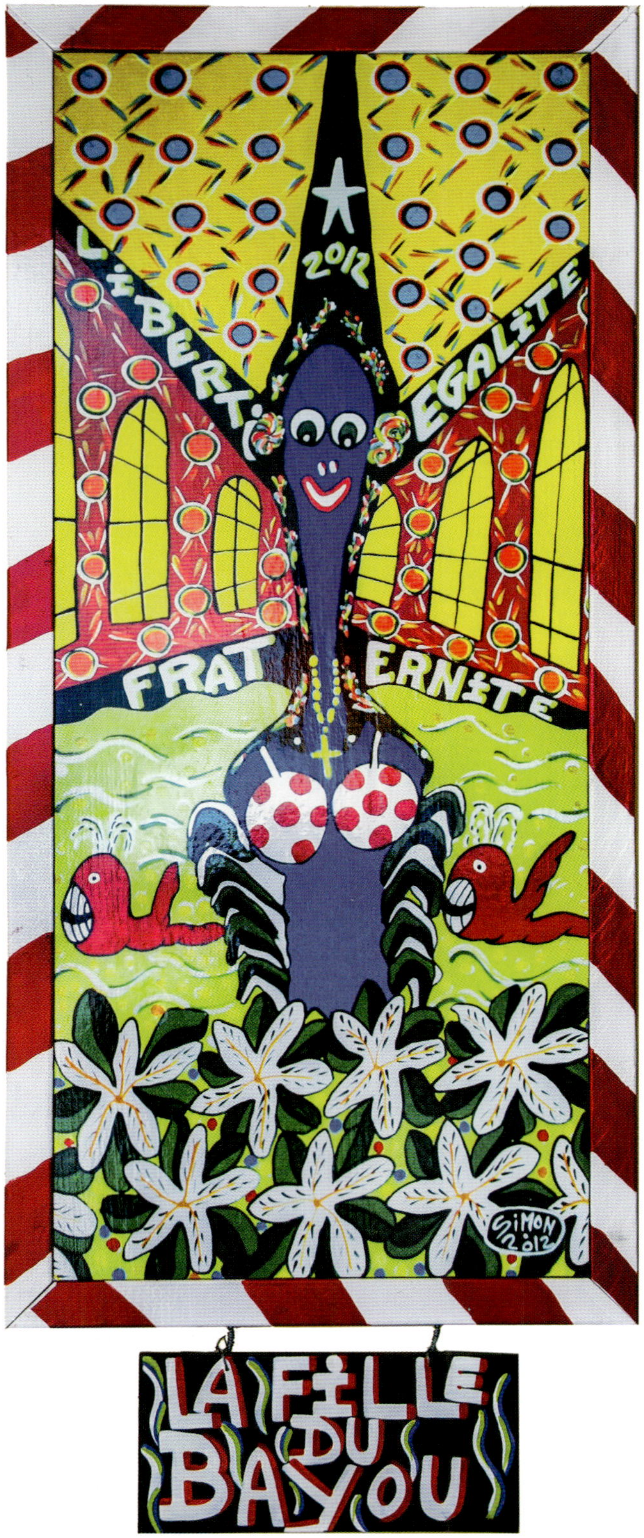

A nearly identical blue maiden is La Fille du Bayou. *She also sports a triple-pronged crown (or hairdo) while whales and windows fill the background. Emblazoned upon the buildings is France's national motto—Liberté, Égalité, Fraternité (Liberty, Equality, Brotherhood)—a maxim with its origins in the French Liberation of the 1940s, in which Simon's father participated. (Joey K's Restaurant, 2012)*

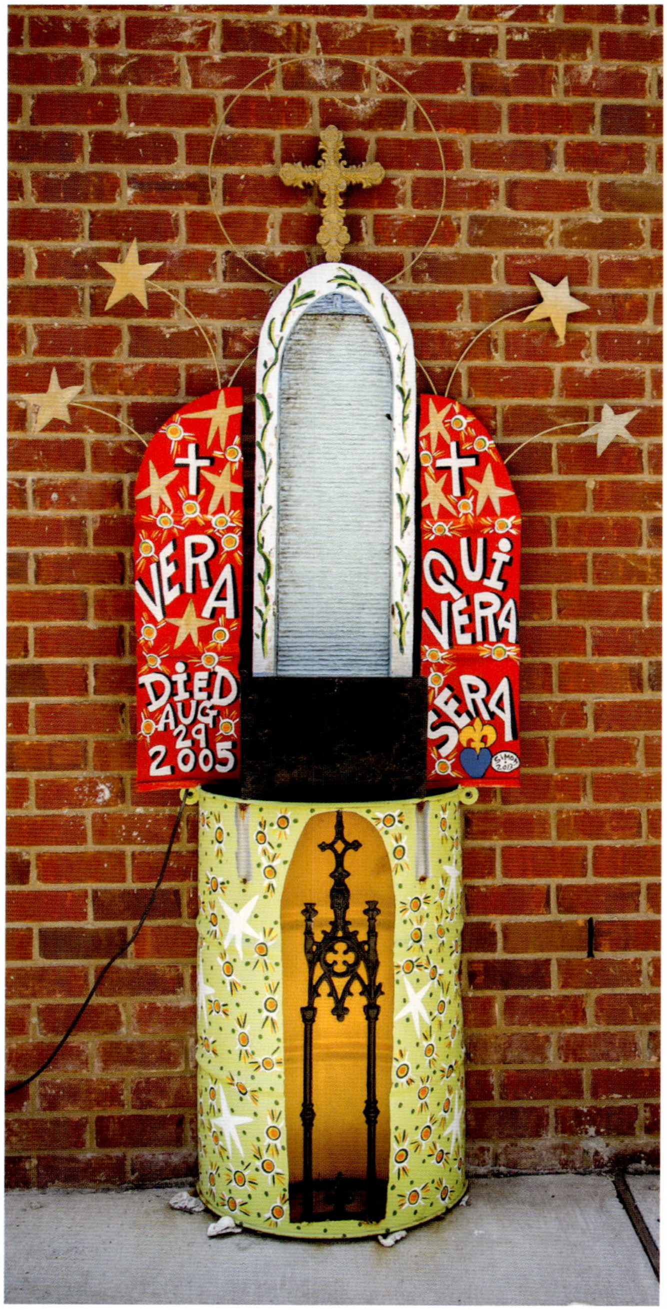

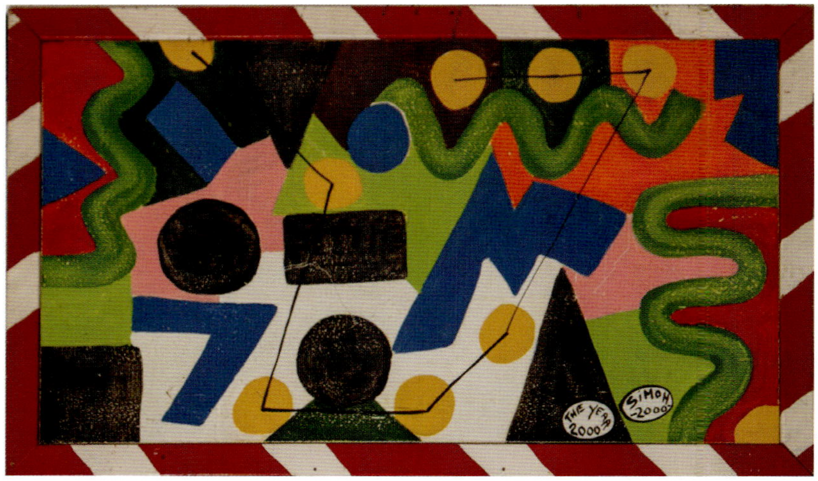

Above: Simon's abstract depiction of The Year 2000 *hangs in his home in the transom above the back door.*

Left: Here Lies Vera *is a noteworthy exception to the nearly universally light-hearted tone of Simon's work. The piece is a memorial to Vera Smith, who died after Hurricane Katrina and whose body was left where she fell, on the corner of Magazine Street and Jackson Avenue, near the location of what is now Simon's studio. After five days and in exasperated defiance of officials who had warned residents not to remove her body or bury her remains, neighbors gave Vera the simple dignity of a makeshift grave. The photo of the brick-lined grave topped by a sheet that read "Here Lies Vera—God Help Us" became one of the iconic images of the hurricane's aftermath. When officials finally removed her remains, neighbors erected a marker at the site while Simon began work on this lasting memorial. (2005)*

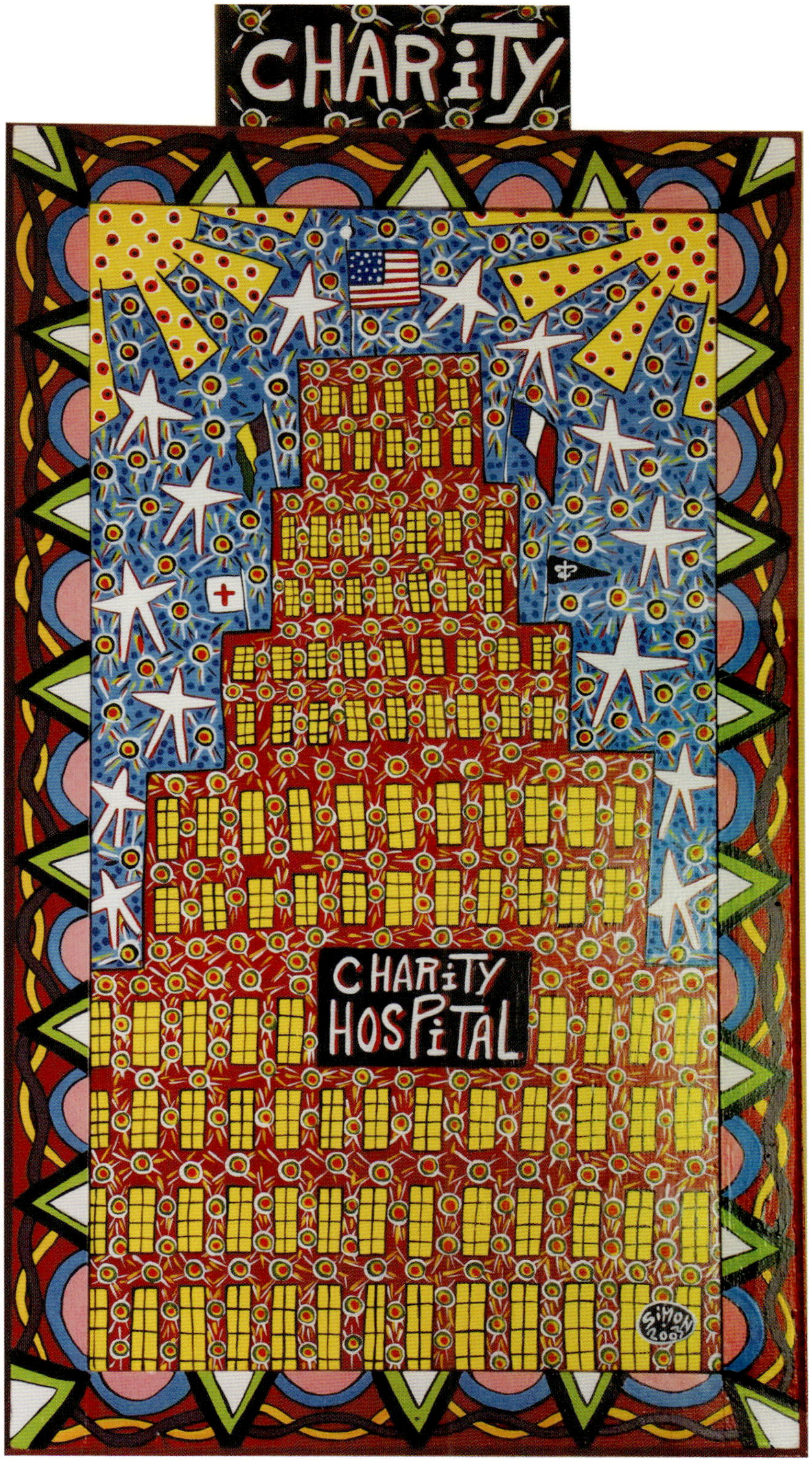

Simon presented this depiction of Charity Hospital to Dr. Tom Nolan, a physician at the hospital until Hurricane Katrina closed the facility. Five flags fly above the hospital beneath a bright sun—the flags of the Red Cross, Mardi Gras, the United States, France, and the Saints football team. (Courtesy Tom and Susan Nolan, Nolan collection, 2003)

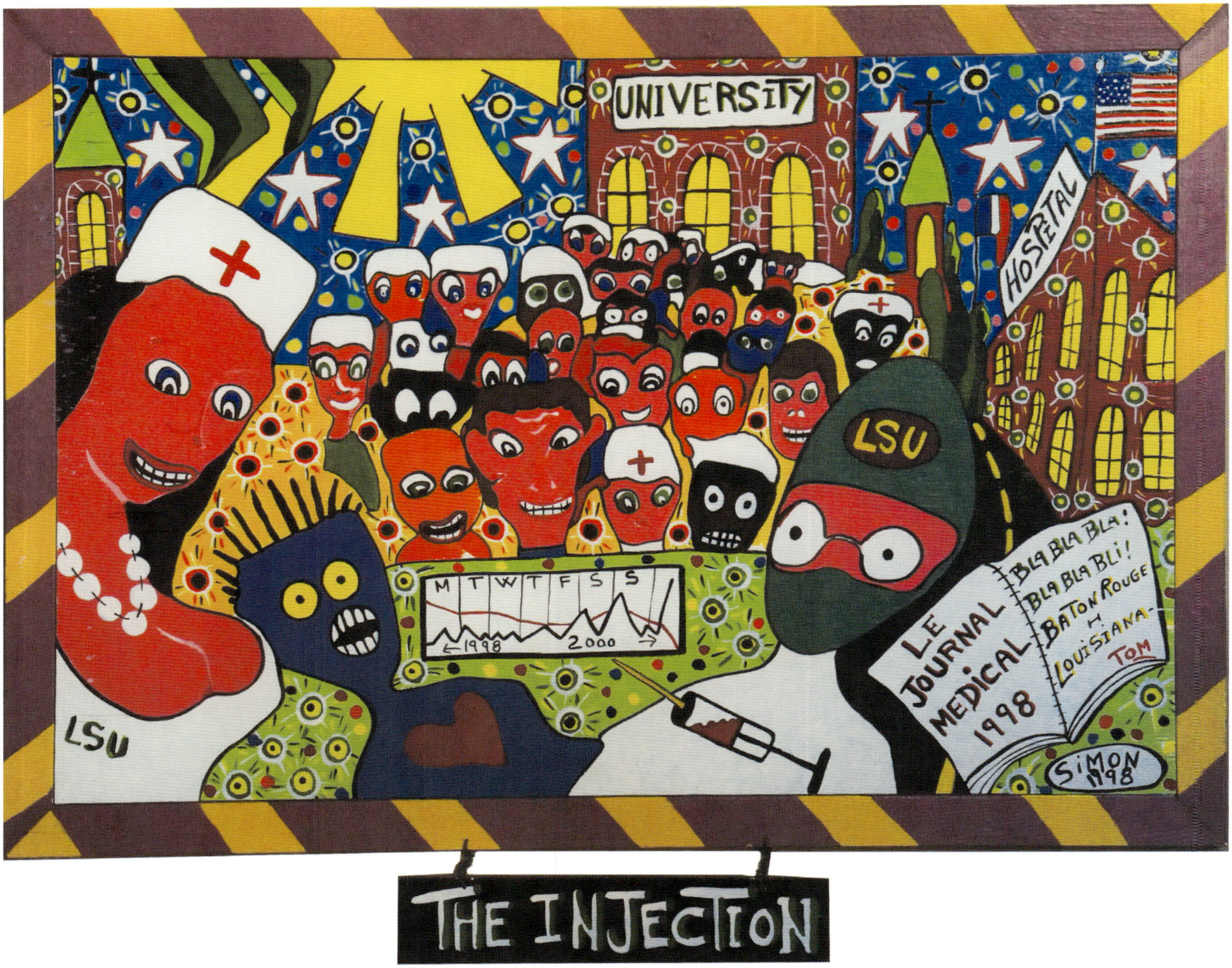

The Injection *was painted for Dr. Tom Nolan, who taught at both Charity and University Hospitals, part of the LSU Health Sciences Center. It is one of Simon's "busiest" works. In addition to a portrayal of Dr. Nolan with a syringe, there is a patient and his medical chart, a buxom nurse, a medical journal* (Le Journal Medical, *1998), and over two dozen onlookers. The scene takes place under a bright sky in front of University Hospital. (Courtesy Tom and Susan Nolan, Nolan collection, 1998)*

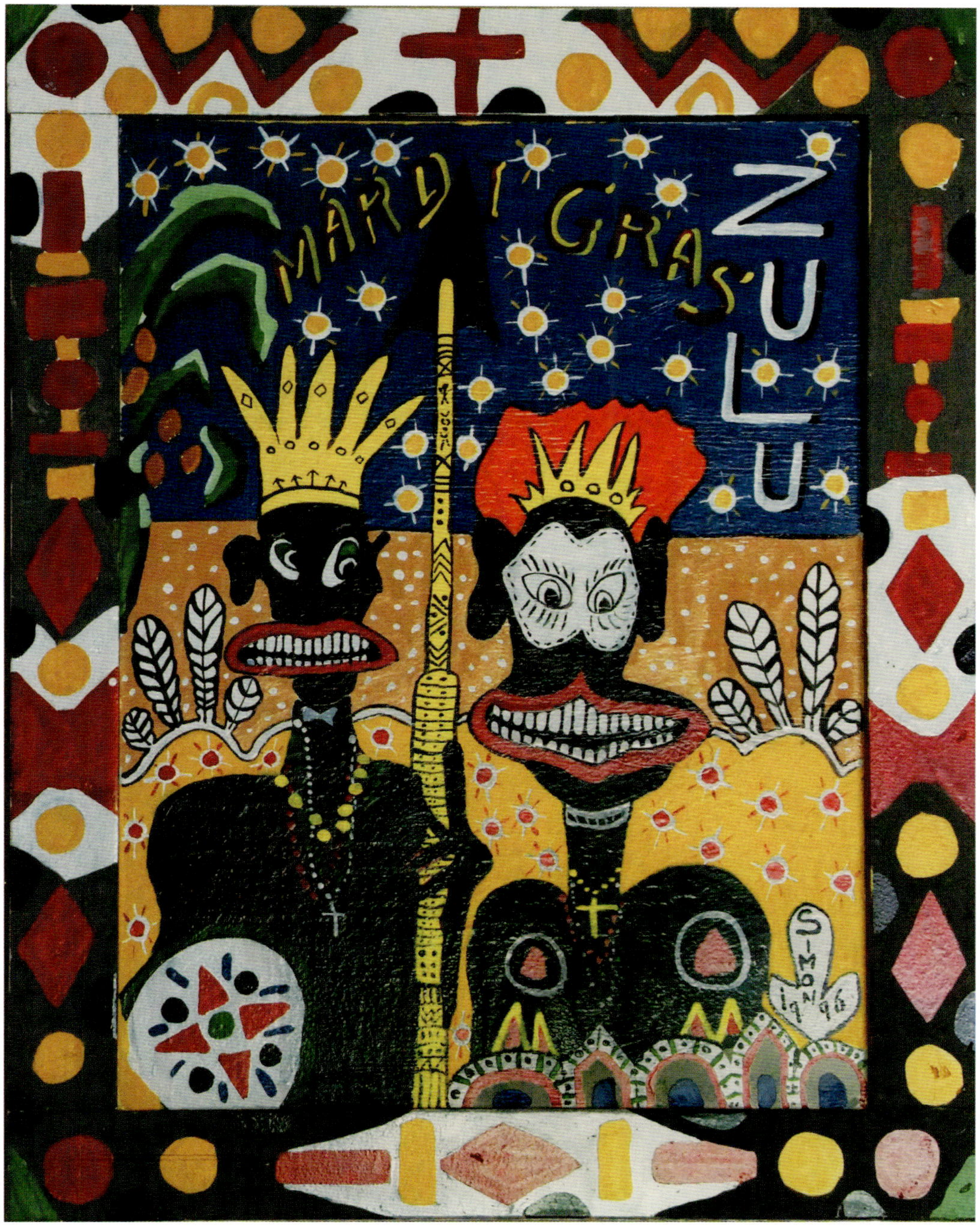

Zulu features the king and queen of that krewe. The king holds an intricately decorated spear and shield. Feathers in the background give a nod to the Mardi Gras Indians. (Courtesy Tom and Susan Nolan, Nolan collection, 1996)

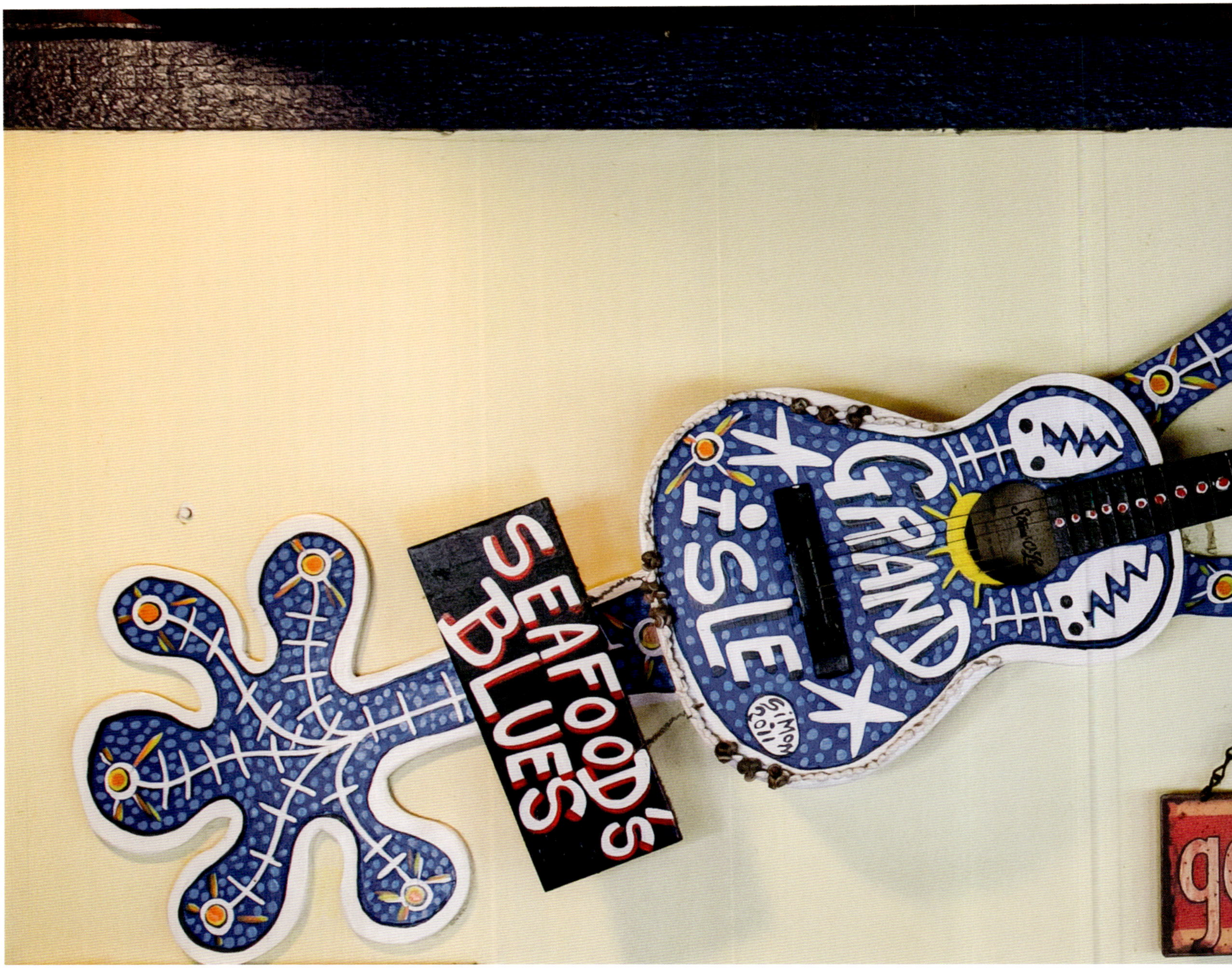

Simon created the seven-foot-long blue crawfish of Seafood's Blues for a fundraising auction to help pay the medical bills of his friend Shanette Edler, the longtime proprietor of Liuzza's Restaurant, who was battling cancer. Edler died in 2011. The piece hangs in the upstairs dining room of O'Henry's Restaurant in the Riverbend area of Carrollton Avenue. This piece is one of Simon's largest creations. Tiny sea shells are threaded along the guitar's edges. The body of the crawfish is a guitar with "Grand Isle" painted on the face and "Laissez les bon temps rouler" around the sides. Oyster shells mark the joints of the crawfish's legs.

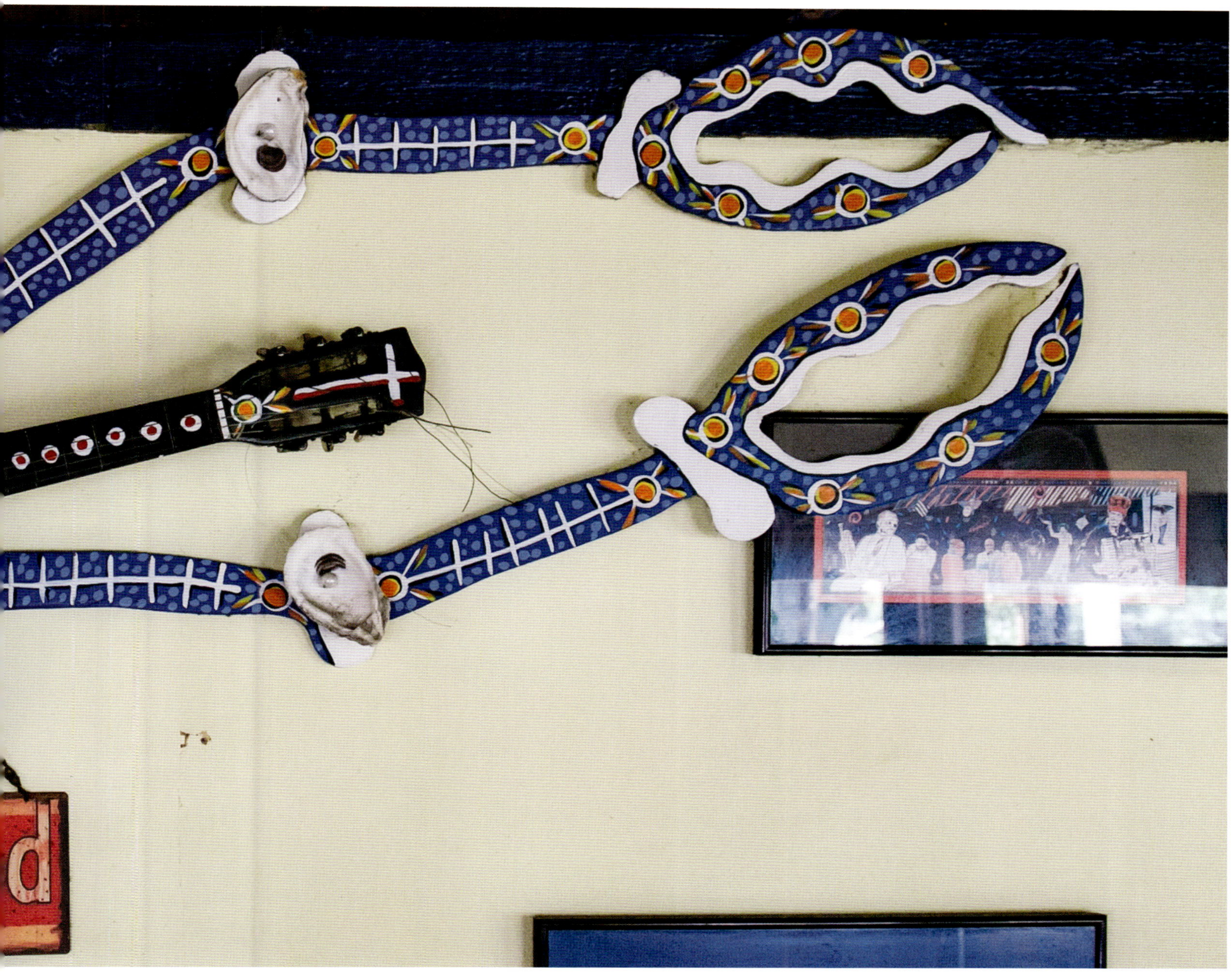

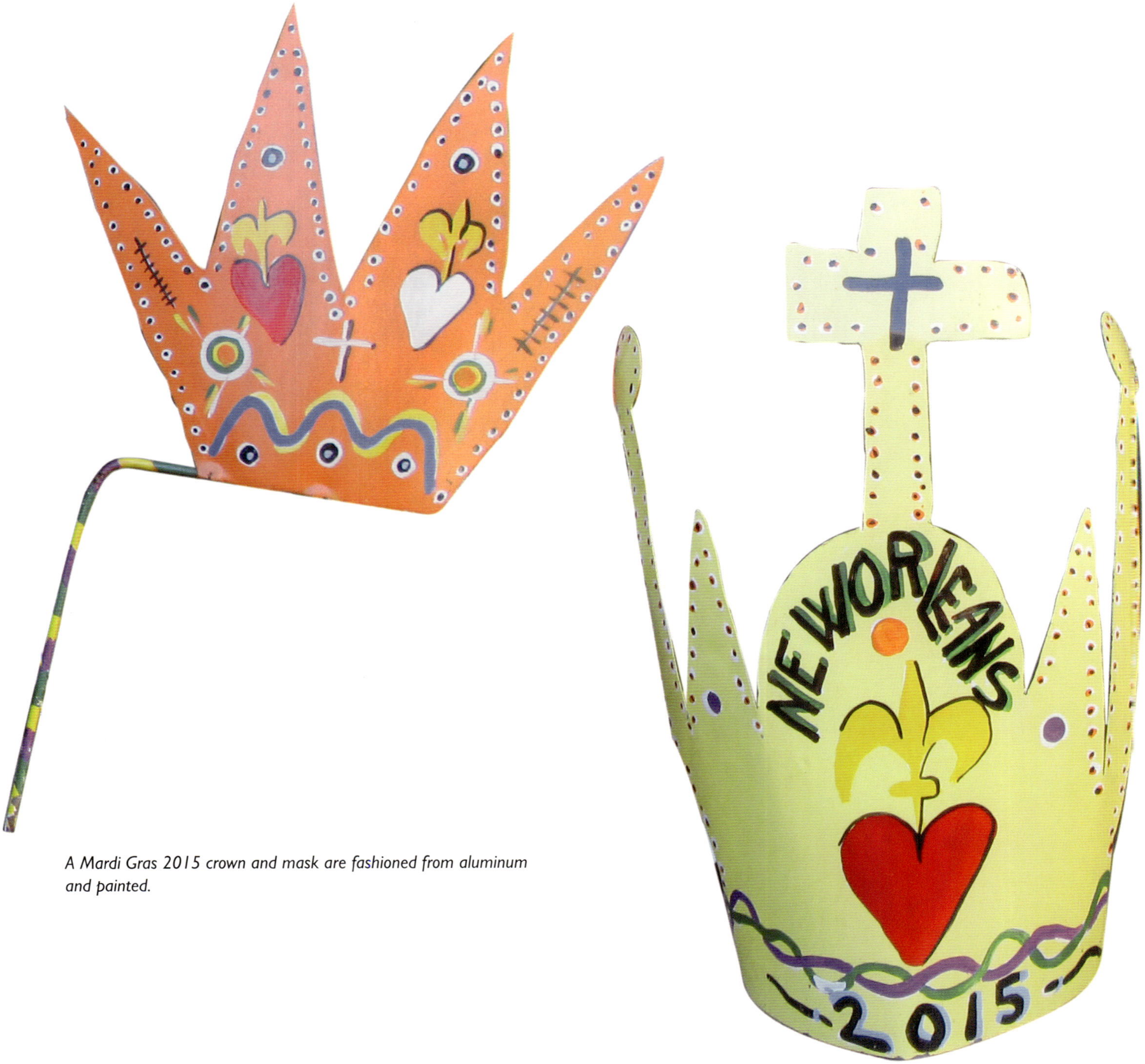

A Mardi Gras 2015 crown and mask are fashioned from aluminum and painted.

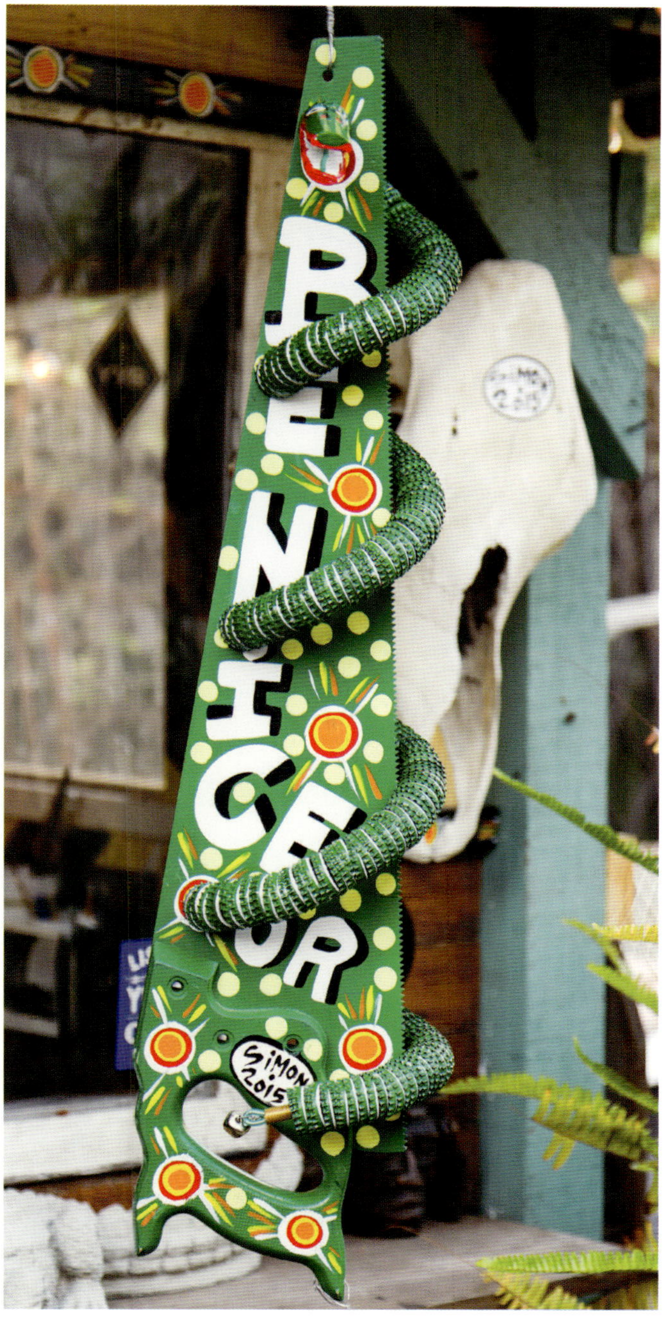

The "snake" curling around this "Be Nice or Leave" sign is crafted from hundreds of Heineken bottle caps.

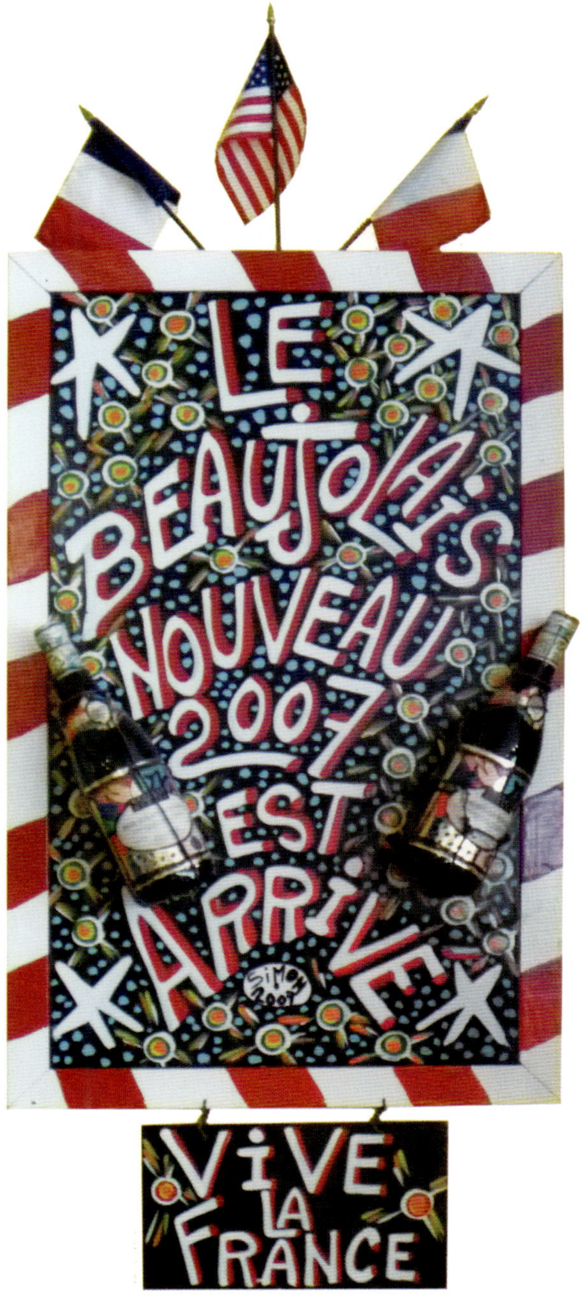

Sporting both French and American flags, this sign announces the arrival of the 2007 vintage of Beaujolais. The piece is complete with two bottles of the wine.

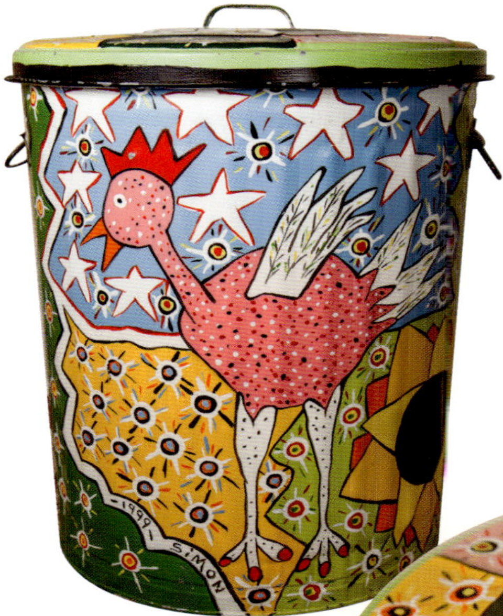

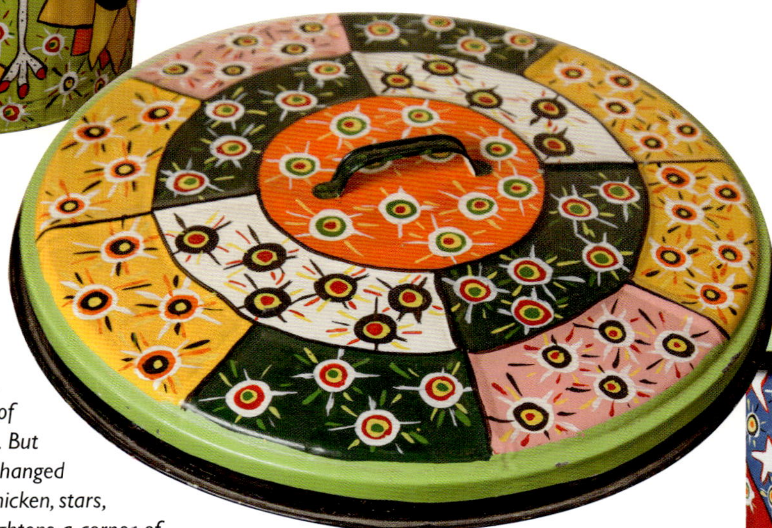

When Dr. Lenny Glade asked Simon to design a trash can for him, the collector had every intention of actually using the artwork as such. But when the creation arrived, Glade changed his mind. Decorated with a cat, a chicken, stars, a sun, and a sunflower, the can brightens a corner of his dining room. (Glade collection, 1999)

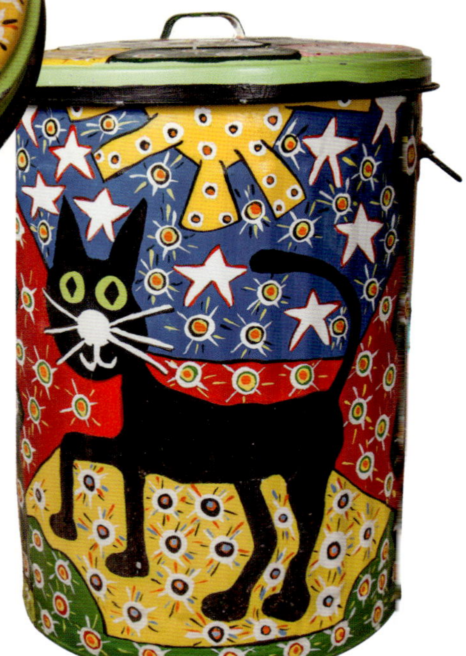

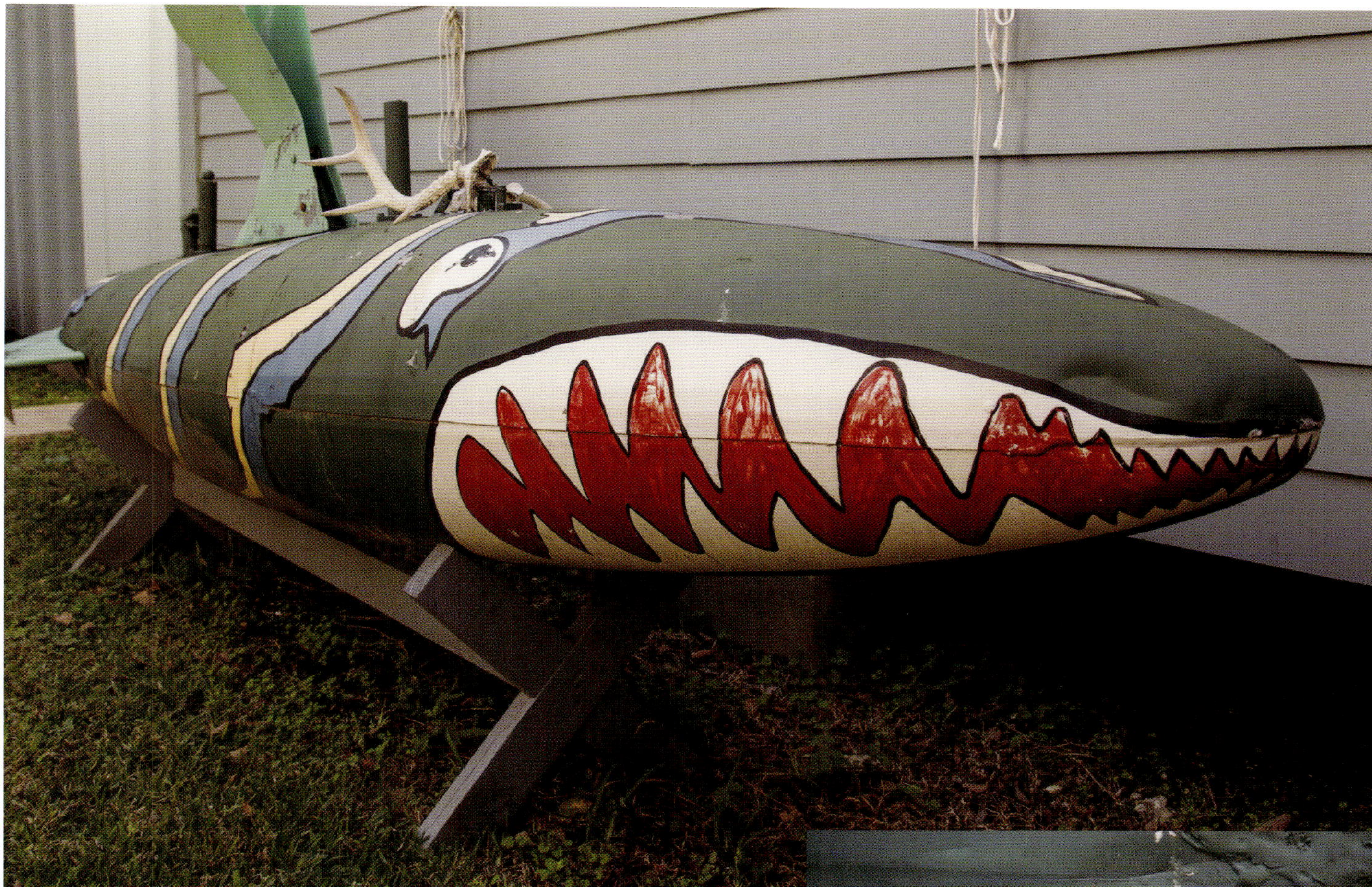

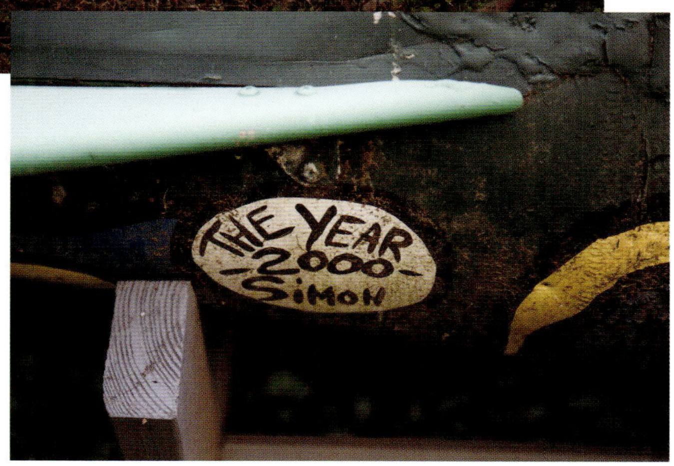

Above and right: Simon crafted this ten-foot shark, complete with dorsal fin, from the pontoon of a seaplane. (Glade collection, 2000)

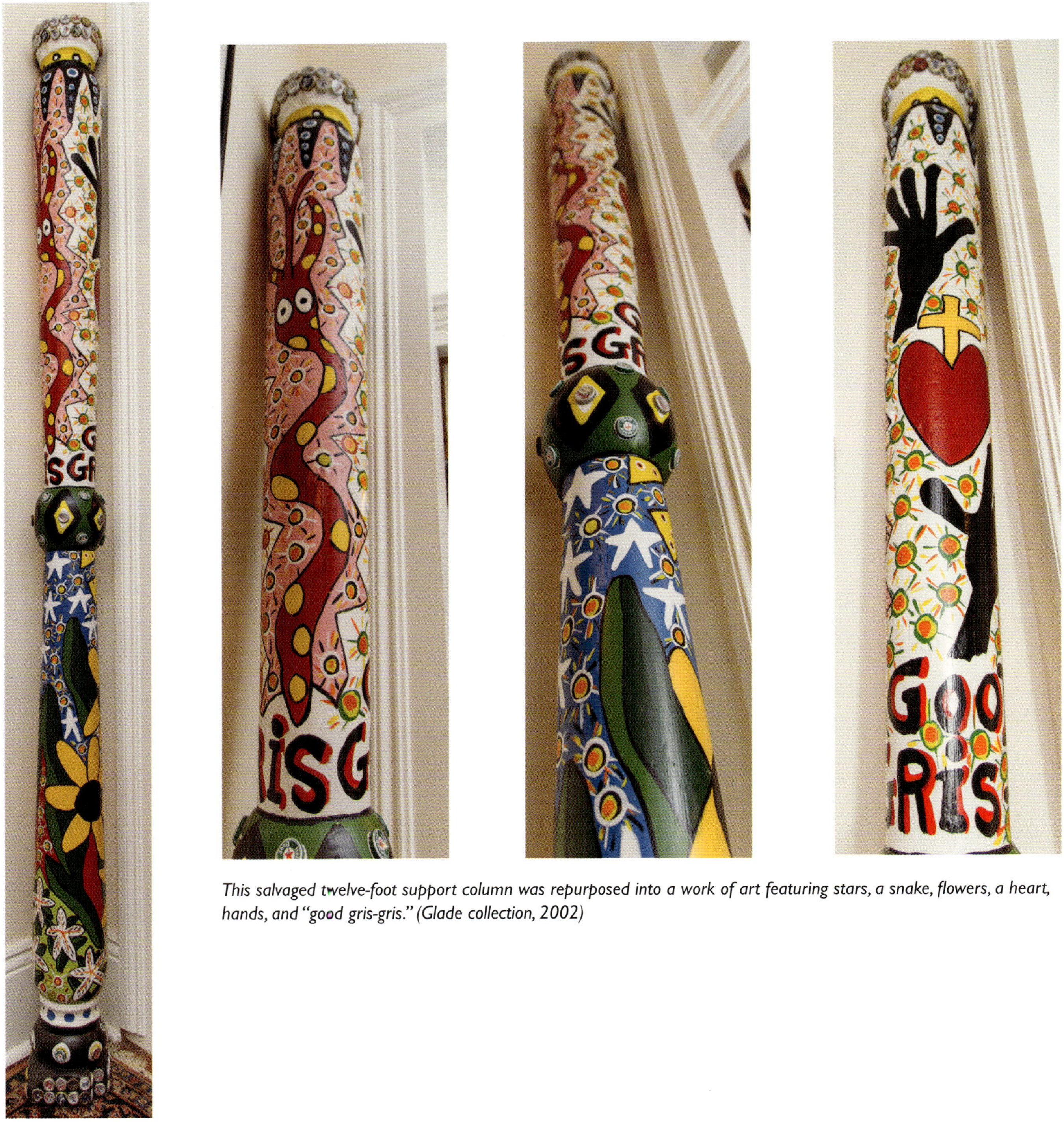

This salvaged twelve-foot support column was repurposed into a work of art featuring stars, a snake, flowers, a heart, hands, and "good gris-gris." (Glade collection, 2002)

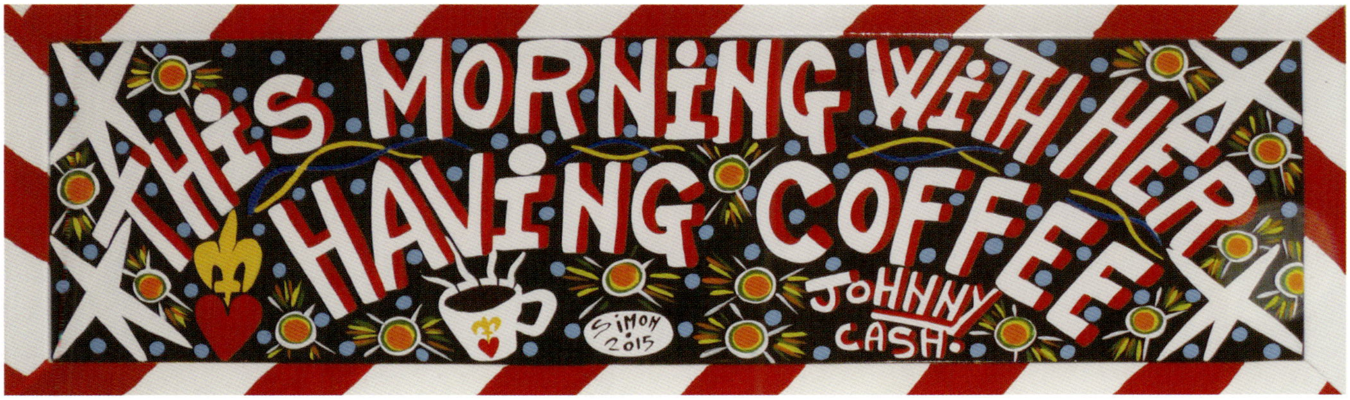
THIS MORNING WITH HER
HAVING COFFEE
JOHNNY CASH.
SIMON 2015

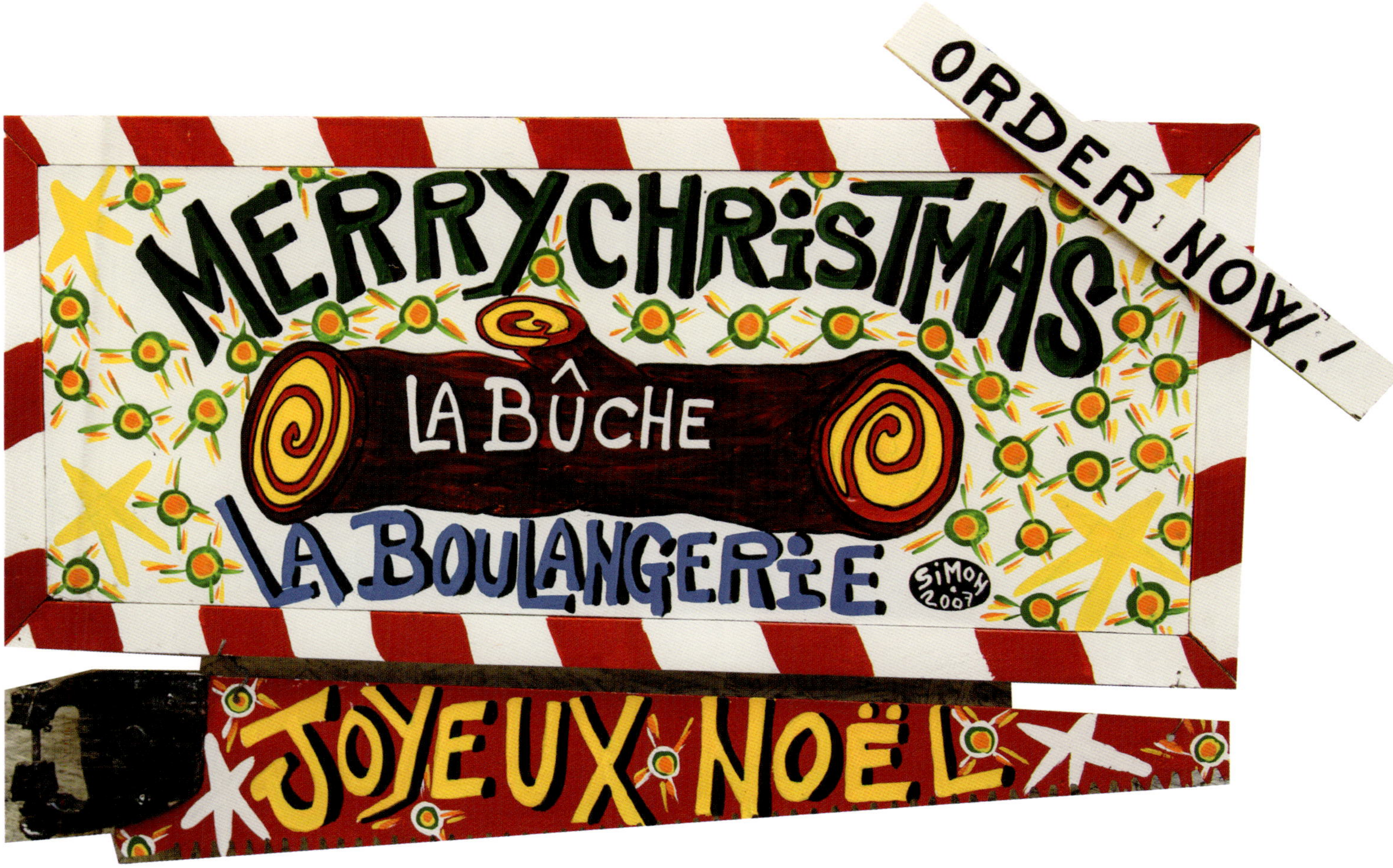
ORDER NOW!
MERRY CHRISTMAS
LA BÛCHE
LA BOULANGERIE
SIMON 2007
JOYEUX NOËL

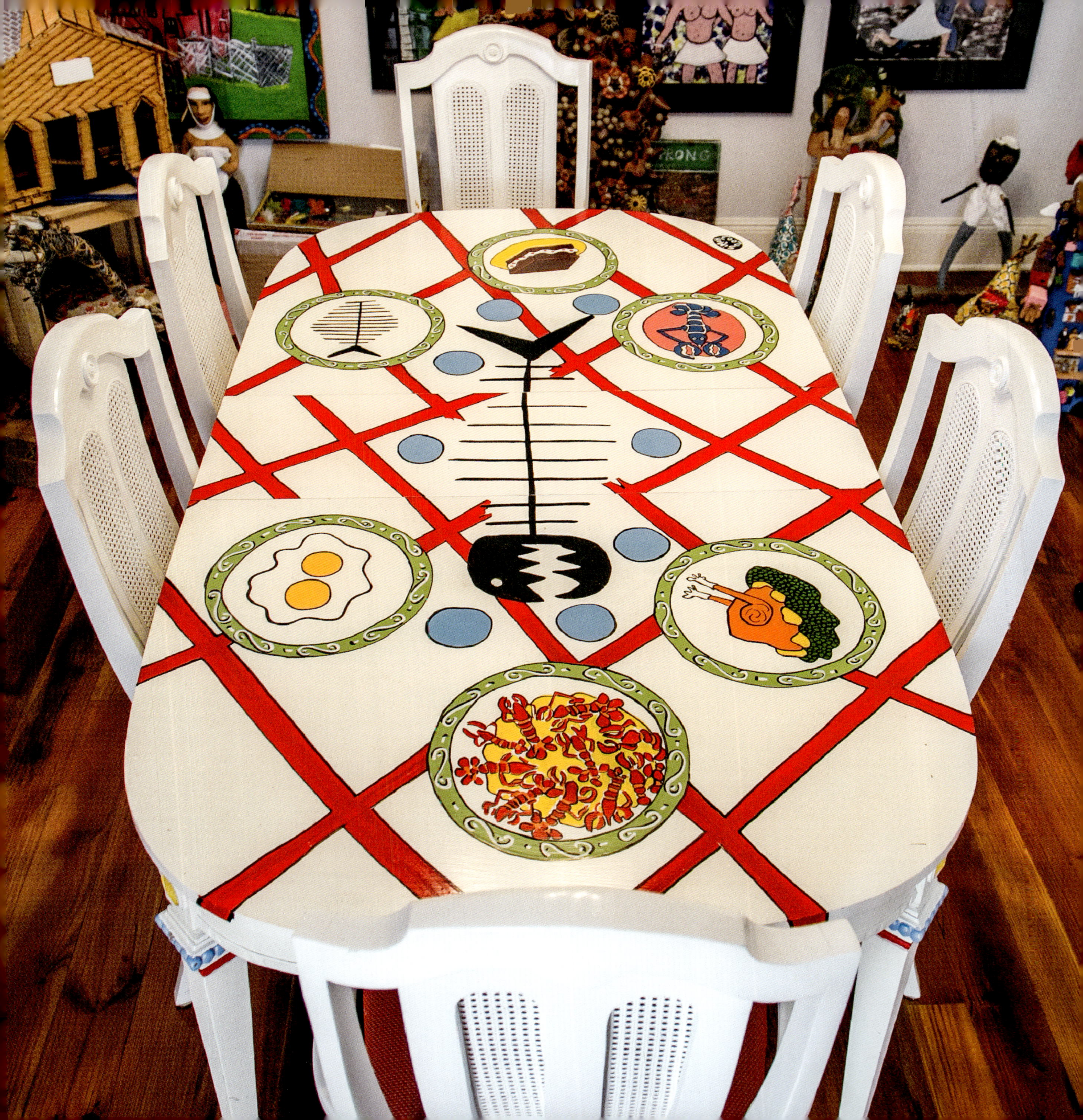

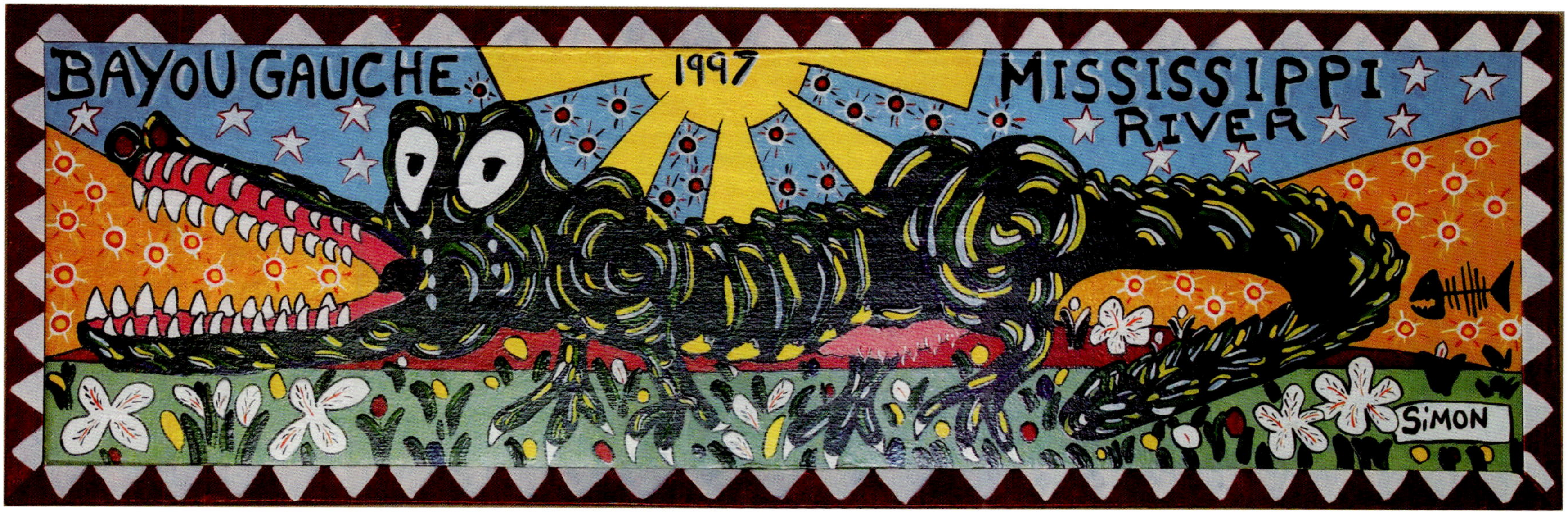

Above: An alligator suns herself in Bayou Gauche, Mississippi River. *Behind her are the bones of a fish she has just enjoyed. (Courtesy Tom and Susan Nolan, Nolan collection, 1997)*

Opposite: The centerpiece of collector Dale Fleishmann's dining room is the birthday gift Simon presented her many years ago: a full-size dining room table painted to look like a complete repast of fresh fish, lobster, crawfish, turkey, fried eggs, and pie. (Fleishmann collection, 2003)

THE ARTIST AT WORK

An integral part of the experience of owning art, according to Simon, is the interpersonal connection between the art creator and the art collector. Thus, unlike many artists, Simon is accessible; he can be found most Mondays through Saturdays working at his Jackson Avenue studio. The studio is open to the public, but there are no signs to designate the location. Instead, there is an archway that reads, "Please Hippies Use Back Door." Find the archway and you have found his studio—the word "studio" being used somewhat unconventionally. Located near Magazine Street, Simon's workplace/gallery is an outdoor complex consisting of several lightly constructed, open-air, tin-roofed sheds brimming with completed works and works in progress. The whole area has a decidedly Caribbean feel to it and a "Don't worry; be happy" ambiance, often with reggae or jazz music playing in the background. There is an unmistakably uplifting atmosphere to the place, with humor and wit everywhere. There are signs with bitingly clever sayings, embellished "found" objects transformed into objects d'art, large sculptures, and architectural pieces.

On a recent sunny Saturday afternoon, a steady stream of people walked in and around the studio. Simon enjoys giving "newbies" a quick whirl around his studio, and he often stops his

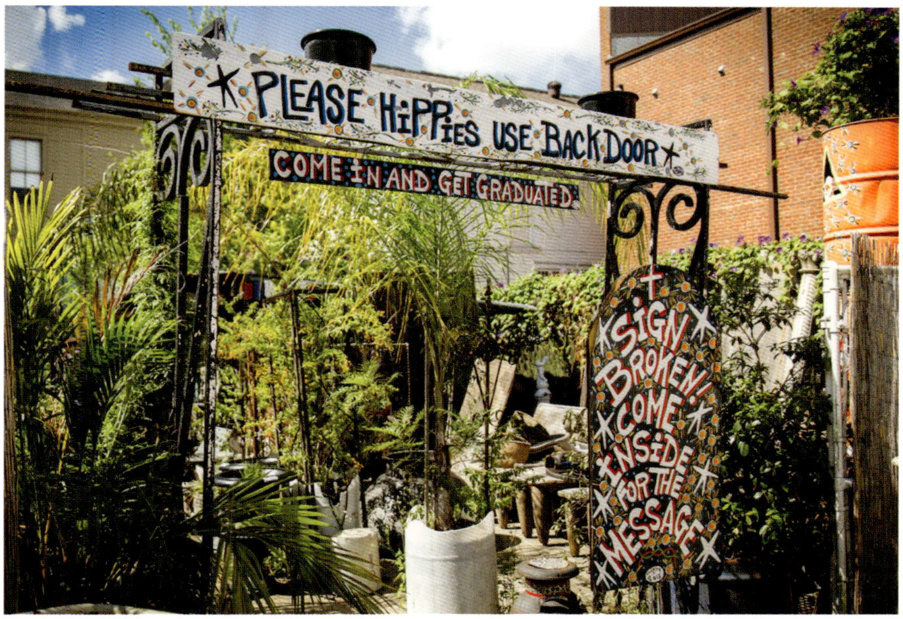

Visitors to Simon's studio pass beneath this unusual archway.

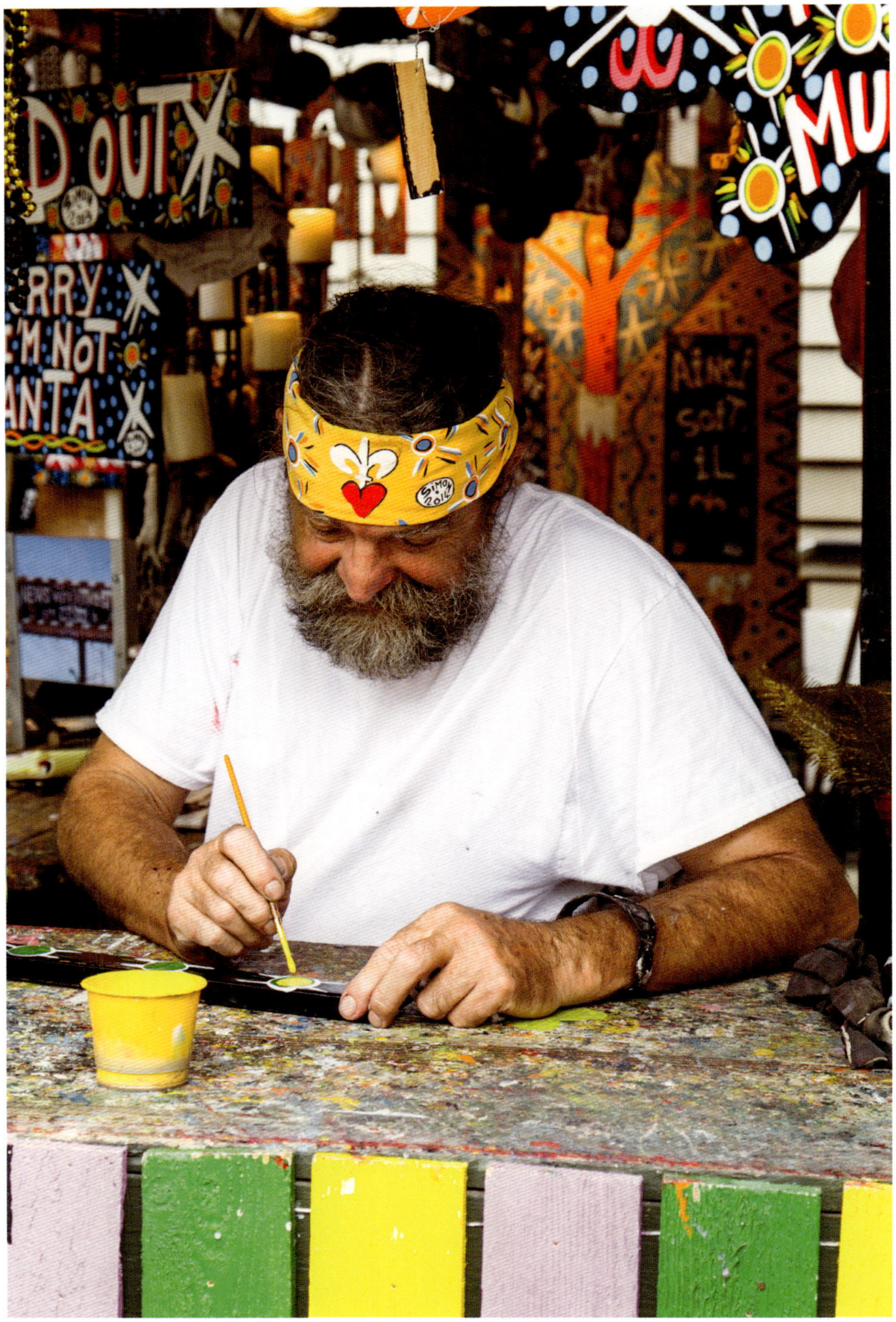

Simon at work in his Jackson Avenue studio.

work to chat with repeat customers and frequent visitors. Consistent with his belief in the personal connection between the artist and the collector, a purchase of any of his art pieces will usually include a photo opportunity with the artist. But the photo is more than just a "selfie" on a cellular phone. In a tradition that was started long before digital photos were the norm, Simon poses for a photo with each buyer and the artwork he or she has chosen. Once the picture is printed, it is placed in a photo album. After years of keeping photographic records of everyone who has purchased one of his works, Simon has amassed literally thousands of photos—and fans. The evidence lies in the four-foot-high stack of bulging photo albums that hold the pictures and crowd his office.

Because the studio is an outdoor complex, it is subject to the weather. New Orleans summers can be brutally hot and humid, but Simon insists he isn't bothered by the heat. "This is what I am used to," he says, shrugging his shoulders. When it rains, he closes up the sheds as much as possible and just keeps on creating. "The rain doesn't hurt the artwork," he says, pointing to the signs displayed outside the work sheds. "It is the sun that is bad for them."

Despite its laid-back atmosphere, the studio is a busy place. Simon sells thousands of art pieces and signs each year, and because he personally designs and executes the main body of each piece of art, the wait time for commissioned pieces is over a year long.

In an era of social media and online promotion and marketing, it is amazing that as busy as his enterprise is, it does not encompass any type of electronic networking. One of the signs in his studio makes Simon's business philosophy succinctly clear: "No Computer. No Web. No Fax. No Virus. Come and See Us." Instead of e-mails and websites, his networking consists of stopping work for a while to chat with those who drop by to visit. Customers who want to commission a piece can call and talk directly to the artist himself or, better yet, take a trip to his studio, which Simon considers a key part of the whole art-buying experience. With so many people heeding his advice, Simon has become an Uptown icon and his studio a community draw.

Although Simon does not feel the need to embrace technology, his work has nonetheless found its way onto the internet, though not of his own volition. One of his fans has created and maintains a Facebook page

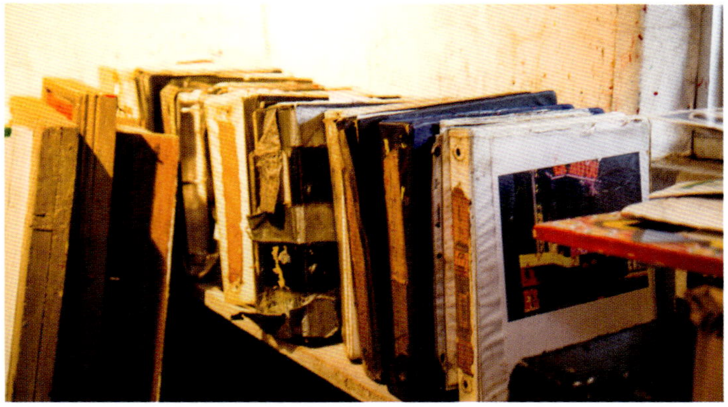

Dozens of albums are filled with photographs of customers standing with Simon and their art purchase.

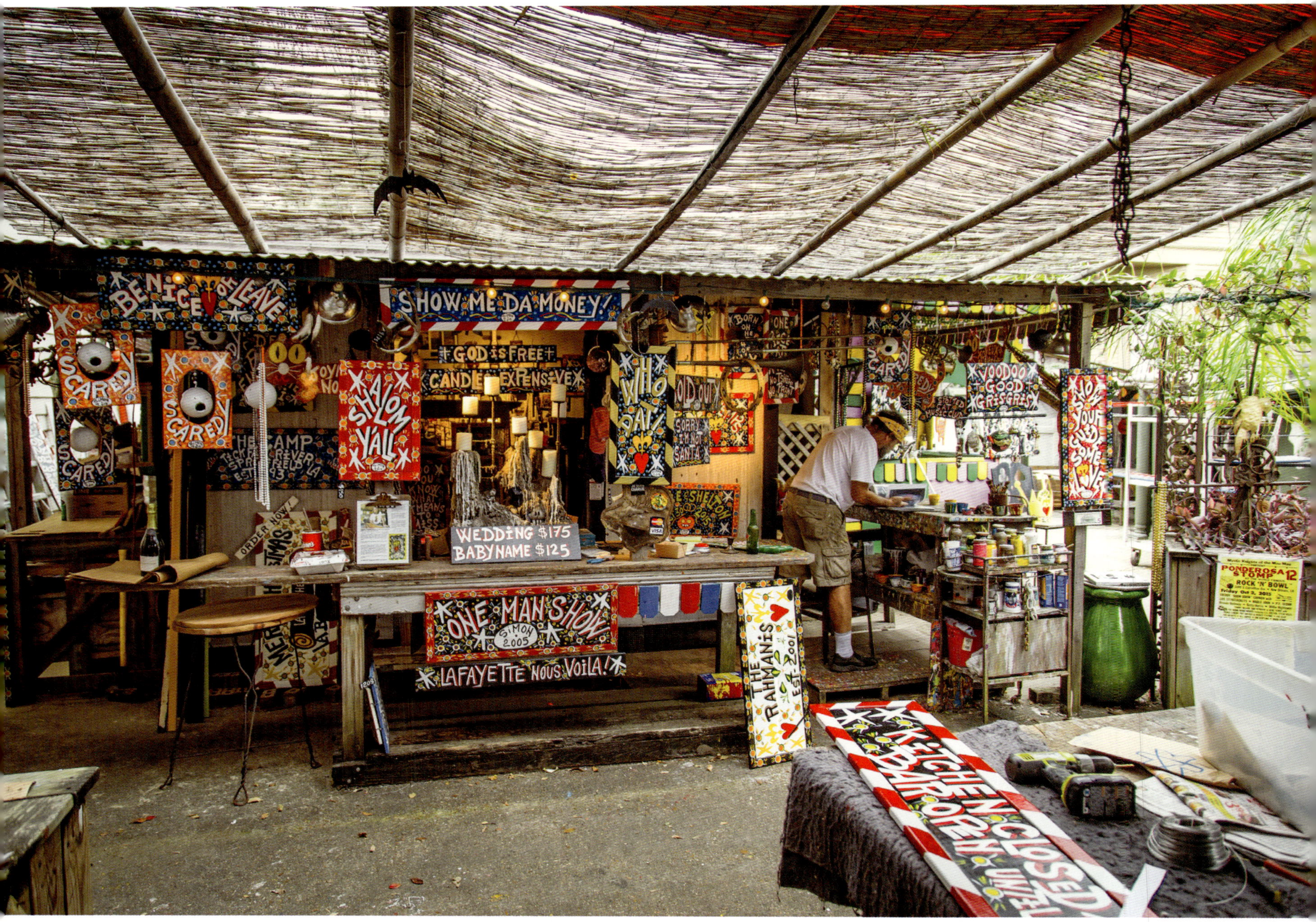

Simon works in a shaded area of his open-air studio.

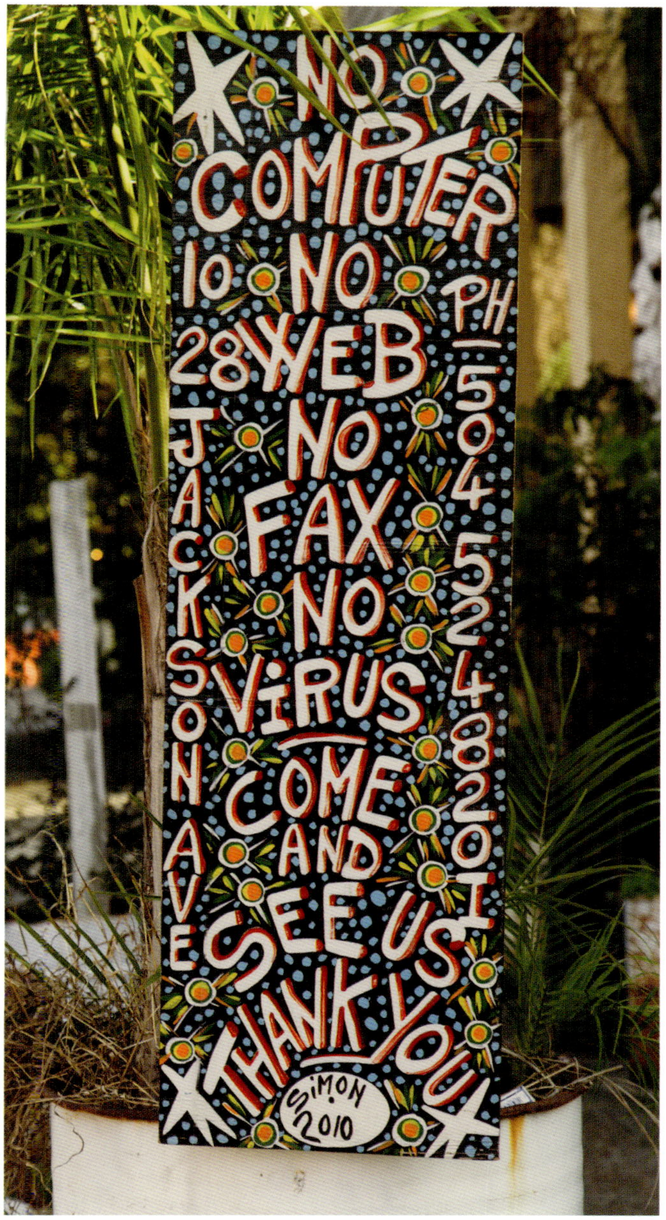

Simon's long-standing policy on using technology in his business is expressed in this sign in front of his studio. "If you want a piece of art, come by and see me," says the artist.

about his work. Lori Bair, co-owner of Cajun Pride Swamp Tours, administers the page titled "Simon of New Orleans." Although the artist doesn't take part in the site's updates, he is pleased that it is frequented by art fans.

Bair owns several of Simon's art pieces, some of which she keeps at home. Others are displayed around the Cajun Pride grounds. "Admission Free for Alligators," declares a sign near the business office. An alligator skull is the focal point of a piece that announces, "Gone Swamping."

"The boat captains are always on the lookout for interesting artifacts to save for Simon," she adds. He carved a spear from an alligator jawbone Bair sent him. Bair often brings Simon the bones from frogs' legs, which he adds to his "gris-gris" collection and uses as needed.

Bair came to know Simon years ago when she visited his studio, and over the years they have become friends. "I love his positive attitude. We both share a love of New Orleans and realize the importance of tourism.

"He is kind and generous, too. I know Simon was not born 'Southern,'" she adds, "but he sure has that Southern charm."

Even without the internet, "Simon is an exciting artist and expert marketer," says collector Dr. Leonard Glade. "It is incredibly unique to find such a dynamic seller, especially in the art world. Selling contemporary art is almost impossible. Simon has done it. It wouldn't be as successful if Simon weren't there. I respect his ability to go from nothing to big sales."

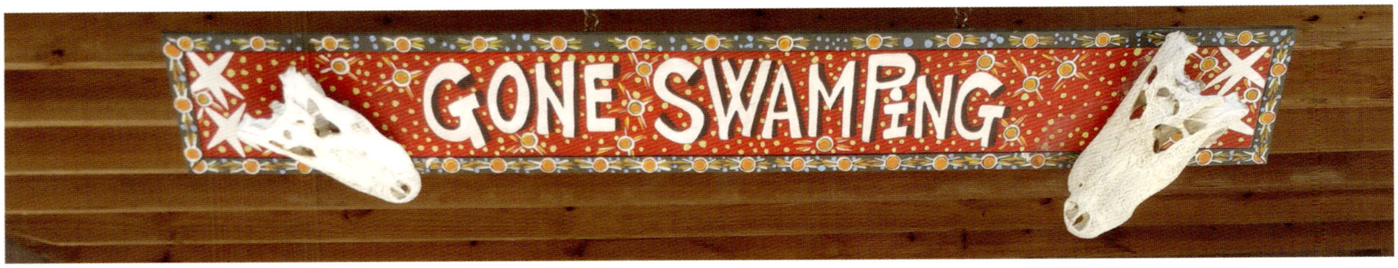

Simon used alligator skulls found by Cajun Pride Swamp Tours co-owner Lori Bair to fashion this sign hanging near the tour boat loading area. (Courtesy Lori Bair)

Simon knows that buying contemporary art can be a daunting prospect for many people, especially those just starting to collect pieces. The prices are often high. The buying process can be intimidating. The paintings themselves can be perplexing. The artist tries to eliminate as many of the roadblocks as possible. He keeps his prices affordable. His easygoing demeanor and accessibility make the process personable and relaxed. And the artwork itself is anything but scary. He hopes to be thought of as the artist who made owning contemporary artwork possible and desirable to a whole new generation, especially a new generation of New Orleanians.

"I want people who appreciate art to be able to own art and to connect with the artist himself," says Simon. "I hope to be their introduction to the world of art."

Glade concurs. "I believe that Simon is responsible for bringing modern art to people in this area. He makes it available and affordable. For young people especially, Simon's work is often their first piece of original art.

"So many people see owning art as not much more than an investment. 'What is its provenance?' they want to know. 'What is its future value?'" continues Glade. "But Simon's art is art for its own sake. You see a piece. You like it. It makes you happy. You don't have to endanger your credit to buy it. You get a good feeling every time you pass it hanging on the wall in your home. That's what owning art should be like. And Simon makes it possible."

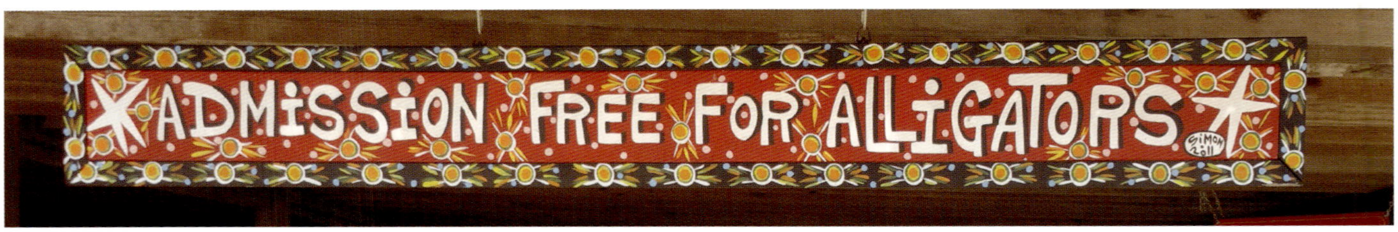

A Simon sign at Cajun Pride Swamp Tours. (Courtesy Lori Bair)

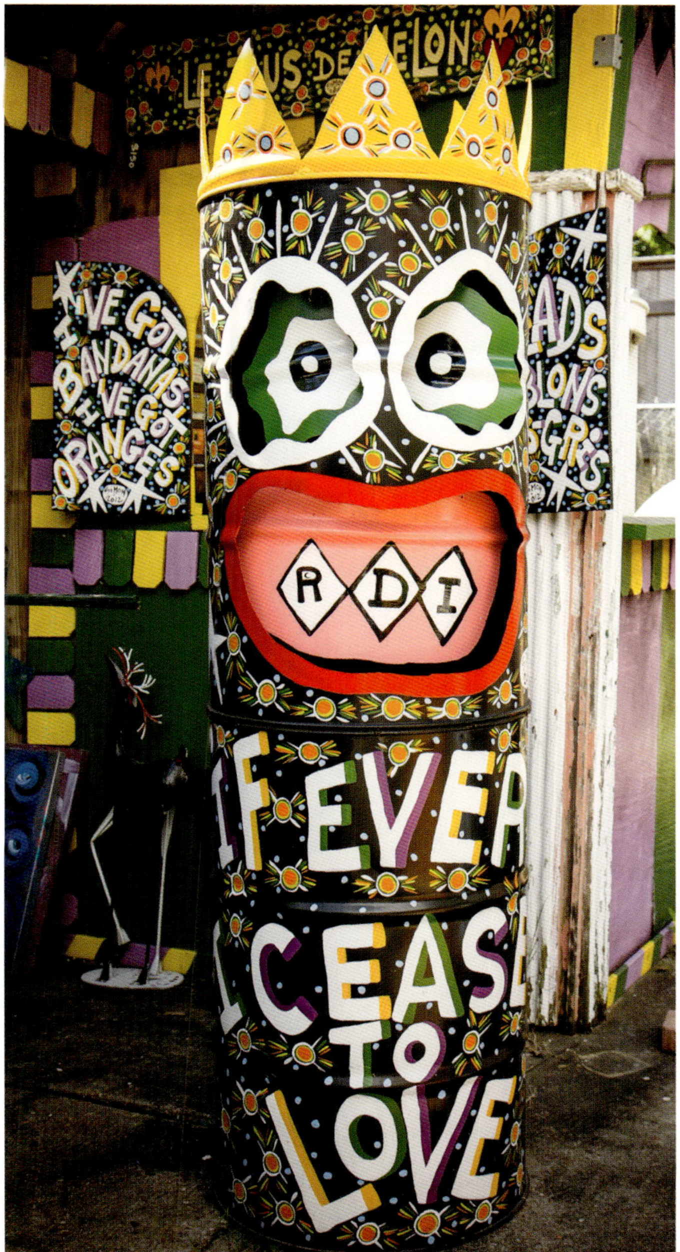

A totem made of oil drums is painted with "If Ever I Cease to Love," the official song of the Krewe of Rex.

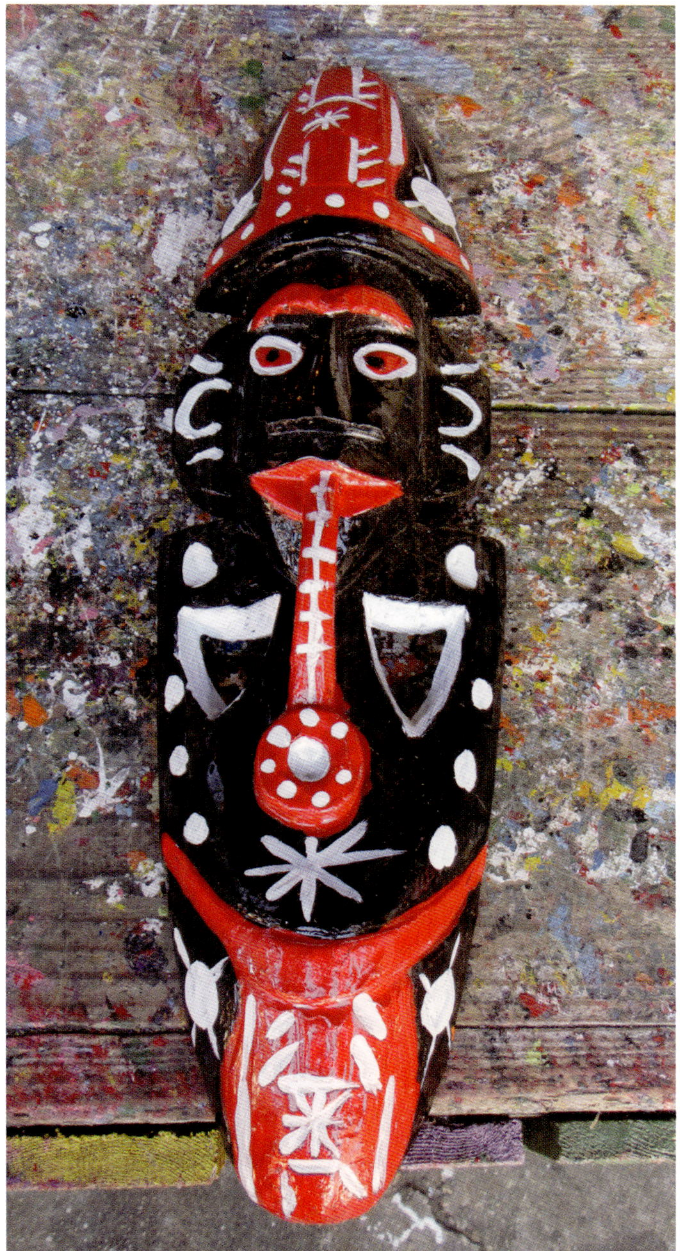

A painted mask.

THE CREATIVE PROCESS

When Simon is struck with inspiration for a new piece, it usually comes as a single, complete visualization of the finished work. He knows what it should look like from the very beginning and then goes with the vision, rarely making changes along the way.

Once he has the basic design elements in mind, the artist begins one of his paintings by cutting a piece of wood to the desired dimensions. At that time he also fashions wooden strips which will be used later in the framing. The pieces are then sanded smooth and painted with a coat of gesso, a thick, white-pigmented primer made from gypsum that has been mixed with glue. The result is a mélange that seals the irregularities in the wood and provides a uniform surface that will accept the paints evenly and smoothly. It also prevents the paint from leaking through into the wood itself, which could cause the colors to lose their brightness. For Simon, it's all about intensity and brightness.

When the initial coat of gesso is dry, the wood is sanded smooth again, and a second

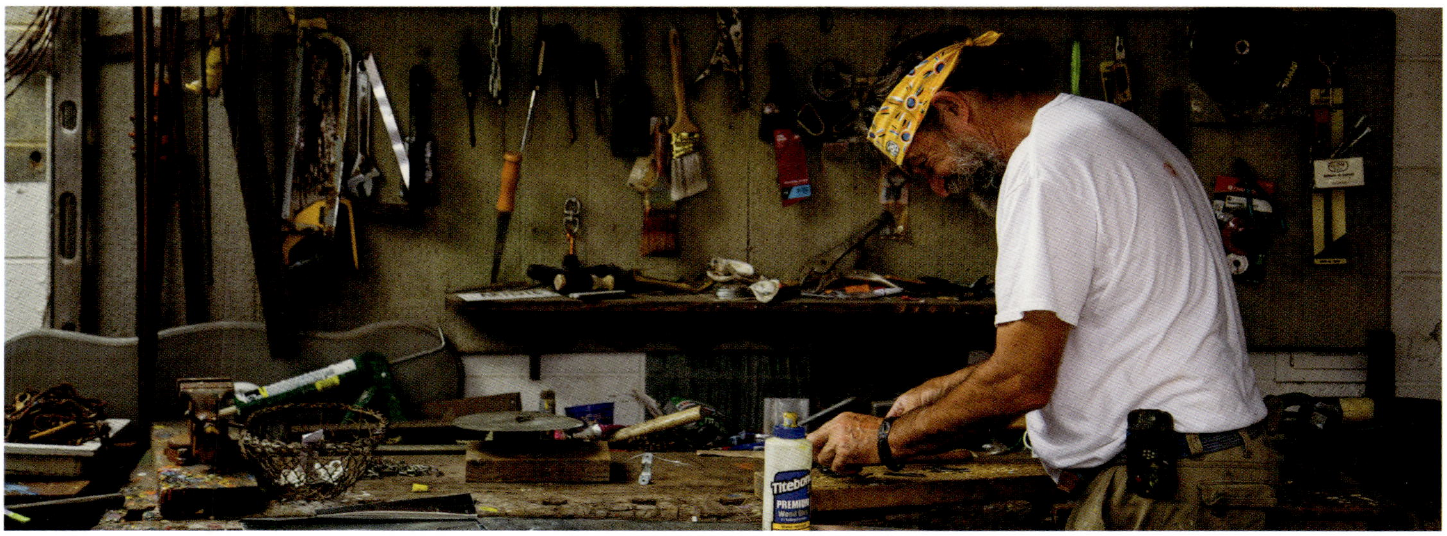

Simon at his workbench.

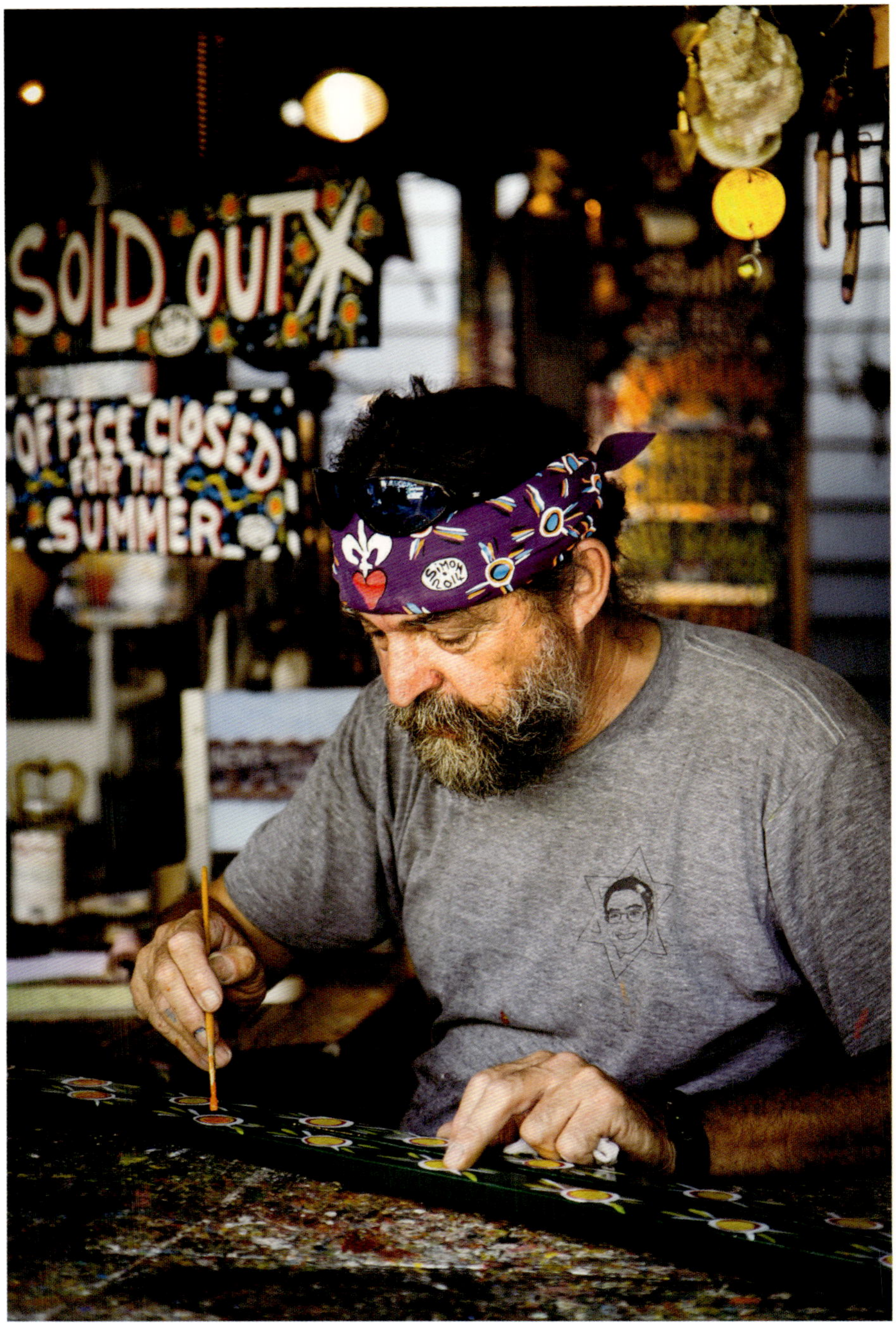

The framing strips are cut to length and the corners are mitered.

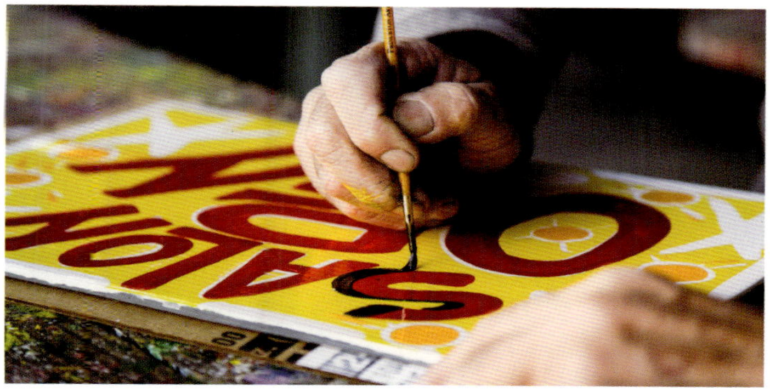

Simon hand paints the distinctive capitals-only lettering and shadows each character.

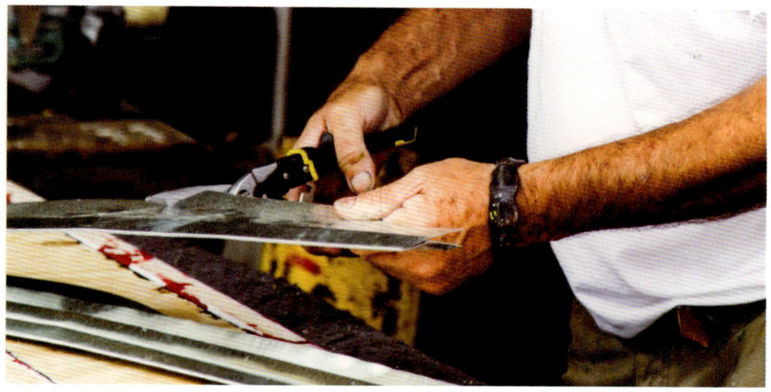

Scrap aluminum is fashioned into hangers.

coat of gesso is applied. If necessary, a third sanding and gesso application follow.

Instead of wood, Simon sometimes uses pressed tin as the "canvas" for his paintings. The tin is cleaned and lightly sanded, but the application of gesso is not usually necessary. He begins by painting the background color directly onto the surface of the tin and then adds his main design over that.

To keep the pieces bright and intense, the artist uses only oil-based enamel paints in vivid primary and secondary colors. He says that these oil-based enamels more closely resemble the types of paints used by the old French and Dutch masters. If the work is to be a holiday-themed piece—Mardi Gras, July Fourth, Bastille Day, St. Patrick's Day, etc.—he chooses the appropriate seasonal colors. After laying down a background color, he paints the main image of the artwork or the words for a sign.

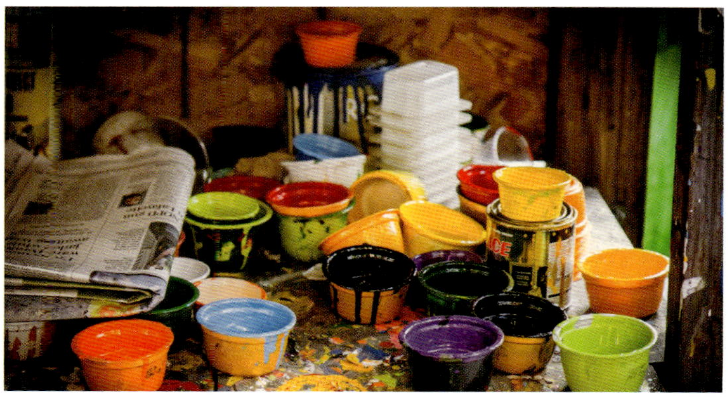

The artist uses only oil-based enamels in bright colors.

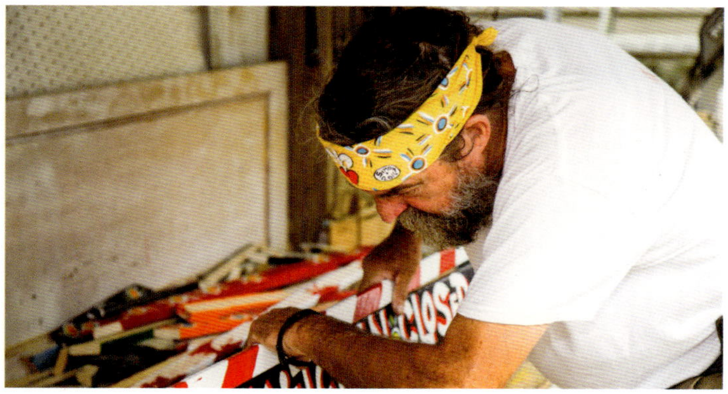

The framing is fitted to the main piece of work.

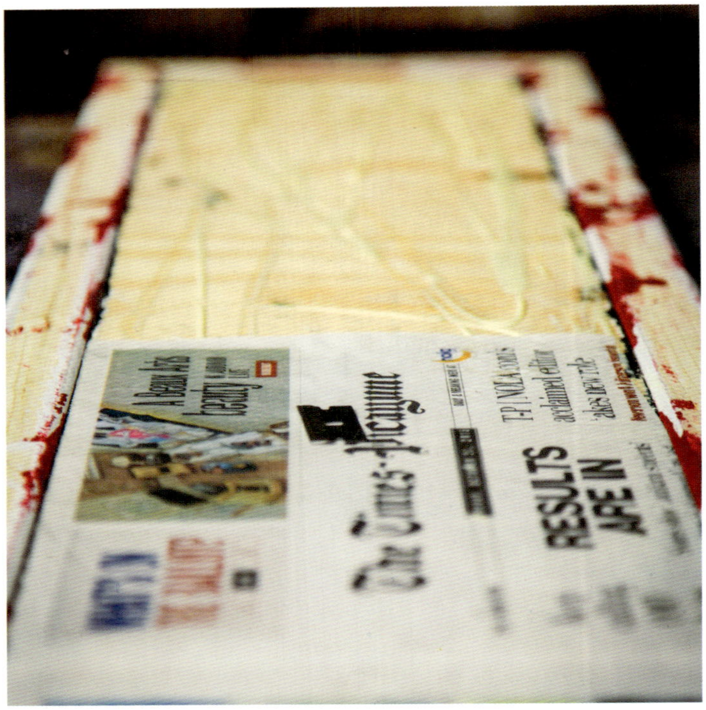

Backing each piece with newspaper documents the date of completion and locale.

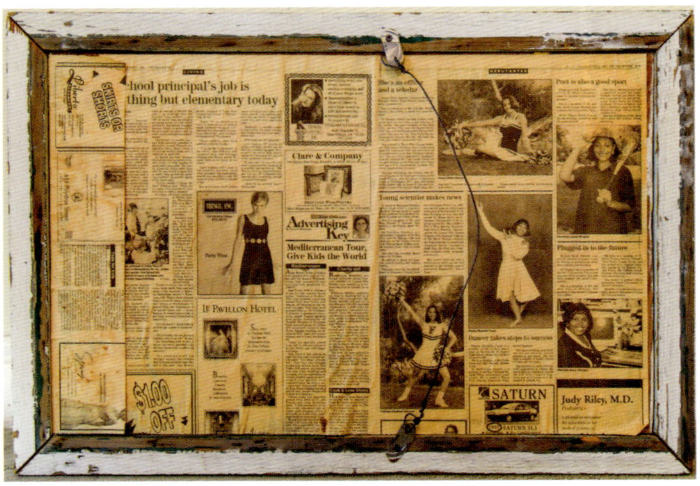

Even his earliest pieces were backed with newspaper, this one in 1996.

Next, he fills any empty spaces with one of his three customary symbols: the asymmetric star, the stylized double- or triple-dot, and the wriggly "chromosome." An assistant, usually a university art student or graduate, is often on hand to help when the workload is heavy, filling in the final coloring details per Simon's instructions. The piece is then framed.

Whether the surface is wood or pressed tin, Simon backs his paintings with pages from local newspapers. He first began this practice because not only were the newspaper pages readily available and inexpensive, but they also documented the date of completion and the locale of the work's origin.

He fashions the hanging apparatus for the art by cutting two pieces of scrap aluminum to the correct size and shape with tin snips, punching holes through the metal, and then nailing them to the back of the frame. Wire is strung between the two pieces.

It takes about two weeks to complete one of his iconic signs. It takes much longer for full-size paintings and large free-standing pieces.

"People often ask me how I know when the piece is finished," says Simon. "That's easy," he explains with a shrug. "It is finished when there is no more room left to paint." He signs each of his finished pieces with an oval containing the name "Simon" and the year of completion. This treatment of his signature is the only part of his works that is trademarked.

Prices for most of his signs and small objects

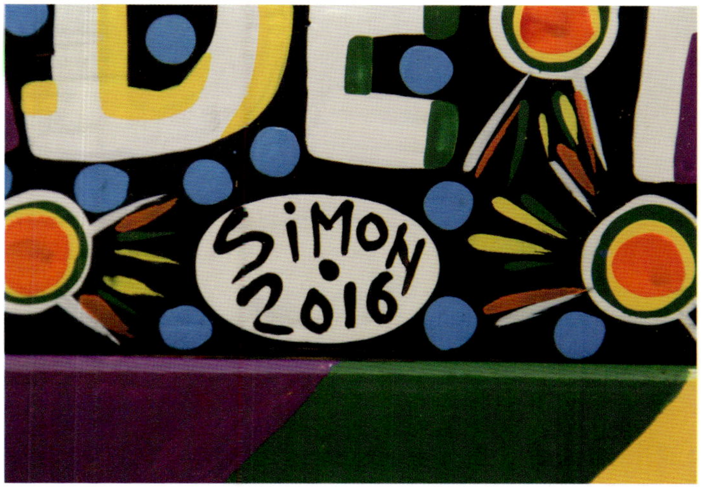

The oval containing "Simon" and the year is trademarked.

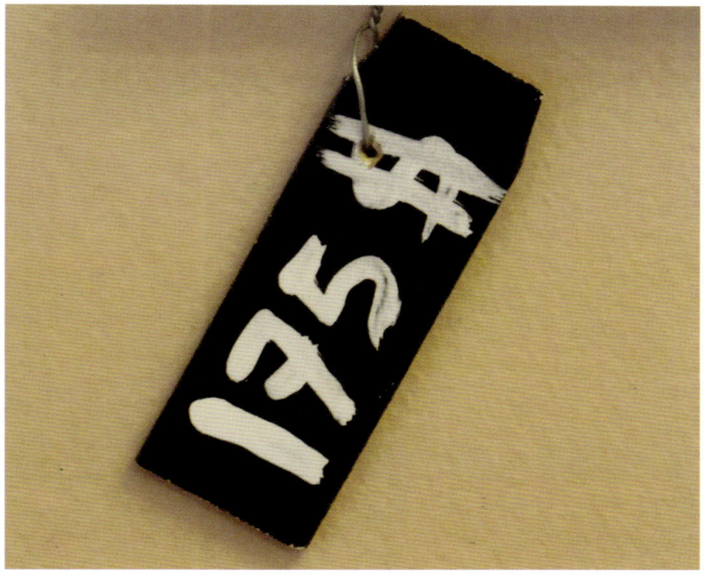

Made of scrap wood, the price tag is large so "people don't have to find their glasses" to read it.

d'art range between $125 and $250. Prices are higher for more complex works, with larger paintings and free-standing pieces priced anywhere from $300 to $800.

In keeping with the light-hearted folk-art tone of his works, the price tag that accompanies each piece is created in the same fashion as the piece itself. Made of a wood scrap about 2 x 3 inches, it is hand painted and then attached to the artwork with a wire loop.

"I make the price tag big," explains Simon, "so people in restaurants where the art is displayed don't have to find their glasses or lean over tables where other people are eating just so they can see the price." Most collectors leave the price tags intact with the artwork.

The completed pieces are destined for various locations. Simon personally delivers to the restaurants and other local businesses that display and sell his work. The deliveries often entail a congenial visit with the business owners, most of whom consider themselves to be not only business partners, but also friends with the artist. If the piece has been commissioned by a local client, Simon calls with an invitation to come by, pick up the art, and pose for a picture. Other commissioned pieces are shipped to worldwide locations. Of course, much of the art is used to replenish the inventory he displays at his Jackson Avenue studio—where the creative process has already begun anew.

LIFE IN FRANCE

Despite his success as an artist, Simon did not originally pursue a career in the visual arts. Instead, it was the culinary arts that dominated his early life. Born in Chamonix, France, Simon grew up in the Hotel Savoie, a ski resort owned by his family. The resort was located at the foot of Mont Blanc in a beautiful area of France with wide-rolling pastures surrounded by snow-capped peaks. His mother, Madeleine, was a classically trained chef who ran the resort's kitchen and restaurant, in addition to her other duties as owner. As such, instead of being referred to as the hotel chef, she was known to all as *"la mère"* (the mother, as in "the mother of the hotel"). Simon's grandfather was the hotel's pastry chef and baker.

With World War II having ended just a few years earlier, there was relative peace in this area of France. Visitors from around the world traveled to the area to ski the nearby mountains. Many came from Paris, returning to the hotel every year during the ski season. (Simon lamented recently that unfortunately there is only limited skiing in the Hotel Savoie area now. The amount of snow has continued to decrease, and the snowline has consistently crept farther and farther up the mountain.) Simon knew the hotel staff and made friends with the guests.

His favorite childhood memories take him back to the hotel and its grounds, where he played with his siblings: two brothers and a sister. The children were close in age and close as a family. Simon, born in 1949, was third out of the four children, with his sister being the baby of the group. They often traveled to their grandparents' home, a seventeenth-century farmhouse in a rural area outside of Paris, and during their visits the children spent time playing with and feeding the animals that roamed the nearby fields.

Simon, along with his brothers and sister and two dozen other local children of various ages, attended classes in Chamonix's one-room schoolhouse. Centrally located in the room was a wood-burning stove which helped provide warmth during the cold winter months. Each day Simon and his siblings walked a considerable distance from the hotel to the schoolhouse in the morning, returned home for lunch, and then walked back for afternoon classes. When school dismissed for the summer, they and their classmates made the long trek by bus to the Atlantic shore near Brest, France, for summer camp.

Simon remains in contact with his siblings, who now live in the Toulouse area of France.

Simon's father, Wilhelm, was a Dutch citizen

who served for eight years in the French Foreign Legion in the 1940s under Charles de Gaulle. During that time Wilhelm led his soldiers in several battles and subsequently became wounded in action in Senegal, Africa, barely surviving eleven days in the desert before he and his men were rescued. Because of his dedication in the fight for the liberation of France, Wilhelm eventually became one of de Gaulle's closest assistants and his personal friend. After leaving the Legion, he rarely spoke of his wartime exploits, but every once in a while, prodded by his children, he would share some of his memories with them. Simon remembers playing with the numerous medals his father had earned, and decades later many of Simon's paintings would pay tribute to his father and to the French Liberation by including the movement's motto, *Liberté, Egalité, Fraternité* (Liberty, Equality, Fraternity), on many of his works. Wilhelm died in 1974.

Simon's parents first met in the Foreign Legion offices in Paris, where his mother had worked as a clerk before becoming a chef. Included in their circle of friends were Simone de Beauvoir and Jean-Paul Sartre, both of whom were French authors, philosophers, and political activists. Sartre was godfather to one of Simon's cousins.

Because his father was Dutch and his mother French, Simon sometimes refers to himself as half-Gauguin and half-Van Gogh, two nineteenth-century post-Impressionist

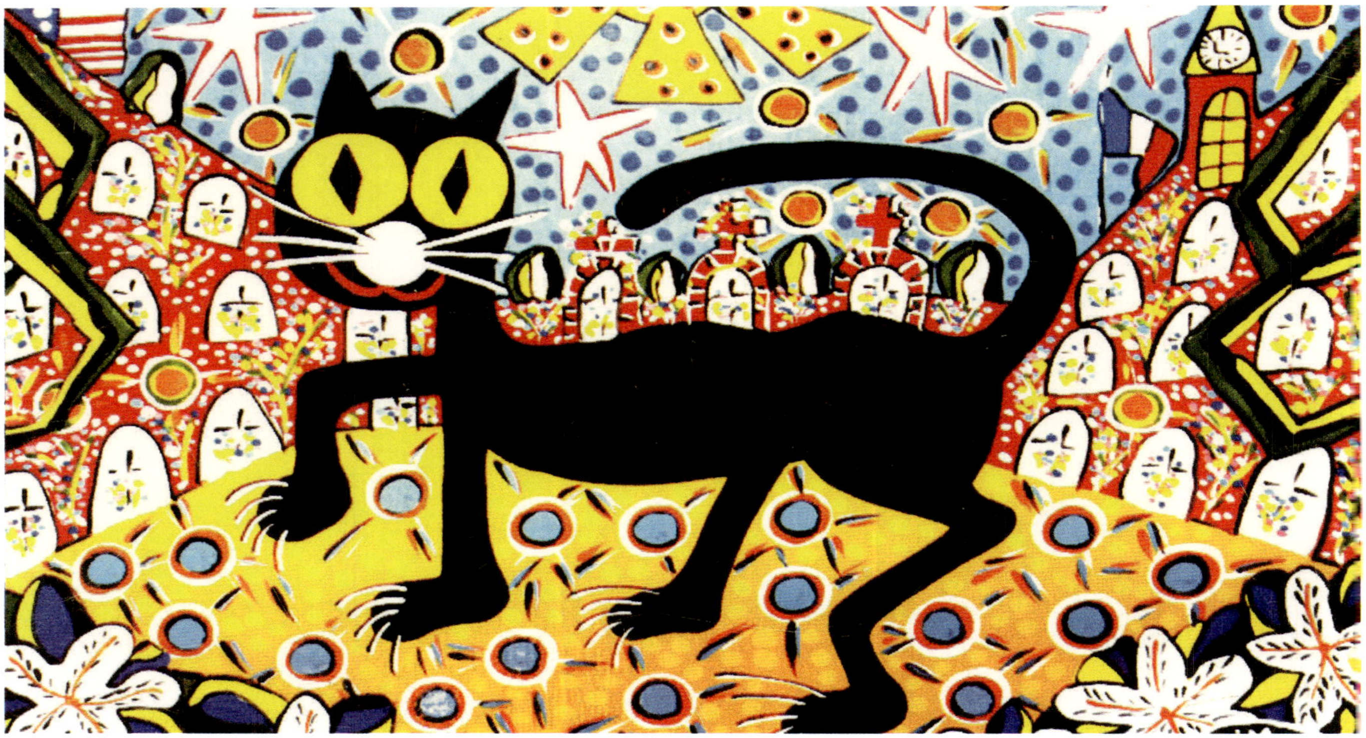

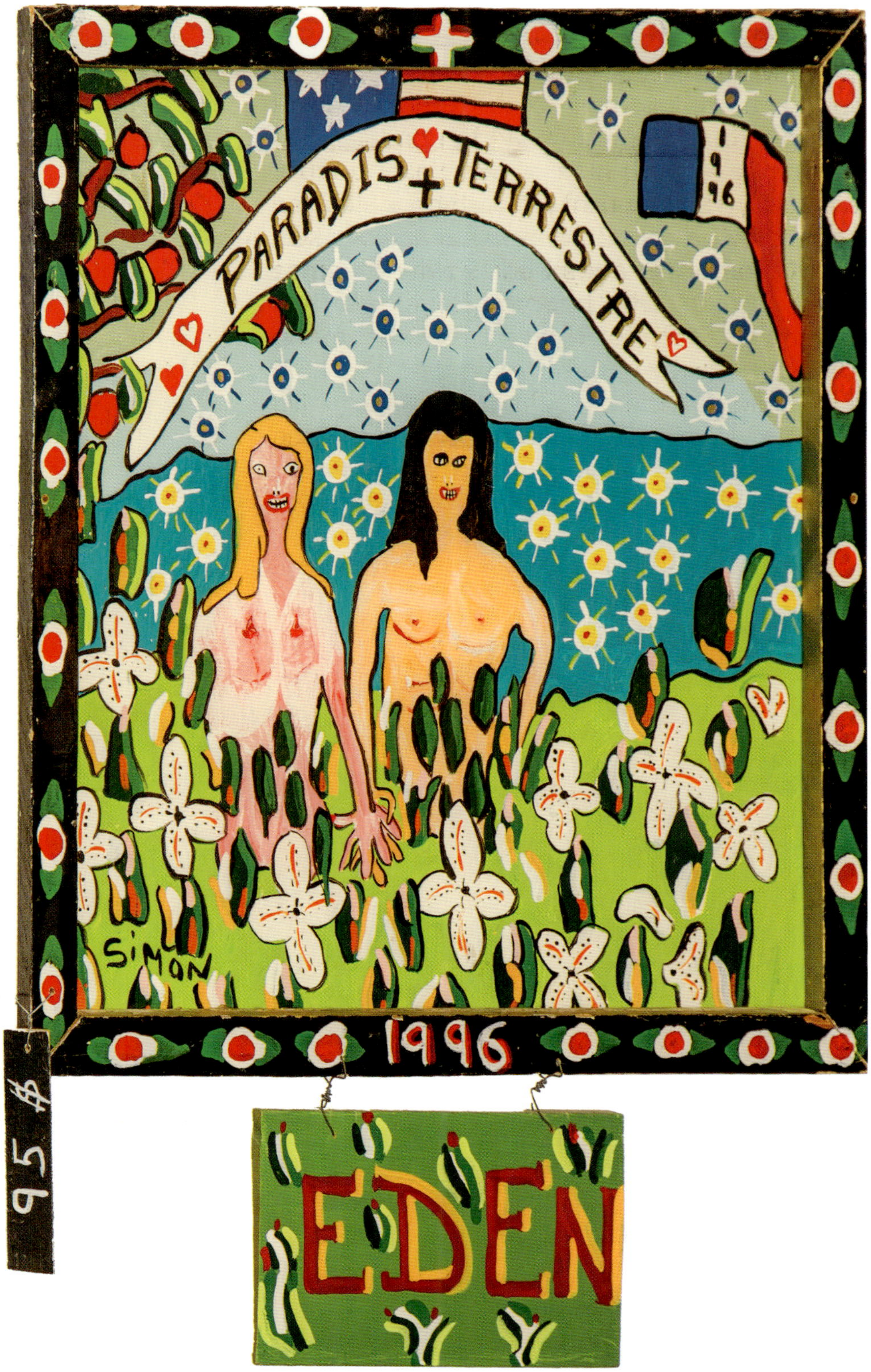

Eden *features Adam and Eve standing beneath a heart-decorated banner proclaiming "Paradis Terrestre" (Earthly Paradise). Somewhat modestly covered by a field of lily-like flowers, the couple holds hands as they pass beneath the apple tree (sans serpent). Earth, sea, and sky are represented, along with both the American and French flags. The expressions on the faces of the famous first couple are left to the interpretation of the viewer. (Fleishmann collection, 1996)*

painters. Paul Gauguin was French and Vincent Van Gogh, Dutch.

Following in the culinary footsteps of his mother and grandfather, Simon eventually became a classically trained chef himself. He ran successful restaurants in Chamonix and Cannes for many years, but a divorce at age thirty-seven prompted him to leave France and seek a fresh start. He headed to the United States, arriving in Florida in 1986, and began to make inroads in the restaurant business in that state.

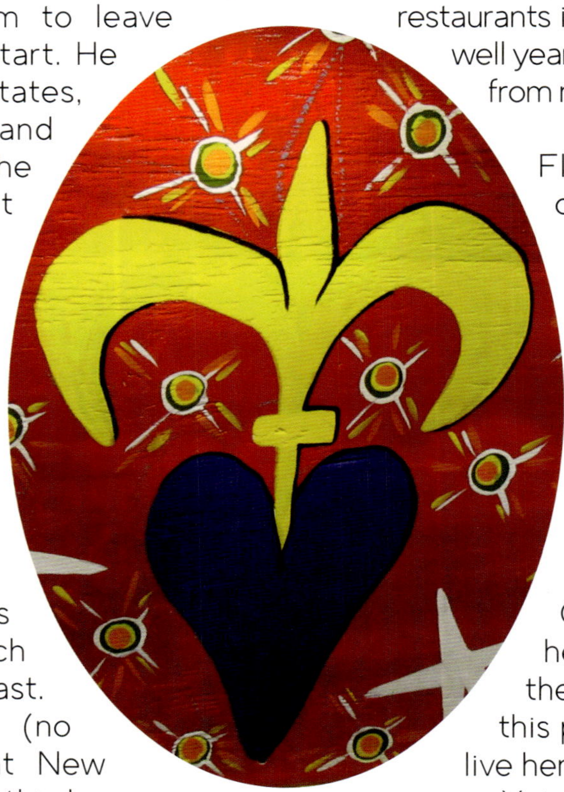

Not long after his arrival in Florida, through mutual friends he met and fell in love with Maria Morse, a native New Orleanian who was working in the area. They married in 1988. With Simon as chef and Maria as manager, the couple opened three restaurants near the West Palm Beach area, on Florida's east coast. Two were Palace Cafés (no affiliation with the current New Orleans restaurant). The third was the Ashley, a restaurant they named after Florida's infamous gang of bank robbers and bootleggers who were led by the notorious thief John Ashley, a.k.a. the "Swamp Bandit." In 1912 the Ashley gang robbed the bank that once occupied the building where Simon and Maria opened their restaurant. The couple renovated the Ashley, taking it down to the studs and remodeling it with a bank theme, complete with brass teller windows for cashier stations. Whenever possible, they supported local artists by hosting art shows and displaying pieces for sale on the restaurant walls. The concept of pairing local art with local restaurants is one that would serve Simon well years later when he switched roles from restaurateur to artist.

During their years in Florida, Maria asked Simon on several occasions to join her for a visit to her hometown of New Orleans, but running the restaurants left scant vacation time, and he repeatedly balked at the idea. When she finally convinced him to accompany her on a short trip to New Orleans (not coincidentally during Mardi Gras season), Simon fell head over heels in love with the city. "I never want to leave this place," he told her. "I want to live here. I want to die here."

Yet they had businesses to run in Florida, and so they returned. Not long after that, however, Maria's mother became seriously ill, and in 1996 they sold the restaurants and moved to New Orleans to help with her care.

Up until this point, Simon was a chef, not an artist. But that was about to change.

Above: This representation of a fleur de lis rooted in a heart symbolizes the artist's love of New Orleans. This emblem appears frequently in Simon's works.

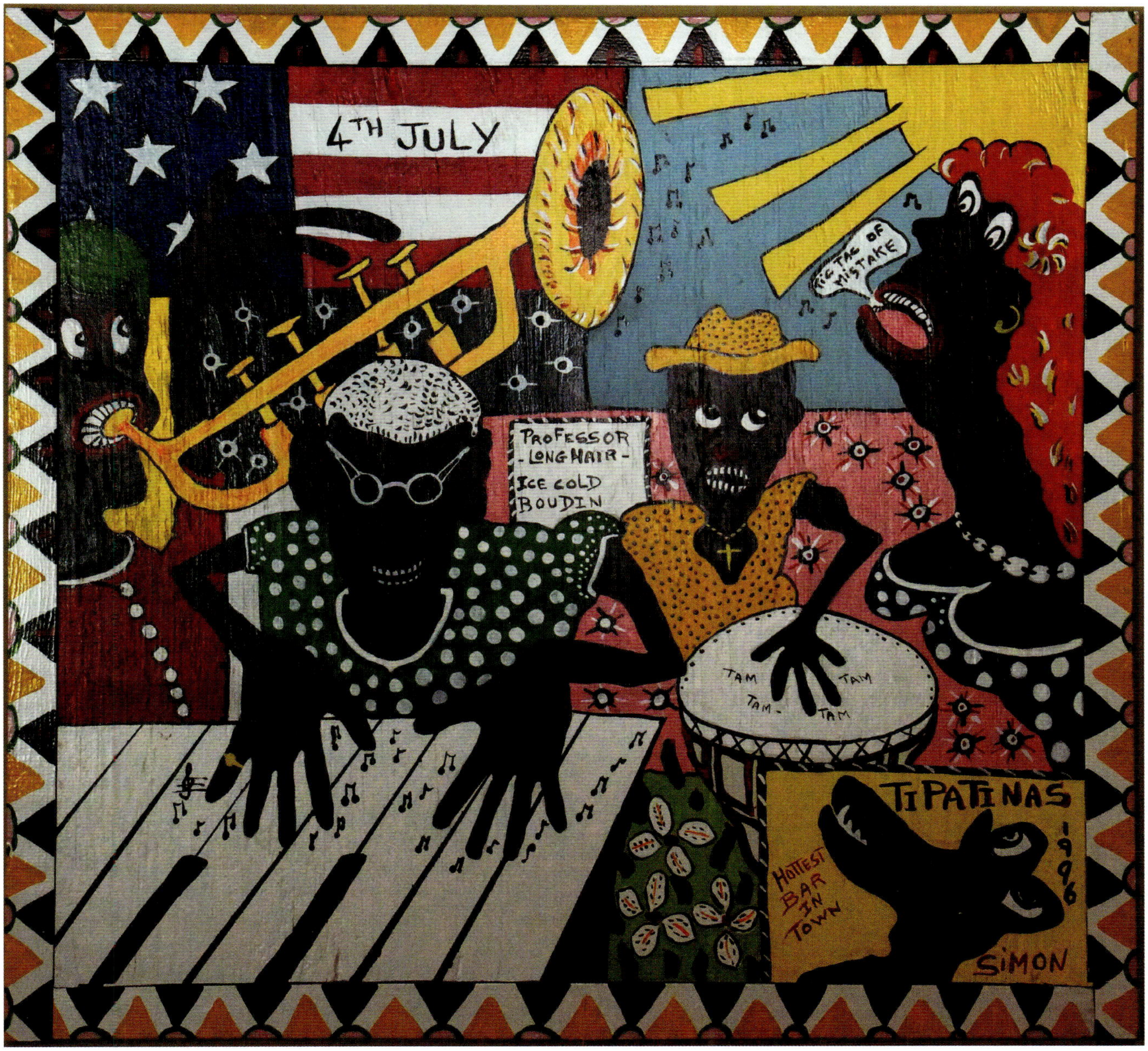

Tipatina's [sic] is the "Hottest Bar in Town" with Professor Longhair tickling the ivories and musical notes flowing from his fingers. In a tribute to Ella Fitzgerald, who passed away the year in which the work was created, Simon shows Fitzgerald belting out her 1938 rendition of "A-Tisket, A-Tasket" (though the lyrics read, "Tic Tac of mistake"). A bongo player adds the beat, and a trumpeter wails away. It is July Fourth and there is "Ice Cold Boudin" available. Simon explains that he had moved to New Orleans just before painting this piece, and he had noticed signs that alternately proclaimed "ice cold beer" and "hot boudin," so he combined the two here. (Courtesy Tom and Susan Nolan, Nolan collection, 1996)

THE CHEF WHO DOESN'T COOK

Soon after his arrival in New Orleans, feeling inspired by the city, its people, its spirited atmosphere, and its affinity with his native France, Simon felt compelled to begin painting, hoping to somehow capture in paint the essence of his newly adopted city.

However, never having painted before, he was unsure of how to start and which direction to pursue. So he began to practice the art by attempting to mimic his favorite artist, Pablo Picasso, and contemporary artists he admired. Among them was George Rodrigue, originator of the Blue Dog paintings. Simon practiced his own versions of the Blue Dog, and it wasn't long before he received via certified mail a "cease and desist" letter from Rodrigue.

Rather than being upset by the letter, Simon took it as an indication that if his work were good enough to spur action from the wildly popular Rodrigue, then perhaps it had potential—though it was now time for Simon to develop a style of his own. He had the letter framed and hung on his office wall. After dabbling with different styles, his own style began to emerge and to coalesce into the types of paintings he does today.

When Simon first started out as an artist,

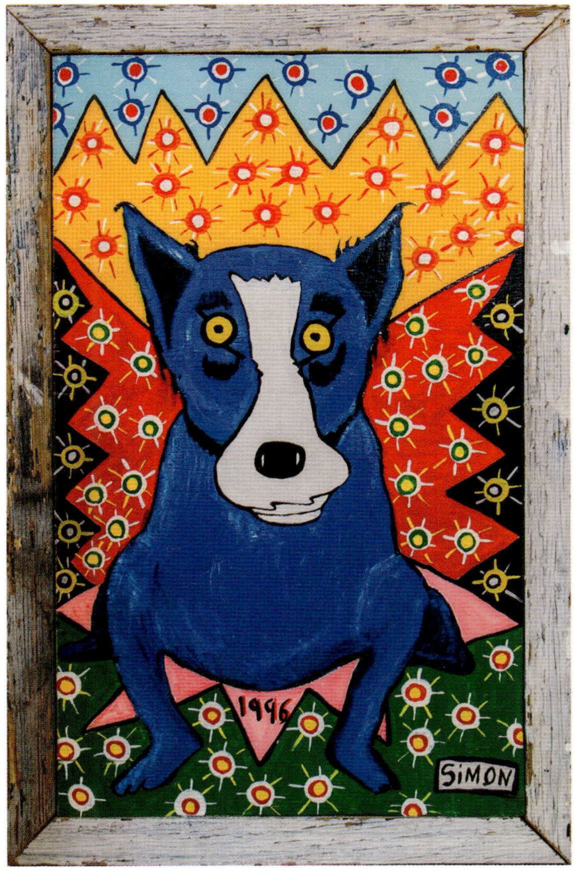

This is a look-alike of the famous George Rodrigue subject. When Simon first started painting, he practiced the art by mimicking popular artists he admired. This piece was completed before he received a "cease and desist" letter from Rodrigue. The collector also has a copy of the letter. (Fleishmann collection, 1996)

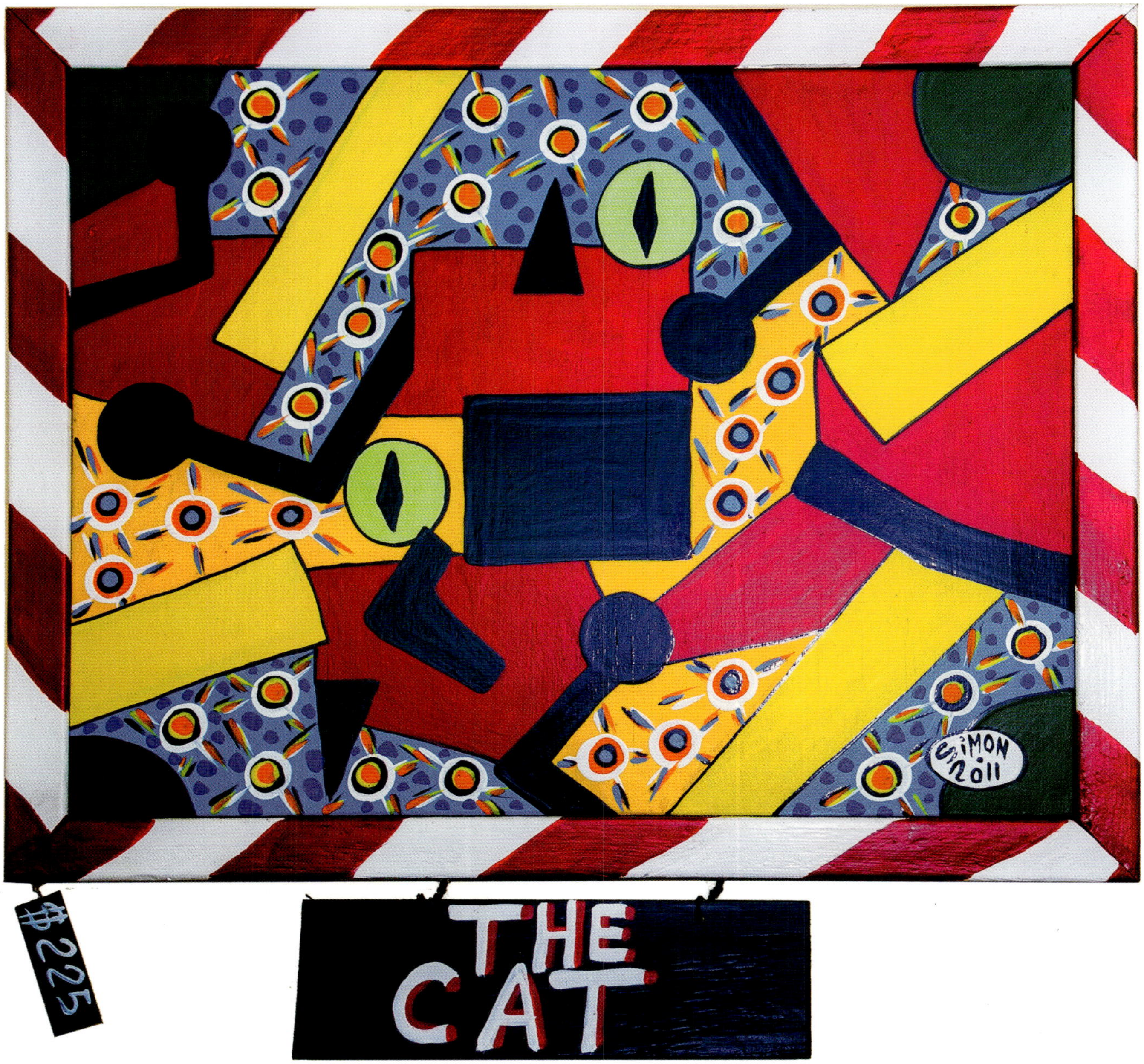

A Picasso-esque style cat.

the sales of his artwork didn't cover the cost of his supplies. To save money, he scoured recycling places for his painting supplies, looking for salvaged auto paints, enamels, and scrap wood and tin. Even now, with the success of his art firmly established, he keeps the creative process as "green" as possible by continuing to repurpose and recycle previously used materials.

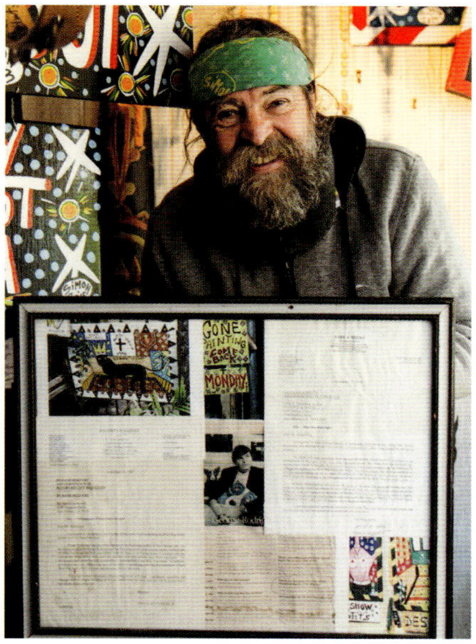

Simon shows off the "cease and desist" order he received from attorneys for George Rodrigue.

As for his "day job," Simon assumed at the time that he would continue to work in the culinary field. Not long after arriving in New Orleans, he applied to work as a chef at a well-known French Quarter restaurant. During the hiring process, he was instructed to observe and assist in the restaurant's kitchen. He dutifully showed up for his first night, assuming that his previous training and experience in classic French cooking would fit right in. But the timing was off, for this was the beginning of the nouvelle Orleans cooking era, when many restaurants were transitioning from Old World French cuisine to lighter, more experimental dishes. He became more and more disappointed as the night wore on. "It's not that the food wasn't good," explains Simon. "It just wasn't my style, not what I was expecting." So after a couple of hours of observing, he quietly slipped out the back door of the kitchen and never returned.

Not long after, Simon and Maria opened a restaurant of their own—a brasserie in the New Orleans suburb of Old Metairie. He decided on the dishes he would offer and then he hand-painted a menu board and some small folk-art pieces and signs with witty sayings. He used his creations to decorate the restaurant's walls. Although the restaurant did reasonably well, it eventually became obvious that people were more interested in the art he produced than in

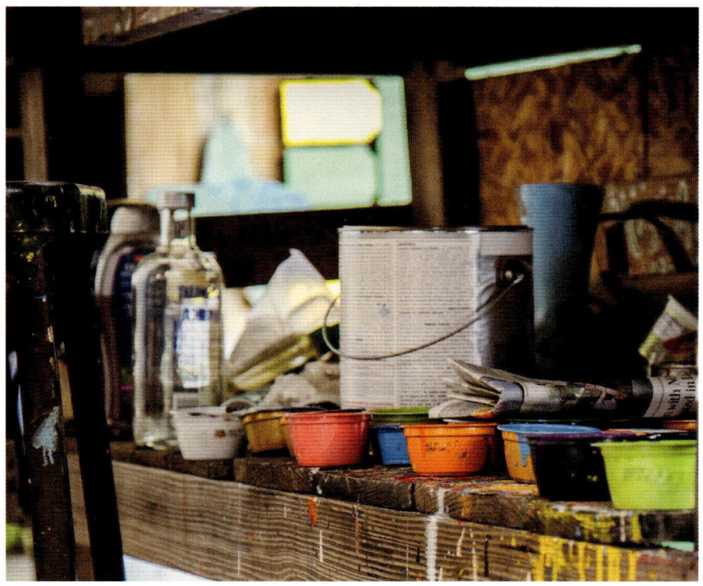

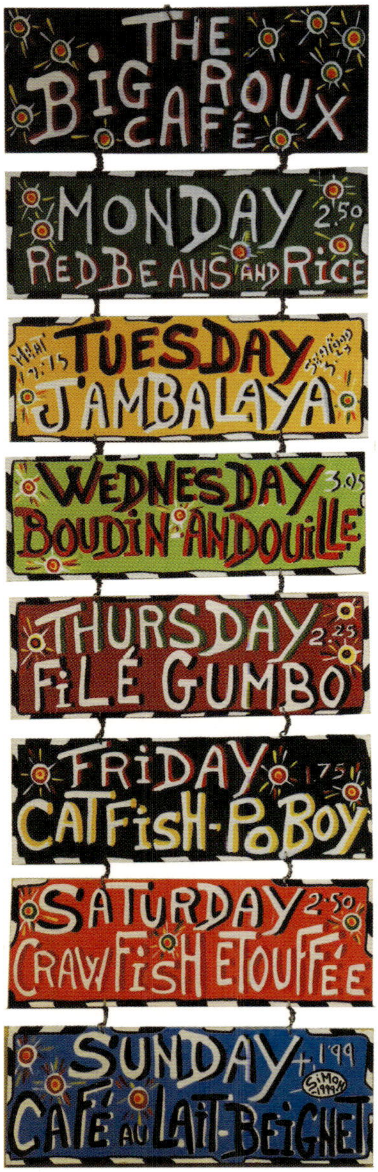

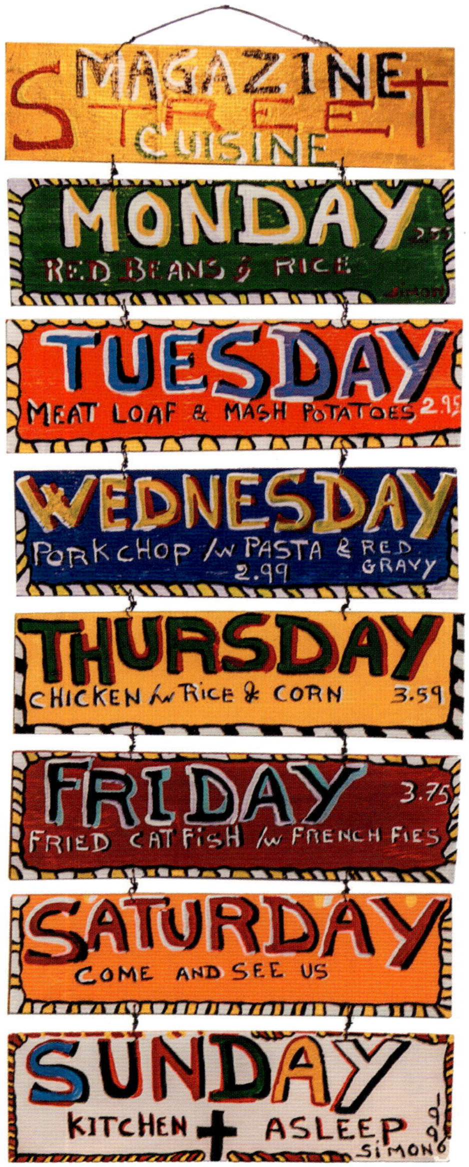

Above left: The colorful menu board has been one of Simon's signature pieces from the beginning of his art career. He started with one in the brasserie he ran in Metairie when he first moved to the area. The menu board remains one of his most requested types of work.

Above right: The days' specials for Monday through Friday are listed, including the prices. Saturday requests, "Come and See Us." Sunday announces, "Kitchen Asleep," along with a cross to represent church day. (Fleishmann collection, 1996)

the cuisine he created. To accommodate the requests, he began painting extra pieces to sell at the restaurant. His artwork repeatedly sold out, but the patrons didn't seem to appreciate the food. So he sold the brasserie and—after decades in the culinary field—he formally ended his career as a chef.

Simon contends that the two fields are not as dissimilar as one might think, saying that his skills as a chef contributed to his career as an artist: "You put this together and you put that together and you see what works."

Meanwhile, his wife, Maria, had begun working at Bush Antiques on Magazine Street. After selling the brasserie, Simon joined her at the antiques shop, working in the courtyard behind the store to help package and ship customers' purchases. In spare moments he continued to work on his art, and the courtyard soon became a neighborhood draw for those interested in his paintings. Allain Bush, owner of Bush Antiques, offered him space in front of her store to display and sell his signs. It was there that his art business began to take off. (The couple remains friends with Allain and continued to help at her store until its closing in 2012.)

Maria soon opened her own antiques store at 2126 Magazine, where Simon continued to produce and sell his art. As Simon's artwork grew in popularity, he began to get requests for commissioned pieces.

His connection to local restaurants also began at this time, starting with a painting of a Chihuahua wearing a sombrero destined for

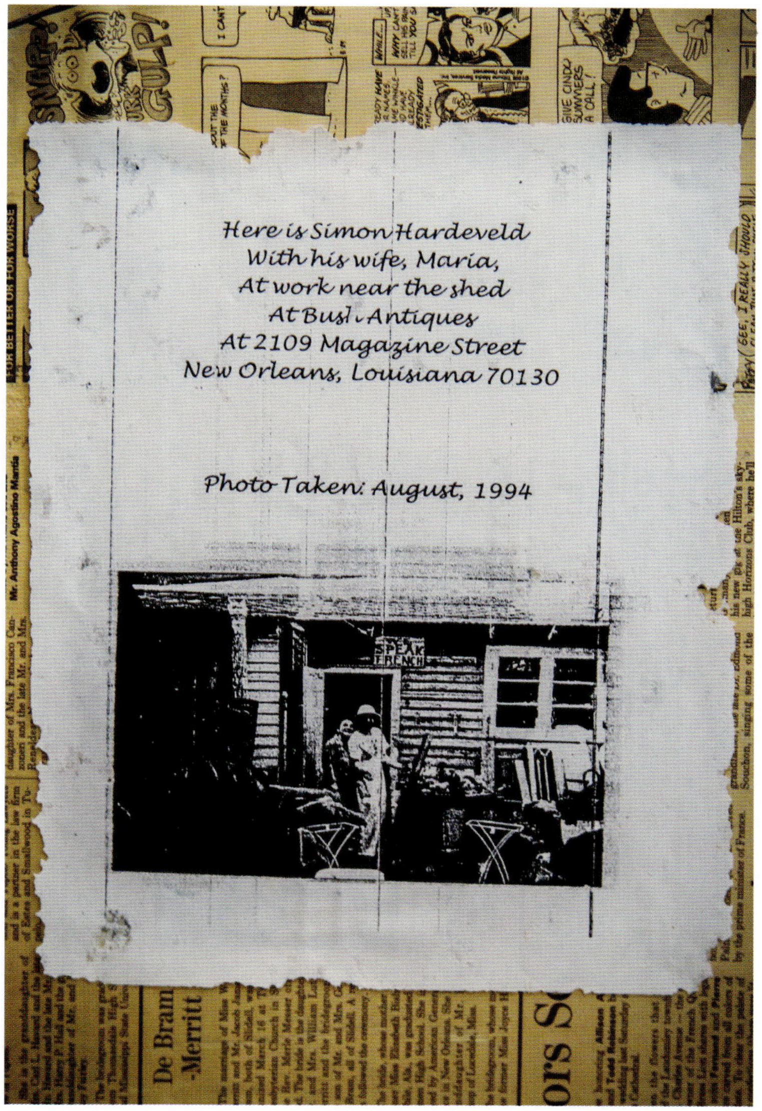

A 1994 flyer of Simon and Maria at Bush Antiques on Magazine Street.

Superior Grill on St. Charles Avenue. He also created various pieces for the House of Blues. Commenting on the chef-turned-artist and the popularity of Simon's work, especially in

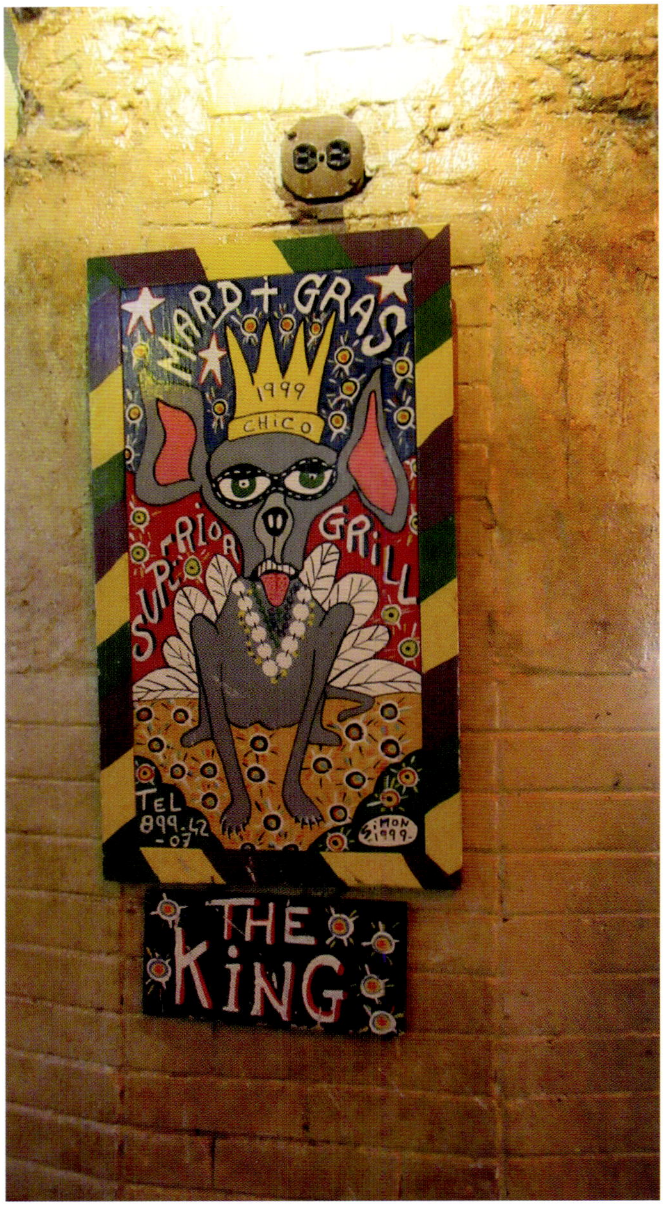

This painting, still hanging at Superior Grill on St. Charles Avenue, was one of Simon's first restaurant placements.

local restaurants, WGNO station news anchor Curt Sprang quips, "He's the chef who doesn't cook, but who has a presence in restaurants all around town."

In keeping with the artist's growing popularity, Simon and Maria quickly outgrew the space, and in 1999 they moved around the corner to their present location at 1028 Jackson Avenue. The Jackson Avenue location was a great find, accommodating both interests. Maria's shop, "Antiques on Jackson," is located in the building at that address, a former Popeyes chicken restaurant; Simon's studio is located in the open area adjacent to the antiques store. The screen door at the back of the shop squeaks open and closed all day as customers wander from one business to the other and Simon and Maria take breaks and visit during the day.

Simon is happy where he is, and he doesn't mourn the passing of his life as a chef. "I don't cook anymore," he says with no regret. "No more cooking, or at least very rarely. The only time I like to go into the kitchen now is to grab a beer," he says with a smile. "Maria cooks more than I do, and she is an incredible cook—especially her Italian meals. Of course, I still love classic French cuisine. The first time I went to Galatoire's, I thought to myself, 'Now, *this* is what I remember from my childhood. This is like the traditional French cooking of fifty years ago.' And it is still so good today." Then he adds quickly, "But I am more than happy to have someone else cook it for me!"

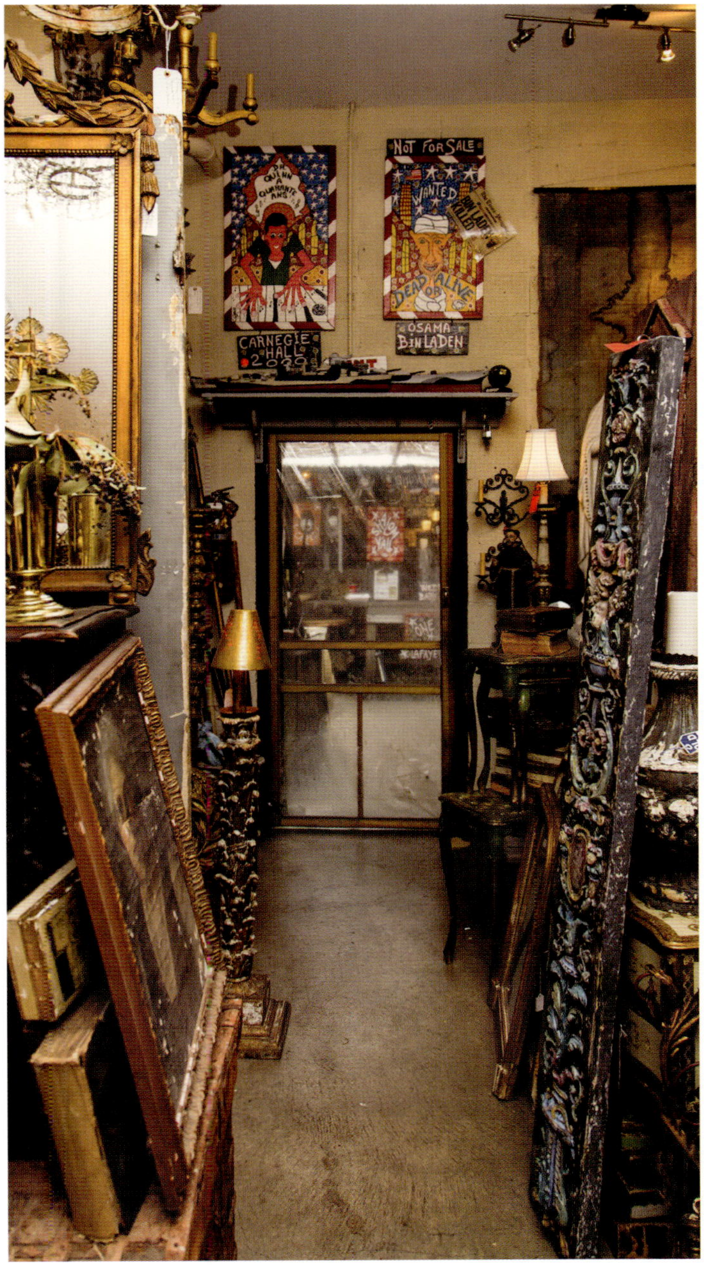

The screen door leads from the antiques shop to the art studio.

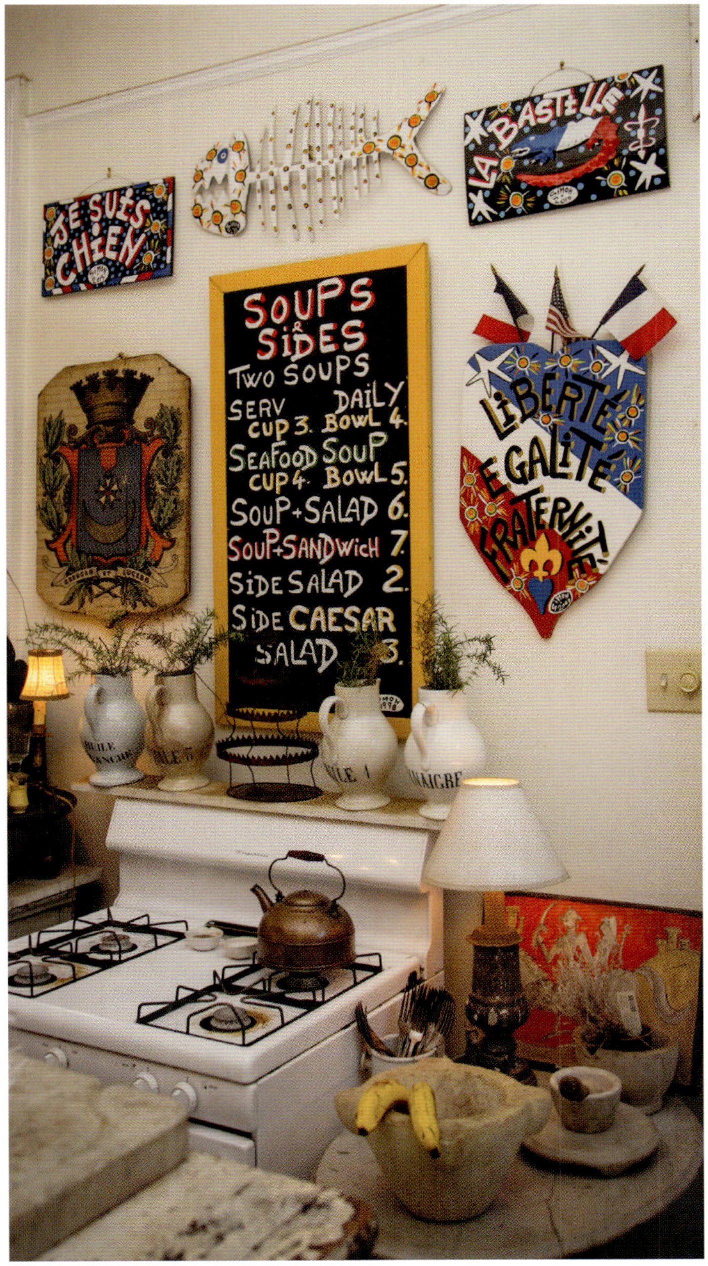

Simon's works brighten the kitchen area of the home he shares with his wife, Maria.

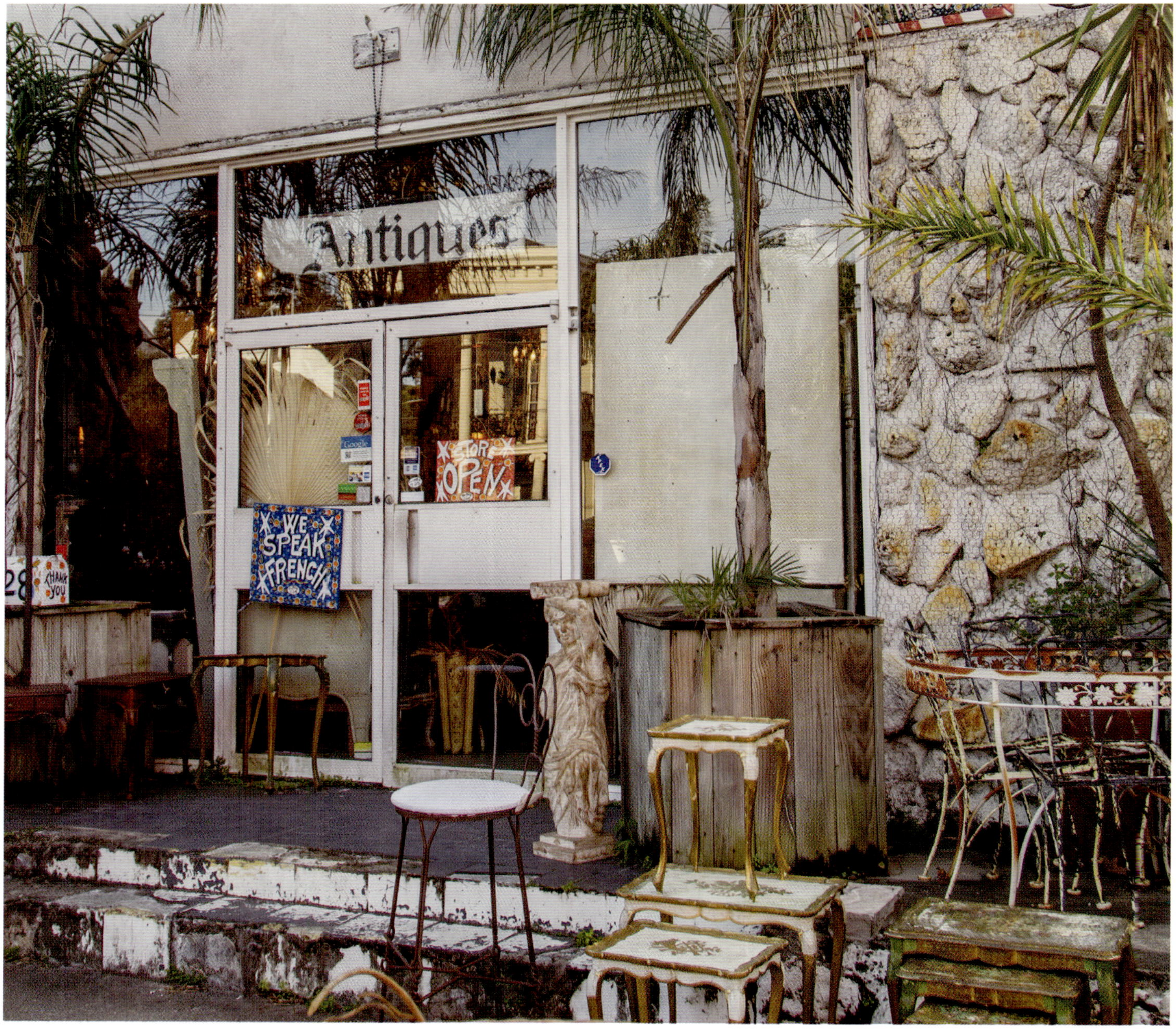

The front of Maria's shop, Antiques on Jackson, which is located in a former Popeyes restaurant.

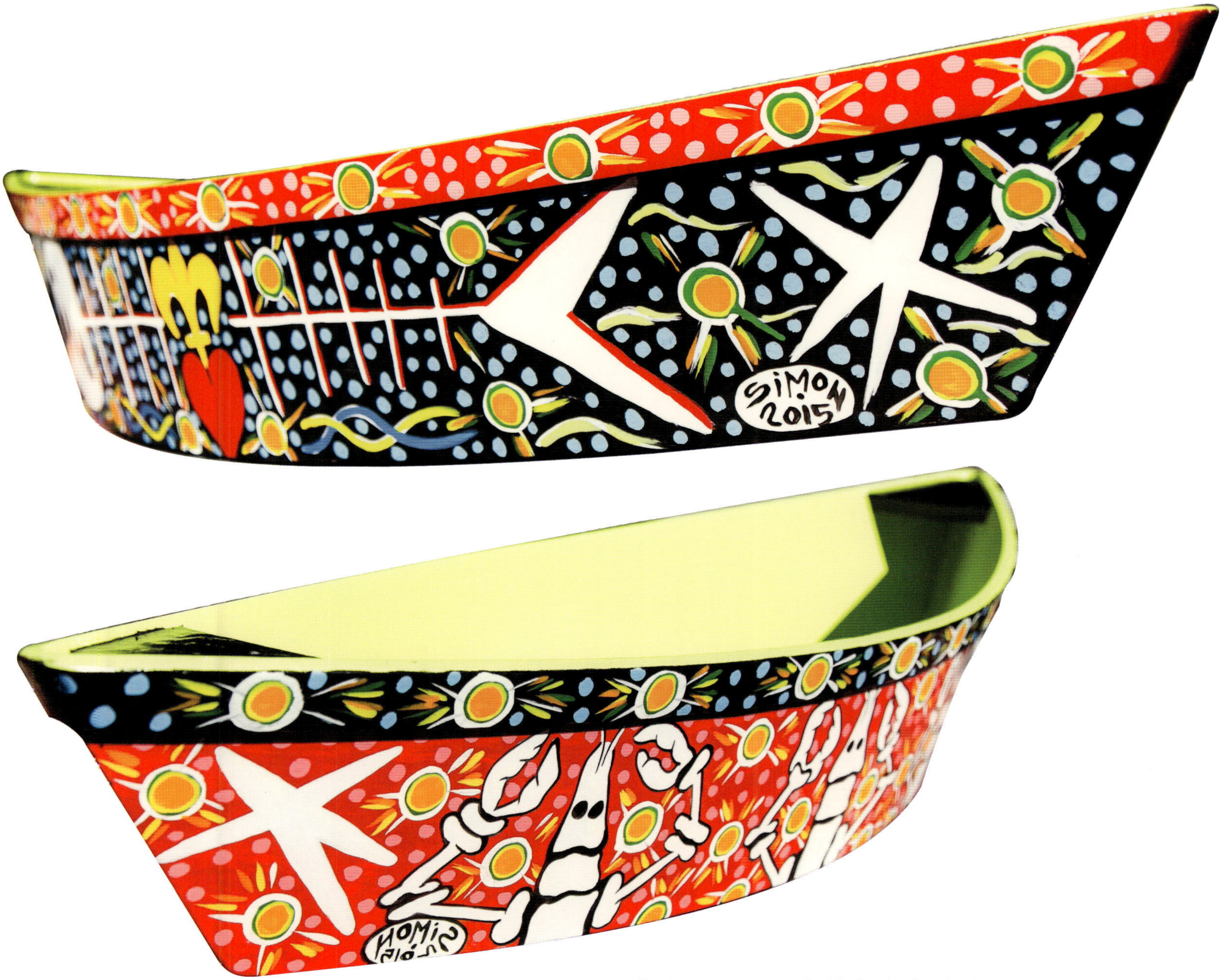

Coming to your next seafood boil is this four-foot-long pirogue, destined to be filled with heaps of steaming, freshly boiled crawfish and shrimp.

AT HOME IN NOUVELLE-ORLÉANS

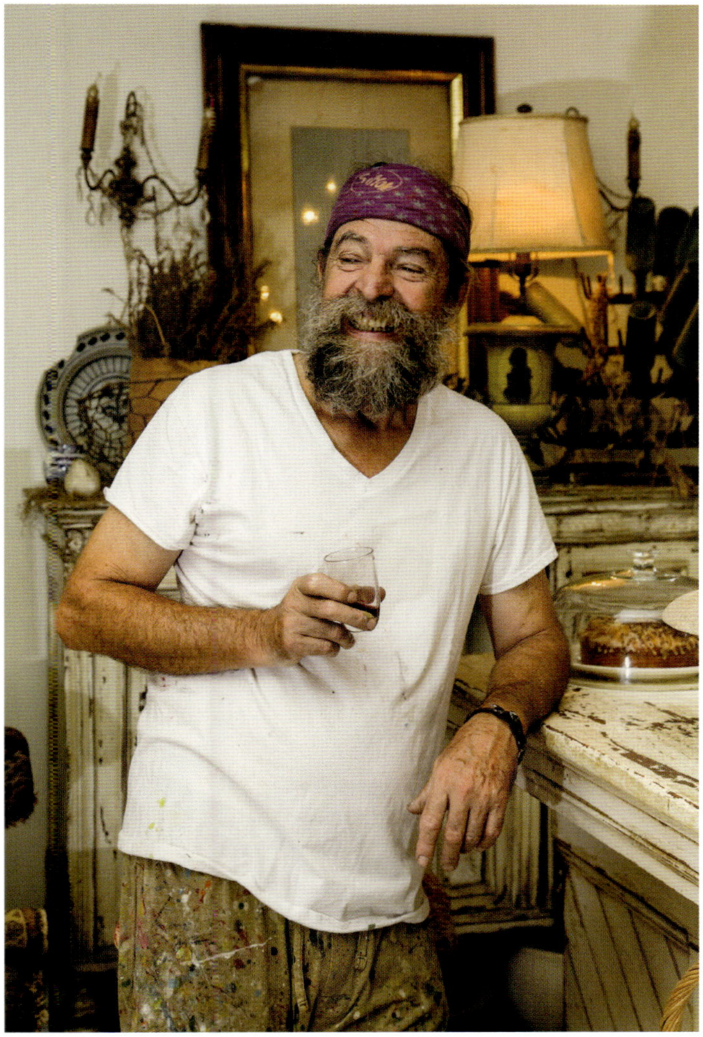

Simor at home, enjoying a glass of wine.

When asked what he wants people to know about him, Simon's answer comes quickly: "That I am married to Maria," he replies.

"Aw, is that what he said?" she asks. "He's so sweet." The pair have been together for almost three decades now. "I love spending time with him. I especially like how we can be together and be apart at the same time," she says. "We might be working side by side, yet we're each involved in our own projects—Simon with his art and me with antiques. And it's just so comfortable."

Born and raised in New Orleans, Maria is a former x-ray technician, but she has had a passion for antiques for as long as she can remember. She recalls that as a child, she and her friends would crawl under the raised shotgun houses in her Mid-City neighborhood and look for "cool stuff." If she found something really good, like a piece of old jewelry, she would wriggle out from under the house and skip down the alley to bring it to her mother. But she also kept many of the finds for herself. Pretty shells, broken vases, chipped china cups, and half-melted candles were used to decorate the rooms of her doll house and her bedroom. "I was happiest when I was decorating," she says. "I guess I was just a homebody," she muses, "and in a real sense, I guess I still am."

With a special fondness for Florentine pieces,

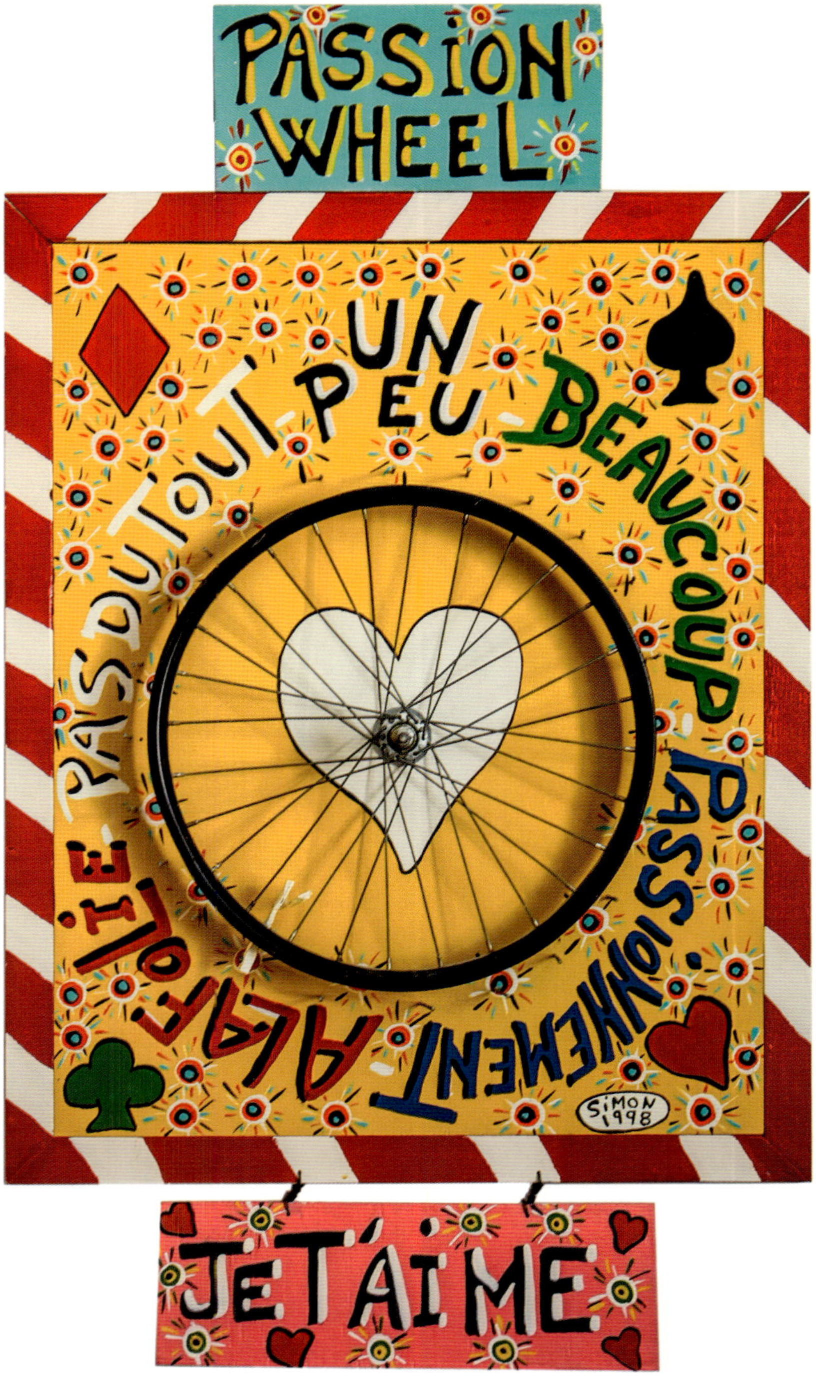

Simon expands on the traditional "loves me; loves me not" concept with his Passion Wheel, *a type of lover's roulette. This interactive piece entices the viewer to take his chances with a spin of the wheel (made from a bicycle tire rim) and find out if his sweetheart loves him Pas du Tout (Not at All); Un Peu (A Little); Beaucoup (A Lot); A La Folie (Madly); or Passionnément (Passionately). Emblazoned across the bottom are the words "Je T'Aime." (Fleishmann collection, 1998)*

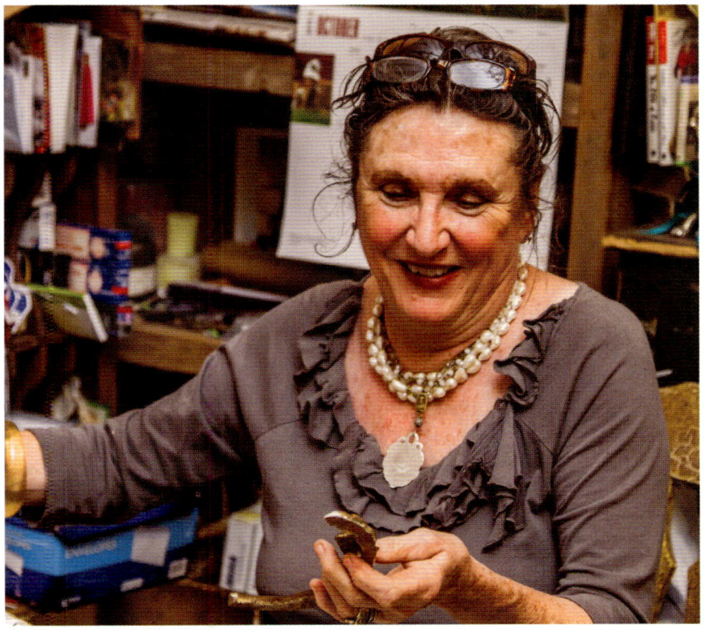

Maria Hardeveld at work in her shop, Antiques on Jackson.

she has filled her shop with antiques and Old World collectibles to be used in home décor by her customers. And, of course, she has decorated her own home in the same style, filling it with her most treasured finds. In fact, she has done so twice.

After relocating from Florida, she and Simon bought a house in Broadmoor and set to work renovating it. But with the meticulous renovation finally nearing completion, Katrina hit, the levees failed, and their home was filled with seven feet of water, ruining their treasured antiques and destroying a lifetime of irreplaceable photos.

After their evacuation, they made the decision to return to New Orleans, but it was back to square one. "We just had to bear down and get to work again. So that's what we did. The entire city did."

After being taken down to the studs, the home is now whole again, and it serves as their oasis. Two English bulldogs, Clover and Peanut, and a "mutt," Houdini (the escape artist), share the space with them, or more correctly, they allow Simon and Maria to share *their* space. Simon is also a fan of antiques and time-worn furniture, and he feels comfortable in the home. "At the end of a long day, I can't wait to get home, relax, and have a glass (or two) of wine with Maria and play with the dogs."

The studio in his home is also an oasis of sorts. Sometimes he uses it to get work done, but it is also a place where he goes when struck with an inspiration. And it is a popular hangout for him and his grandchildren, a place where he encourages them to design and create their own artwork.

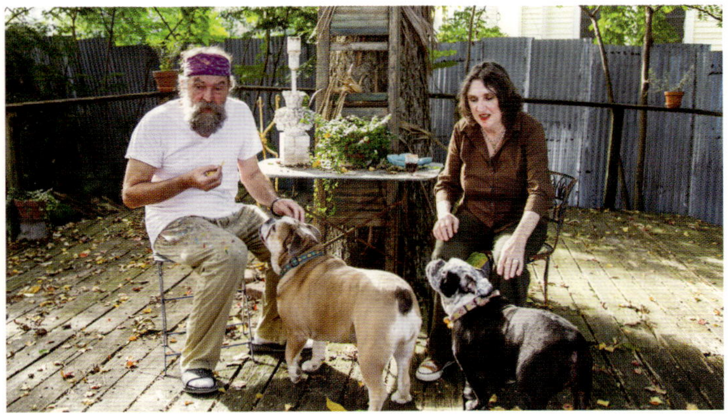

Avid dog lovers, the couple enjoys spending the evenings in the backyard of their home where their three dogs, Clover, Peanut, and Houdini, join them.

"To see Simon's true personality," says Maria, "all you have to do is look at his art. It is full of playful humor and clever wit. So is Simon."

It's been a long, improbable journey that has taken a classically trained chef from the foothills of the French Alps and transformed him into a renowned folk artist loving life in the lowlands of Louisiana. But Simon feels there is a reason that the journey has brought him to where he is. "I hope to capture in my art the story of this period in New Orleans history," he says.

Those who know and appreciate his work might add that not only has he done just that, but he has also captured—in bright colors—the soul and spirit of the city.

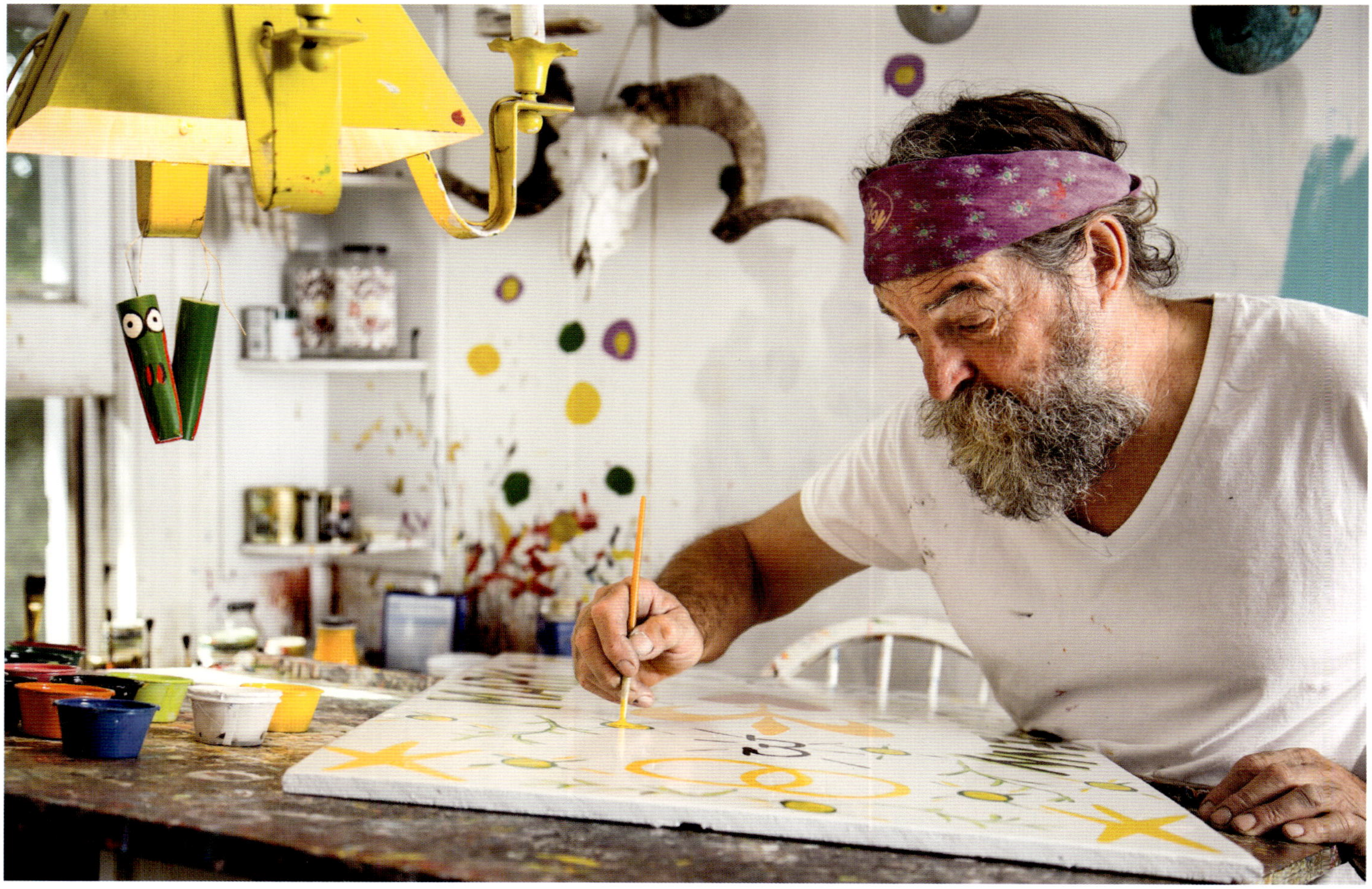

Many of Simon's inspirations come to him while working in the quiet upstairs studio of his home in Broadmoor.

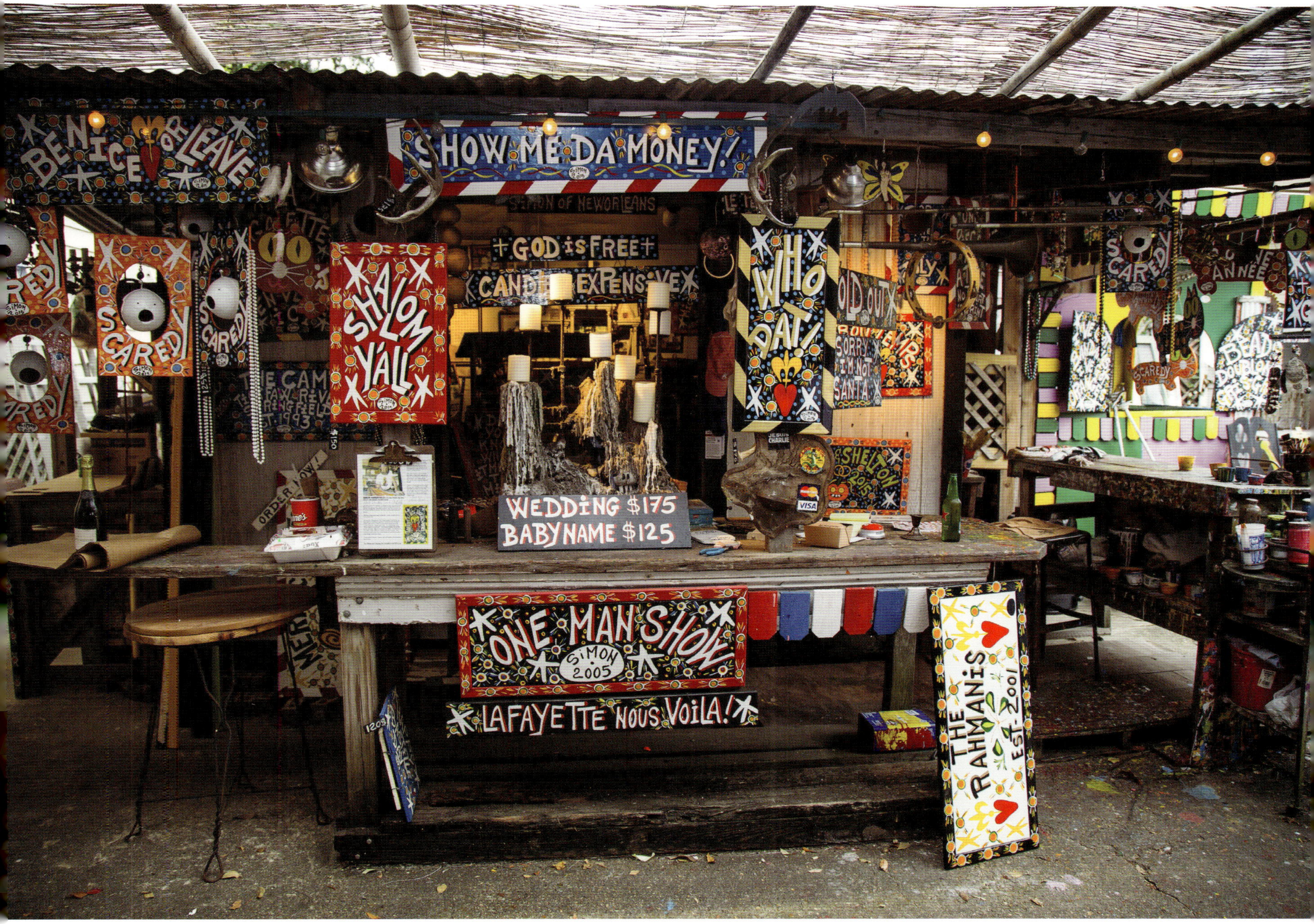

The main work area in Simon's studio on Jackson Avenue.

THE CUISINE-ART CONNECTION

In a move that combines a feast for the palate with a feast from the palette, Simon has struck a symbiotic relationship with many area restaurants. His artwork is displayed on the walls of local establishments, putting a definitive New Orleans stamp on the restaurant's ambience. In return, his art reaches a larger audience.

Simon's first experiences in combining local art with local cuisine began when he was a restaurateur in Florida and hosted art shows for local artists in his restaurants. When he arrived in New Orleans, he again sought relationships between local restaurants and local art, this time as the artist instead of as the restaurateur.

It's been a successful liaison for both, and according to Simon, a providential one too. "My signs are good luck," he insists with a wink. "Every business that has put up my signs, they have all done well."

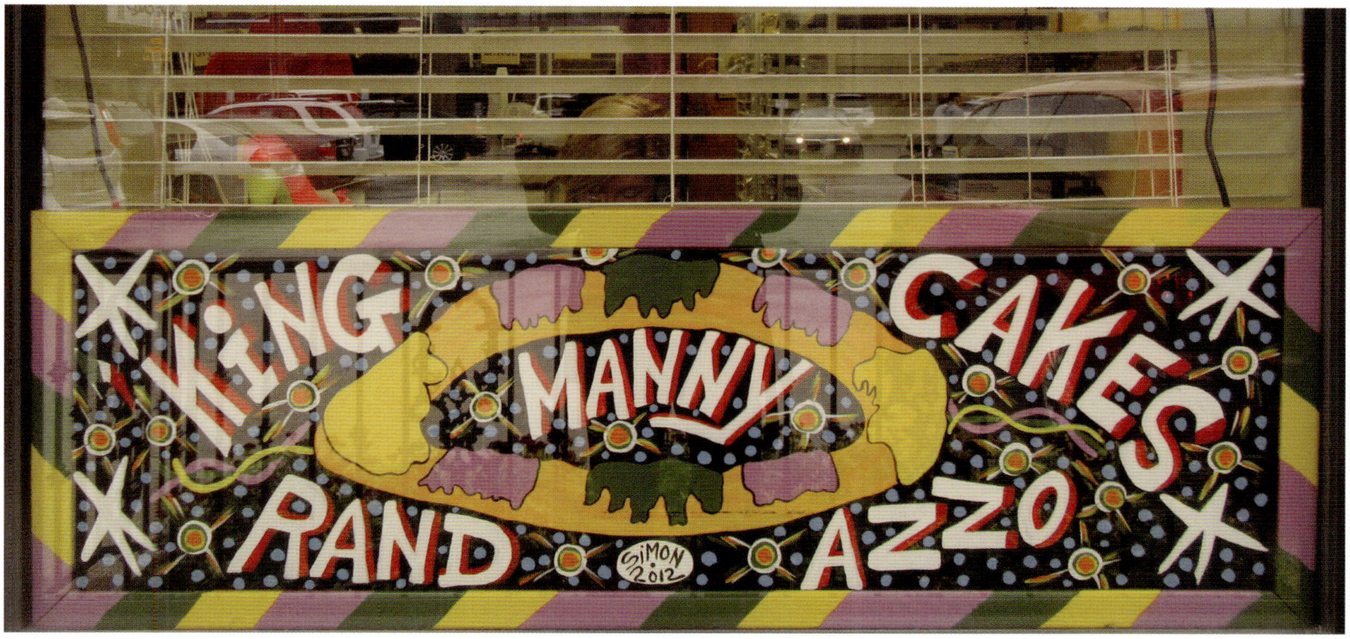

Manny Randazzo's King Cakes in Metairie, Louisiana.

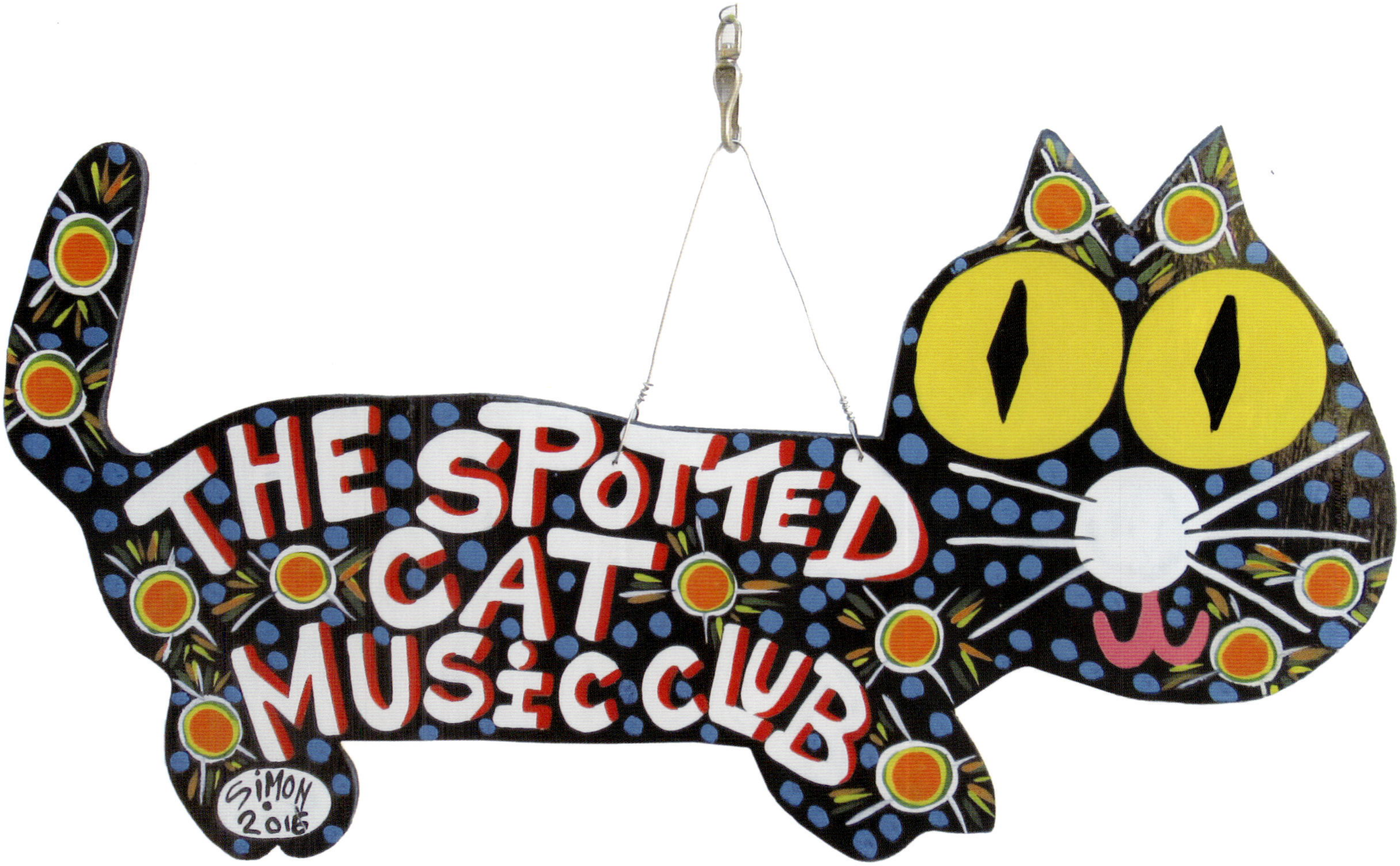

Many local businesses use Simon's hand-painted custom signs.

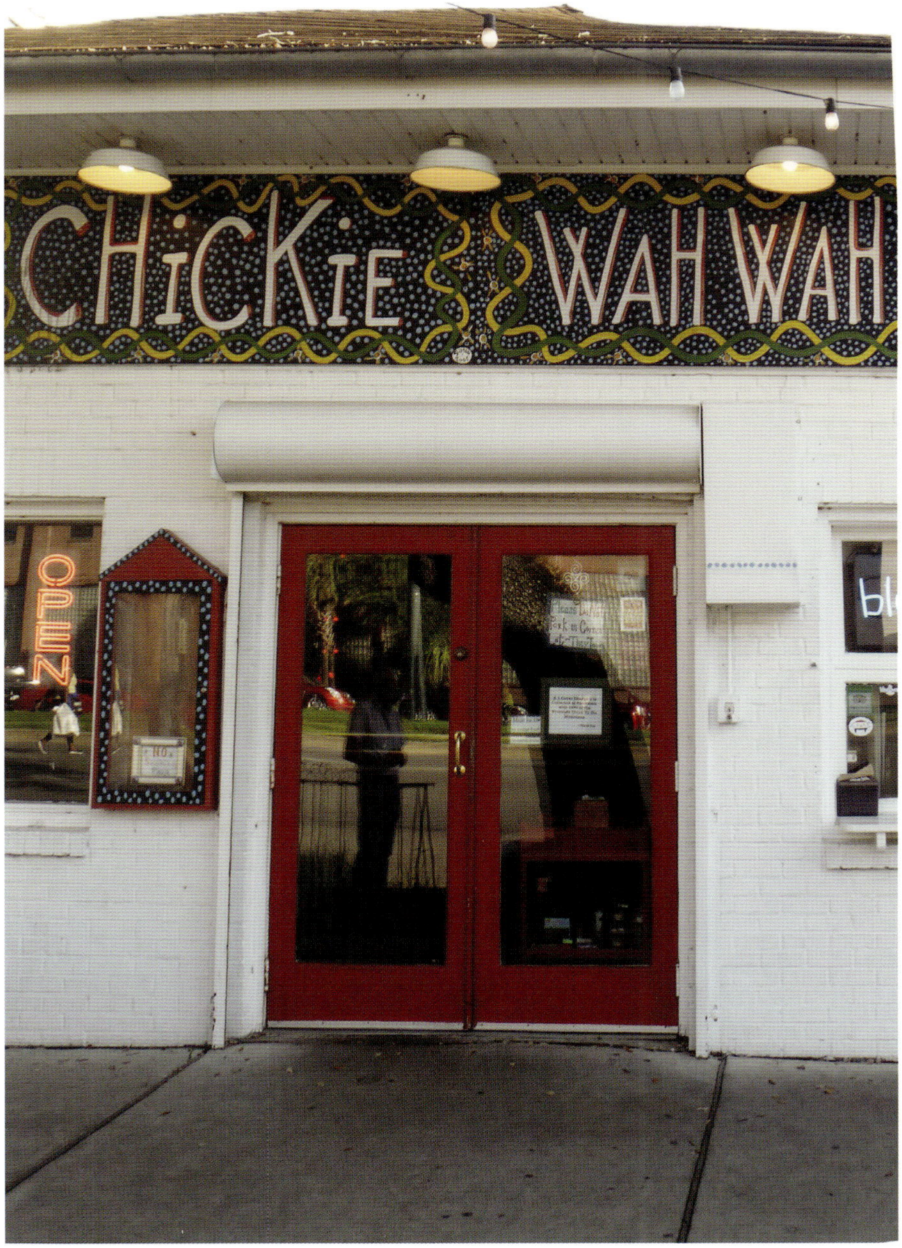

Chickie Wah Wah's on Canal Street.

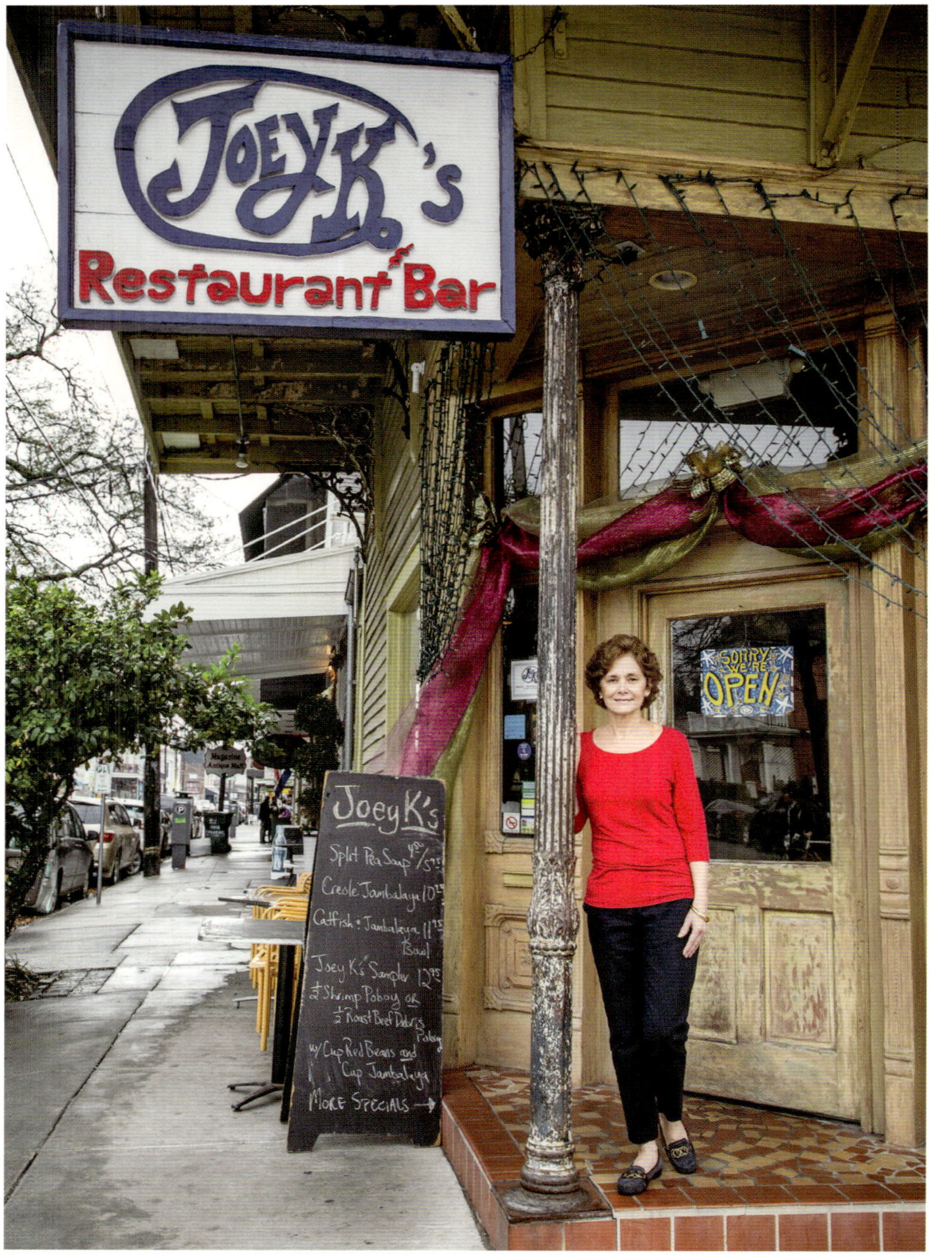

Co-owner Cindy Farnet outside Joey K's.

JOEY K'S

3001 MAGAZINE STREET NEW ORLEANS

Not long after Sam and Cindy Farnet bought the property at 3001 Magazine Street and assumed ownership of Joey K's Restaurant, they became friends with Simon and Maria, neighbors in the same Magazine Street community. At one point, they had discussed with Simon the possibility of placing a couple of his signs in their restaurant.

Then Hurricane Katrina hit. The restaurant was closed for a time while the city struggled to get back on its feet and the Farnets struggled to get Joey K's up and running again. Not long after Joey's reopened, Simon stopped by and brought a few signs, and then a few more signs. Before long he had filled the walls. Cindy, who had dreaded the task of having to come up with and execute a new decorative theme, was delighted that Simon had taken care of it for her. And the look was an instant hit. His work is now an iconic part of the appearance and feel of the restaurant.

Cindy states that locals and tourists alike enjoy Simon's art and the upbeat, casual tone it brings to the restaurant. She says that

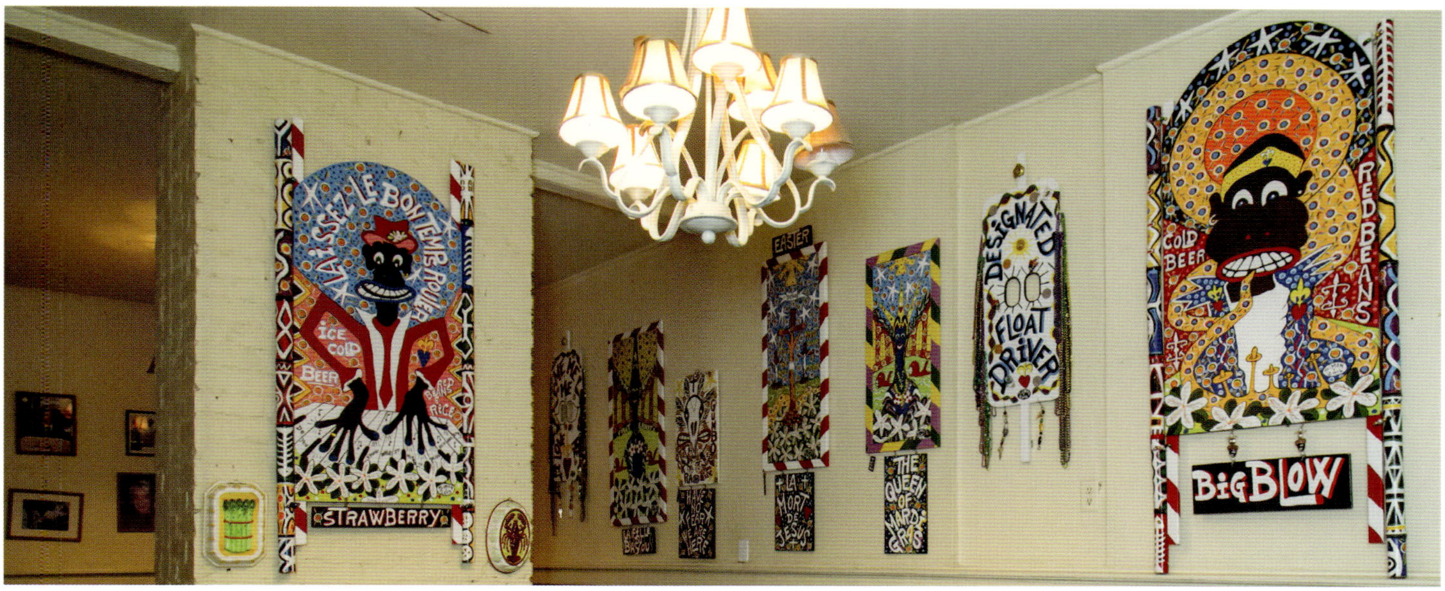

Large works by Simon fill the walls of the back dining room.

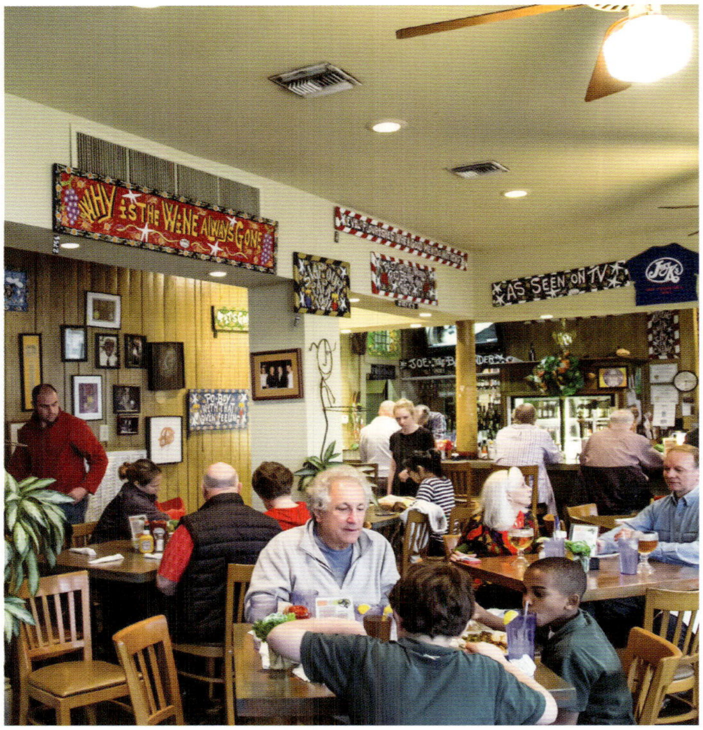

The front dining room is filled with customers and Simon signs.

sometimes the diners scratch their heads (especially the tourists) when they first read some of the signs. Then a smile emerges when they finally "get" it.

As the pieces sell—and they sell quickly—Simon refills the empty spaces. Farnet says that one of the most popular signs is the one that proclaims "Parade Route." Another popular piece is the "Bar-macy" sign that hangs over the restaurant's front door, but usually it does not remain there for long. For some reason, people just have to have this one, and it must be replaced regularly.

The building at Magazine and Seventh Streets that now houses Joey K's has a long history as a restaurant. More than fifty years ago, Tony's opened in the same location. The lady who owned it had a son named Joey who helped her run the establishment, and she turned it

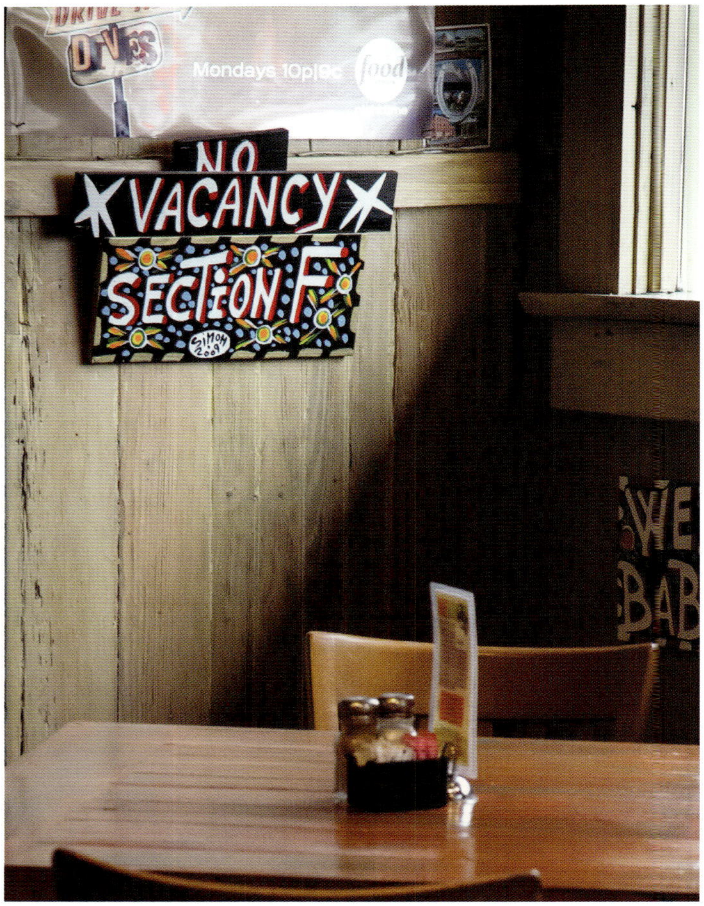

The Honorable Dennis Waldron, longtime judge for Orleans Criminal Court, Section F, ate lunch at this corner table every workday for many years. When Waldron retired, Simon painted a sign to designate the table where the judge had held court of a different kind, socializing and bantering with other restaurant patrons.

over to him in the 1970s. When Joey had a daughter, he named her Joey K and decided to rename the restaurant in his daughter's honor. It has remained Joey K's ever since. When the Farnets bought the property, they decided to keep the name.

They are only the third family to own the building. The structure, originally built in 1847, remained with the original family, passing from generation to generation, for well over a century. Family members finally sold it around

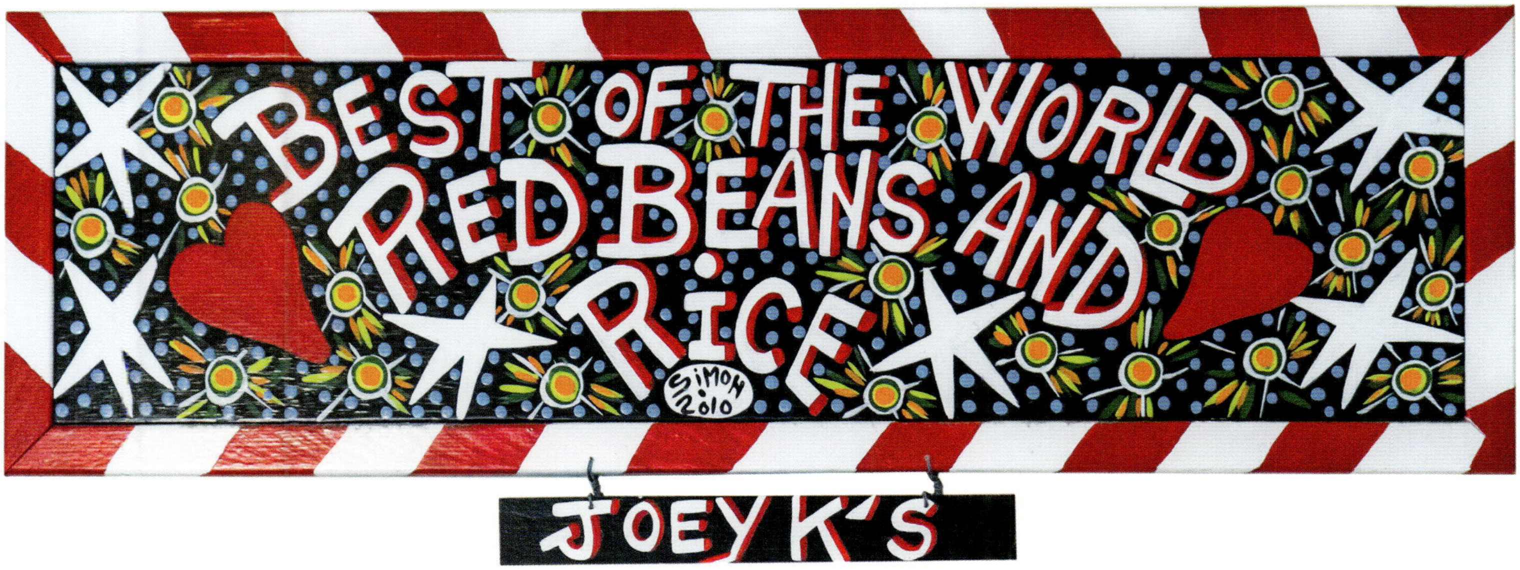

Best of the World Red Beans and Rice *is a winner's plaque painted by Simon to commemorate the honor bestowed on Joey K's by the readers of* Gambit, *who named the restaurant their favorite purveyor of the city's traditional Monday dish.*

1960, and the Farnets bought it from those second owners in 1989.

The restaurant is perennially popular. *Gambit* readers have bestowed it with the titles "Best Lunch Specials" and "Best Red Beans and Rice" in the magazine's annual "Best of New Orleans" poll. And it has been showcased on the Food Network's *Diners, Drive-Ins and Dives.*

Cindy recalls that when they first moved into the area and took over operation of Joey K's, the Magazine Street corridor was not the bustling, popular area it is today. There were far too many empty shops and abandoned residences. Sometimes they felt alone on the block and often asked themselves, "What were we thinking?"

Then one by one the empty buildings were bought and renovated. New businesses ventured into the area. By the early 2000s the renaissance had taken hold, only to become a genuine "boom" in the rebuilding after Katrina.

"Now it has become a real neighborhood," says Farnet. "We've gotten to know so many wonderful people." The young couples and families are back, living and working in the neighborhood. The commercial area bustles with both locals and tourists. It is a walking neighborhood with most necessities within easy distance.

The Farnets remain friends with Simon. "With Simon, what you see is what you get," Cindy says. "And what you get is upbeat and genuine."

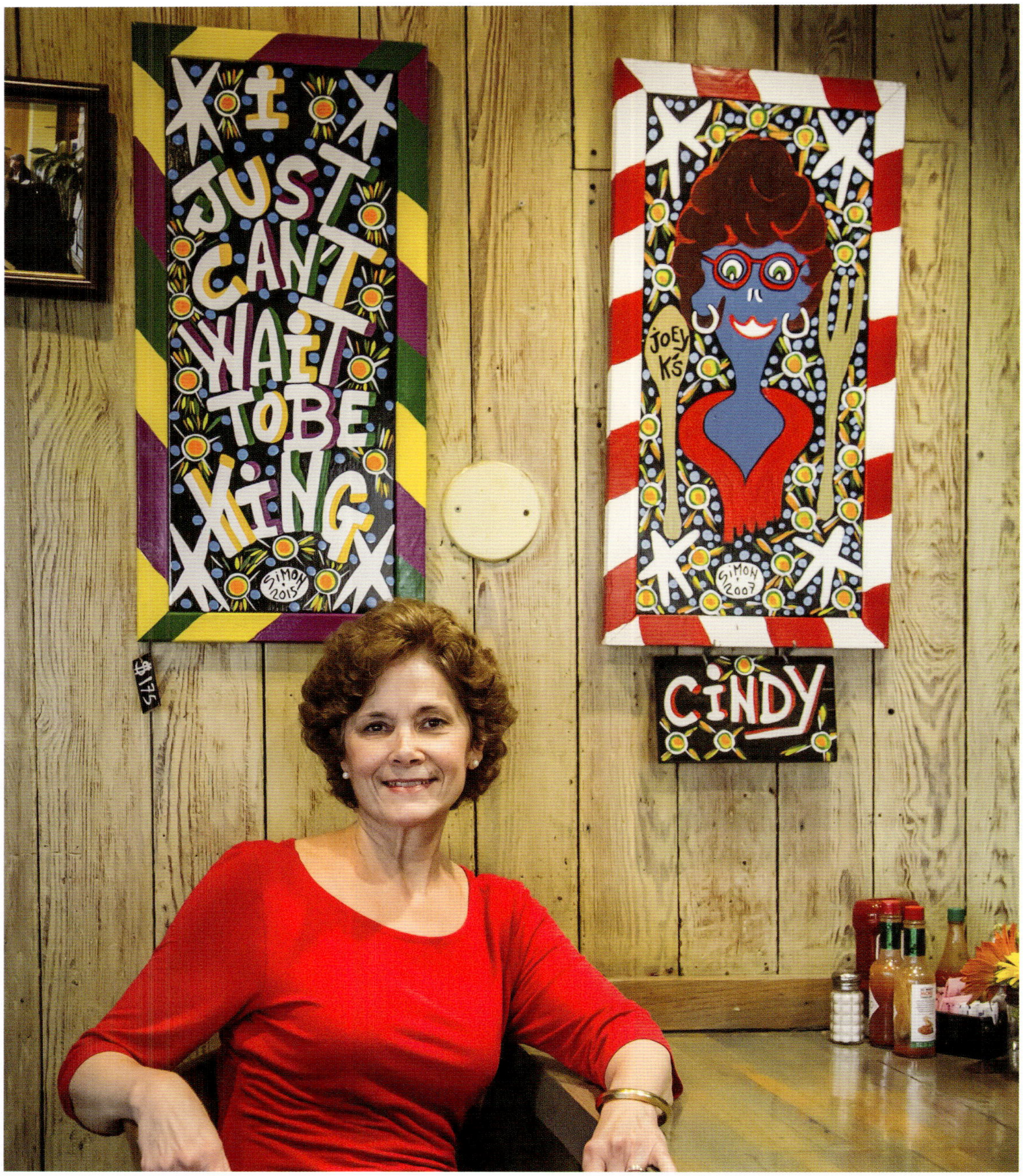

Cindy Farnet of Joey K's poses with with her portrait, painted by Simon.

SHRIMP MAGAZINE

One of Joey K's most popular dishes.

1 lb. large shrimp, peeled
Flour for dredging (seasoned with salt and pepper)
1/4 cup olive oil
1 tbsp. fresh garlic, minced
8 slices of ham, chopped
1 can of quartered artichoke hearts
1/4 cup white wine
1 stick butter, melted
1 tbsp. Worcestershire sauce
1 tbsp. Cajun seasoning
1 tbsp. fresh basil
Capellini (angel hair) pasta
Green onion
Parmesan cheese
Fresh parsley

Dredge shrimp in seasoned flour. Heat oil in a large sauce pan and sauté shrimp for about a minute, until shrimp are almost pink. Add garlic, ham, artichoke hearts, white wine, butter, Worcestershire sauce, Cajun seasoning, and basil. Stir to combine. Sauté for a few more minutes until shrimp are fully cooked. Serve over pasta. Garnish with green onion, parmesan cheese, and parsley. Serves 4.

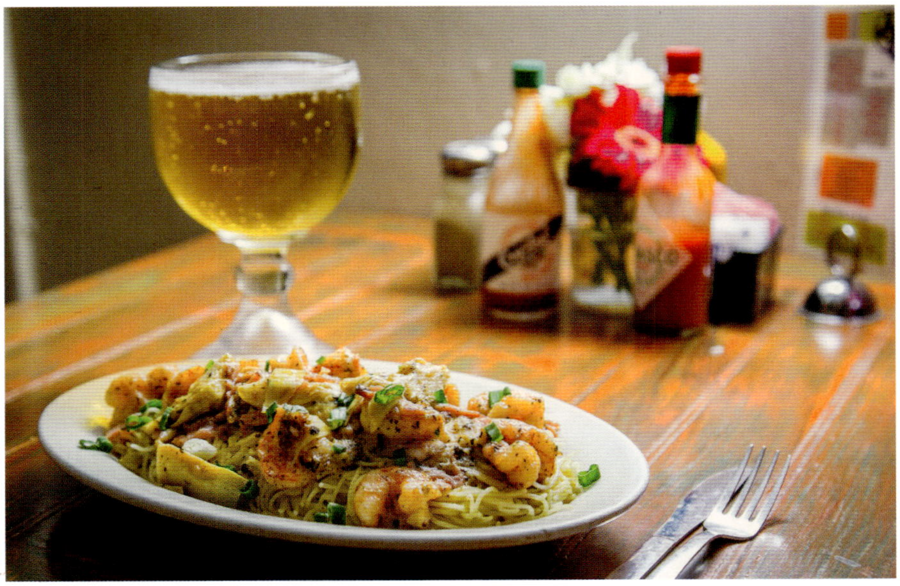

Shrimp Magazine, one of Joey K's most popular menu items.

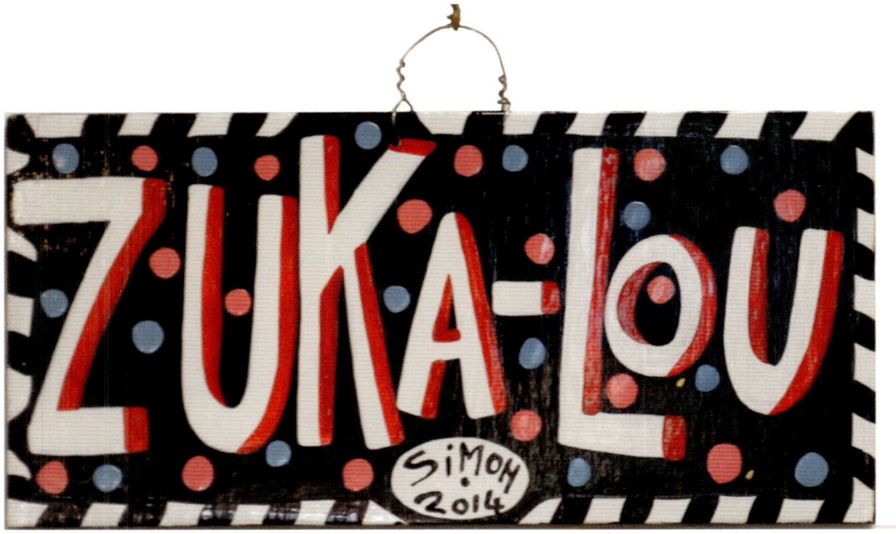

The restroom at ZukaBaby sports this Zuka-Lou sign, a humorous nod to the British term for a bathroom.

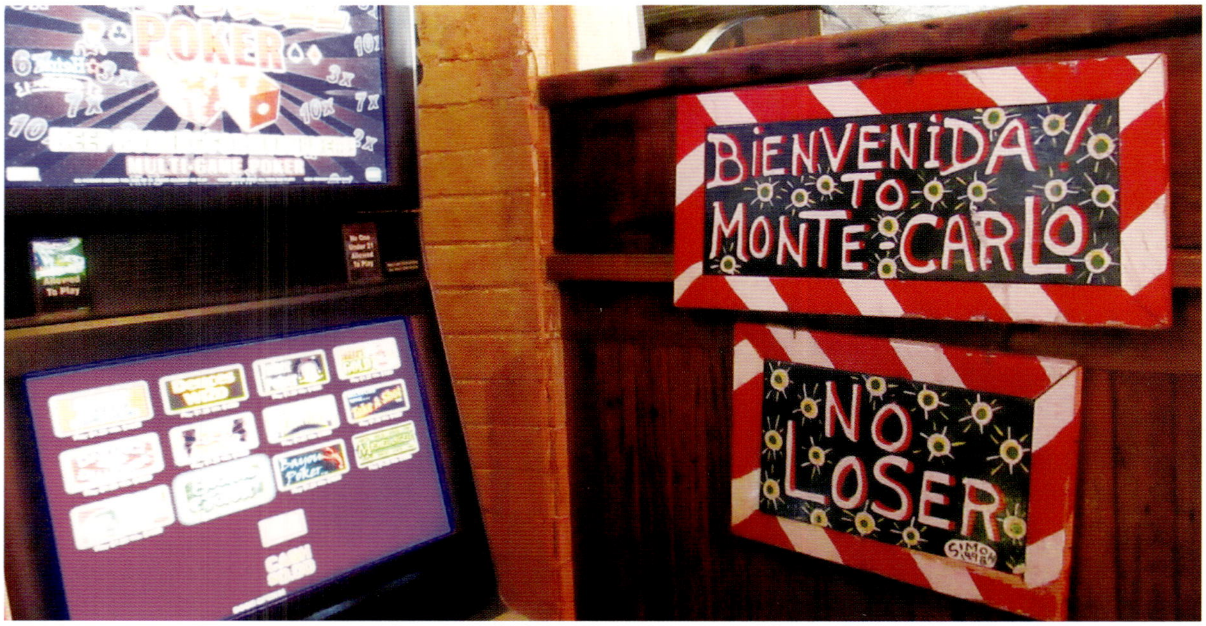

The gaming area at Superior Grill on St. Charles Avenue.

LOLA'S

3312 ESPLANADE AVENUE
NEW ORLEANS

Angel Miranda, a native of Seville, Spain, opened his first New Orleans restaurant, Altamira, in the Warehouse District across from the Hilton Hotel in the 1980s. Angel, an art aficionado, hand painted the restaurant's tables and its dining room walls. When Altamira closed, Angel opened Lola's Restaurant on Esplanade Avenue in Faubourg St. John, naming the restaurant after his mother.

Not long after, Angel met Simon, who had just moved to the city from Florida. Finding they shared a love of art and wine, the two became friends, and Angel asked Simon to supply the paintings that embellish the restaurant's walls.

Lola's current owner, Juan Miranda, was just a child when his father and Simon became friends, and he remembers the two men spending evenings discussing art and drinking wine while Simon painted originals for display at the restaurant.

Opened in 1994, Lola's occupies a small space, but it has a large following. It was the first restaurant to offer true Spanish fare to

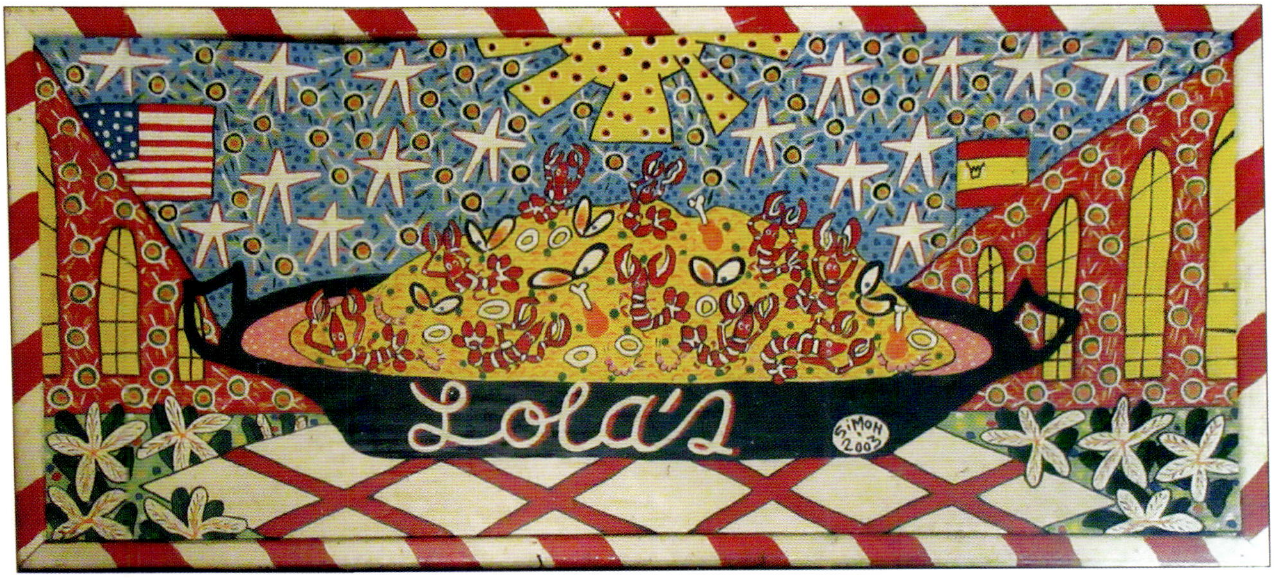

A painting of a large platter of paella hangs above the kitchen at Lola's. (Photo by author)

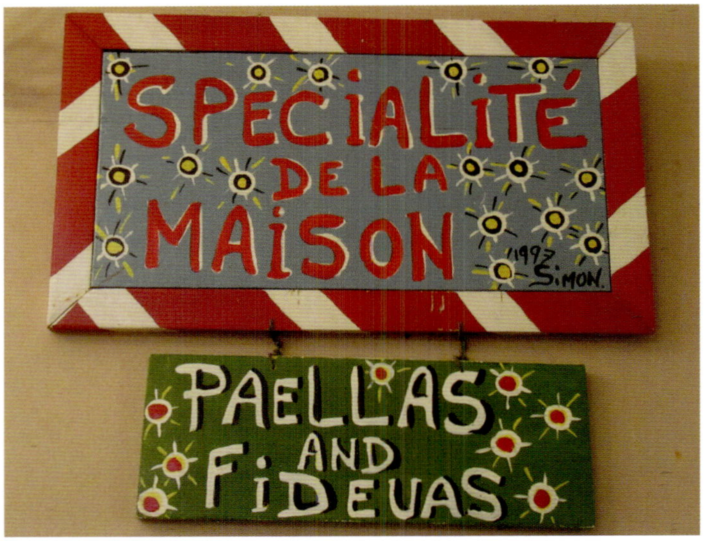

Painted in 1997, this sign advertises the specialties of the house. (Photo by author)

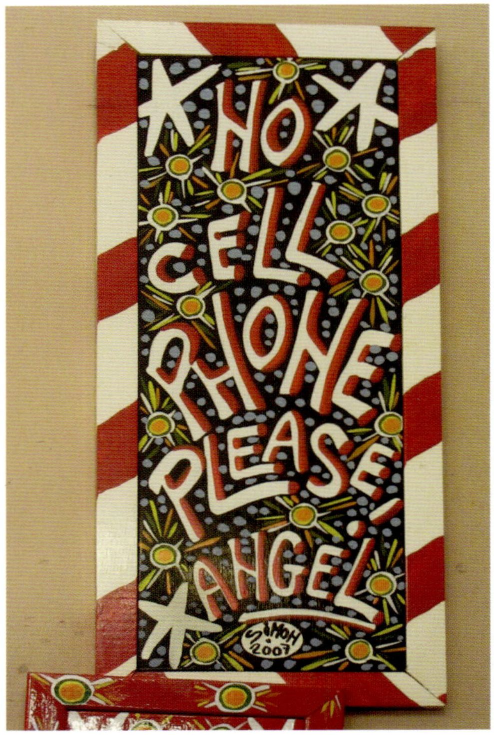

This sign is special to Miranda because it was painted by Simon at his father's request. The sign also contains his father's name. (Photo by author)

New Orleans diners. "My dad worked so hard to make Lola's a successful place," says Juan. Angel operated the restaurant as its owner and chef until his death in 2011.

"Angel was a nice guy," says Simon. "And a great chef. He made sure that his restaurants were true to the cuisines of Spain and Cuba."

The restaurant still displays and sells Simon's artwork. One of Juan's favorite pieces has his father's name on it. Simon is well known for his anti-technology stance, and apparently Angel had a similar leaning back in the 1990s. The sign, prominently displayed, reads: "No cell phone please! Angel." Another sign that Juan likes is *"Not You Again"*—which Angel had hung over the bathroom door as a joke.

Juan also remembers a large piece of Simon's artwork that featured a poem written in French and decorated with paintings of French flags and a French woman. Completed in 1997, the art adorned the restaurant wall for years, and Juan grew fond of it. He was sad to see it go when it was eventually bought by a customer.

"Simon is just a great guy," says Juan. "Although I don't know him quite as well as my Dad did, he was around quite a bit when I was growing up, and it doesn't take long to figure that out."

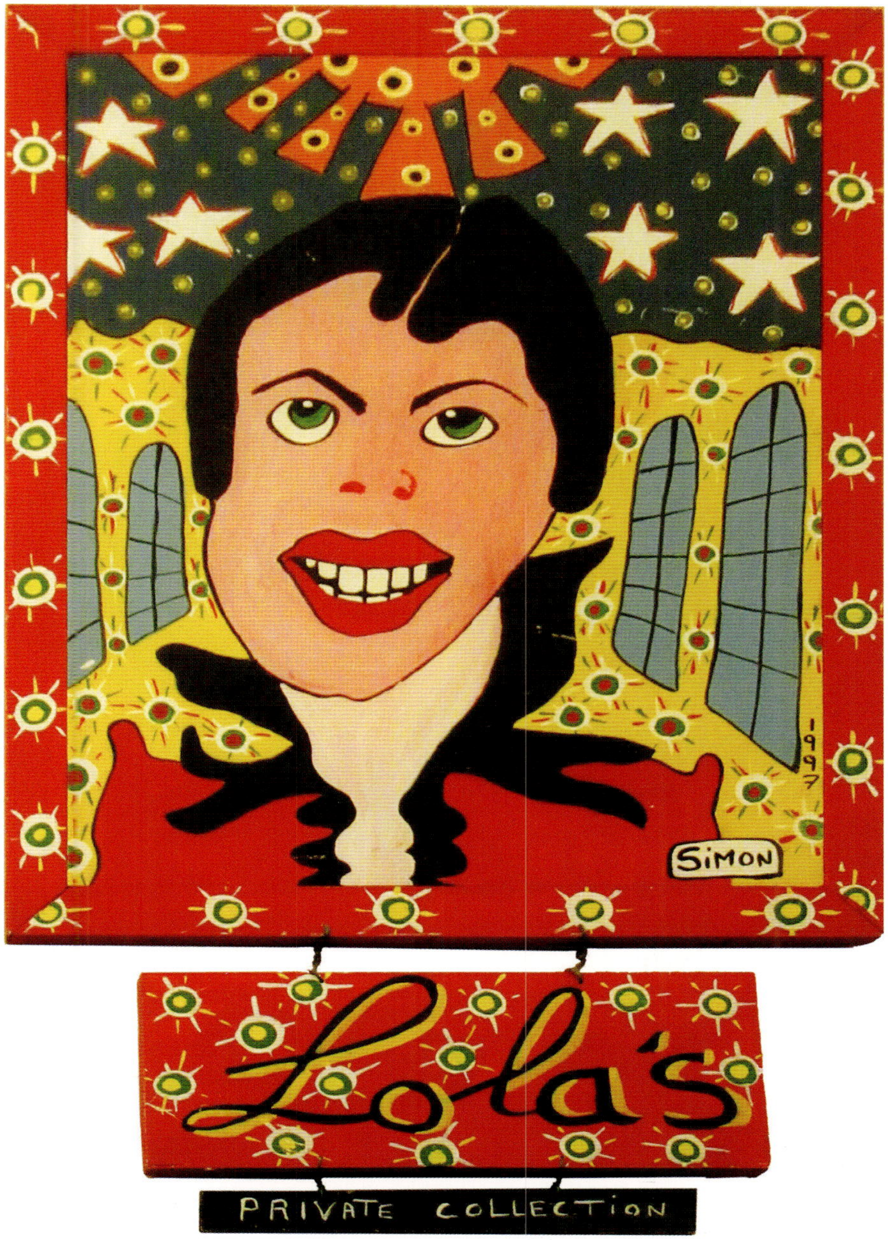

Lola Miranda, the subject of this painting and the namesake of the Esplanade Avenue restaurant, was the mother of Angel Miranda, the restaurant's founder, and grandmother of the current owner, Juan Miranda. (Photo by author)

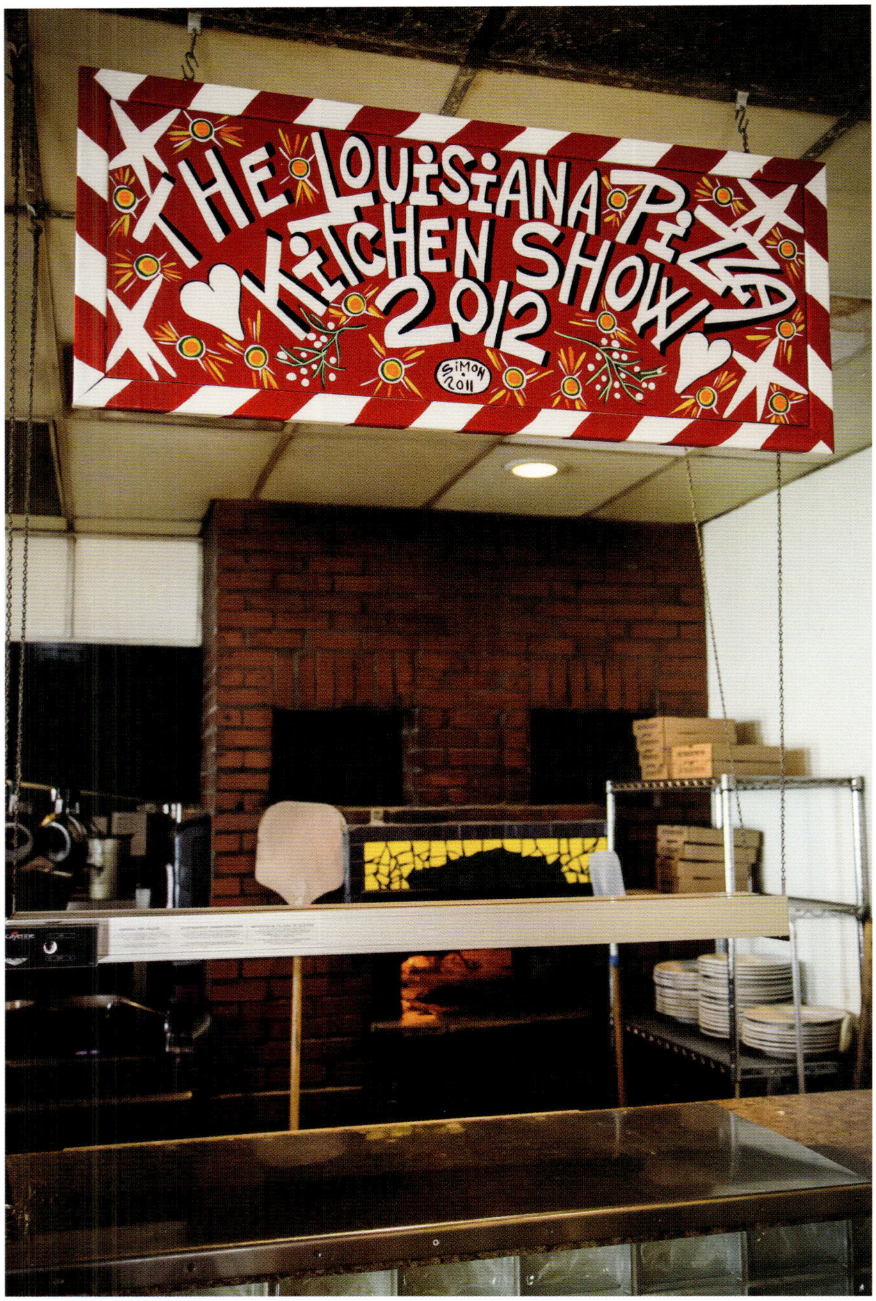

By design, the kitchen at Louisiana Pizza Kitchen is visible to customers.

LOUISIANA PIZZA KITCHEN

615 S. CARROLLTON AVE NEW ORLEANS

Rob Gerhart, owner of the Louisiana Pizza Kitchen on Carrollton Avenue, had noticed the somewhat unconventional-looking guy in his restaurant on previous occasions. Because the man was a regular customer, Gerhart decided it was time to get to know him; so one afternoon he joined the man at his table. Thus began his friendship with Simon.

Up until that point, Gerhart hadn't known that Simon was an artist or that many of the artworks he had noticed around the city had been created by the customer sitting at one of his tables enjoying a pizza. This first meeting took place in the late 1990s, when Simon's work was just beginning to gain popularity.

The restaurant had long maintained a policy of supporting local artists by offering them a venue in which to showcase their work and then forwarding all proceeds to the artist. Not long after getting to know Simon, Gerhart asked him why he hadn't asked to have his art displayed on the restaurant's walls. Simon shrugged and said he was there for the pizza, not for a place to display his art.

But in the end, his art *was* displayed there. In fact, not only were Simon's works placed around the restaurant and featured on its website, for several years the Louisiana Pizza Kitchen also sponsored a showing of his art every year at Christmas.

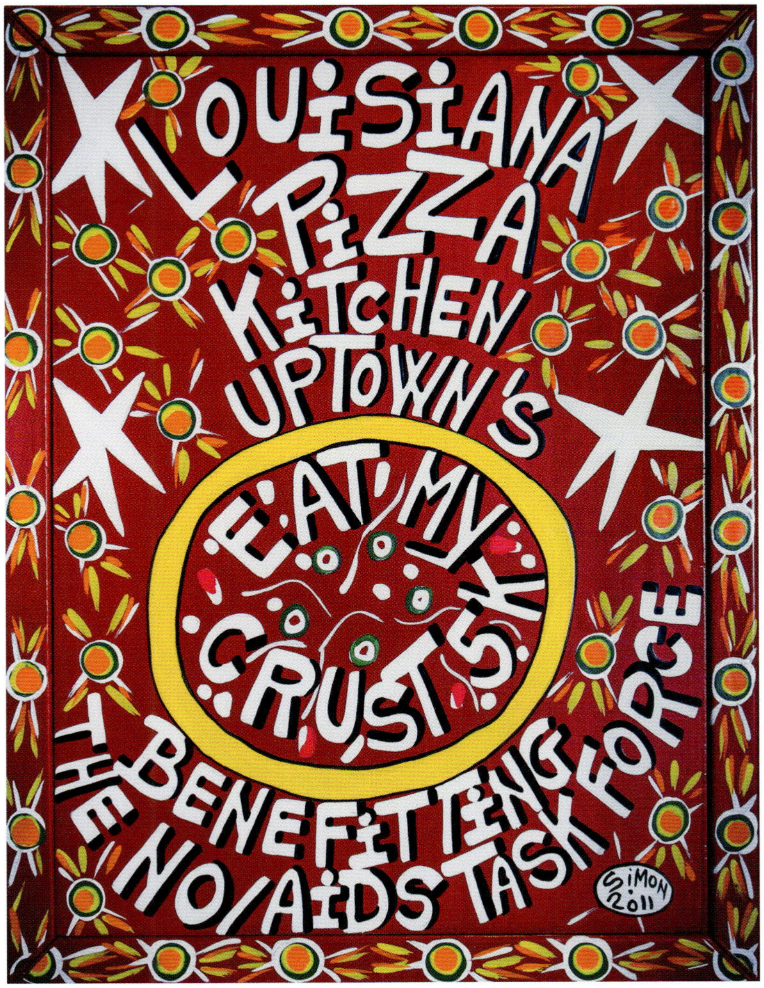

Louisiana Pizza Kitchen and Simon have collaborated on events to benefit the community.

Many of Simon's signs are still displayed on the website and at the restaurant, especially behind the bar. They include "Oh No! Not You Again!" and "Please God, Don't Sue Me." Although there are signs for sale, Gerhart now owns many of them himself and has taken them off the market in order to keep them as permanent fixtures in the pizzeria. In addition, he has a collection of Simon's seasonal pieces which he displays at certain times of the year, including Thanksgiving, Christmas, Mardi Gras, and the Fourth of July.

Over the years Simon has designed and executed pieces specifically for Gerhart and the restaurant. The large sign stating "Louisiana Pizza Kitchen Show" hangs over the open entrance to the kitchen, which—by design—is visible to the customers in the dining area.

One day Gerhart mentioned to Simon that earlier in the week singer Willie Nelson had stopped in to eat at the restaurant. The next time Simon returned, he brought with him a sign featuring a large red, white, and blue guitar and the proclamation: "Willie Nelson Eat Here. Me too."

Gerhart says that Simon's artwork functions as conversation pieces in the restaurant, and he enjoys telling customers that he and Simon are friends.

"Simon is a fantastic individual," says Gerhart, "and he has such an intense love for this city. It's always great to talk with him, not only because of his amazing accent, but also because he is such a wonderful listener." He offers this tip: "I always find it easier to understand Simon's accent after we've had a couple of drinks. I don't know if his English gets better or my French gets better—but I don't speak French."

Gerhart originally worked at the Esplanade and Broad location of Louisiana Pizza Kitchen after his graduation from LSU in 1991. When the owners split the multi-location corporation into separately owned and operated restaurants, Gerhart took over the Riverbend location. In the years since, it has become a staple of the Uptown and university area. He is proud to point out that, with the help of friends, family, and a skeleton crew, the South Carrollton Louisiana Pizza Kitchen was one of the first area restaurants to reopen after Hurricane Katrina.

Gerhart is also proud that his restaurant is very involved in the community, and that includes its ongoing support of local artists. "It's so cool to think that we may have played even a small part in helping a local artist make it big."

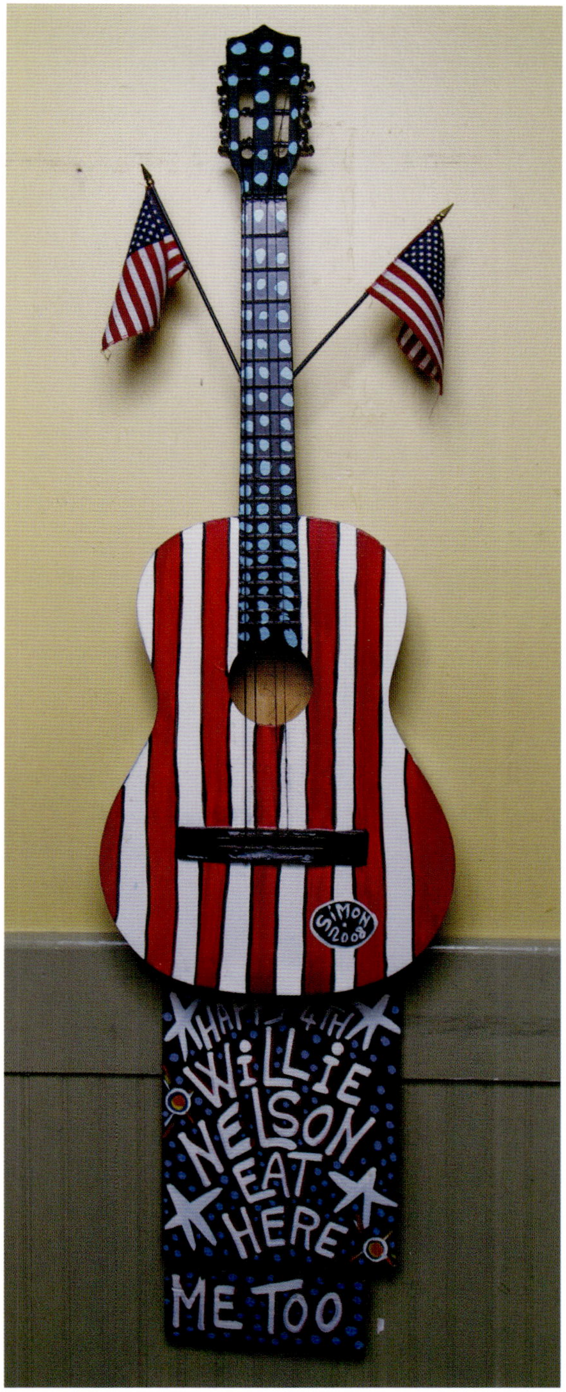

Simon commemorated Willie Nelson's visit to the Carrollton Avenue Louisiana Pizza Kitchen with this piece.

ROASTED DUCK PIZZA

Gerhart reveals the ingredients for one of the restaurant's most popular menu choices:

Duck breast
Mushrooms
Roma tomatoes
Grapes
Grape demi-glace
Mozzarella cheese

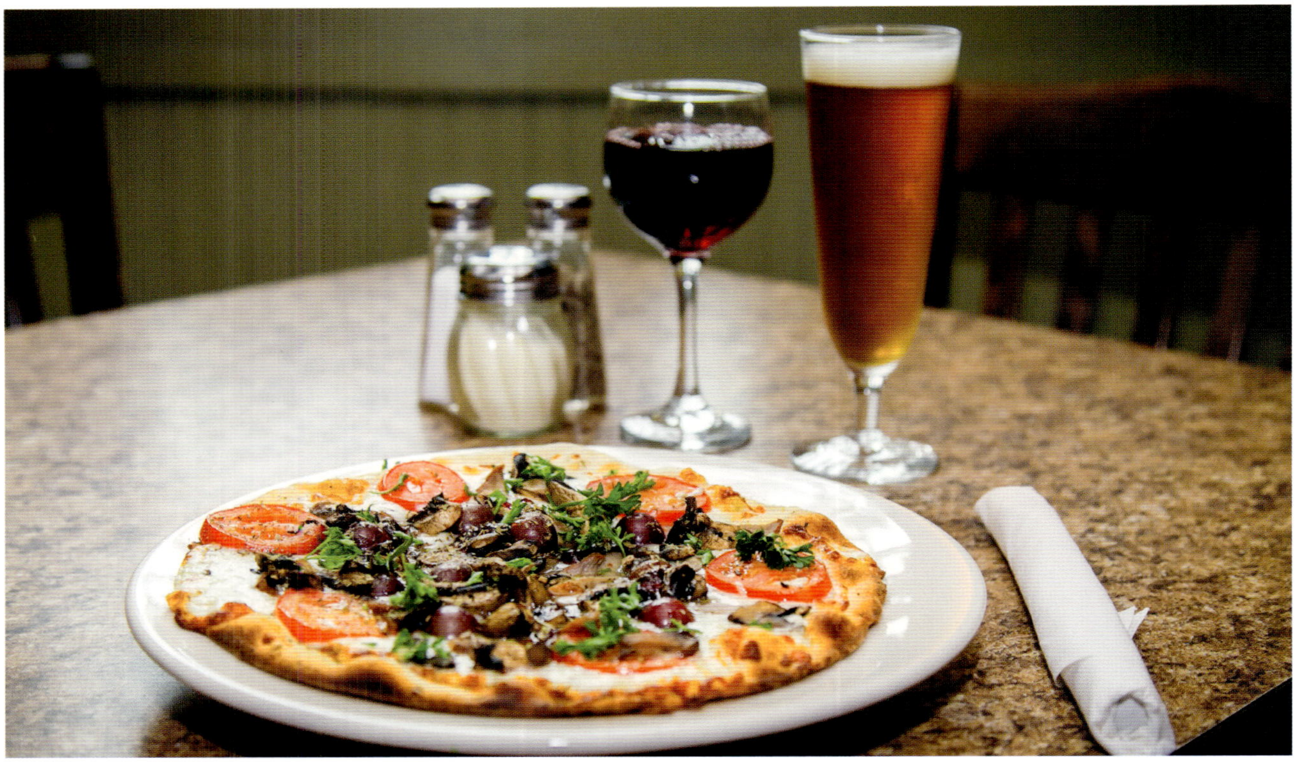

Roasted duck pizza

DAT DOG

5030 FRERET STREET
NEW ORLEANS, LA

The broadest smile in the city comes cradled in a bun and drizzled with ribbons of mustard and ketchup. It's the Simon-created, mouth-watering, grinning hot dog logo that identifies the city's Dat Dog restaurants: two locations Uptown, one in the Marigny, one in Metairie, and one in Lafayette.

Dat Dog owner and co-founder Constantine Georges and former co-owner Skip Murray brought Simon into the picture early on, just as they were opening the first Dat Dog in a small shed on Freret Street in 2011. Georges had met the artist through friend and fellow restaurateur Wolfram Koehler, owner and brewmaster of Crescent City Brewhouse and a Simon devotee.

Simon and the owners discussed logo designs and eventually settled on the now well-known hot dog smile, along with other Simon pieces which were prominently displayed at the original location. "Simon's designs were 'spot-on' for what I was looking for," says Georges. "His art is more than just

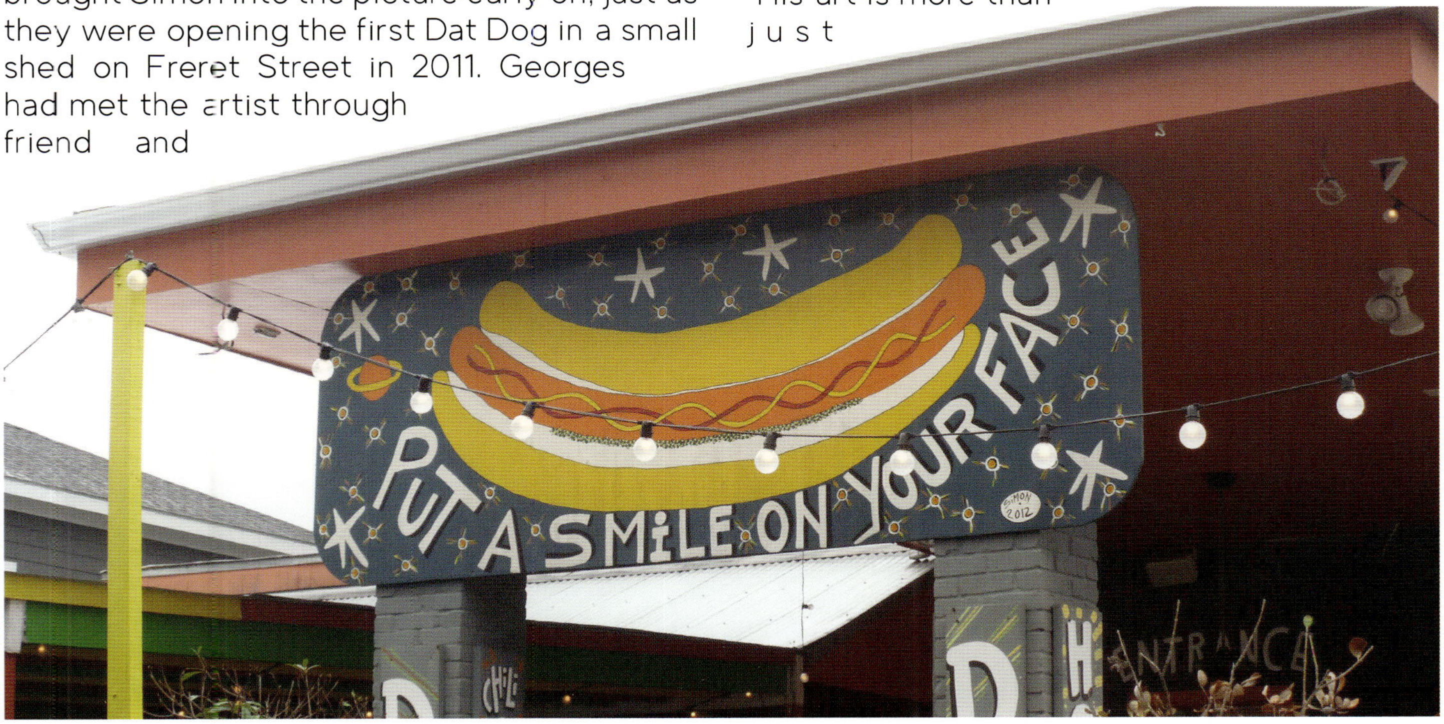

The familiar Dat Dog logo smiles over the location at the Freret Street location. (Photo by author)

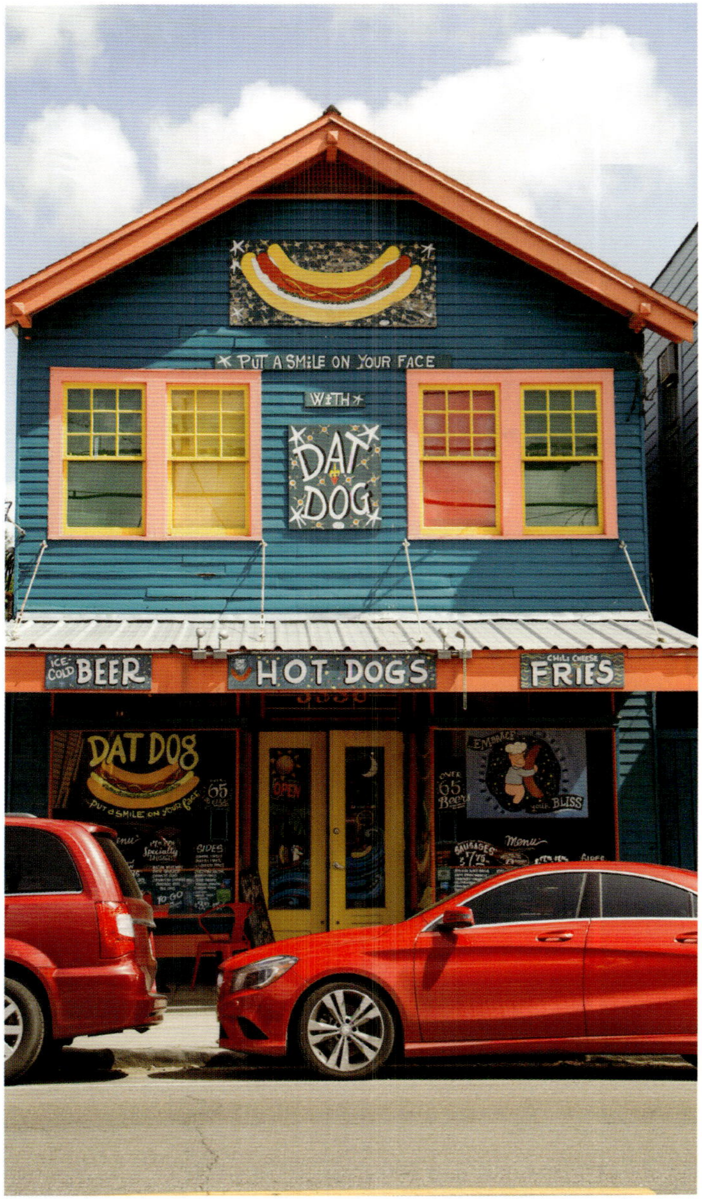

The façade of the Magazine Street location of Dat Dog is festooned with signs Simon created for the chain. The sign just below the roofline is from the original location at 5031 Freret Street.

art; his art is entertainment." Georges remains fond of some of the other early ideas proposed by Simon, one of which is framed and displayed in his office.

Before long, the popular gourmet hot dog restaurant outgrew its original cramped venue and moved across the street to its present location at 5030 Freret Street. The only artwork left from the original Freret location is now displayed at the Dat Dog on Magazine Street. The restaurant's popularity continues to grow. In addition to the four established locations in the city, there is now a Dat Dog in Lafayette, and there are plans to expand throughout southeast Louisiana.

Georges values Simon and his positive outlook. "He was one of our earliest, most supportive fans," states the owner. "The guy is always upbeat. He's so creative, and always in a positive way. Just a joy to be around."

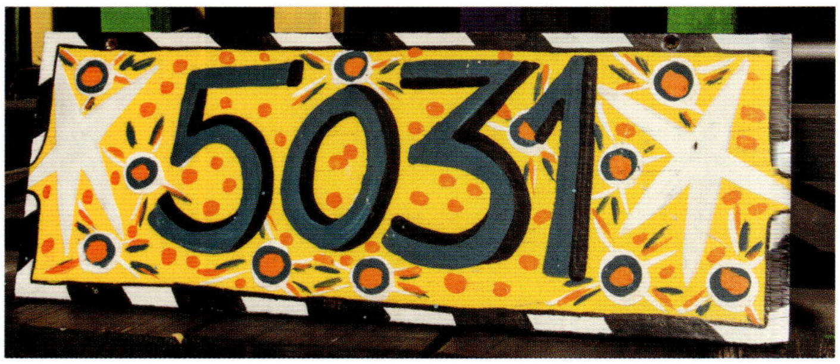

The address of the original Dat Dog location in the "shed" at 5031 Freret, across the street from the restaurant's current location. (Photo by author)

THE SIMON HOT DOG

In tribute to the artist, Georges worked with his executive chef, Alex Ventura, to create the official Simon hot dog, incorporating Simon's favorite ingredients. The new menu item was first offered to coincide with the release of this book.

The all-beef dog is cooked in crab boil, then topped with a house-made sauerkraut, a unique satsuma/dat-biere mustard, and ketchup. It is served in a steamed-then-toasted sourdough bun and finished with a parsley garnish.

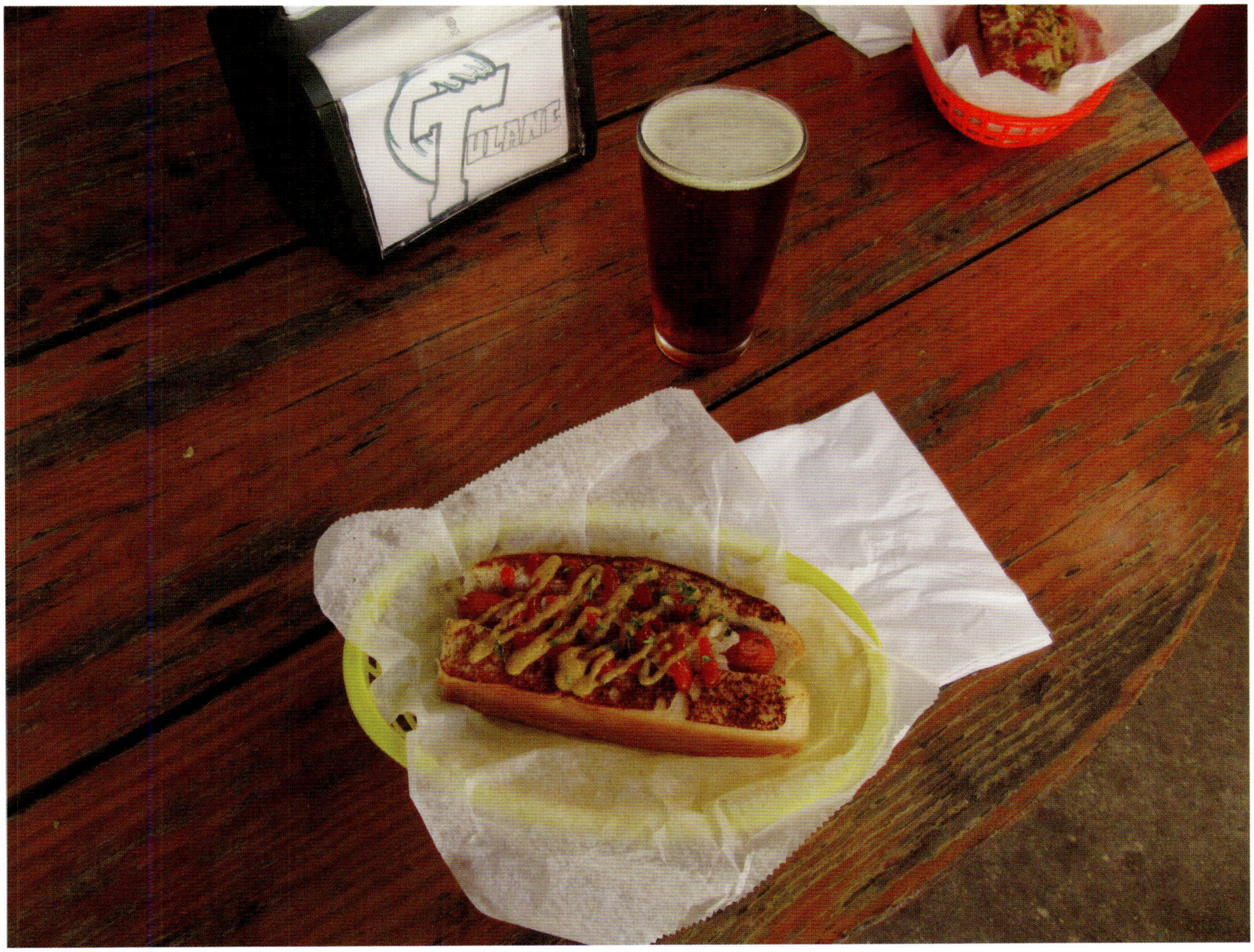

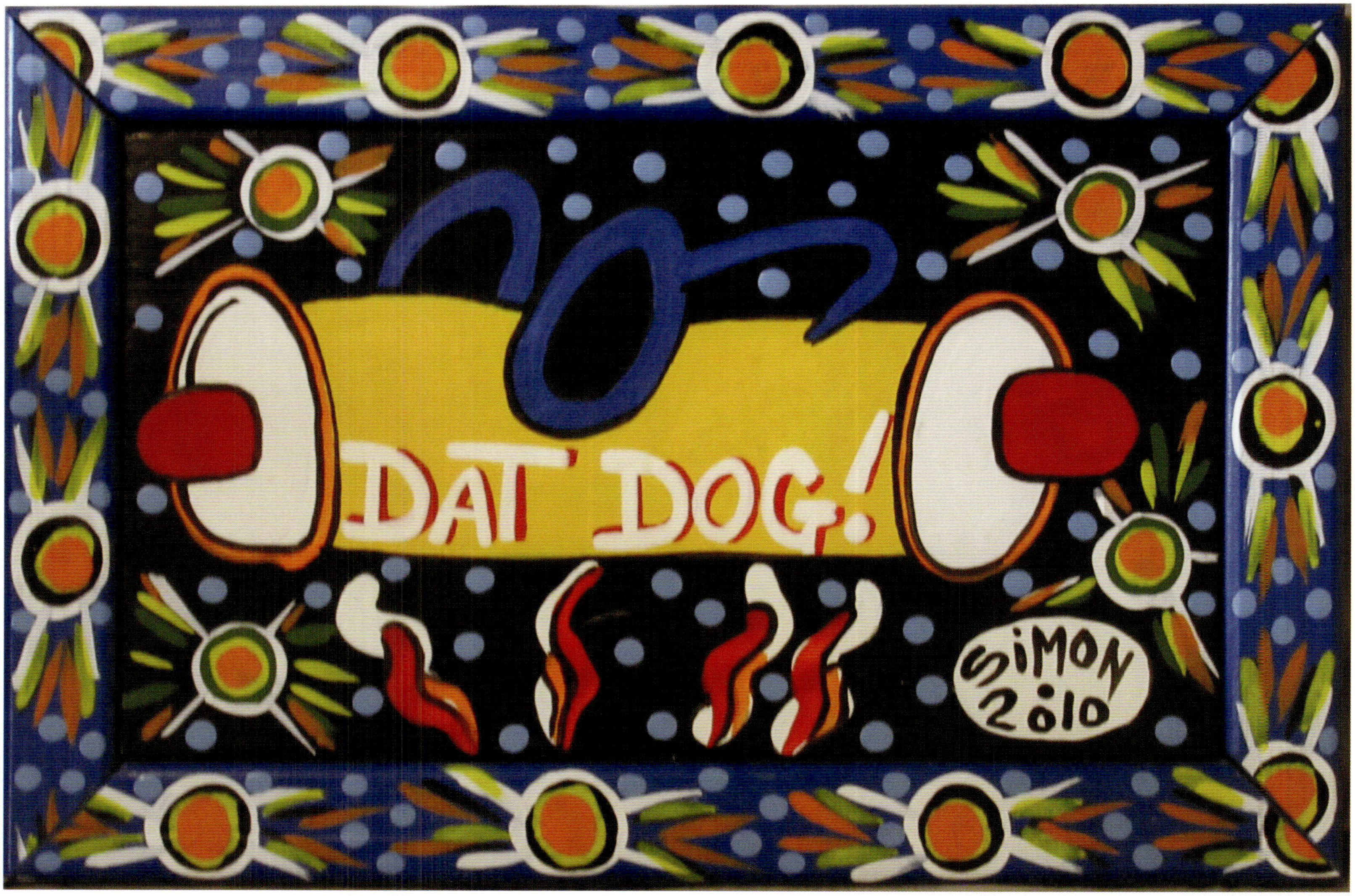

One of the earlier designs for the Dat Dog logo. (Photo by author)

CRESCENT CITY BREWHOUSE

527 DECATUR STREET
NEW ORLEANS

Located in a legendary, two-hundred-year old French Quarter building, the Crescent City Brewhouse opened in 1991. The seventeen-barrel state-of-the-art brewery was the city's first real brewpub and the first new brewery to open in New Orleans in more than seventy years. The renovation of the building has earned awards for maintaining the integrity of the historic property, and the pub has signaled a revival of the brewing industry that had once flourished in the New Orleans area.

From the beginning the Brewhouse owners chose to feature different local artists every month, displaying their artwork at the restaurant and hosting a party in their honor. Crescent City Brewhouse founder and brewmaster Wolfram Koehler, a native of Germany, first met Simon many years ago during Koehler's soccer-playing days. "A group of former Europeans—we called ourselves 'the foreign guys'—used to play informal pick-up games every week. Now Simon is a great friend. He has a big and open heart. He is always smiling, and he never stops working."

Simon first exhibited his work at the Brewhouse in the early 2000s and has since been invited to display his pieces annually. Koehler is happy to have forged so many new relationships with the New Orleans art world in the last twenty-five years, and Simon is one of

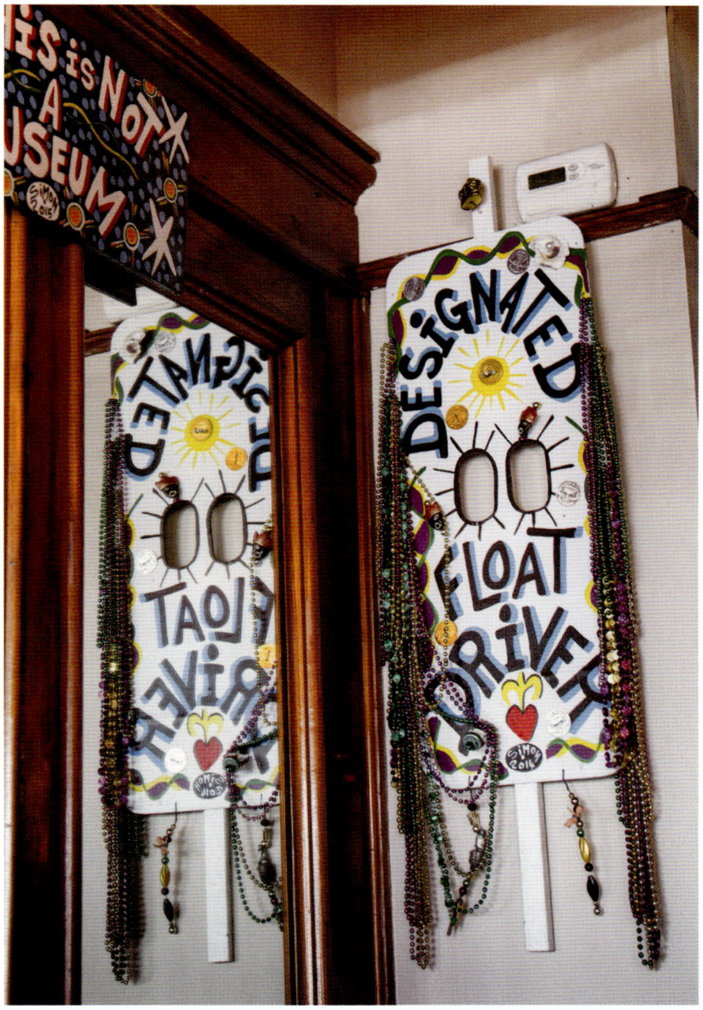

A Simon sign and Mardi Gras mask hang in Crescent City Brewhouse.

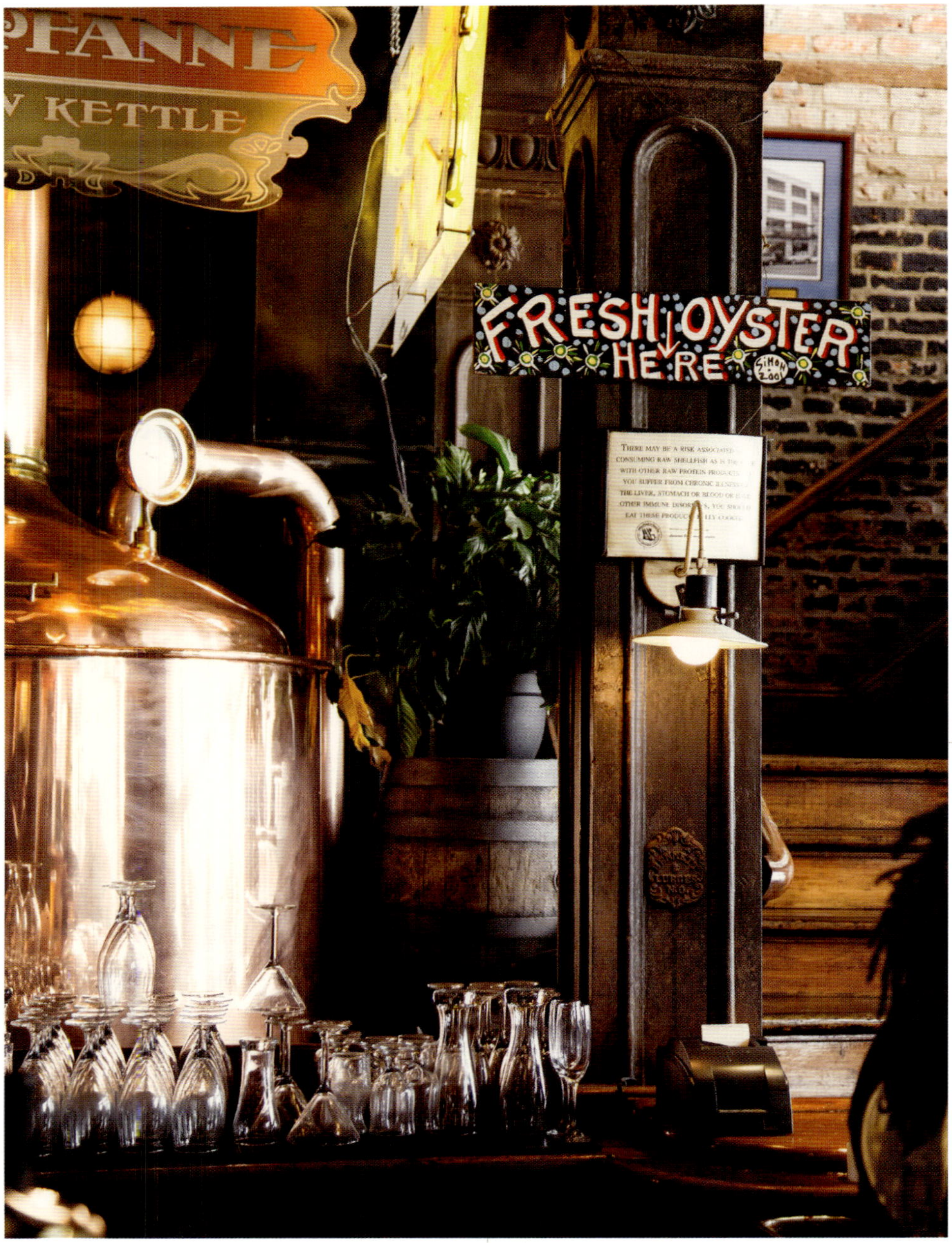

The Oyster Bar.

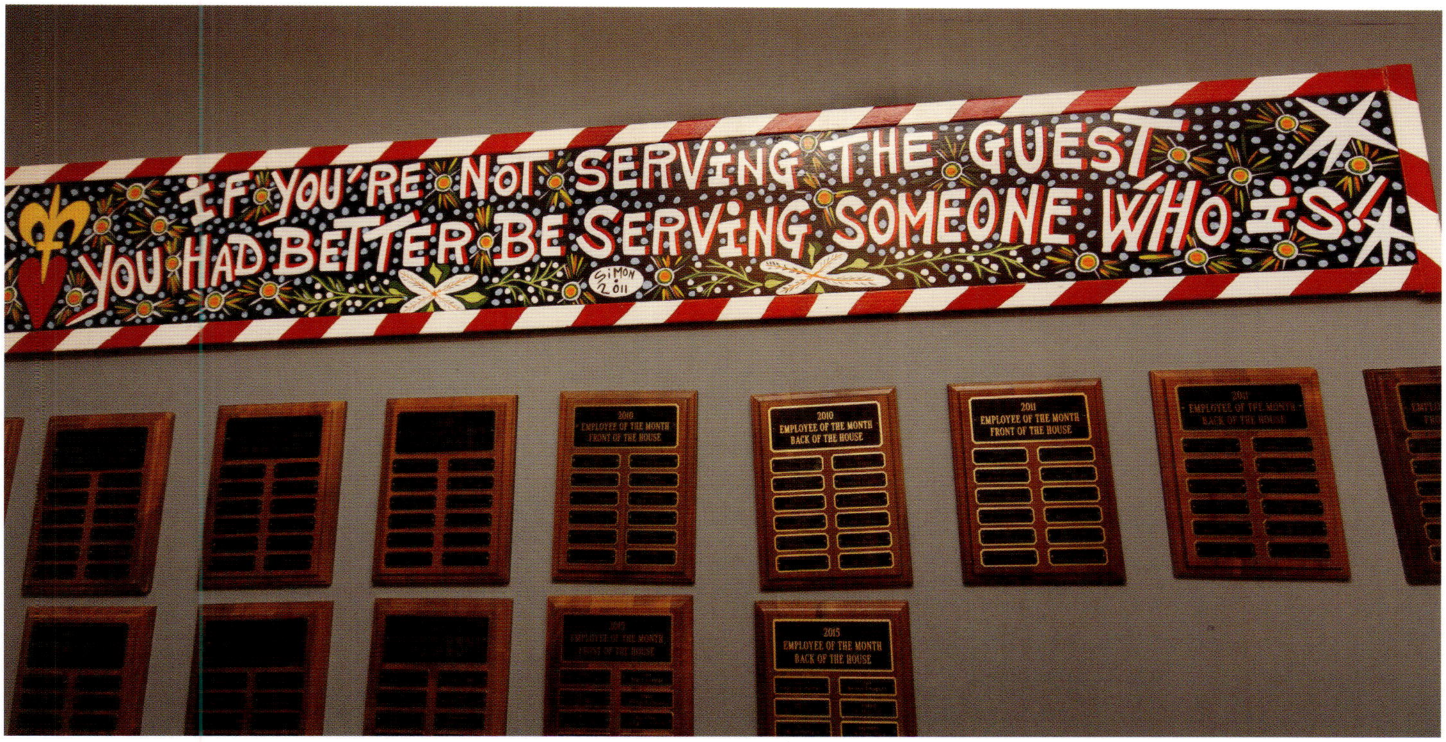

Hanging above the plaques honoring the "Employees of the Month" is this reminder from the management.

his favorites. "He fills the place with whimsical and poignant signs and paintings during his exhibits. Even though some are satirical comments on our times, he always finds a conciliatory note or a positive spin." Koehler reports that Simon's work sells better than any other artist they profile, usually between fifty and sixty pieces at each of his shows.

Earning a permanent place in the restaurant are artworks Simon has dedicated to the staff over the years. "My personal favorite," notes Koehler, "is the piece that says, 'Not All Those Who Wander Are Lost.' It was displayed at one of Simon's numerous exhibits here, and now it is in my home."

At the owners' request the artist designed and built a piece to hold go-cups for patrons exiting the restaurant with unfinished drinks. The imaginative dispenser is conspicuously featured near the front door.

"Simon is an artist who created an art form that has become a part of modern New Orleans culture, just like I hope the Brewhouse has contributed in its own way. A perfect match."

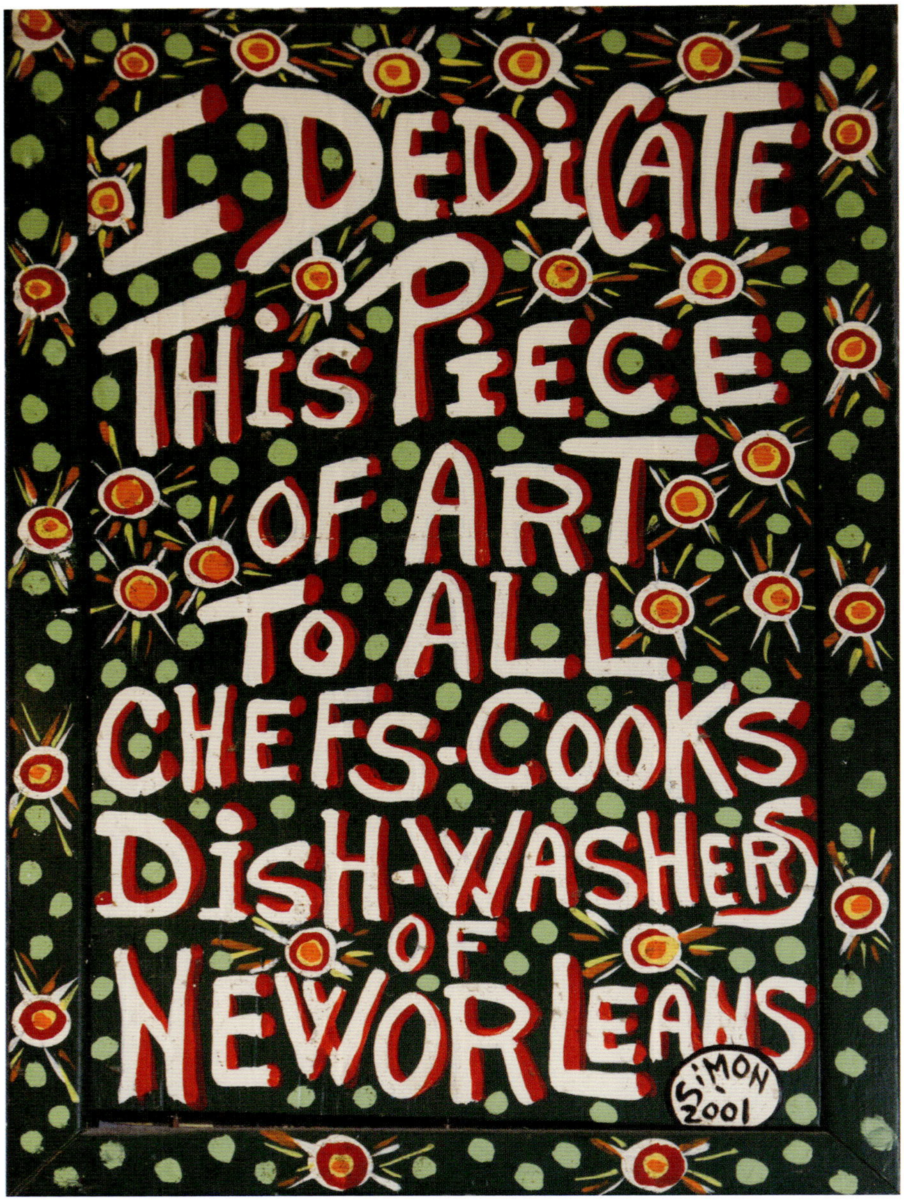

Simon, a former chef himself, salutes the city's restaurant workers.

DIS & DEM RESTAURANT

2540 BANKS STREET
NEW ORLEANS

From the very beginning, it was important to Skip Murray that his restaurant Dis & Dem have a neighborhood heart and soul to it. He wanted it to fit in with the unique culture of New Orleans that has strangers greet each other with "How ya doin', dawlin?" or "Where y'at, sugah?" And he insists that the owner-operator presence is vital. "You will 'eat mo' better' if the owner is present," he says.

Located in the burgeoning "bio-district," Dis & Dem is just such a place. The Mid-City "burger and slider joint" is the latest in a progression of restaurants that Murray has established.

While living in London, the New Orleans native launched the Real American Hot Dog Company. With the success of the chain, he became known as "The Hot Dog Guy of the U.K." After Hurricane Katrina, he moved back to New Orleans to help his family recover from four feet of floodwater in their home. Then in 2011, with the encouragement of family and friends, Murray co-founded the first Dat Dog in a small shed on Freret Street. Though no longer involved with the Dat Dog restaurants, Murray returned to the concept of the New Orleans neighborhood eateries that he remembers

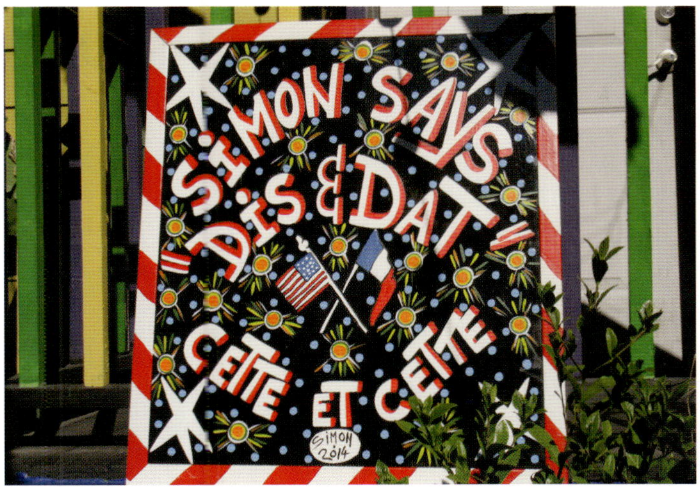

"Cette et Cette" *translates to "This and That," or "Dis and Dat" in New Orleans-speak. Murray had originally planned to name the restaurant Dis & Dat but changed the name to Dis & Dem. (Photo by author)*

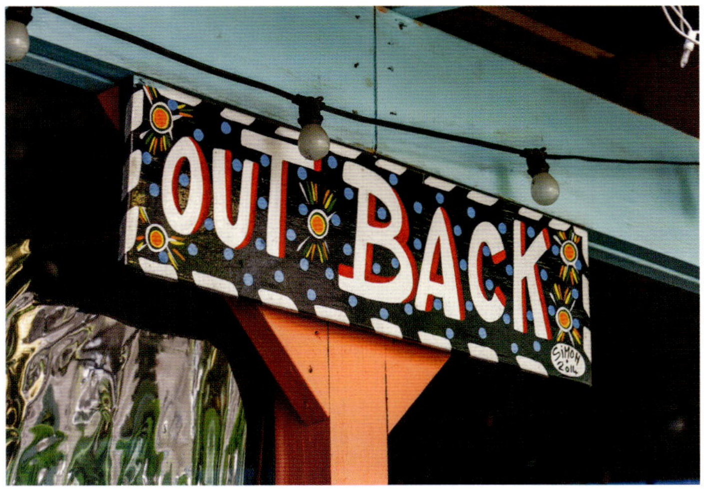

The Outback is a covered patio dining area behind the restaurant. (Photo by author)

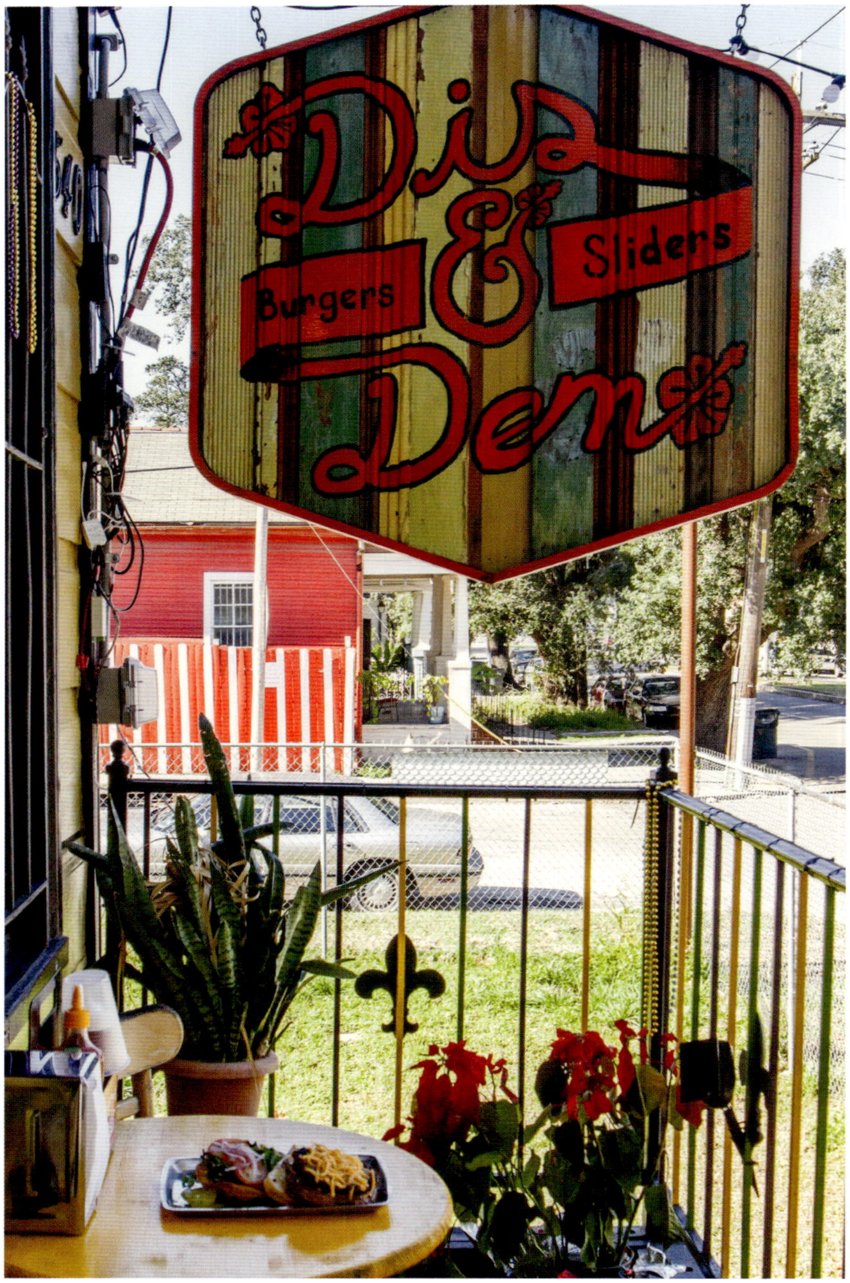

The Dis & Dem Burger features a grilled beef patty slathered in a house-made glaze, then topped with a spicy second patty and dressed with cheese, lettuce, tomato, onion, and mayonnaise. The signature burger is served on a sweet sourdough onion bun and served with house-made pickles. (Photo by author)

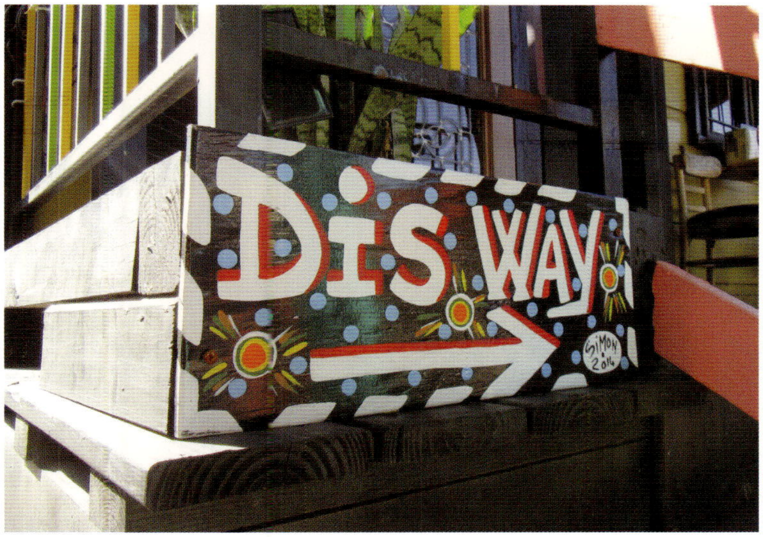

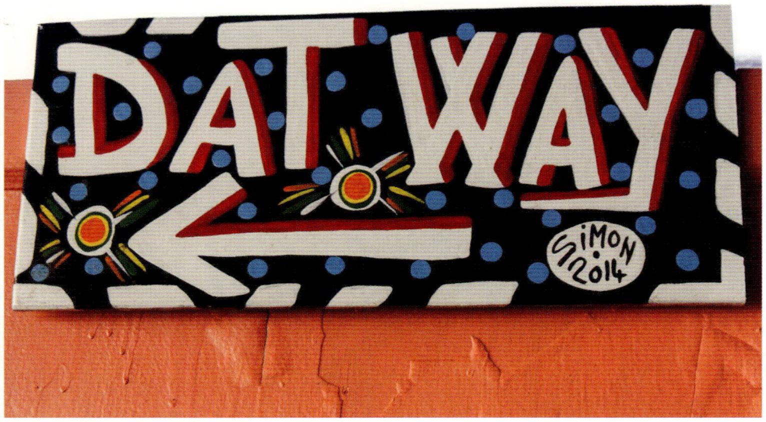

After Murray mentioned to Simon that customers had trouble finding the restaurant when it first opened, the artist decided to help out with some tongue-in-cheek directional signs: First you go dis way. Den you go dat way. (Photo by author)

from his youth, and he opened Dis & Dem in October of 2014.

Simon's signs fit in perfectly with the neighborhood feel that Murray fosters. The bright colors are friendly, the look is casual, and the style is so identifiably New Orleans. With many people seemingly unfamiliar with the evolving area where the restaurant is located, Murray has asked Simon to create some tongue-in-cheek "directional signs," including ones that lead diners to walk "Dis Way" and "Dat Way." Another indicates the direction of the North Pole and South Pole.

Murray feels fortunate to know Simon. "We connected from the very beginning. Simon is a natural for me. The guy is always smiling. He just brings out the best in other people.

"He has an unshakable sense of humor, but I pay for it at times," says Murray. The restaurateur, who spent a year in France and picked up French words when he worked at Brennan's, says he often makes a concerted effort to speak to Simon in French. Simon always answers in English, just to aggravate Murray.

Murray believes Simon has a great story with his French background and his training as a chef. The painter has reinvented himself to become part and parcel of everything that makes this city quirky and special.

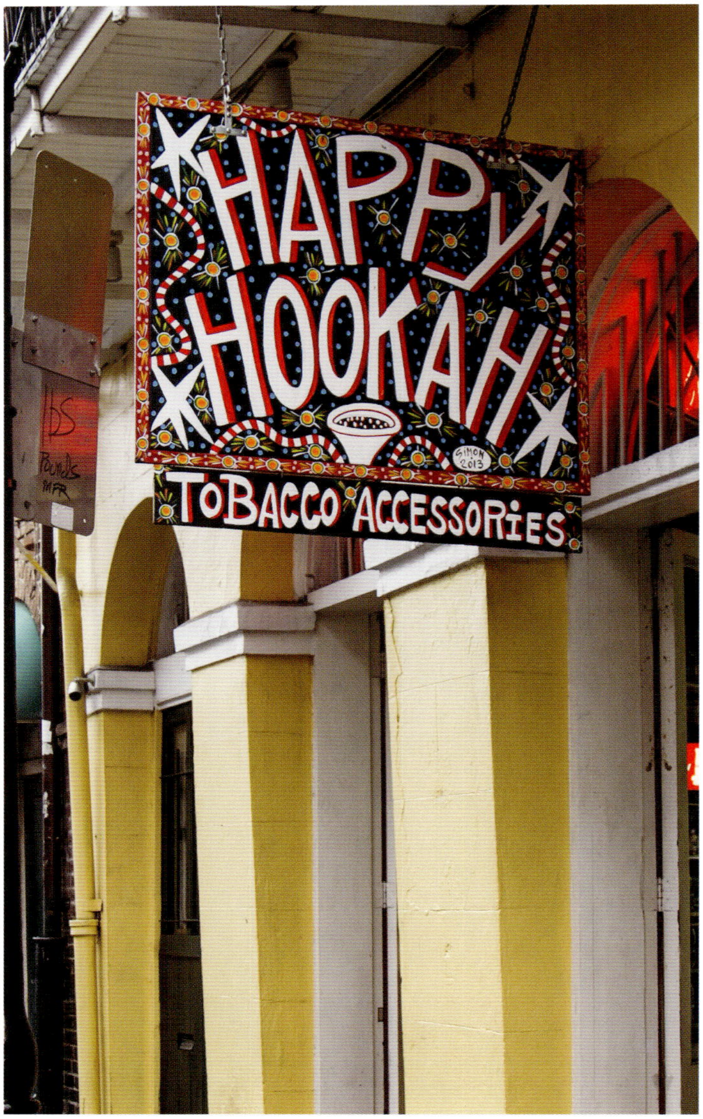

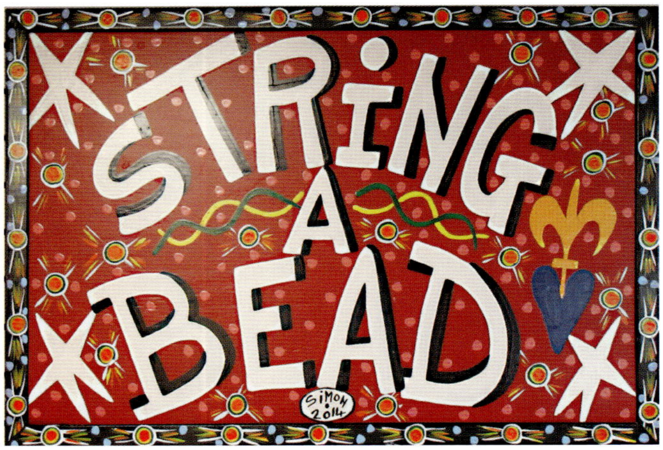

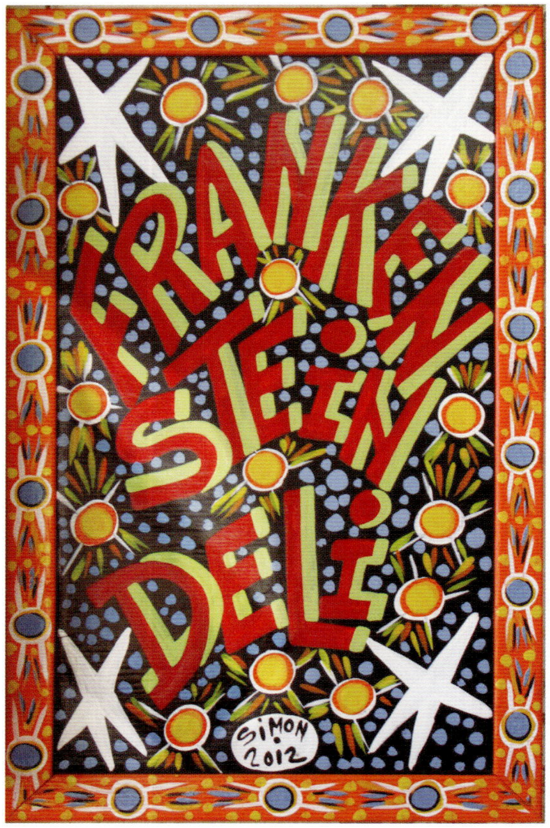

Happy Hookah, New Orleans French Quarter.

Above right: String a Bead shop, Metairie, Louisiana.

Bottom right: Simon added a bit of a fiendish twist to this sign in Stein's Deli on Magazine Street.

CHARCOAL'S GOURMET BURGER BAR

2200 MAGAZINE STREET NEW ORLEANS

"Simon's been nothing but great—a great friend and a great neighbor," says Blaine Prestenbach, who along with Craig Walker, Jr., co-founded Charcoal's Gourmet Burger Bar in 2013. The restaurant, located at the corner of Magazine Street and Jackson Avenue, is adjacent to Simon's studio.

"Our whole culinary concept is to put forth the best of Louisiana. So, we went out and found the finest of local and Louisiana products, like the best boudin, the choicest hogshead cheese, the freshest local seafood, etc.

"Somehow, however, the exterior of the restaurant doesn't convey its local connection," bemoans Prestenbach. "It's a new building, built after Katrina, and it just doesn't have that 'old New Orleans look' to it." So Prestenbach and Walker have filled the eatery with local artwork, mostly Simon's. "Simon is a great fit. He is so local, so New Orleans. His works give the interior a 'totally New Orleans' look and feel."

The owners, both Cajun, spend a lot of time at a hunting camp in Golden Meadow. One of Simon's signs greets those who visit the camp, named the Ridge: *"Bienvenue a la Ridge 2 Venez Passer un Bon Moment."* A sign with the English version, "Welcome to the Ridge 2 Come Pass a Good Time" hangs in the restaurant. "Jesus was a fisherman, too" proclaims another Simon work at the camp. The sportsmen often return bearing gifts for Simon: fresh-caught fish and ducks.

One of Prestenbach's favorite pieces is Simon's painting of Charcoal, the beloved thirteen-year-old black lab, which is displayed at the entrance to the restaurant. The dog, who passed away in 2015, was the restaurant's namesake and a lifelong hunting companion.

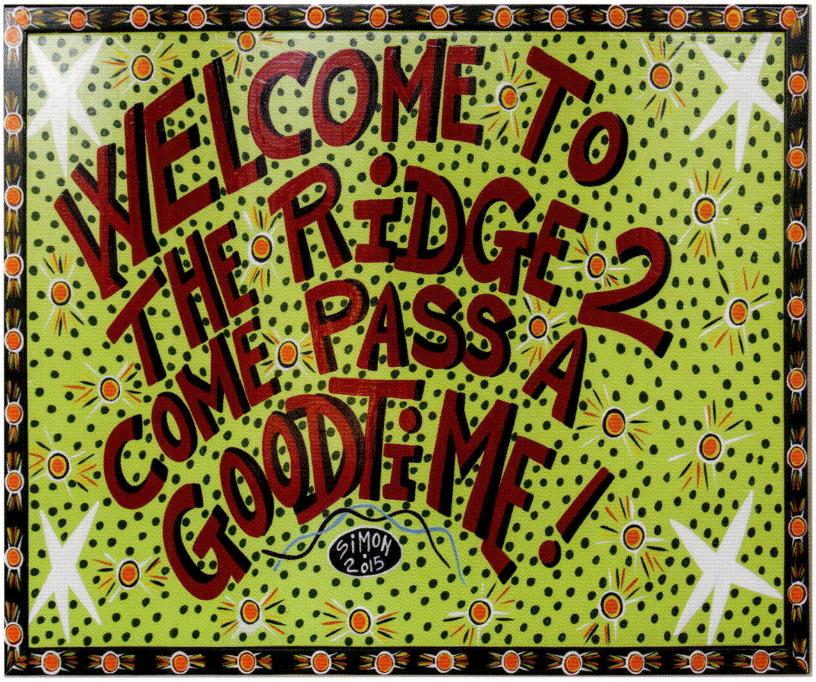

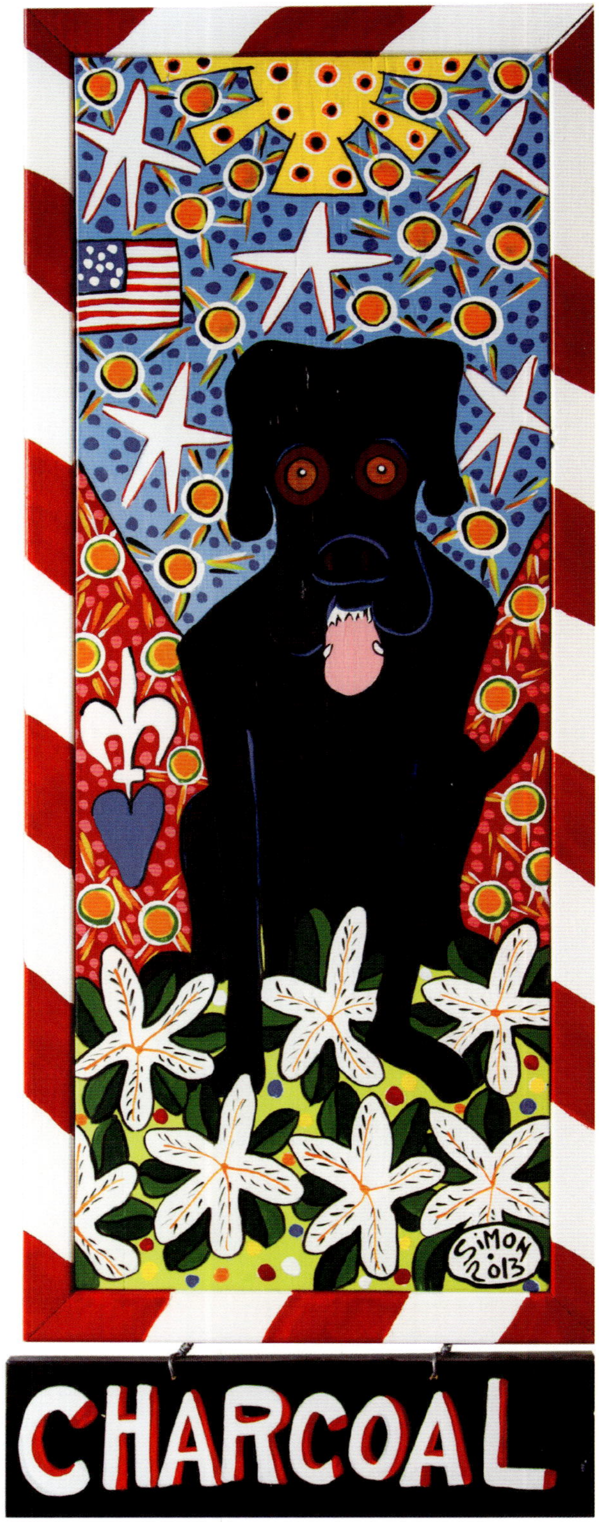

In 2015, Simon painted a portrait of Charcoal, the canine namesake of the gourmet burger restaurant.

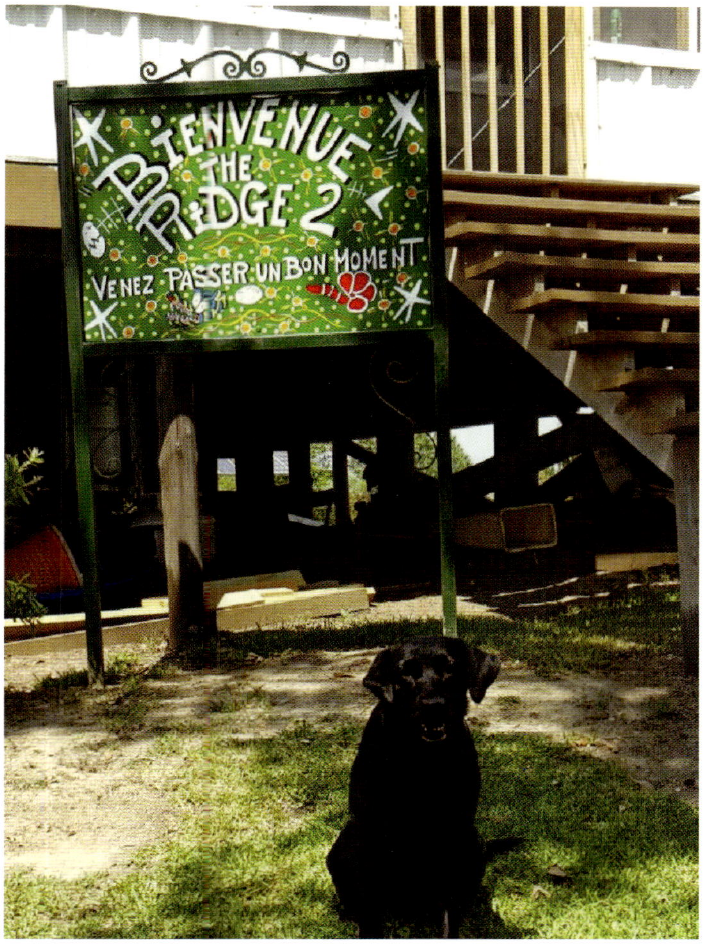

Charcoal poses in front of the Ridge, the restaurant owners' hunting camp in Golden Meadow.

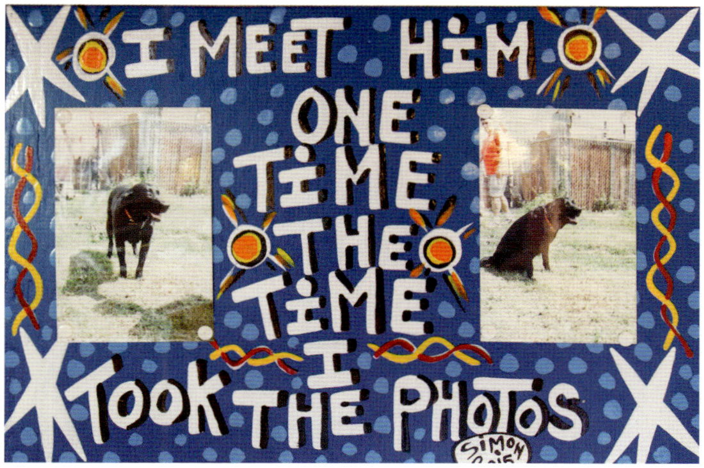

When Charcoal died in 2015, Simon framed the photos he had taken of the chocolate lab. The tribute is displayed in the restaurant.

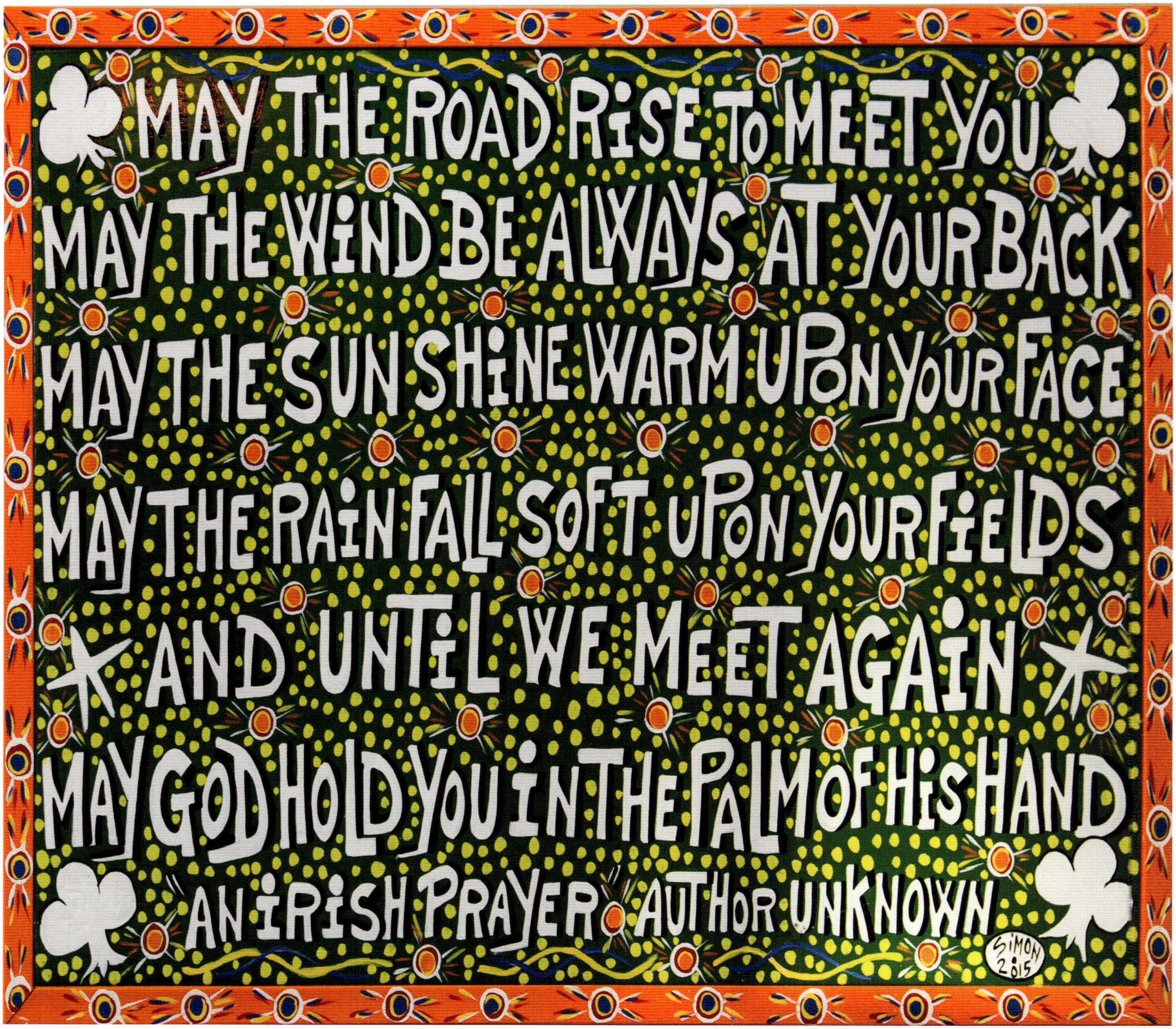

Diners climbing the stairway to the restaurant's second floor are given thoughts to ponder.

GOURMET SHRIMP BURGER

Prestenbach and Walker share the recipe for one of the restaurant's most-requested items.

Fresh Louisiana shrimp, peeled and deveined
Seasonings to taste
Salt and pepper to taste
Hawaiian sweet bun
White cheddar cheese slices
Guacamole
Bacon, cooked
Iceberg lettuce
Tomato, sliced
Condiments to taste

Grind fresh Louisiana shrimp in a meat grinder. Season to taste using Creole seasonings, salt, and pepper. (Charcoal's uses a proprietary mix of spices.) Divide the shrimp mix into equal size patties, and place on a very hot grill. Grill until cooked thoroughly (no gray in the middle).

Place burger on a bun and dress with white cheddar, guacamole, bacon, iceberg lettuce, and tomato. Charcoal's adds their own special sauce; at home use mayonnaise, specialty mustards, or your favorite sauce.

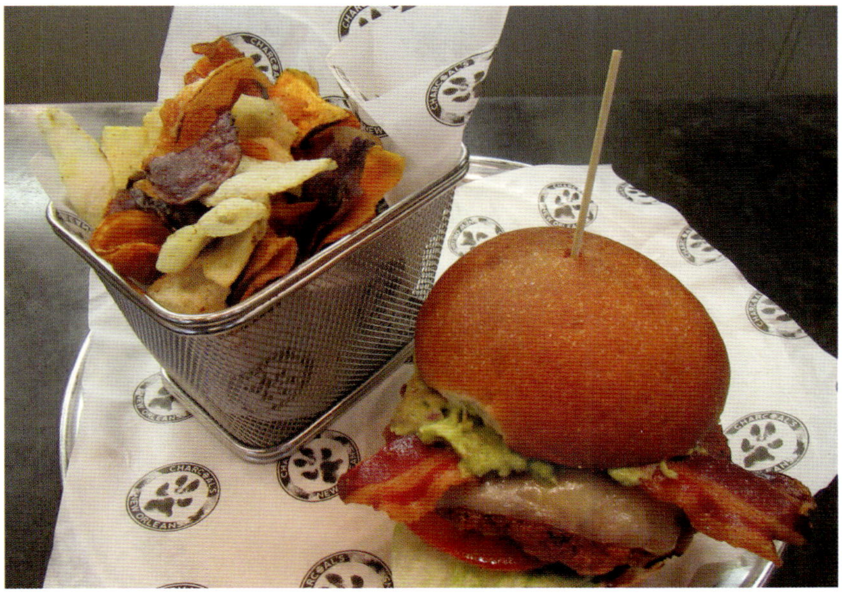

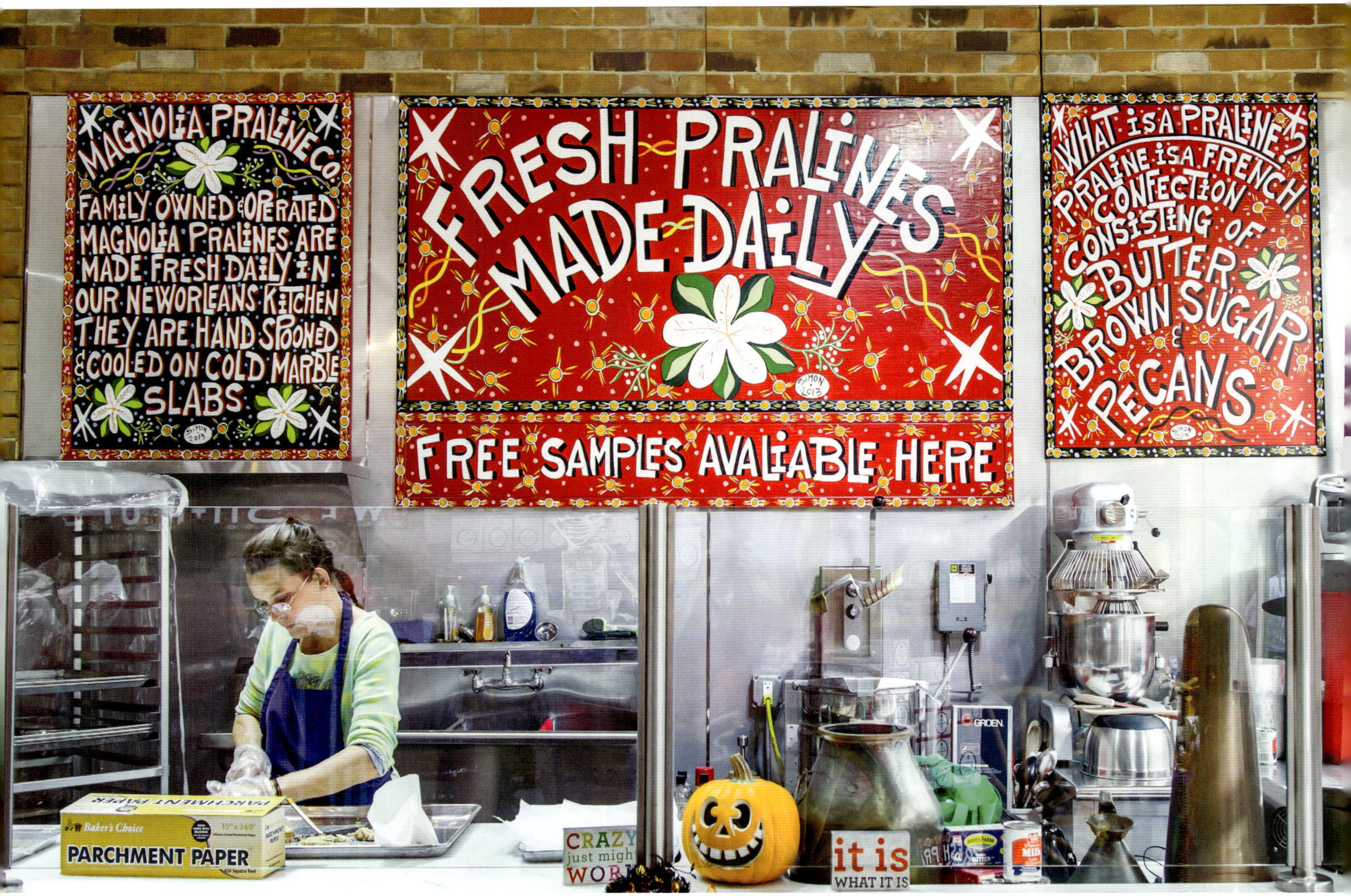

Simon's signs behind the counter of the Magnolia Praline Company in the French Quarter explain the process and the ingredients for making the famous New Orleans confection.

PJ'S COFFEE OF NEW ORLEANS

5432 MAGAZINE STREET NEW ORLEANS

Of the sixty-plus PJ's coffeehouses in Louisiana and Mississippi, the oldest continuously operated location is found at 5432 Magazine Street. It is one of the original handful of sites opened by the company's founder, Phyllis Jordan, in the late 1970s. Aubry Miller, owner of the Magazine Street location, has filled the walls with Simon's art.

"It's not something I planned on when I first assumed the operation of this location," she muses. "It's just a happy accident, I guess."

Miller explains that she had wandered into Simon's art studio on Jackson Avenue one day looking to purchase a sign for an acquaintance. She left with a piece of art and a new friend. "Simon was so cheery and positive. We got to talking, and before long, we realized that a business alliance would benefit both of us," she explains. "His artworks lend a friendly, decidedly New Orleans feel to the shop, and people recognize them right away."

Customers who fall in love with a particular piece can purchase it right then and there. At any given time, there are a dozen or more Simon pieces in the store, along with Simon-designed coffee mugs and magnets.

"Simon is a kick," says Miller. "The employees and customers just love it when he stops by to replenish the pieces that have sold. He connects so easily with everyone," she continues, "though sometimes it takes a minute for first-timers to get past his unconventional looks and realize how down-to-earth he really is."

Since taking ownership of the Magazine Street location, Miller has completed renovations to the front of the shop facing Magazine Street, to the courtyard located behind the building, and to the interior of the shop. "The building has a long history," explains Miller. "We think that, at some point, it could have been an automobile

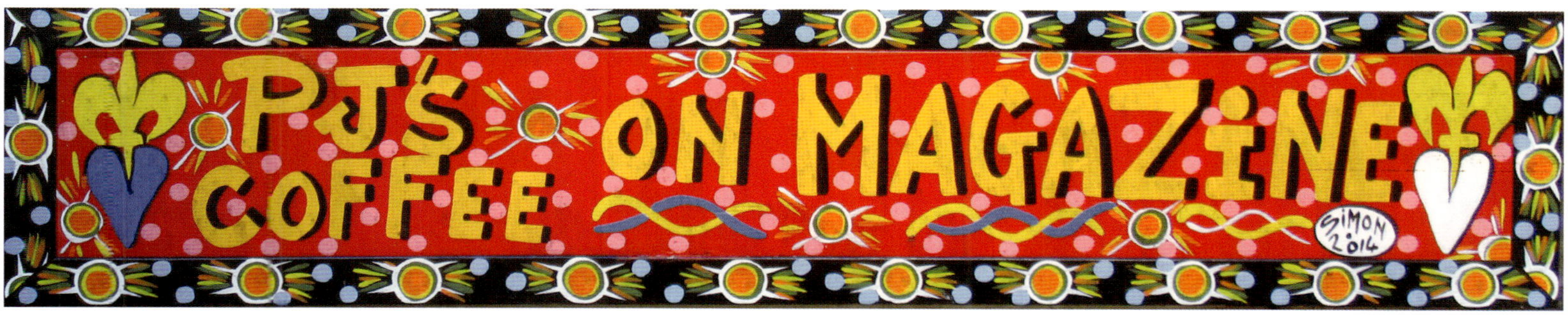

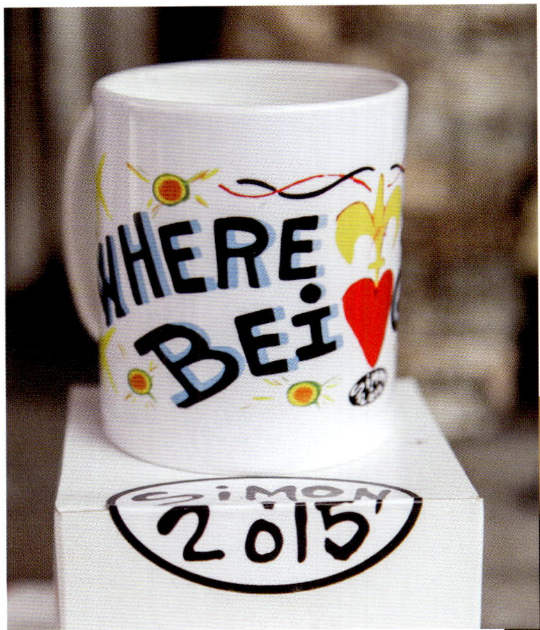

Simon has put a few of his sayings on coffee mugs. "Where Is My Beignet."

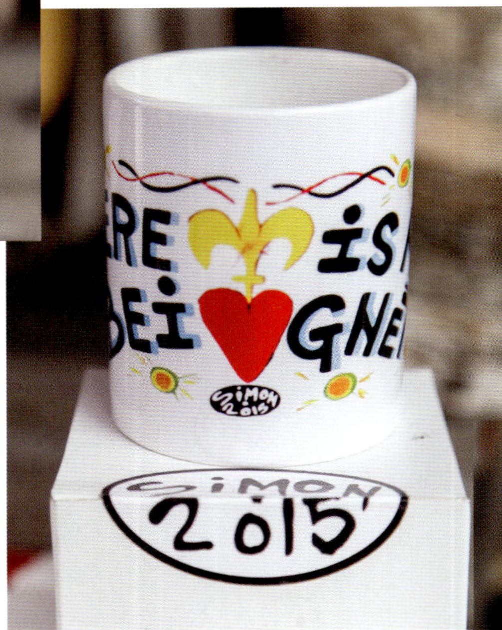

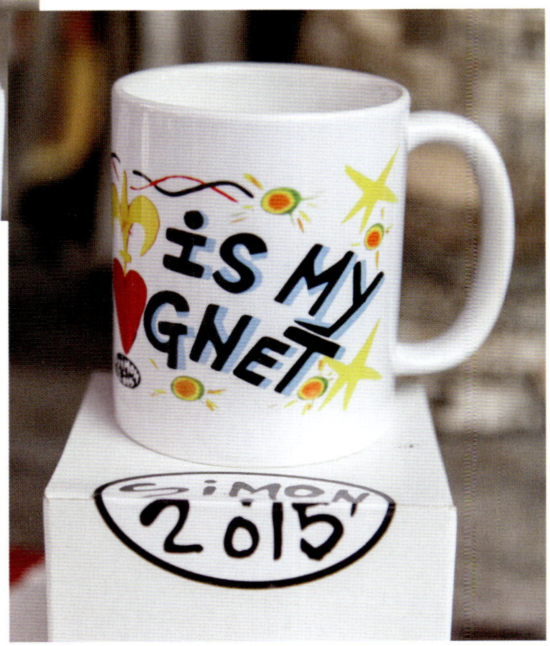

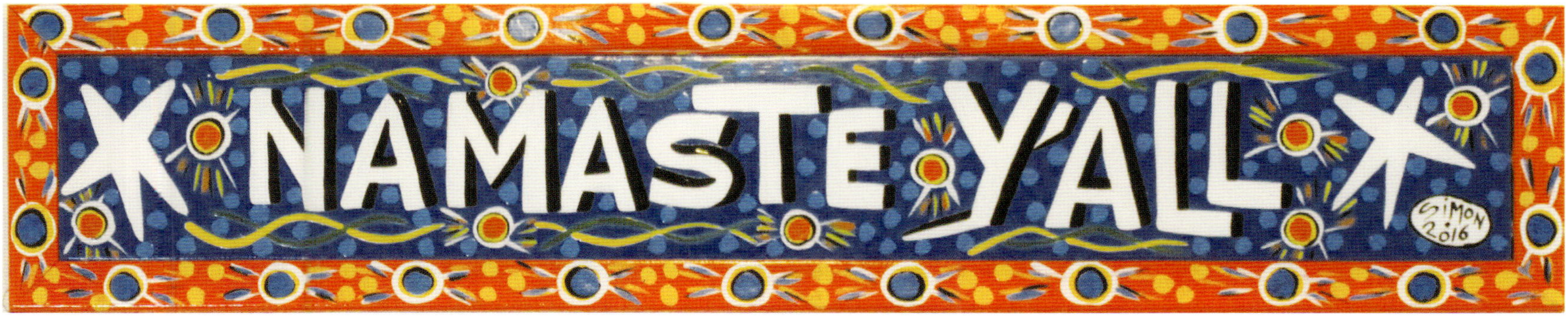

On the back wall is a Hindu greeting with a local twist, "Namaste, Y'all."

service shop." The front of the building once housed an open bay area where cars could be driven in to be serviced. Workers removing the old flooring in that area discovered and refurbished a herringbone-patterned brick floor beneath "It's also possible it was a grocery or butcher shop at one time," she adds. When the courtyard was dug up, animal bones were found in a condition that would be consistent with those discarded by a butcher.

Whatever its history, the shop is now a popular gathering place on Magazine Street, where people go to enjoy coffee, conversation, and Simon's art.

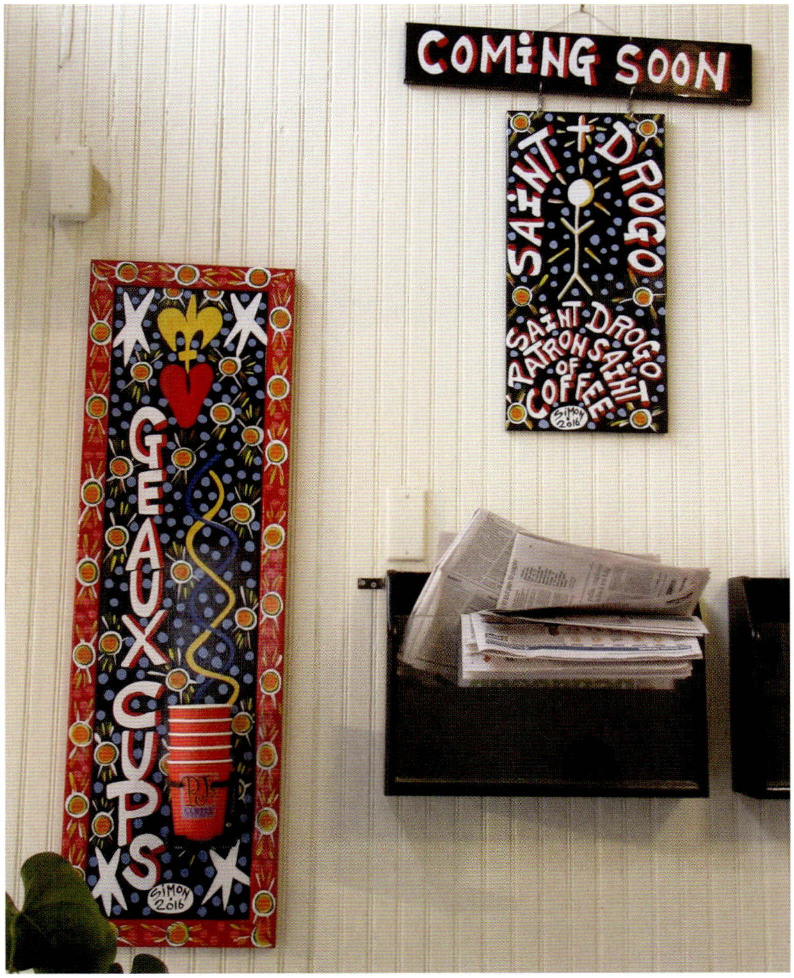

Near the front entrance on the wall holding reading material for customers are two Simon pieces. One is "Geaux Cups," complete with PJs take-out cups; the other is dedicated to Saint Drogo, a tenth-century penitent who is the patron saint of baristas and coffee house owners.

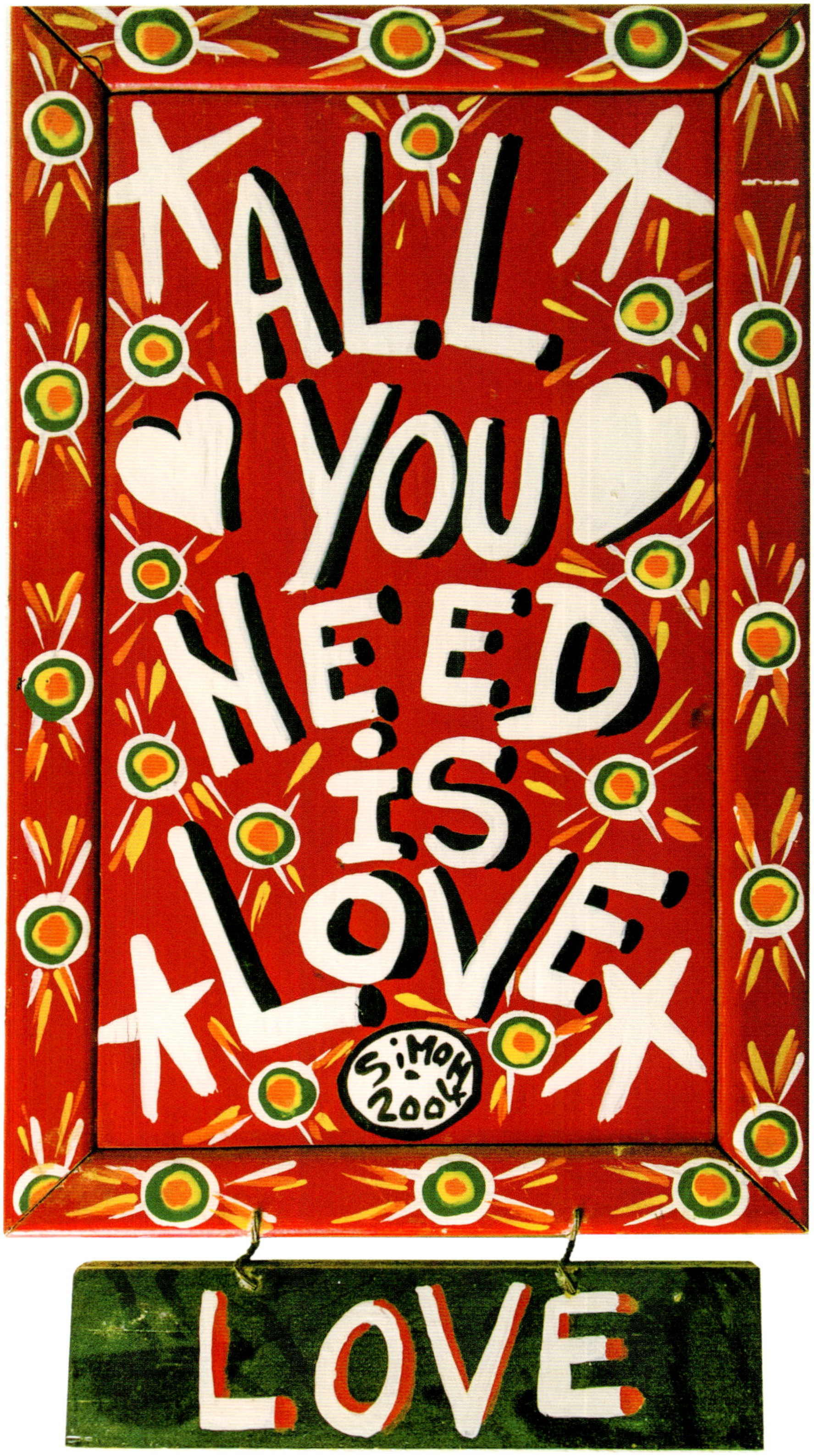
ALL YOU NEED IS LOVE
SIMON 2004
LOVE

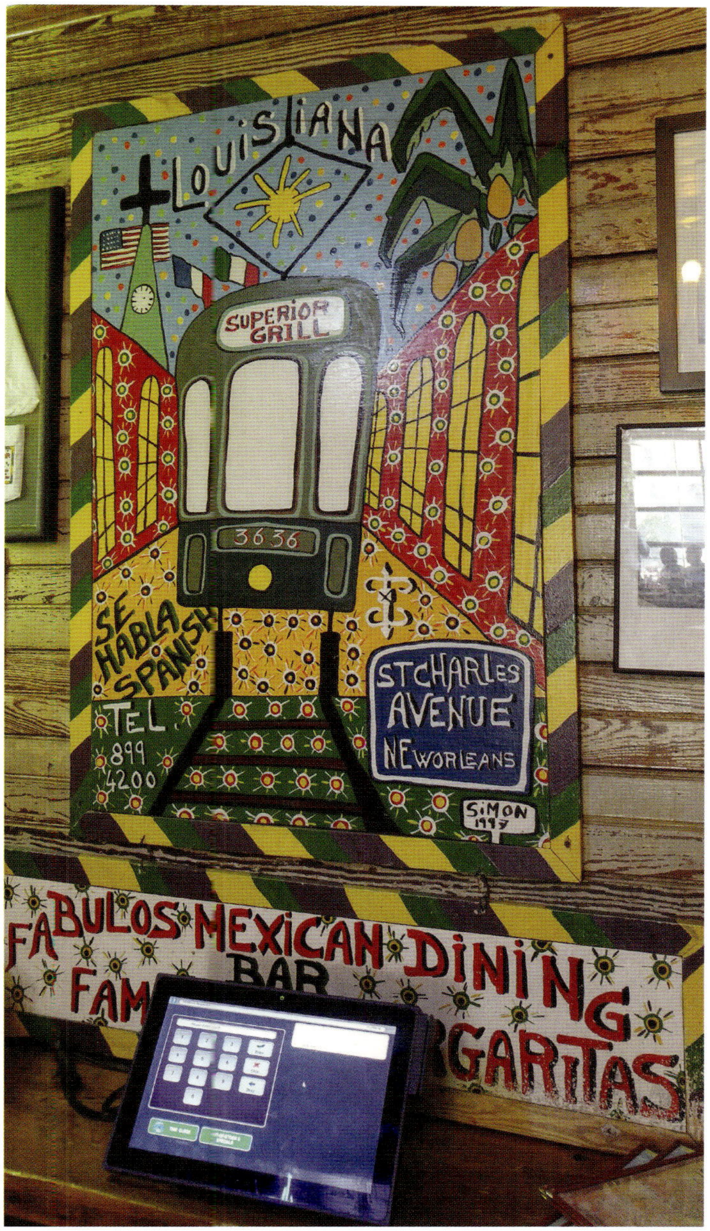

Simon's artworks surround the cashiers station at Superior Grill on St. Charles Avenue

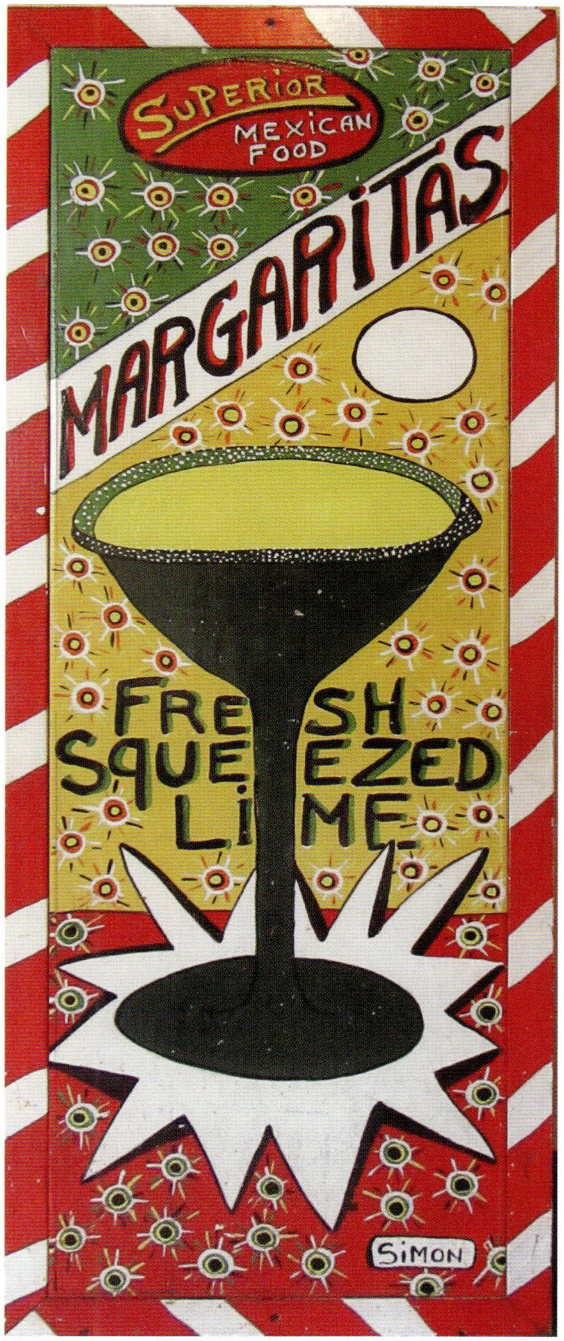

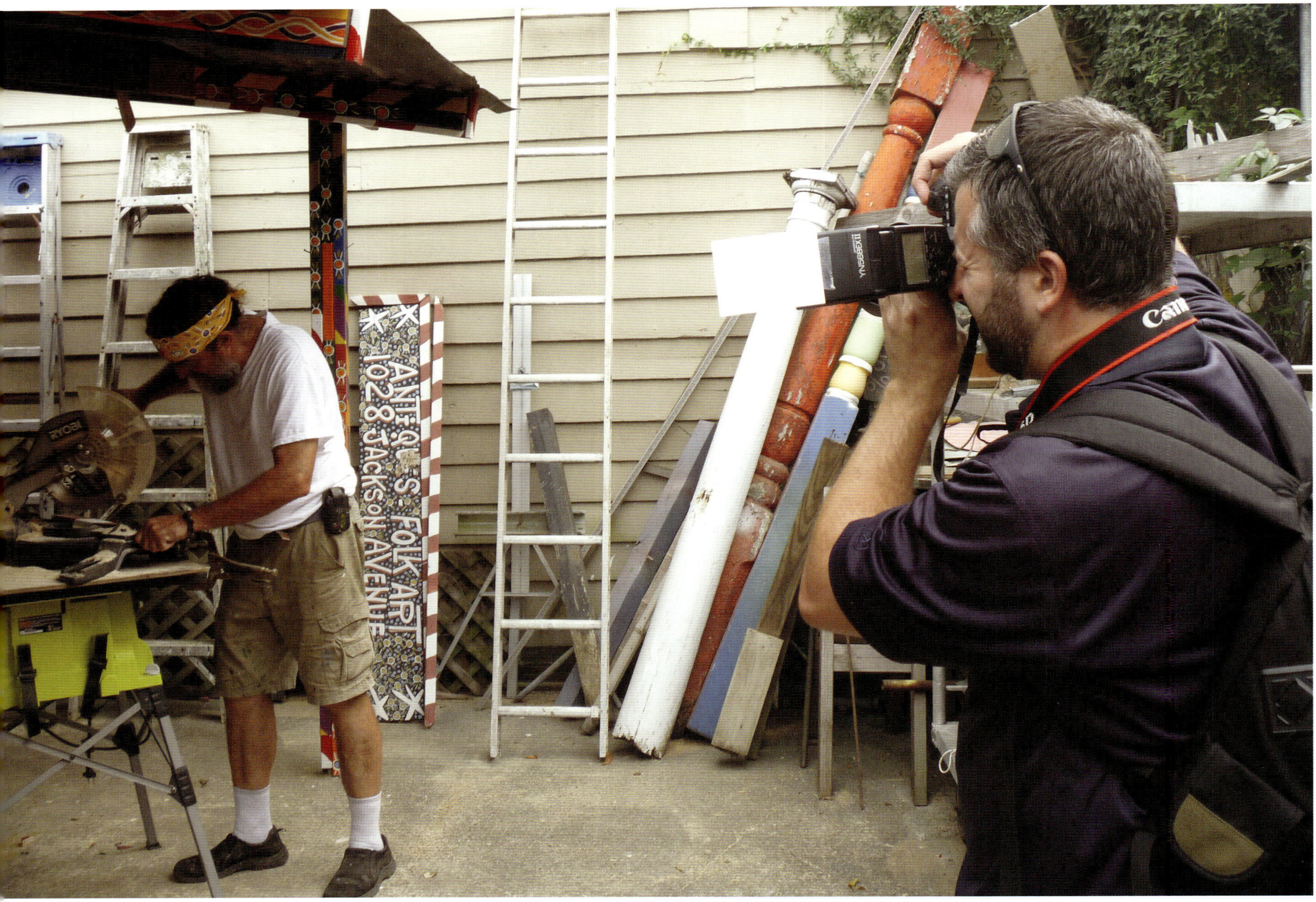

Photographer Paul Perret captures Simon at work.

ACKNOWLEDGMENTS

We gratefully acknowledge the contributions of the following:

★

Grégor Trumel, Consul général de France à La Nouvelle-Orléans, for sharing his enthusiasm for Simon, his art, and the French culture he tirelessly promotes; for generously donating his time, ideas, and resources; and for penning the foreword to this book.

★

The staff of the French Consulate who provided their kind assistance:
Béatrice Germaine, Chargée de mission artistique et audiovisual, for her unwavering support; Olivia Lamy; Meagan Moreland-Taliancich; Laetitia Bussy; and Marie-Agnes Scialfa.

★

Collectors Dale Fleishmann, Dr. Leonard Glade, Dr. Tom and Susan Nolan, who shared their stories and welcomed us into their homes to photograph their collections of Simon's art.

★

The staff of WGNO-TV, especially Susan Roesgen, LeBron Joseph, and Curt Sprang, hosts of *News with a Twist*, who broadcast each day from within a Simon-created world; John Cruse, Station General Manager; Mark Deane; Rick Erbach; Jeff Kent; Jeff Funk; and Kris Cusanza.

★

Lycée Français de la Nouvelle-Orléans, especially:
Keith Bartlett, Principal; Marina Schoen, Director of Academics; Marie Enjalbert, professeur, for her editing and translation assistance.

★

Ecole Bilingue de la Nouvelle-Orléans, especially:
Pauline Dides, Principal.

★

Marci Schramm, Director of the New Orleans French Quarter Festival.

★

Allain Bush, of Bush Antiques, the starting point in Simon's art career.

★

Charlie Camm, who provided his insights on collecting Simon's artworks.

★

Paul and Lori Bair (Cajun Pride Swamp Tours and administrators of Simon's Facebook page)
Cindy Farnet (Joey K's Restaurant)
Constantine Georges and Alex Ventura (Dat Dog restaurants)
Rob Gerhart (Louisiana Pizza Kitchen)
Wolfram Koehler (Crescent City Brewhouse)
Marcy McCall (The Grocery Deli)
Aubry Miller (PJ's on Magazine)
Juan Miranda (Lola's Restaurant)
Skip Murray (Dis & Dem Restaurant)
Katell Oijubin and Dominique Rizzo (La Boulangerie)
Blaine Prestenbach and Craig Walker, Jr. (Charcoal's Gourmet Burgers)

★

Maria Morse Hardeveld, Simon's biggest fan.

★

Cindy Sevin and Eugenie Fenerty, for their valued assistance to the author.

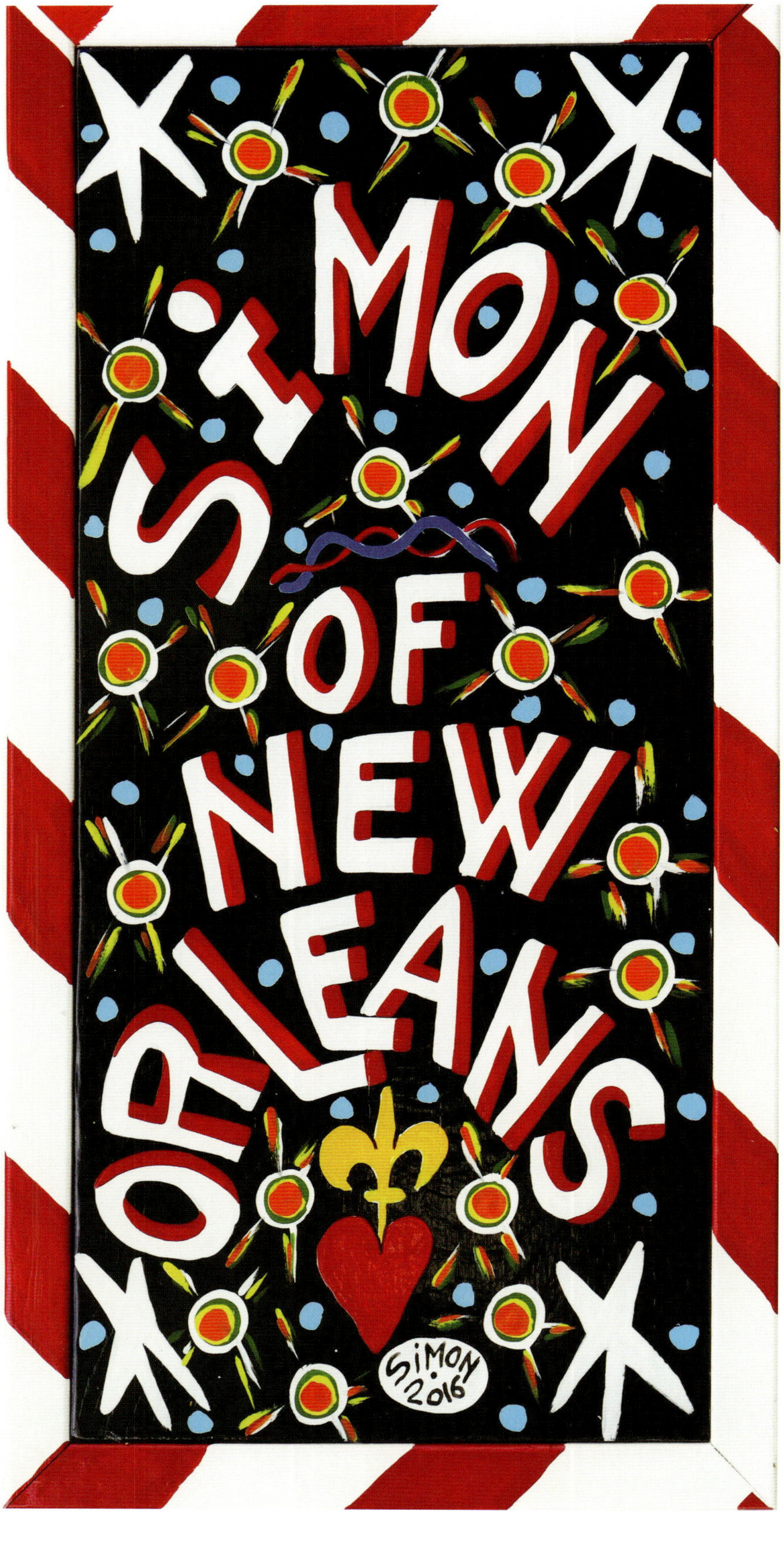
SIMON
OF
NEW
ORLEANS
SIMON
2016

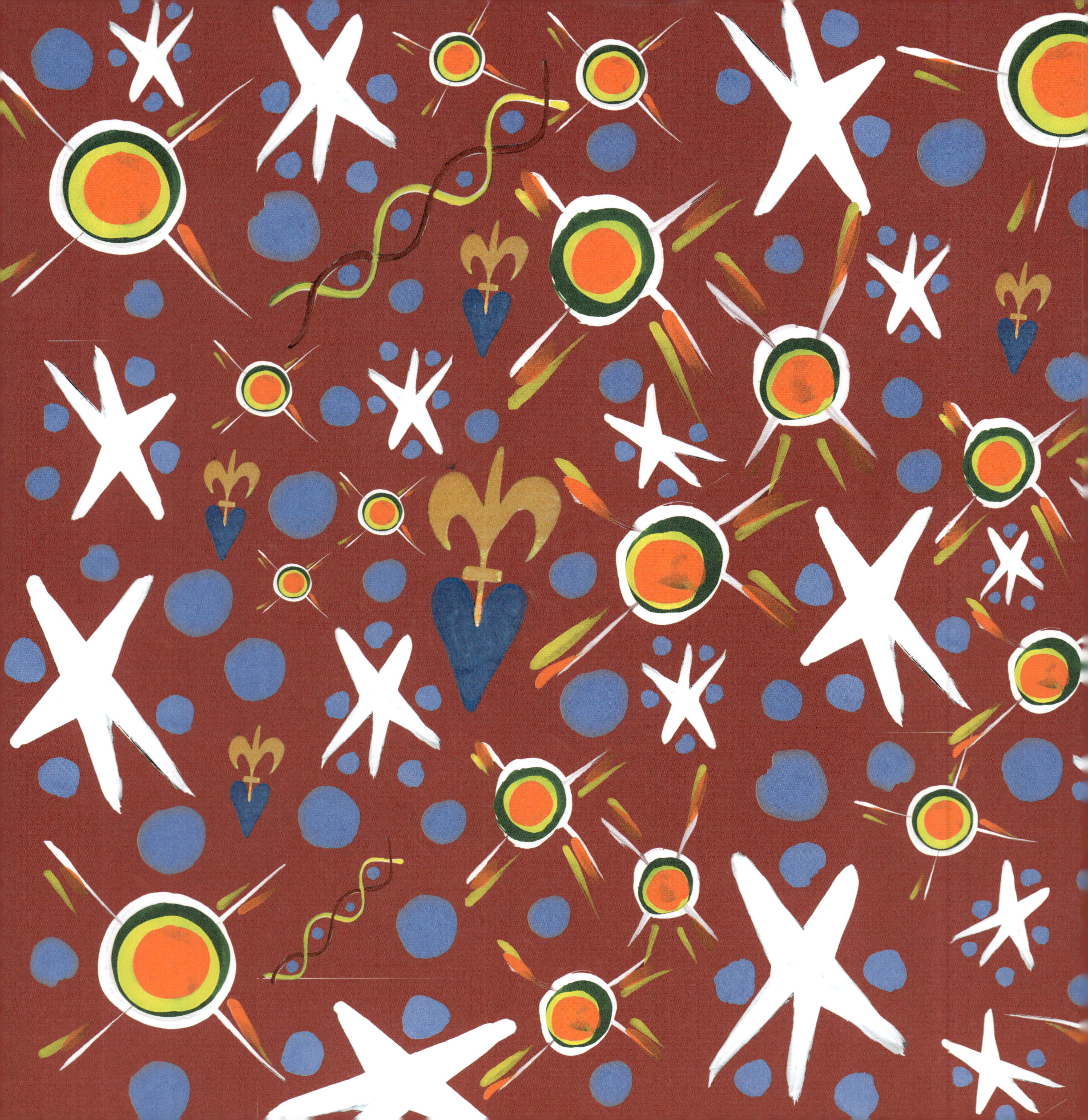